Economic Origins of
Jeffersonian
Democracy

Economic Origins of
Jeffersonian Democracy

How Hamilton's Merchant Class
Lost Out to the Agrarian South

Charles A. Beard

Foreword by
Clyde W. Barrow

DOVER PUBLICATIONS, INC.
Mineola, New York

FOREWORD

THE *Economic Origins of Jeffersonian Democracy*
(1915) was published by Charles A. Beard just over 100
years ago as the second installment of a planned series of
books that would apply the method of economic interpretation to each major period of United States history.[1] The
first book of this planned series was Beard's more widely
known and controversial, *An Economic Interpretation of
the Constitution of the United States* (1913). In this first
book, Beard explained the origins, form, and content of
the U.S. Constitution as the outcome of a class struggle
between capitalistic and agricultural interests in the early Republic. According to Beard, capitalistic interests
had dominated the constitutional convention of 1787 and,
consequently, they authored a founding document that
appealed "directly and unerringly to identical interests in
the country at large."[2] Beard's *Economic Interpretation
of the Constitution* was unquestionably one of the most
controversial scholarly works of his generation,[3] because
populists, progressives, liberals, socialists and, later, even
communists, would all cite his book as evidence that the
Constitution was of the capitalists, by the capitalists, and
for the capitalists.[4]

In contrast to the political controversy of Beard's first
book on economic interpretation, *Economic Origins of Jeffersonian Democracy* was generally warmly received by
reviewers in the leading journals of political science, eco-

nomics, and history[5] even though one of its two main ob-
jectives was to document that the class struggle organized
around ratification of the U.S. Constitution continued to
define the main lines of political conflict in the new American republic. The Federalists, led by Alexander Hamilton,
breathed life into their Constitution with policies designed
to facilitate the emergence of a capitalist economy and to
institutionalize the Constitution as a capitalist state, while
former Anti-Federalists gradually coalesced into an opposition agrarian Republican party. However, in document-
ing this claim, Beard was pursuing a second related objec-
tive and that was to debunk the idea that "the Jeffersonian
party was founded not on any set of economic doctrines but
upon some general principles of American liberty."[6]

At the time, this claim was being advanced quite aggres-
sively by the historian Orin G. Libby so *Economic Origins* is
set up as a polemic against Libby's claim. Libby responded
with an angry and inaccurate review of *Economic Origins*.[7]
He had also decried Beard's earlier book as a "partisan appeal to class prejudice," while chastising Beard "for arous-
ing class feelings over questions that have long since passed
into history."[8] However, Beard argued that Libby's claim
about the high-minded origins of Jeffersonian democracy
was based on an uncritical reading of Thomas Jefferson's
early declarations, who at first "attributed the antagonism
between Federalists and Republicans to divergences in theories of state. 'Fear and distrust' of the people was the principle which dominated the former, while the latter rested
their cause on 'the cherishment of the people'".[9] However, in
his own reading of Jefferson's writings on politics, Beard was
convinced that "as Jefferson watched the progress of Hamilton's measures in Congress, he [Jefferson] became more and
more convinced that the members who supported them rep-

resented their own personal interests rather than the mass of the voters – particularly, the agrarian interests."[10] Thus, in practice, Beard concludes that "Jeffersonian Democracy simply meant the possession of the federal government by the agrarian masses led by an aristocracy of slave-owning planters and the theoretical repudiation of the right to use the Government for the benefit of any capitalistic groups, fiscal, banking, or manufacturing."[11]

Moreover, Beard challenges Libby's claim that such questions have long since passed into history. Beard notes that a belief in the concept of Jeffersonian democracy as one anchored in "the cherishment of the people...is still accepted with a whole heart wherever the magic of Jefferson's name remains undiminished. In wide circles it is an approved axiom."[12] Thus, understanding the real content of "Jeffersonian democracy" remains important to understanding contemporary political movements that invoke the myths of Jefferson's populist republicanism. In *Economic Origins*, Beard not only documents that Jeffersonian democracy found its social base in an agrarian, landed, and realty interest, he simultaneously documents Jefferson's own profound distrust of the urban and industrial working classes. Beard documents Jefferson's "avowed hostility to a working-class" through a review of his own writings.[13] Beard observes that "confidence in the reasonableness and virtue of man which Jefferson made the basis of his party's faith, wide as it was, did not extend to all men regardless of their economic interests and occupations, but was restricted to the free, stalwart, farmer secure in his economic basis."[14] In other words, Jeffersonian "democracy" was to be narrowly confined to independent landed proprietors, including small famers and the slave-owning class of plantation masters. The Jeffersonian democratic republic did not extend to women, African-Americans, Native Americans, or essentially anyone beyond a narrowly defined group of white middle class and upper class real estate-owning males. It was a narrowly circumscribed concept of a democratic republic, which excluded large swaths of the population from citizenship in that republic.

Beard never got past the second volume of his planned series. Instead, Beard spent the following two decades collaborating with his wife on the *magnum opus* that was to solidify his reputation as an icon of the new history. In 1927, the Beards published the first two volumes of *The Rise of American Civilization*, a general history which extended his earlier thesis by interpreting the course of American political development in terms of its transition from an agricultural era (1620 - 1877) to an industrial era (1877 - present). A dialectical clash between agricultural interests (Jeffersonianism) and capitalist interests (Hamiltonianism) had been the engine of American political development during this entire time. A decade later, the Beards published a third volume, *America in Mid-Passage* (1939), which developed a theme introduced in the last chapter of *The Rise*, where Beard predicted that the United States was on the verge of a transition to a new phase of social and industrial democracy.[15]

Consequently, while completing his *magnum opus*, Beard continually threw barbs at agrarian populists and Wilsonian liberals for their archaic economic conception of the United States as a middle class society and, consequently, what he called their fuzzy Jeffersonianism.[16] He warned contemporary readers that is a mistake to identify contemporary concepts of working class or social-democratic radicalism with Jeffersonian democracy, because from a *contemporary* standpoint, Jeffersonian populism was wedded to an economic theory that was reactionary even in its own time — always seeking the return to a mythical past — so to carry it uncritically into the present day merely obstructs the pursuit of more modern concepts of democracy in American politics.[17]

Clyde W. Barrow
University of Texas Rio Grande Valley

ENDNOTES

1. In the Preface, Beard (p. vii) observes that *Economic Origins of Jeffersonian Democracy* "is intended to be a modest contribution" to fulfilling Carl L. Becker's earlier prophesy "that American history will shortly be rewritten along economic lines." .On the method of economic interpretation, see, Clyde W. Barrow, *More Than a Historian: The Political and Economic Thought of Charles A. Beard* (New Brunswick, NJ: Transaction Publishers, 2000), Chaps. 2-3.

2. Charles A. Beard, *An Economic Interpretation of the Constitution of the United States* (New York: Free Press, 1913), p. 188

3. Richard Hofstadter, *The Progressive Historians: Turner, Beard, Parrington* (Chicago: University of Chicago Press, 1968), p. 181.

4. Eric F. Goldman, "A Historian at Seventy," *New Republic* 111 (November 27, 1944), p. 696.

5. E.L. Bogart, "Review of *Economic Origins of Jeffersonian Democracy* by Charles A. Beard," *The Annals of the American Academy of Political and Social Science* 63 (January 1916): 298-99; Frank I. Schecter, "Review of *Economic Origins of Jeffersonian Democracy* by Charles A. Beard," *The American Political Science Review*, Vol. 10, No. 1 (February 1916): 175-77; Charles H. Levermore, "Review of *Economic Origins of Jeffersonian Democracy* by Charles A. Beard," *The American Economic Review*, Vol. 6, No. 2 (June 1916): 352-53. Charles H. Hull, "Review of *Economic Origins of Jeffersonian Democracy* by Charles A. Beard," *The American Historical Review*, Vol. 22, No. 2 (January 1917): 401-03

6. Charles A. Beard, *Economic Origins of Jeffersonian Democracy* (New York: The Macmillan Company, 1915), p. 19.

7. Orin G. Libby, "Review *Economic Origins of Jeffersonian Democracy* by Charles A. Beard," *Mississippi Valley Historical Review*, Vol. 3, No. 1 (June 1916): 99-102.

8. Orin G. Libby, "Review of *Economic Interpretation of the Constitution of the United States* by Charles A. Beard." *Mississippi Valley Historical Review* Vol. 1, No. 1 (June 1914): 113-17. Libby was a professor of history and well-known protégé of Frederick Jackson Turner. Libby is best known for his dissertation, which was published as *The Geographical Distribution of the Vote of the Thirteen States on the Federal Constitution, 1787-1789* (Madison: University of Wisconsin Press, 1894).

9. Charles A. Beard, "Some Economic Origins of Jeffersonian Democracy," *The American Historical Review*, Vol. 19, No. 2 (January 2014), p. 282.

10. Ibid., p. 282.

11. Beard, *Economic Origins of Jeffersonian Democracy*, p. 467.

12. Beard, "Some Economic Origins," p. 282.

13. Beard, *Economic Origins of Jeffersonian Democracy*, pp. 427.

14. Ibid., pp. 424-25.

15. It is well established that the Beards maintained a strict division of labor in writing *The Rise of American Civilization*. Charles authored the sections and chapters dealing with economic and political history. Mary authored the sections and chapters dealing with cultural and intellectual history, see Nore, *Charles A. Beard*, p. 112; Nancy F. Cott, "Two Beards: Coauthorship and the Concept of Civilization," *American Quarterly*, Vol. 42, No. 2 (June 1990): 274-300.

16. Charles A. Beard, "Review of *The New Freedom: A Call for the Emancipation of the Generous Energies of a People*, by Woodrow Wilson," *Political Science Quarterly* 29 (September 1914): 506-507; Charles A. Beard, "Jefferson and the New Freedom," *New Republic* (November 14, 1914), p. 18; Charles A. Beard, "Review of *Property and Contract in their Relation to the Distribution of Wealth* by Robert T. Ely," *Political Science Quarterly* (September 1915), p. 511; Charles A. Beard, "The Myth of Rugged American Individualism," *Harper's Monthly Magazine* (December 1931), pp. 19-22; Charles A. Beard, *Jefferson, Corporations, and the Constitution* (Washington, D.C.: National Home Library Foundation, 1936), pp. 26-32. For extensive criticisms of Woodrow Wilson and Theodore Roosevelt, see, Beard, *Contemporary American History*, 1877-1913, pp. 254-377, passim.

17. Beard observes in his last book that he was certain the Founders of the American Republic "intended to set up a government endowed with broad national powers and that they expected their posterity to use those powers in dealing with questions, crises, and disturbances arising from generation to generation." He exemplified his claim by pointing to the Hamiltonian program of 1792-1798, which he called a "Federalist new deal" that had successfully pulled the country out of economic, financial, and political chaos through the adoption of strong national policies. Thomas Jefferson, James Madison, and former anti-Federalists opposed these policies, which led to the formal organization of Jefferson's Democratic-Republican party. See, Charles A. Beard, *The Republic*, with a new introduction by Clyde W. Barrow (New Brunswick, NJ: Transaction Publishers, 2008 [1943]), pp. 115, 124, 270.

"We may trace the contest between the capitalist and the democratic pioneer from the earliest colonial days."

PROFESSOR FREDERICK J. TURNER, in the American Historical Review, Vol. XVI, p. 227.

PREFACE

ONE of the most brilliant of the younger historians in the United States, Professor Carl L. Becker, of the University of Kansas, has prophesied that American history will shortly be rewritten along economic lines. This collection of essays on the first decade of politics under the Constitution is intended to be a modest contribution to the fulfilment of that prophecy.

In the preparation of the volume I have been laid under deep obligation to one of my students, Mr. C. J. Hendley, who spent many weeks with me examining pamphlets and newspapers.

CHARLES A. BEARD.

COLUMBIA UNIVERSITY,
July 30, 1915.

TABLE OF CONTENTS

ECONOMIC ORIGINS OF JEFFERSONIAN DEMOCRACY

CHAPTER I

THE FEDERALIST-REPUBLICAN ANTAGONISM AND THE CONFLICT OVER THE CONSTITUTION

An examination into the origins of Jeffersonian Democracy naturally opens with an inquiry whether there was any connection between that party and the large body of citizens who opposed the establishment of the Constitution of the United States. In the struggle over the adoption of that instrument, there appeared, it is well known, a sharp antagonism throughout almost the entire country. The views of competent contemporary observers and of modern students of the period are in accord on that point. Of this there can be no doubt. Chief Justice Marshall, a member of the Virginia ratifying convention and a Federalist of high standing, who combined with his unusual opportunities for personal observation his mastery of President Washington's private correspondence, informs us that the parties to the conflict over the Constitution were in some states evenly balanced, that in many instances the majority in favor of the new system was so small that its intrinsic merits alone would not have carried the day, that in some of the adopting states a majority of the people were in the opposition, and that in all of them the new government was accepted with

1

reluctance only because a dread of dismemberment of the union overcame hostility to the proposed fundamental law.[1] A half a century after Marshall thus described the contest over the ratification of the Constitution, Hildreth, a patient and discriminating student of the Federalist period, on turning over the sources in a fresh light, came to the same conclusion.[2] He frankly declared that it was exceedingly doubtful whether, upon a fair canvass, a majority of the people, in several of the states which ratified the Constitution, actually favored its adoption; that in the powerful states of Massachusetts, New York, Pennsylvania, and Virginia, the majority in favor of the new frame of government was very uncertain, so uncertain, in fact, as to raise the question whether there had been any majority at all; and that everywhere the voters of the states were sharply divided into two well-marked political parties. Bancroft, whose devotion to the traditions of the Constitution is never to be questioned, was no less emphatic than Hildreth in his characterization of the contest for the new political order as a hard-fought battle ending in victory snatched from the very jaws of defeat.[3] From the day of Hildreth and Bancroft to this, no serious student of the eighteenth century has doubted at least the severity and even balance of the conflict over the Constitution. Only those publicists concerned with the instant need of political controversies have been bold enough to deny that the fundamental law of the land was itself the product of one of the sharpest partisan contests in the history of the country.

This stubbornly fought battle over the Constitution was in the main economic in character, because the scheme of government contemplated was designed to effect, along

---

[1] *Life of Washington* (2d ed.), Vol. II, p. 127.
[2] Hildreth, *History of the United States* (1856), Vol. IV, pp. 25 ff.
[3] *History of the Constitution of the United States* (1882), Vol. II, pp. *passim*.

with a more adequate national defence, several commercial
and financial reforms of high significance, and at the same
time to afford an efficient check upon state legislatures
that had shown themselves prone to assault acquired property rights, particularly of personalty, by means of paper
money and other agrarian measures. To speak more
precisely, the contest over the Constitution was not primarily a war over abstract political ideals, such as state's
rights and centralization, but over concrete economic
issues, and the political division which accompanied it was
substantially along the lines of the interests affected — the
financiers, public creditors, traders, commercial men, manufacturers, and allied groups, centering mainly in the larger
seaboard towns, being chief among the advocates of the
Constitution, and the farmers, particularly in the inland
regions, and the debtors being chief among its opponents.
That other considerations, such as the necessity for stronger
national defence, entered into the campaign is, of course,
admitted, but with all due allowances, it may be truly said
that the Constitution was a product of a struggle between
capitalistic and agrarian interests.

This removal of the Constitution from the realm of pure
political ethics and its establishment in the dusty way of
earthly strife and common economic endeavor is not, as
some would have us believe, the work of profane hands.
It has come about through the gathering of the testimony
of contemporary witnesses of undoubted competency and
through the researches of many scholars. Although in the
minds of some, the extent of the economic forces may be
exaggerated and the motives of many leaders in the formation and adoption of the Constitution may be incorrectly
interpreted, the significant fact stands out with increasing boldness that the conflict over the new system of

government was chiefly between the capitalistic and agrarian classes.

Occupying an influential position in the former of these classes were the holders of the state and continental debt amounting to more than all the rest of the fluid capital in the United States. No less an important person than Washington assigned the satisfaction of the claims of the public creditors as the chief reason for the adoption of the Constitution, for he held that unless provisions were made for the payment of the debt, the country might as well continue under the old order of the Articles of Confederation. "I had endulged the expectation," he wrote to Jefferson, "that the New Government would enable those entrusted with its administration to do justice to the public creditors and retrieve the National character. But if no means are to be employed but requisitions, that expectation will be in vain and we may well recur to the old Confederation." [1]

Without doubting the fact that the standard of honor which Washington here set up was a consideration in the minds of many, it is no less a fact that the numerous holders of the public debt themselves formed a considerable centre corps in the political army waging the campaign for the adoption of the Constitution. For instance, a prominent Federalist of Connecticut, Chauncey Goodrich, a man placed by his connections and experience in a position to observe closely the politics of that and surrounding states, wrote, in 1790, that "perhaps without the active influence of the creditors, the government could not have been formed, and any well-grounded dissatisfaction on their part will make its movements dull and languid, if not worse." [2] The will-

---

[1] *Documentary History of the Constitution*, Vol. IV, p. 40.
[2] Gibbs, *Administrations of Washington and Adams*, Vol. I, p. 37.

ingness of a number of Northern men to break up the Union before the new government was fairly launched because they could not secure a satisfactory settlement of the debt is proof that Goodrich had correctly gauged the weight of the public creditors in the battle for the Constitution. To the testimony of Virginia and Connecticut in this matter of the influence of public creditors and allied interests in the formation and ratification of the Constitution we may add that of New York, then as now one of the first financial centres, speaking through a witness of such high authority that the most incredulous would hardly question it, — Alexander Hamilton, the first Secretary of the Treasury under the new system. He had been a member of the Convention which drafted the Constitution. He was intimately associated with the leaders in the movement for ratification. He shared in the preparation of that magnificent polemic, *The Federalist*. But above all, he was, as Secretary of the Treasury, in full possession of the names of those who funded continental and state securities after the Constitution was adopted. No one in all the United States, therefore, had such excellent opportunities to know the real forces which determined the constitutional conflict. What Goodrich could surmise, Hamilton could test by reference to the Treasury ledgers at his elbow. That the public creditors were "very influential" and the allied property interests, that is, in the main, capitalistic interests, were "very weighty" in securing the adoption of the Constitution, he distinctly avowed, although he wisely refrained from estimating exactly their respective values in the contest. In an unfinished manuscript on the funding system, he considered this matter at length, saying: "The public creditors, who consisted of various descriptions of men, a large proportion of them very meritorious and very influential, had had a considerable agency in promoting the adoption of the new Constitution, for this peculiar reason, among the many weighty reasons which were common to them as citizens and proprietors, that it exhibited the prospect of a government able to do justice to their claims. Their disappointment and disgust quickened by the sensibility of private interest, could not but have been extreme [if the debt had not been properly funded]. There was also another class of men, and a very weighty one, who had had great share in the establishment of the Constitution, who, though not personally interested in the debt, considered maxims of public credit as of the essence of good government, *as intimately connected by the analogy and sympathy of principles with the security of property in general*, and as forming an inseparable portion of the great system of political order. These men, from sentiment, would have regarded their labors in supporting the Constitution as in a great measure lost; they would have seen the disappointment of their hopes in the unwillingness of the government to do what they esteemed justice, and to pursue what they called an honorable policy; and they would have regarded this failure as an augury of the continuance of the fatal system which had for some time prostrated the national honor, interest, and happiness. The disaffection of a part of these classes of men might have carried a considerable reinforcement to the enemies of the government." [1]

Other contemporaries stressed other features in the conflict, but nevertheless agreed that it had been primarily economic in character. For instance, Fisher Ames, of Massachusetts, who had been a member of the state ratifying convention, laid emphasis upon the commercial rather

---

[1] Hamilton, *Works* (Lodge ed.), Vol. VII, p. 418. The smaller edition, not the Federal edition, is cited throughout this volume.

than the financial aspects of the constitutional battle. Speaking in the House of Representatives, on March 28, 1789, he said : "I conceive, sir, that the present Constitution was dictated by commercial necessity more than any other cause. The want of an efficient government to secure the manufacturing interests and to advance our commerce, was long seen by men of judgment and pointed out by patriots solicitous to promote our general welfare." [1] The inevitable inference from this remark is that, in Ames's opinion, men of commercial and manufacturing interests must have seen the possibilities of economic advantage in the adoption of the Constitution, and naturally arrayed themselves on its side.

More than a decade after the conflict over the Constitution, when many of the great actors in that drama had passed away, and there had been ample time and opportunity to reflect deeply upon the nature and causes of that struggle, Chief Justice Marshall described it, in effect, though not in exact terms, as a war between mercantile, financial, and capitalistic interests generally, on the one hand, and the agrarian and debtor interests, on the other. [2] Half a century later, Hildreth, whose work has been cited above, came to substantially identical conclusions. He declared that "in most of the towns and cities, and seats of trade and mechanical industry, the friends of the Constitution formed a very decided majority. Much was hoped from the organization of a vigorous national government and the exercise of extensive powers vested in it for the regulation of commerce." In North Carolina and Rhode Island, the states which first rejected the Constitution, Hildreth continued, the trouble was the state paper money which de-

[1] P. W. Ames, *Speeches of Fisher Ames*, p. 12.
[2] Beard, *Economic Interpretation of the Constitution*, p. 296.

stroyed the rights of creditors. In Massachusetts he found the "weight of talent, wealth, and influence" on the Federal side. In Virginia, the opponents of the Constitution included many of the great planters and "the backwoods population almost universally," and the opposition of the planters was to be, in part, ascribed to the fear of having to pay their debts due to British merchants in case the Constitution went into effect. In New York it was the City and the southern counties, not the interior agricultural regions, that supported the new scheme of national government.[1]

By a strange coincidence, Charles Francis Adams gave to the world the same economic interpretation of the Constitution in the very year that Hildreth published his history. In his life of his grandfather, the President, Mr. Adams, who enjoyed the unrivalled advantage of having access to documents closed to all his contemporaries, represented the adoption of the fundamental law of the United States as a triumph of property over the propertyless. The social disorder which preceded the federal Convention of 1787, Mr. Adams attributed to "the upheaving of the poorest classes to throw off all law of debtor and creditor," and the Convention itself, he declared, "was the work of commercial people in the seaport towns, of the planters of the slave-holding states, of the officers of the revolutionary army, and the property holders everywhere. . . . That among the opponents of the Constitution are to be ranked a great majority of those who had most strenuously fought the battle of independence of Great Britain is certain. . . . Among the federalists, it is true, were to be found a large body of the patriots of the Revolution, almost all the general officers who survived the war, and a great number of the substantial citizens along the line of the seaboard towns

[1] *Op. cit.*, Vol. IV, pp. 25 ff.

and populous regions, all of whom had heartily sympathized in the policy of resistance.   But these could never have succeeded in effecting the establishment of the Constitution, had they not received the active and steady coöperation of all that was left in America of attachment to the mother country, as well as of the moneyed interest, which ever points to strong government as surely as the needle to the pole." [1]

That which representative men of the eighteenth century definitely understood, and Hildreth implied in a somewhat rambling fashion was completely demonstrated by Professor O. G. Libby in his study of the *Geographical Distribution of the Vote on the Constitution in the Thirteen States:* the support for the Constitution came from the centres of capitalistic interest and the opposition came from the agrarians and those burdened with debts.   To adduce further evidence in support of Professor Libby's thesis is merely to add documentation to that which has been satisfactorily established.[2]

Inasmuch as the country was sharply divided over the ratification of the Constitution, and along fairly definite economic lines, it is natural to assume that these divisions did not disappear when the new government began to carry out the specific policies which had been implied in the language of the instrument and clearly seen by many as necessary corollaries to its adoption.[3]   It was hardly to have been expected that the bitter animosities which had been

---

[1] C. F. Adams, *The Works of John Adams*, Vol. I, p. 441.

[2] Beard, *Economic Interpretation of the Constitution.*   It is curious that this volume raised such a storm of criticism in certain quarters when the leading ideas set forth in it had long been accepted by students of the economic aspects of American history.

[3] *Economic Interpretation*, Chap. XI.   "In the friends of the new constitution, denominated federalists, as well as in its opponents, called anti-federalists, are to be seen the germs of the great political division of the country, which now sprang up and continued to prevail during the existence of at least one generation of men." C. F. Adams, *Works of John Adams*, Vol. I, p. 442.

aroused by that contest could be smoothed away at once and that men who had just been engaged in an angry political quarrel could join in fraternal greetings on the following morning. Many of the older historians assumed, therefore, without a detailed analysis of the facts in the case that the party division over the adoption of the Constitution formed the basis of the Federalist-Republican antagonism which followed the inauguration of the government.

Nevertheless, two careful students, Professor Bassett and Professor Libby, have recently given their support to the proposition that the political alignments which ensued over the ratification of the Constitution were not carried over into Washington's administrations but disappeared when the instrument was actually adopted. Professor Bassett informs us that "the Federalist party of 1787–1788 was not the same as the Federalists of 1791 : the former embraced all those who desired to save the country from the chaos of the government under the Articles of Confederation ; the latter included those who supported Hamilton in his plans for conducting the affairs of the country. Many who acted with Hamilton in 1788 were not with him three years later ; but this does not mean that if the old problems had to be faced again such men would be opposed to their former position. The problems of 1791 were new problems ; they had to do, not with union or chaos, but with two clearly defined lines of internal policy. After the completion of the ratification of the Constitution in 1788, anti-Federalism died because its *raison d'être* was gone. Although a few threats were made later to dissolve the Union, notably by Massachusetts when it seemed that assumption was defeated, such a policy received no serious support from any considerable number of men." [1]

---

[1] *The Federalist System*, p. 42. As a matter of fact, very few of the Anti-Federalists ever favored the complete dissolution of the Union.

This is a strong statement and it is so fundamental for the purposes of the study before us that it deserves the most careful and critical examination. A part of it is highly speculative, to say the least. We are informed that the constitutional Federalists were not identical with the Federalists of 1791, and that the later Federalists included in their ranks only those who supported Hamilton. Of course the statistical materials for demonstrating such a proposition — which rests of course upon facts susceptible of enumeration — are not forthcoming, and indeed cannot, from the nature of our records, ever be forthcoming in any adequate manner. But letting the statement stand, we may ask: "Were not those who supported Hamilton's fiscal measures drawn almost wholly from 'those who desired to save the country from the chaos of government under the Articles of Confederation'?" Again we may ask: "Did not those who were opposed to saving the country from chaos constitute the bulk of the party that opposed Hamilton's measures?" It might be possible, therefore, by one interpretation to accept Professor Bassett's dictum on this point and yet hold that the party division over the ratification of the Constitution formed, in the main, the basis of the division into Federalist and Republican after 1789.

Finally, serious objection may be justly taken to the statement that the problems of 1791 were "new problems." On the contrary, they were exactly the problems which had been raised during the conflict over ratification: the adjustment of the federal and state debts, the regulation of commerce, the enforcement of the terms of the British treaty, the settlement of land titles in Virginia and other Southern states, the payments of debt due principally in the South to British creditors, the establishment of the currency on a sound basis, and the restraint of the states in their attacks or property. Men divided during ratification because they knew that the adoption of the Constitution meant in a general way the settlement of these momentous matters, and after the new government was inaugurated men divided over the concrete measures which expressed the principles laid down in the Constitution. After all, principles must find their embodiment in certain men or groups of men, and the question in 1791 was practically the same as in 1787: "Who shall rule and how?" Hamilton knew this, Washington knew it, the wisest men of the time knew it, and that accounts for their extreme solicitude about the election of the "proper" persons to form the living expression of the new instrument of government.[1]

Professor O. G. Libby, whose work on the adoption of the Constitution gives special weight to his words on the subject, is no less emphatic than Professor Bassett on the point that the Federalist and Anti-Federalist division of 1787–1788 was not the basis of the later Federalist-Republican cleavage.[2] He flatly says that it is a "fallacy" to hold that the divisions obtaining during the struggle over the adoption of the Constitution were continued into Washington's administration, and adds: "In considering the factional divisions during the administrations of Washington, one must bear in mind that the issue that had divided Federalist from Anti-Federalist, namely, the adoption of the new Constitution, no longer existed in 1789, with the inauguration of our first President. Consequent upon the passing away of this particular issue, the two parties that had fought over it had also passed away in every one of the original thirteen states, except perhaps in the faction-ridden state of Rhode

---

[1] See below, pp. 87 ff.

[2] Articles in The Quarterly Journal of the University of North Dakota, Vols. II and III.

Island. So simple and plain a proposition as this seems to have given endless trouble to historians." [1]

Professor Libby goes even further. He denies that there was any real party cleavage during the administrations of Washington and Adams. Factional controversies and personal animosities, he admits, were abundant, but genuine party divisions did not exist. The funding and assumption measures did not produce parties. Jefferson labored in vain during Washington's first administration to build up an organization; but Washington by his judicial conduct and skilful management prevented the formation of national parties. "The almost immediate success of the new bank and the general satisfaction it gave to the taxpayers as well as to the moneyed interests put it out of reach as a party issue for the future.[2] . . . The immediate success of Hamilton's initial revenue and financial measures and the wise caution of Washington's foreign policy left no room for party organization. In characterizing this period, therefore, we may call it a purely transitional one as far as party organization is concerned. It was fruitful in private jealousies and factional and sectional animosities. Men were intolerant of each other and the newspapers poured the foulest abuse upon opponents, sparing not even the most blameless. The experiment of administering the national government under the new instrument had proved a success."[3]

It was not until the administration of John Adams, according to Professor Libby, that a real political party began to come into existence, and it was the alien and sedition laws that afforded Jefferson the opportunity to create a genuine

---

[1] *Loc. cit.*, Vol. III, p. 294.

[2] The pamphlet and periodical literature of the decade from 1790 to 1800 does not bear out this assertion. On the contrary the Bank was one of the leading issues of the period. See below, Chap. VII.   [3] *Loc. cit.*, Vol. II, pp. 218, 219.

political organization. "Jefferson, alone, of all the public men in America, grasped the full significance of the mistake made by Adams and his supporters. He saw as clearly as did Hamilton the storm of denunciation which would descend upon them for their unwarranted severity towards our alien residents and for the inexcusable blunder of the Sedition laws, that menaced freedom of speech and of the press. . . . From his long residence in Europe and his travels in several countries, he was conversant with industrial and social conditions there as was no one else in America. The French Revolution had opened his eyes to the grievances of the down trodden masses. He was aware how their thoughts had been turning toward America, as the land where liberty and equality were more than a theory and where there was land and a home for all. He had watched the diplomatic situation of France carefully and had sensed the meaning of that long and exhausting war which had already begun to rage in Europe. The interruption of peaceful occupations and the devastation wrought by hostile invasion would inevitably turn adrift numberless artisans, farmers, and day laborers. Their natural goal was America. . . . As a typical Virginian he had unbounded faith in the potentialities of the new West and he realized how vitally important it was that every possible stream of population should be made to flow into these vacant lands. With prophetic insight he saw the forward sweep of population farther and farther westward. . . . Thus he launched the new Republican party on the ample platform of national expansion. The French Revolution had proclaimed liberty and equality for all mankind. Jefferson now made concrete application of the principle by announcing as the surest basis of national well-being the free citizens living under its laws, the men of many nations, assembled under

our flag to enjoy the blessing of a free state.   In the march
of events having a world-wide import, Jefferson had seized
the psychological moment to offer himself as a leader with
a message of deepest moment for the humble and oppressed
of every land. . . . The Presidential election of 1800 marks
a turning point in our national history no less important
than does the adoption of our present Constitution.   It
signalized the initial victory of the first political party which
professed to represent the American people.   The career of
this party is in complete contrast with the vacillating course
of the shifting factions described in the administrations of
Washington and Adams." [1]

After these generalities, Professor Libby descends to
particulars.   Starting with a somewhat strict definition of
the term "party," he analyzes the votes in the first House
of Representatives during Washington's administrations.
Of the measures which arose in the first Congress he selects
twenty-one "that may properly be considered as national,
as having a bearing on the central administration in any
vital way."   He then treats these as "administration
measures," and records the vote for and against each one.
Grouping the votes, he finds twenty-four members consistently supporting the government, seven consistently opposing, and thirty-one divided in their votes.   Applying the
same method to the votes in the House during the second
Congress, Professor Libby finds "that thirty-two gave a
large majority of their votes to the support of the administration, twenty-three were in the opposition, and fourteen
were fairly divided in their vote."   Commenting on this,
he adds : "Compared to the showing in the first Congress,
there seems to have been a very decided grouping into something approaching parties.   But the defeat on the culmi-

[1] *Loc. cit.*, Vol. II, pp. 221 ff.

nating issue at the end of the session [censuring the Secretary of the Treasury] showed conclusively how transitory were the affiliations that had so far held the groups together."

In the third and fourth Congresses, Professor Libby finds even a greater lack of uniform party voting. In the third Congress, seventeen members supported the government, eight opposed it, while seventy-six were divided in their votes. In the fourth Congress, twenty-four supported the government, thirty-five were in the opposition, and fifty-three were divided. "In summing up the votes for all four Congresses, it will be found that the Federal Government was supported by ninety-seven members and was opposed by seventy-three members, a total of 170. Those members of Congress having a vote divided in the ratio of two to one numbered 177, a most significant fact with reference to the nature of the factions during this whole period."

Finally, Professor Libby attacks the conclusion of Hildreth, Schouler, and Henry Adams to the effect that Federalism in 1800 was supported by professional, mercantile, and capitalistic classes representing wealth and talents, particularly in New England, — those sections which had carried the Constitution to a successful ratification more than a decade before. The election results of 1800, says Professor Libby, do not in the least bear out this conclusion. "From the returns of the vote by towns in the election for governor in 1800 in Massachusetts, it can be seen from a town map of the state that the Republicans carried Boston and practically the entire eastern half of the state except Essex county. . . . The Massachusetts Federalists in 1800 are from precisely the same general region as the Anti-Federalists in 1788 and the Shays rebels of 1786. If the opinions quoted above [from Adams] are correct, then the wealth, talent, learning and social rank of Massachusetts must have migrated wholesale into the back country districts of the state since 1788. But if we keep clearly in mind the policies and methods of the supporters of Adams in their reckless assault on the rights of citizens and aliens in 1798, it will be easy to reconcile such unwisdom with the constituencies who are their strongest supporters in 1800. Such temper is not at all incompatible with that which inspired the attempted overthrow of law and order in 1786 and resisted the establishment of central government in 1788. On the other hand, the voters in eastern Massachusetts were far too intelligent and progressive to support the un-American course of the Federalists. . . . The situation in Massachusetts may be taken as fairly typical for New England.[1] In the middle section, Pennsylvania was so clearly with Jefferson in spite of the conservatism of her upper house, that we must turn to New York for a comparison of the two parties in this election. The vote of the New York Legislature for presidential electors, November 6, 1800, shows approximately the location of the parties at that date.[2] Thirty-nine votes, representing twelve counties, were cast for the Federal candidates and sixty-one votes, representing fourteen counties, were cast for the Republican candidates. An examination of the respective areas controlled by the two parties shows that the Federal area had a per capita population of 9.9 per square mile and the Republican area a per capita population of 20.9 per square mile. A similar comparison for the value of real estate for 1799 shows that the Federal area, omitting the very extensive and thinly populated western county of Ontario (Federal) had a per capita valuation of $134 and the Republican area a per capita valuation of $179.2. It is clear

[1] Compare, however, the vote in Connecticut and Rhode Island in 1800. See below, p. 379.
[2] See below, p. 30, for an examination of the accuracy of this statement.

that we have here a similar situation to that ascertained for Massachusetts. The Federal party in New York represented country constituencies in sparsely settled regions remote from the activity of business life and out of touch with national progress along every line. The source of the misapprehension concerning the election of 1800 has been two-fold : first, the confusing of issues with party names, so that the Federal party of 1788 is assumed to be the same ten years later ; second, the entire omission of any transitional period following the adoption of the second constitution, during the administration of Washington. Added to this has been the faulty method of investigation upon which rested the conclusions reached. Apparently, no effort has been made by the historians cited to examine such returns of the elections as are available and to determine the geographical location of the constituencies supporting the opposing parties." [1]

The important conclusions advanced by Professor Libby on the basis of his researches may be summarized as follows :

1. No substantial party divisions were manifested during Washington's administration, as tested by the votes in the House of Representatives.

2. The Republican or Jeffersonian party sprang forth in full panoply only after the enactment of the alien and sedition laws.

3. Jefferson built his party on "a group of issues involving fundamental principles in American politics and citizenship," offered by the alien and sedition laws.

4. There is apparently no relation at all between the Federal party of 1788 and the Federal party of 1800, for the votes in the latter year show the regions of wealth and talent to be on Jefferson's side.

[1] *Loc. cit.*, Vol. II, pp. 227 ff.

5. The Jeffersonian party was founded not on any set of economic doctrines but upon some general principles of American liberty.

The documentation and methods of reasoning upon which so remarkable a thesis rests deserve careful examination. First, let us consider his denial of the existence of parties during Washington's and Adams' administration. Of course everything here depends upon the definition of the term "party," and Professor Libby has not left it undefined. On the contrary, he says : "A political party can hardly be said to have an existence unless some issue of more than passing or local importance lies back of its appearance and upon which a majority of its members have taken their stand. A second essential in a political party is that its members and representatives are sufficiently intelligent to stand together on all votes and elections involving the issue or issues of the day which the party has accepted as its own. The presence of a party leader or leaders is generally considered essential to successful continuance in the field of politics, though this is a variable factor, subject to considerable fluctuation from time to time. Lastly the parties of a given period cease to exist when the issue that divides them, for sufficient reason, has ceased to have any further importance." [1]

It is not often useful to quarrel over niceties in terms, but it may be said in passing that it would be difficult, if not almost impossible, to find in any age or any country a political party in the strict sense used in Professor Libby's articles.[2] If we take the votes in Congress on tariff schedules (not the formal vote on the entire bills), more frequently than not we find a shattering of the ranks of the Republican

[1] *Loc. cit.*, Vol. III, p. 294.
[2] See Lowell, *The Government of England*, Vol. II, pp. 71 ff. *American Historical Association Report* for 1901.

and Democratic parties, and yet it must be admitted that the tariff is an issue of more than local importance over which "parties" have divided. In the state of New York where voters are rigidly enrolled in parties and the rank and file have been under disciplined leadership for years, anything like strict and continuous party divisions in the legislature have been far more rare than such divisions in the first Congress.[1] We even find the anti-militarist Social-Democrats in Germany voting for increased military expenditures, not because they are on that side from "principle," but because they know that in case of a defeat of the government's proposal, a dissolution of the Reichstag would occur and an election be held during a "patriotic" fervor.[2] Indeed, it is one of the evidences of skilled leadership if a party is able to formulate its measures in such a manner as to break the ranks of the opposition.

A far more fundamental objection may be urged against Professor Libby's conclusions on the ground that his methods are not altogether invulnerable. In the first place, the measures which he has selected as the basis of testing the votes in the House of Representatives cannot all be treated with the same degree of certainty as "administration measures" to which "opposition" would naturally be expected. For example, in the first Congress the establishment of a Department of Foreign Affairs, the compensation of members of Congress, the salaries of officers in the executive department, the appropriation of money for goods to be used in negotiating Indian treaties, and the United States mint were not propositions on which we should expect a division based upon any fundamental interests such as those raised by the funding, bank, and revenue bills. If we should

---

[1] Colvin, *The Bicameral Principle: a Study of the New York Legislature* (N. Y., 1913).   [2] This was written before the great events of August, 1914.

eliminate a number of the laws which cannot properly be called administration measures and which affected no economic interests directly, we should find far more consistency in voting and something approaching more nearly to Professor Libby's strict definition of a party system. The same objection may be brought against the measures of the other Congresses employed as tests of party alignment, and particularly in the second Congress. In this Congress there was a degree of consistency in voting which Professor Libby admits almost amounted to a party division, but he claims the defeat on the culminating issue at the end of the session showed conclusively "how transitory were the affiliations that had so far held the groups together." Now these last measures, six in number, were resolutions condemning the conduct of the Secretary of the Treasury, Hamilton. It is entirely reasonable to expect a strong defection from the opposition on these propositions, because men who differed from Hamilton on fiscal policies did not question his personal honesty. Furthermore, so many members of Congress were themselves security holders and personally involved in the operations of the Treasury that a condemnation of Hamilton's Treasury administration would have been a condemnation of themselves.[1]

Now let us take the measures selected by Professor Libby to try out the party vote in the third Congress. For example, he treats as "an administration measure" the resolution of non-intercourse with Great Britain, introduced on April 7 by Clark, of New Jersey, but it is difficult to discover what valid reason can be assigned for including this among the propositions employed to test the opposition vote. In fact, we know from a long and important letter written by Hamilton to Washington on April 14, 1794,

[1] See below, p. 202.

seven days after Clark introduced his resolution, that non-intercourse with Great Britain was not deemed an organic part of Federalist policy. The views of his party Hamilton sums up as follows: "to take effectual measures of military preparation, creating, in earnest, force and revenue; to vest the President with important powers respecting navigation and commerce for ulterior contingencies — to endeavor by another effort of negotiation, confided to hands able to manage it, and friendly to the object, to obtain reparation for the wrongs we suffer, and a demarkation of a line of conduct to govern in future; to avoid till the issue of that experiment all measures of a nature to occasion a conflict between the motives which might dispose the British government to do us the justice to which we are entitled and the sense of its own dignity. If that experiments fails, then and not till then to resort to reprisals and war."

Having thus stated the policy of his party, Hamilton then takes up a consideration of the non-intercourse resolution, and treats it as entirely contrary to the letter and spirit of the Federalist programme: "The proposition for cutting off all intercourse with Great Britain has not yet sufficiently developed itself to enable us to pronounce what it truly is. It may be so extensive in its provisions as even to include in fact, though not in form, sequestration, by rendering remittances penal or impracticable. Indeed, it can scarcely avoid so far interfering with the payment of debts already contracted, as in a great degree to amount to a virtual sequestration. But, however this may be, being adopted for the express purpose of retaliating or punishing injuries, to continue until those injuries are redressed, it is in a spirit of a reprisal. Its principle is avowedly coercion — a principle directly opposite to that of negotiation, which supposes an appeal to the reason and justice of the party. Caustic and stimulant in the highest degree, it cannot fail to have a correspondent effect upon the minds of those against whom it is directed. It cannot fail to be viewed as originating in motives of the most hostile and overbearing kind; to stir up all the feelings of pride and resentment in the nation as well as in the Cabinet; and, consequently, to render negotiations abortive.[1] "

The policy here outlined by Hamilton was accepted by Washington in full, as the subsequent negotiations through Jay, and the maintenance of the Jay treaty, conclusively show. To treat the non-intercourse resolution, therefore, as an administration measure and to charge the New England members with vacillation and factional spirit because they supported the carriage tax designed to sustain public credit and voted against non-intercourse with Great Britain which meant the destruction of New England commerce is surely unwarranted. The votes recorded for this measure should be recorded against the administration and those against the resolution should be treated as administration votes.

There is likewise just ground for questioning the warrant for including as tests the votes taken on the bill levying tonnage duties on American and foreign ships, in May, 1794. This measure was one of a long list of provisions designed to increase the public revenue and support the public credit; but it was not an essential or vital part of them. The representatives from the New England and middle commercial states did not relish any tax on shipping and they were able to strike it out, with the aid of some representatives from Southern states that were not vitally

[1] *Works* (Lodge ed.), Vol. IV, pp. 282 ff.

interested one way or another. The resolutions of which the tonnage duties formed a part were reported to the house from the committee of the whole on May 7, 1794, and it is difficult to say with what justice they, in particular, may be called administration measures.[1] Even if they were to be so included, we should naturally expect to find the commercial interests of the Northern states against them.

Similar exceptions may be taken to Professor Libby's classification of measures of the fourth Congress. Why, for instance, should the admission of Tennessee be treated as an administration measure? Professor Libby does not explain. The resolution in question grew out of a presidential message sent to Congress on April 8, 1796, transmitting papers submitted by Governor Blount, including a census report and the new constitution of the state. Washington cautiously remarked that, among the rights enjoyed by the inhabitants of that territory under the act of cession of 1792, "appear" to be the right of forming a constitution and entering the Union. There is no proof at all that he or that little group of advisers who constituted the heart of the administration regarded the admission of Tennessee as a party measure in any sense.[2] The resolution to admit the state was prepared and introduced by a select committee appointed at the time Washington transmitted the papers to Congress. Under the circumstances one has little warrant for charging the members of the commercial states with factional inconsistency because they voted against admitting to the Union a backwoods agricultural region (certain to be Republican) and

---

[1] *Annals of Congress*, 3d Con., 1793–1795, p. 653.

[2] In fact the Federalists opposed the admission of Tennessee because it was a measure intended to help Jefferson to the presidency. American Historical Review, Vol. IV, p. 652.

voted in favor of upholding the Jay treaty which guaranteed the continuance of commercial relations with Great Britain.

The truth is that it is difficult to classify all of the acts of Congress during Washington's administration. The measures providing for the funding of the debt, establishing the bank, maintaining the army and navy at a high standard, keeping trade and commerce with Great Britain open, sustaining the public credit, and clearing the Indians off the frontier were really the only measures which can be called "administration" in any strict sense of that term, and on these propositions there was a striking degree of unanimity among the commercial and financial sections as opposed to the agrarian regions.

In fact, the politics of the period would show the sharp party alignments required to meet Professor Libby's tests only if the administration group had uniformly introduced measures designed wholly in the interests of a certain class or section. This would have been impossible, even if the leaders in that group had thought it desirable or expedient. After the funding of the debt and the establishment of the Bank, revenue measures were among the leading propositions advanced by the administration. Revenue was indispensable to the maintenance of the public credit and the stability of the Bank and all the fiscal and financial operations built upon them. Doubtless Hamilton and his party would have preferred to raise revenue by means entirely acceptable to all sections and classes of the country, and they relied as far as possible upon indirect taxes as impalpable as could be devised. But such taxes were not adequate to meet the demands for revenue, and resort to other forms was necessary. To have refused the grants of new duties and taxes would have been repudiation of the debt, in a degree at least. In view of the large number of security holders in Congress itself [1] this had become impossible, even if there had been popular sanction for it. Consequently every economic resource in the country had to be reached by federal taxes, and under the circumstances compromises and a resultant breaking of party lines inevitably followed.

To show how the subsidiary measures of the Federalist leaders often cut athwart the ranks of their own party and enlisted support from those ordinarily classed among the opposition is an easy matter. An incident which illustrates the process is described by Madison in a letter written to Jefferson, on May 11, 1794. He tells us that the report of the committee searching for additional revenues was the work of a subcommittee, "in understanding with the Fiscal Department," and included besides stamp duties, excises on tobacco and sugar manufactured in the United States, and "a tax on carriages as an *indirect* tax." These measures were highly objectionable to Madison and yet he was compelled to admit, to his chagrin, that "the aversion to direct taxes, which appeared by a vote of seventy odd for rejecting them, will saddle us with all those pernicious innovations, without ultimately avoiding direct taxes in addition to them. All opposition to the new excises, though enforced by memorials from the manufacturers, was vain. And the tax on carriages succeeded, in spite of the Constitution, by a majority of twenty, the advocates for the principle being reinforced by the adversaries to luxury. Six of the *North Carolina* members were in the majority. This is another proof of the facility with which usurpation triumphs where there is a standing corps always on the watch for favorable conjunctures, and directed by the policy of dividing their

[1] See below, Chap. VI.

honest but undiscerning adversaries." [1] Certainly, we are not warranted in assuming that the opposition members of the North Carolina group who thus voted for a Federalist measure underwent any change in their general partisan feelings.

But granting, for the sake of argument, Professor Libby's contention that there was no sharp party antagonism in the House of Representatives during Washington's administration, we need not accept his conclusion that there was no substantial party division in the country at large, that there was no fairly consistent body of voters in general support of the government and no fairly consistent body of voters in general opposition to it. Why the hot battles at the polls in nearly every important constituency if there were only "factions" and no parties? Why did the newspapers of the time classify candidates into Federalists and Anti-Federalists, if such groupings were imaginary? Moreover are we to reject the abundant testimony of such competent observers as Hamilton, Madison, Marshall, Ames, Jefferson, and even Washington himself,[2] in favor of testimony derived from tables of votes in the House of Representatives, tested by measures arbitrarily selected and tried by partisan concepts which have never been realized anywhere in practice? That there was great uncertainty of opinion on the part of many people and that there was considerable movement from one side to the other will not be questioned. These things appear under the most decided party régimes. But the burden of proof is still upon the historian who asserts that there was not in the United States, during Washington's administrations, two fairly consistent and substantial groups, one indorsing and the other opposing, in the main, the policies of the federal government.

[1] Madison, *Writings* (1867 ed.), Vol. II, p. 14.   See below, pp. 62 ff.

If we remain unconvinced by Professor Libby's important tables designed to show that there were no parties, we may be even less moved by his declaration that the conflict over the Constitution bore no relation to the partisan struggle which later arose. The difficulties of proving by mathematical politics the existence or non-existence of such a relation are well-nigh insuperable. In the first place, when we compare the map of the vote on the Constitution with a map showing by districts the vote in the House of Representatives, we have to remember that all of the members of the House were not elected by districts as were the members of the state conventions which ratified the Constitution. In the first Congress in which the votes were cast on Hamilton's crucial measures, the Representatives from New Hampshire, Connecticut, New Jersey, Pennsylvania, and Georgia were elected at large. Delaware and Rhode Island had only one Representative each. In Maryland, each voter cast his ballot for the whole list of six Representatives, but it was required that he should vote for one member living in his district. Massachusetts, New York, Maryland, Virginia, North Carolina, and South Carolina elected by districts, but the congressional district was so much larger than the state convention district [1] of 1787–1788 that identical measurements of the popular vote cannot be taken.

In the second place, it must be remembered that our local election figures for the period are painfully meagre. The statistics of the votes in the New England towns in the election of delegates to the state ratifying conventions are so scanty as to be almost negligible. A few returns for the larger towns are reported in the newspapers. The

---

[1] In New England the town was the unit of representation in the state conventions which ratified the Constitution.

records of the town meetings seem merely to show that certain men were elected to the conventions, and do not state by what vote or what majority.[1] For New York we have only fragmentary returns and from the Middle and Southern states meagre newspaper reports. Our figures for the first congressional elections seem almost as scanty. For the election of 1800 a surprisingly large number of returns are available, but they are at best unsatisfactory.

Such figures as we have, however, completely demonstrate the impossibility of proving Professor Libby's broad thesis that there was no substantial relation between the antagonism over the Constitution and the party antagonism which followed, because these figures show a very light vote on the Constitution as compared with the vote in the crucial election of 1800, and thus prevent our tracing the movements of electors from one side to the other. In Boston, for example, only 760 men, out of some 2700 entitled to vote, took the trouble to express any opinion at all on the adoption of the Constitution, whereas over 3000 voted in the election of 1800. That is, four times as many voted on the Jeffersonian issue as voted on the Constitution. In New York county, with all property qualifications removed, 2869 electors participated in the choice of delegates to the state convention in 1788, but in the election of 1800, 5757 votes were cast in New York City alone, to say nothing of the county, and that with the property qualifications applied. It is readily apparent that every man who voted for the Constitution in 1787–1788, in these cities, may have voted for Adams, the Federalist candidate, in 1800, and the victory have still remained with the Republicans. How can we say, therefore, that the Federalists of 1788 went over to

[1] I am indebted to Mr. Spencer Miller, Jr., for examining Massachusetts records on this point. The Connecticut records which I have investigated are no more explicit.

Jefferson or the Anti-Federalists over to Adams by merely comparing the colors on a map? More than once New York state has gone Democratic because the rural Republicans remained away from the polls; in other words, the political map has been completely changed without any appreciable change in party feeling or convictions. Political maps must always be checked up by reference to other sources of information, for standing alone they are often misleading.

Certainly the proposition that the party alignments of 1788 were reversed or even indiscriminately broken in 1800 cannot be established on the few figures which Professor Libby adduces in support of his thesis.[1] A far closer analysis of the election returns than he presents will have to be made. There is, for instance, great danger in treating the vote in such large areas as he does. This is illustrated by the figures given below relative to the vote in the wards of the city of New York in 1800.[2] Professor Libby taking a large area as his working unit rightly puts the city and county of New York in the Democratic column in the election of 1800, but the maps printed below, based on a study of the wards and streets of New York, show that the heart of the old city, Broad Street, Whitehall, Maiden Lane, Pearl Street, William, State, and Wall streets, where the wealth and culture of the city were located, were loyal to Federalism in 1800 as in the contest over the ratification of the Constitution. The truck gardeners, laborers, and farmers of the outlying districts overwhelmed the men of trade and finance at the lower end of Manhattan. If we had such detailed figures for other areas, we might come to the mathematical conclusion which is so much to be desired.

Another illustration of the inconclusive character of Professor Libby's statistical methods is his treatment of the election of 1800 in Boston. He informs us that "from the returns of the vote by towns in the election for governor in 1800 in Massachusetts it can be seen from a town map of the state that the Republicans carried Boston." On the basis of the vote as represented by the map he assumes that the wealth, talent, and social rank of the state turned to Jefferson, and his explanation is that the alien and sedition laws of Adams' administration produced a reaction in the minds of the cultured classes of Boston not unlike that produced by Shays' attack on the social order. Now as a matter of record, Boston went Republican in 1800 by the narrow margin of twenty-four votes and Strong, the Federalist candidate for governor, polled 1531 votes;[1] that is, more than twice the entire number cast in the town in 1787 when the delegates to the state convention called to ratify the federal Constitution were chosen. It is apparent, therefore, that every Federalist of 1787 who was living in 1800 may have cast his vote for the Federalist party for anything that we know or can discover.

To recapitulate, we may say, therefore, that Professor Libby's tests of partisan alignments in the first Congresses cannot all be accepted, that his definition of a political "party" is too strict, and that the crossing of party lines in the legislature on many measures is such a common matter, even where fairly definite party government is acknowledged, as to excite no surprise at all when we find it in the period of Washington's administrations.

In the second place, in view of our meagre figures for the vote on the Constitution and the certain smallness of that vote as compared with the vote in the election of 1800, we must hold that Professor Libby's contention that the

---

[1] A. E. Morse, *The Federalist Party in Massachusetts*, p. 179 n.

Federalist and Republican parties of the latter date were not the lineal descendants of the Federalist and Anti-Federalist parties of the constitutional conflict yet remains to be proved. Indeed, we may say that it cannot be proved by the comparative political map-making process, for the reason (among others) that there was an enormous increase in the vote of 1800 over that of 1787–1788, an increase altogether out of proportion to the increase in population. It may very well be that the Federalists who supported the Constitution were in the main loyal to the Federalist party, and were simply overwhelmed by a new army of the opposition raised up by the concrete measures realized under the Constitution and by the profound agitation which stirred America when the floods of the French Revolution were loosened.

Finally, with reference to Professor Libby's whole contention that there were no political parties between 1789 and 1800, we may say that contemporaries, no less capable and penetrating than Jefferson, Hamilton, Washington, Madison, and Gerry, thought there were political parties. Men constantly spoke of the Federalist and Republican or Anti-Federalist parties. Organizations representing these two groups put up candidates in the important constituencies and soon began to wage hot electoral battles in behalf of their favorites. And after the elections the newspapers recorded so many votes for the Federalist and so many for the Republican candidates, and the mathematical politicians set to work to figure out the strength of the respective parties in Congress and in the state governments. That lines were sometimes confused on measures of slight importance or on measures which, of necessity, cut across both capitalistic and agrarian interests there can be no doubt, but unquestionably there was within each of the contending groups a large corps consistently loyal to its standards — a corps so large and so coherent as to deserve the name "party." Notwithstanding the able arguments of Professors Bassett and Libby, we are still fully justified in asking the question: "Was there not a fundamental relation between the division over the adoption of the Constitution and the later party antagonism between Federalists and Anti-Federalists?"

CHAPTER II

IN the absence of adequate statistical material on the relation of the constitutional parties to the later political parties, we must resort to circumstantial evidence. If there was no relation between the party alignment of 1787–1788 and that which followed the inauguration of the new government, then by the law of probability, we should find the men whose views on the adoption of the Constitution are positively known to us, distributed with a fair degree of equality between the two parties. That is, Federalists of the constitutional conflict should be fairly divided between the Federalist and Republican parties, and Anti-Federalists of that conflict likewise fairly divided. Indeed, if we should take Professor Libby strictly at his word, we might expect to find the former party connections entirely reversed.

The roll of distinguished men of the period whose political history may be most easily traced is that of the Convention which drafted the Constitution and it is peculiarly appropriate that we should inquire what were their party affiliations during the decade which followed the establishment of the Federal system. We shall, therefore, take them up in alphabetical order.

Abraham Baldwin, of Georgia, a signer of the Constitution, was a Representative in the first, second, third, fourth, and fifth Congresses and served in the United States Senate from 1799 until his death in 1807. Baldwin voted against the assumption of state debts, but it cannot be discovered whether he voted for or against the general proposition to fund the continental debt at face value, for there is no record of the votes on that matter. Baldwin was in the opposition from the beginning and remained a consistent Republican until his death. It is not apparent, however, that he desired to carry Jefferson's cherishment of the people doctrine [1] to extreme lengths, for in the Philadelphia Convention he had contended that the Senate should represent property and that in constituting the upper house "some reference ought to be had to the relative wealth of their constituents and to the principles on which the senate of Massachusetts was constituted." [2] At the time, the senate of Massachusetts rested on property qualifications and representation was distributed among the districts on the basis of the taxable property in each. Baldwin therefore evidently thought that property needed a defence against "the people" in the upper house of the new government.

Richard Bassett, of Delaware, a signer of the Constitution, was a member of the Senate during the first Congress, 1789–1791, and he voted for the Judiciary Act although he is recorded against the funding bill. He was chief justice of the court of common pleas in his state from 1793 to 1799 and in the latter year he was elected as a Federalist to the office of governor. In 1801 he was among the midnight appointees selected by President Adams to fill the new circuit courts recently erected for the purpose (among other things) of intrenching the Federalists in the judicial department of the government. Bassett was, therefore, among the judges deposed by the Republicans when they repealed

---

[1] Jefferson said that the party cleavage was due to the fact that the Federalists feared and distrusted the people and Republicans cherished them. See below, p. 417.

[2] Farrand. *Records*, Vol. I, p. 469.

the Judiciary Act in Jefferson's first administration.[1] It appears that he consistently adhered to his early Federalist opinion until his death in 1815.[2]

Gunning Bedford, of Delaware, a signer of the Constitution, was appointed to a federal district judgeship by Washington and remained on the bench until his death. Bedford was a zealous Federalist. He supported Chase during his impeachment by the Republicans and he thought it not incompatible with his judicial office to preside at a meeting at which a toast to Jefferson, as President of the United States, was voted down. His biographer tells us that Bedford "undoubtedly sympathized with Federalist principles" and that he "disliked French doctrines and habits of dress. He never adopted trousers, but adhered to short breeches, knee buckles, and wore a queue with powdered hair." [3]

John Blair, of Virginia, was among the signers of the Constitution and he labored valiantly in Virginia to secure its ratification, serving in the state convention and recording his vote there in favor of the new plan. When Washington was casting about for judges of the first Supreme Court organized in 1789 he selected Blair for a position as Associate Justice because of his eminent services as Chief Justice of the Virginia Court of Appeals. As a member of the state court he had agreed with his colleagues in the case of Commonwealth *v.* Caton that the tribunal "had power to declare any resolution or act of the legislature, or either branch of it to be unconstitutional and void." [4] Blair resigned his Associate Justiceship in 1796 and retired to Virginia, where he died in 1800. It seems, however, that he never surrendered

---

[1] For Bassett's protest against the repeal of the Judiciary Act which deprived him of his office, see *American State Papers: Miscellaneous*, Vol. I, p. 340.

[2] W. T. Read, *Life of George Read*, p. 557.

[3] J. P. Nields, *Gunning Bedford, Jr.* A pamphlet in the New York Public Library.   [4] Thayer, *Cases in Constitutional Law*, Vol. I, p. 55.

his Federalist principles, for he was nominated for presidential elector on the "American" Republican party which was bitterly opposed to Jefferson and was loyal to Washington's system.[1]

William Blount, of North Carolina, a signer of the Constitution, was appointed by Washington to the office of governor of the Territory South of the Ohio in 1790 and he retained that post until 1796, when he was chosen to represent the state of Tennessee in the United States Senate. The following year he was expelled from the Senate on the ground that he was implicated in a treasonable plot in the Southwest. This unhappy ending of his senatorial career had no effect upon his position in Tennessee, for he was at once elected president of the senate in that state, and maintained a high political standing until his death in 1800. In view of Blount's record in the Republican state of Tennessee, it might be surmised that he was not unacceptable to the Republican party, but we have high authority — The Aurora — for setting him down among "the anglomonarchic, aristocratic faction." [2]

[1] Connecticut Courant, June 16, 1800.

[2] The Aurora, August 7 and 8th, 1800.   Nevertheless it is stated on good authority that no public man at the time in Tennessee dared to admit that he entertained Federalist principles. American Historical Review, Vol. IV, p. 563.   Blount's half-brother, Willie Blount, early declared his allegiance to Jefferson in the following curious letter preserved among Jefferson's manuscripts:

KNOXVILLE, November 14, 1801.

Sir, Being disengaged this evening from such pursuits as generally engage my attention, and it occurring to me that I might not be considered an intruder, since I am one of those who admire your doings and quite willing and desirous that you should continue to preside as President of the United States so long as you may feel disposed to act in that way and feeling desirous that you should know merely for my own gratification that there does exist within the limits of the United States a man of my name, have written you this letter to which I in language of the purest sincerity subscribe it, as

Your unfeigned, and
unalterable friend,
WILLIE BLOUNT.

Jefferson Papers, 2d Series, Vol. VIII, No. 18.

David Brearley, of New Jersey, a signer of the Constitution, was appointed by Washington to the post of United States district judge in 1789. He was thus brought into the service of the government which he had labored to create, but his death the following year, 1790, cut short his career at the early age of 44.

Jacob Broom, of Delaware, a signer of the Constitution, was a business man rather than a politician, and his biographer does not inform us concerning his later partisan views. Like most of his colleagues in the Convention he was willing to accept office under the new government and he actually sought the position of collector at Wilmington. It appears that he had to be content with the smaller office of postmaster.[1] Judging from his interests and affiliations, Broom probably remained a loyal Federalist, but for the present he must be put among the unclassified.

Pierce Butler, of South Carolina, a signer of the Constitution, served in the United States Senate from 1789 to 1796. He voted for the funding bill and for a short time he seems to have shared the conservative Federalist views of his colleague Ralph Izard, but he was opposed to the tariff and the tonnage measures and soon drifted over into the Anti-Federalist party.[2] In other words, he remained with the party of the Constitution until the securities in which his Charleston friends and supporters were so deeply interested were firmly established under Hamilton's system, and then he refused to accord to the Northern states those commercial concessions which had also been a part of the nationalist plan of government. Butler was stanch in his defence of slavery and he thought the United States Senate should be

[1] W. W. Campbell, *Life and Character of Jacob Broom*, Papers of the Historical Society of Delaware, Vol. LI, p. 25.

[2] Professor Phillips, in the American Historical Review, Vol. XIV, p. 731 (July, 1909).

frankly based upon property interests.[1] It does not appear that Butler's democratic susceptibilities were offended by the "high toned" policies of the Federalists or that Jefferson's cherishment of the people attracted his impetuous nature.

Daniel Carroll, of Maryland, a signer of the Constitution, was elected as a Federalist to the first Congress. He voted once against taking over the state debts, but was induced to change his view, probably as a result of the secret negotiations over the trading of the capital for assumption. He was one of the federal commissioners who laid out the District of Columbia and was instrumental in the location of the capitol on land which he owned.[2] He died in Washington in 1796. The records readily available do not seem to contain any definite expressions of his party opinions during the closing days of his life.

George Clymer, of Pennsylvania, a signer of the Constitution, was a member of the House of Representatives in the first Congress and voted in favor of assumption, supported the protective tariff measures, and assisted the administration party during both sessions. At the expiration of his term of service in Congress he was given a federal appointment as collector of excise, but he resigned this position after the Whiskey Rebellion. He remained a consistent, though not a very active, Federalist until his death in 1813.

William R. Davie, of North Carolina, did not sign the Constitution, but he was a member of both of the North Carolina conventions and worked to secure the ratification of the new instrument of government. He was appointed a federal district judge by Washington in 1790, but declined. Adams selected him as ambassador to France in 1799, and

---

[1] *Economic Interpretation*, p. 192.

[2] Scharf, *History of Western Maryland*, Vol. I, p. 679; H. Crew, *History of Washington*, p. 108.

he was chosen by Jefferson in 1802 to negotiate a treaty with the Tuscarroras.   This appointment by Jefferson did not imply, however, that Davie had any Democratic leanings. To him the whole "jacobin creed" was vile,[1] and he stood as a Federalist candidate for Congress in 1803 only to be defeated by Willis Alston, a Republican.[2]   Shortly after this defeat, he retired to private life and remained there until his death in 1820.   Though time may have softened his antipathy to democratic doctrines, there can be no doubt that he never relinquished his strong Federalist principles.

Jonathan Dayton, of New Jersey, a signer of the Constitution, was a Representative in the second, third, fourth, and fifth Congresses and he was Speaker in the fourth and fifth.   He supported Hamilton's measures,[3] but he was very politic in the expression of his views and for a time some of the Republicans thought that he was veering in the direction of their party.   However, in 1796 he wrote to Sedgwick expressing great fear of the election of Jefferson and his hopes for the success of Adams.[4]   Later, he again showed Republican tendencies and on account of his conciliatory attitude received many votes from Republican members when he was a candidate for Speaker of the House.   But shortly afterward, Jefferson counted him as wholly lost,[5] and when he was brought under a cloud in connection with the Burr conspiracy, he was reckoned a Federalist.[6]

[1] *Life and Correspondence of Iredell*, Vol. II, p. 577.

[2] J. H. Wheeler, *Historical Sketches of North Carolina*, Vol. II, pp. 188–199; Peele, *Lives of Distinguished North Carolinians*, pp. 59 ff.

[3] Hamilton Mss., August 26, 1792.

[4] *Ibid.*, November 12, 1796.

[5] Jefferson, *Works* (Washington ed.), Vol. IV, p. 211.

[6] The Aurora for September 9, 1800, contains the following "Anglo-Federal Compact of New Jersey" in which Dayton figures as a Federalist:

John Dickinson, of Delaware, a signer of the Constitution, did not actively engage in politics after the inauguration of the federal government, but he was no doubt in general sympathy with Washington's administration. Nevertheless, he was on excellent terms with Jefferson and was regarded by the latter as an "orthodox advocate of the true principles of our new government." [1] He definitely went over to the Republican party on the withdrawal of Washington, for he hated John Adams with a cordiality that is difficult to describe, because Adams had attacked him during the Revolutionary period as a man afraid of his convictions and too timid in coming to the open conflict with Great Britain.[2] It would have been impossible for Dickinson to have associated himself with any party headed by Adams, even if his sympathies with Jefferson's views had been merely academic.

Oliver Ellsworth, of Connecticut, although not among the signers of the Constitution, was a stanch defender of that instrument and as a delegate in the Connecticut ratifying convention he contributed powerfully to its adoption. Ellsworth was a member of the Senate in the first Congress ; he was appointed Chief Justice of the Supreme Court by Washington in 1796 ; and was later named ambassador to France by Adams. While in the Senate, he drafted the Judiciary Act of 1789, voted for the funding bill, and

First. Andrew Bell, collector of customs at Amboy. Had been private sec'y to Sir Guy Carleton at the time British evacuated New York.
Second. Judge Patterson, U. S. Sup. Ct. judge. Married Bell's sister.
Third. Jonathan Dayton, U. S. senator from N. J., promoted Bell over one Halsey a Revolutionary patriot.
Fourth. Dayton's brother, a commissary officer.
Fifth. Dayton's nephew, a quartermaster.
Sixth. Col. Ogden, related to Dayton by marriage; a deputy-quartermaster.
Seventh. Brother-in-law of Ogden, a medical appointee.

[1] *Works* (Washington ed.), Vol. V, p. 249.
[2] *Life and Works of John Adams,* Vol. I, p. 183, and Vol. II, p. 410.

supported all of the economic measures of the new government. To the last he remained a firm Federalist, despising everything that savored of "Jacobinical Democracy."

William Few, of Georgia, a signer of the Constitution, was a member of the state ratifying convention and gave his support there to the new instrument of government. He was a member of the Senate of the first Congress (1789–1793) and voted with the rest of the Georgia delegation in Congress against assumption. Few moved to New York in 1799 and three years later he was appointed by Jefferson to the office of commissioner of loans which he held until 1810. He also served in the New York state legislature from 1802 to 1805. He may be reckoned as a consistent Republican from the adoption of the Constitution until his death.[1]

Thomas Fitzsimons, of Pennsylvania, a signer of the Constitution, was a Representative in the first, second, and third Congresses where he warmly supported all of the fiscal, commercial, and tariff measures advanced by Hamilton and his group. After retiring from Congress Fitzsimons continued a strong Federalist and was active in the campaign of 1800 against Jefferson.[2]

Benjamin Franklin, of Pennsylvania, a signer of the Constitution, was accounted by many as lukewarm in his support of the new system, and he was put forward as an opposition candidate for member of the Pennsylvania ratifying convention, only to be defeated. His correspondence shows, however, that while he disapproved of some parts of the Constitution, he thought it the best instrument that could have been devised under the circumstances. His extreme old age and his death in 1790 precluded his taking any part

---

[1] Autobiography, in the Magazine of American History, Vol. VII, pp. 343 ff.
[2] The Gazette of the United States, August to November, 1800.

in the political controversies which speedily followed the inauguration of the new government.

Elbridge Gerry, of Massachusetts, refused to sign the Constitution and although not a member of the state convention, he labored with great zeal to defeat ratification. He was a member of the House of Representatives of the first Congress and, in common with his other security-holding colleagues from Massachusetts, he voted in favor of the funding bill and assumption. He vigorously denounced Madison's proposal to discriminate against the speculative purchasers and he supported the fiscal and commercial policy of the new government. Nevertheless, for reasons which it is impossible to fathom, he became a strong Anti-Federalist in Adams' administration. It would appear, however, that it was no extreme "cherishment of the people" which drew him into Jefferson's party, for, in the Convention at Philadelphia, he had declared that the evils which they had experienced flowed "from the excess of democracy," and that while he was still Republican, he "had been taught by experience the dangers of the levelling spirit."[1] When the proposition relative to the election of United States Senators was before the Philadelphia Convention, Gerry "insisted that the commercial and monied interest would be more secure in the hands of the State legislatures, than of the people at large. The former have more sense of character, and will be restrained by that from injustice. . . . Besides in some States there are two Branches in the Legislature, one of which is somewhat aristocratic. There wd. therefore be so far a better chance of refinement in the choice."[2] It is true that Gerry opposed the ratification of the Constitution on the ground, among others, that there was grave danger of usurpation on the part of the judiciary

[1] Farrand, *Records*, Vol. I, p. 48.   [2] *Ibid.*, Vol. I, p. 154.

as contemplated by the new instrument, but his spoken words within the secret confines of the convention hall may quite justifiably be taken as representing his genuine feelings on the subject of democracy. Without accepting the view of his contemporary opponents, that personal ambition and chagrin at not securing the funding of continental paper money at par value were responsible for his Anti-Federalism,[1] we may safely say that equalitarian principles did not carry him over to Republicanism.

Nicholas Gilman, of New Hampshire, a signer of the Constitution, was a Representative in the first, second, third, and fourth Congresses and was a Senator from 1805 until his death in 1814. Gilman voted against the assumption bill, but it does not appear that he was opposed to Hamilton's entire fiscal system, for he voted in favor of chartering the first United States Bank which was extremely popular with the security holders, among whom he was himself to be reckoned.[2] Why Gilman went over to the Republican opposition is not clear. He was not a man given to expounding his political principles. He was silent in the Convention which drafted the Constitution and he was not among the talking members of Congress.

Nathaniel Gorham, of Massachusetts, a signer of the Constitution, stood as a Federalist candidate for the House of Representatives against Gerry at the first Congressional election, and was counted a Federalist until his death in 1796. There can be no reasonable doubt as to the stand he would have taken had he lived until the great battle of 1800.

Alexander Hamilton, of New York, a signer of the Constitution, was a member of the ratifying convention in his

[1] Ford, *Essays on the Constitution*, p. 174.
[2] *Economic Interpretation*, p. 94.

state, and did more than any other member to wring the approval of the new instrument from delegates practically instructed by their constituents to vote against it.   Hamilton was appointed first Secretary of the Treasury by Washington and held that office until all of the great fiscal measures associated with his name were firmly established.   He was employed by the government in 1796 to defend the constitutionality of the carriage tax when it was assailed by Virginia Republicans.   He was called to the service of the nation in 1798, when war with France was impending, and in the stirring battle of 1800 he was the most trusted leader and adviser in the Federalist party.   During his life Hamilton's devotion to the Federalist principles which he early espoused never weakened, and he met his unhappy death at the hands of a political opponent, Aaron Burr, whose lack of skill in intrigue prevented him from becoming the first Republican President.[1]

William C. Houston, of New Jersey, was prevented by ill-health from remaining through the sessions of the Convention, and he died in 1788 before the new government was set in motion.

William Houstoun, of Georgia, did not sign the Constitution, but he gave his support to it.   Reasonable care in the examination of the available biographical materials fails to reveal any important particulars concerning his career or political views after the inauguration of the new government.   If he followed the example of the other members from Georgia, he went over to the Republican party, and this is highly probable.   Nevertheless, he must at present be classed as doubtful.

Jared Ingersoll, of Pennsylvania, a signer of the Constitution, apparently did not seek any public office after his

[1] Below, p. 408.

services in the Convention. He was early nominated to the post of United States district attorney, but declined to serve. Adams offered him a federal judgeship in 1801, but he refused it. He was selected as the Federalist candidate for Vice-President in 1812, and no doubt he remained a firm Federalist until his death.[1]

Daniel of St. Thomas Jenifer, a signer of the Constitution, from Maryland, died in 1790, and therefore took no part in the political controversies which began to rage early in Washington's administration.

William Samuel Johnson, of Connecticut, a signer of the Constitution, was also a member of the Connecticut convention and there voted in favor of ratifying the Constitution. He was elected to the first Senate of the United States and served from 1789 to 1791, giving his powerful support to the funding bill, the judiciary act, and the other measures which were designed to afford stable foundations for the new system. After his term of service in the Senate, Johnson devoted himself to his labors as President of Columbia College, until his resignation in 1800. Like all the stalwart Federalists of his native state, Johnson remained faithful to his party until his death in 1819. After his retirement from Columbia College he seems to have taken little or no part in political discussions,[2] but Dr. Dwight, of Yale, said of him in 1815 that he might be considered "as the representative of his contemporaries of a former age, whom time has spared for the purpose of pointing out to their children the true policy of this state." [3]   If Johnson had betrayed in public discourse or private conversation any sympathy with the party of Jefferson, he would hardly have received this praise from the valiant warrior against atheism.[4]

---

[1] H. Binney, *Leaders of the Old Bar of Philadelphia*, p. 86.

[2] Beardsley, *Life and Times of Johnson*, p. 165.

[3] *Ibid.*, 167.   [4] See below, p. 365.

Rufus King, of Massachusetts, a signer of the Constitution, moved to New York in 1788 and was at once elected to the United States Senate, where he served from 1789 to 1796. In the Senate he was a thoroughgoing and powerful supporter of Hamilton's fiscal and commercial measures. At the expiration of his term, King was appointed minister to Great Britain and represented the United States there until 1803. He was the Federalist candidate for Vice-President in 1804; he ran for governor of New York on the Federalist ticket in 1815; and he had the honor of being the last candidate ever nominated for President of the United States by the Federalists, in 1816. Although unable to secure an office by popular vote, King was elected as a Federalist to the Senate in 1813 and remained there until 1825. In that year he was sent for a second time to the Court of St. James as minister of the United States, but he held this post for only one year. He died in 1827.

John Langdon, of New Hampshire, a signer of the Constitution, was a member of the state ratifying convention and it was largely by his skilful engineering that the convention was adjourned when it was found that a majority were instructed to vote in the negative, and reassembled when enough converts to the Federalist party had been secured. Langdon was elected to the first Senate and he took an active part in the management of Hamilton's fiscal measures in Congress. He remained loyal to the Federalist group until 1794 when he broke with Washington's policies. The following year he opposed the Jay treaty and for this action the commercial town of Portsmouth voted him thanks and gave him a public dinner. From that time forward he was a strong opponent of the administration; he attacked Adams with extraordinary vehemence; and at length he attached himself to Jefferson's party, believing that it was time for all men of "property and influence" [1] to follow the leadership of the great Virginian. His biographer says of him: "He courted popularity with the zeal of a lover and the constancy of a martyr." [2]

John Lansing, of New York, left the Philadelphia Convention before the Constitution was finished, because he contended that the delegates had exceeded their powers in casting aside the Articles of Confederation and drafting a national system.[3] He was a member of the New York convention and there worked and voted against the ratification of the Constitution. Lansing was appointed justice of the New York supreme court in 1790, and eight years later was elevated to the post of chief justice, which he occupied until 1814 when he became a regent of the University of New York. He remained a consistent Anti-Federalist until the end of his days, but he was not an active politician, and he declined to become a candidate for governor in 1804 when the Anti-Federalists unanimously nominated him.

William Livingston, of New Jersey, a signer of the Constitution, was offered a post as superintendent of federal buildings as soon as the new government was established, but he declined the appointment. He was shortly afterward asked by Washington to go to Holland as the minister of the United States, but this he likewise declined. He died in 1790.

James McClurg, of Virginia, was an eminent physician at Richmond, and does not seem to have taken a prominent part in national politics. Washington thought so highly of his abilities that he might have appointed him Secretary of

---

[1] The Aurora, November 14, 1800.   Langdon wrote, on October 18, 1800, "I am greatly rejoiced to see gentlemen of property and influence coming forward at this eventful moment."

[2] Batchellor, *State Papers of New Hampshire*, Vol. XXI, pp. 806 ff.

[3] Farrand, *Records*, Vol. III, p. 244.

State on Jefferson's resignation, but was deterred by the rumor that he was a speculator.[1] McClurg was elected a director of the Bank of the United States in 1791, and all of his affiliations were Federalist in character. But without conclusive documentary evidence as to his later political views, McClurg must remain for the present unclassified.

James McHenry, of Maryland, one of the signers of the Constitution, was also a member of the convention of his state and voted in favor of ratification. He early expressed his willingness to accept office under the new government.[2] He served as Secretary of War, under Washington for a time, and also for a short period under Adams. McHenry was active in politics, particularly during the campaign of 1800 in which he supported the Federalist cause with great ardor. The defeat of his party in no way diminished his devotion to Federalist principles and he remained loyal to them until his death in 1816. To the end, he hoped that enough Federalists might be found to protect the Constitution against radical changes and to restore it to its original form, and he never ceased to lament the low estate into which the nation had fallen through the triumph of "democratical" doctrines. To Lafayette, he wrote in 1803 in a tone akin to despair: "Were you to come among us, you would find yourself in many points of view, as it were, in a new world. Most of your old friends in private life, friends tremblingly alive to whatever is likely to affect their popu-

---

[1] Jefferson, *Works* (Washington ed.), Vol. IX, p. 168.

[2] "I asked appointments for some honest but poor federals of this place and the President has been very attentive to my recommendations. I asked nothing for myself because in fact I am very easy in my circumstances. Still, however, I am not wholly lost to ambition and would have no objection to a situation where I might indulge and improve at the same time my literary propensities with perhaps some advantage to the public. Will you therefore be good enough to feel (if a resident or even chargé des affaires is to be appointed to London or France) whether the President has thought of me or would in such a case nominate me." Hamilton Mss., October 27, 1789.

larity. The people too changed, that is because more democratical. Great and lesser demagogues in every state and district and the prejudices and violence of party, leaving little or no room for moderation or social intercourse between men of opposite politics. . . . These are no doubt evils in themselves, and what is worse may lead to still greater. We cannot tell what further changes such democratical opinions may produce in the public mind, in the government itself. When the people are made to believe that they are everything, and have a right to have everything fashioned to their own way of thinking, they are in a sure road of alternately ruling their demagogues and being ruled by them, and the fundamental laws and institutions of the state disregarded or trampled upon as they stand opposed to the passions or interests of their leaders. Such has generally been the consequences of flattering the multitude in republics, for in republics any deviation in the people from their prescribed rights and the government from the free exercise of its authorities leads rapidly to democracy, in other words confusion and licentiousness. As yet, however, such consequences are more feared than felt; and feared only by the most reflecting part of the community, those in power excepted, who act as if they thought they could manage the multitude according to their views of public interest. . . . With respect to myself I would not say that I am an unconcerned spectator, or indifferent to all that passes. Having an interest at stake, loving real liberty, and wishing for its maintenance, I cannot without regret look upon any conduct in rulers or the people which tends to endanger and finally destroy it. In my eyes, despotism of the multitude is the most terrible of tyrannies." [1]

[1] Steiner, *Life and Correspondence of McHenry*, p. 527.

James Madison, of Virginia, a signer of the Constitution, labored valiantly in the Virginia convention for its ratification. He would have been elected to the first United States Senate had it not been for the Anti-Federalist opposition to him in the state legislature. Under the circumstances he was compelled to be content with an election to the House of Representatives. As is well known, he turned very early against Hamilton and his policies ; he fought for a discrimination between the original holders of securities and the speculative purchasers ; he opposed the assumption of state debts ; and he soon became an avowed partisan of Jefferson. Why Madison made this radical change has long been a subject of conjecture among historians, but no universally accepted answer to the enigma has been found. Many have ascribed it to his personal ambitions and his discovery that there was no hope for him in the Federalist party, in view of the Anti-Federalism of Virginia. Others ascribe it to his antipathy to the fiscal measures of the Secretary of the Treasury, and this seems more plausible, for Madison held no securities and was not engaged in the private financial operations which were extensively connected with Federalism. Certain it is that it was not difference in fundamental principles of government which carried Madison into opposition to Hamilton, for no member of the Philadelphia convention more earnestly believed in a thoroughgoing economic interpretation of politics, more profoundly distrusted majority rule, more assiduously sought for some devices to check the assaults of the masses upon the rights of property, or more anxiously feared the great experiment of universal manhood suffrage.[1]

The most plausible explanation of Madison's change would seem to be the following. During the constitutional struggle

[1] *Economic Interpretation*, pp. 25, 156–158.

he displayed as much anxiety about providing adequate checks on the state legislatures which had been assaulting property rights as about the positive achievements of the national government. When the federal system was inaugurated he discovered that a more active capitalistic policy than he had contemplated was determined upon, and that policy he found to be particularly offensive to his agrarian state which had barely ratified the Constitution. In other words, it was the capitalistic views of the Federalists, not their "fear of the people," that drove him into the opposition. It is an interesting commentary on the quality of Jefferson's democracy that he chose Madison as his successor.

Alexander Martin, of North Carolina, left the Convention in August and was not among the signers of the Constitution. Martin took little part in the proceedings of the Convention and one of his colleagues, Hugh Williamson, suggested that he had so exhausted his fund of political wisdom as governor of the state "that time must be required to enable him again to exert his abilities to the advantage of the nation." [1]   Martin seems to have been an adroit politician, for he was elected governor of his state in 1792 by a Federalist legislature but with the support of both parties.[2] The following year he was elected to the Senate of the United States as a moderate Republican, although he was charged with being aristocratic in his sympathies and known to have been in harmony with Davie, Johnston, Spaight, and other advocates of a reformed federal system.[3]   He may be set down therefore as a conservative Republican by force of circumstances.

Luther Martin, of Maryland, refused to sign the Constitu-

[1] Farrand, *Records*, Vol. III, p. 55.
[2] J. W. Moore, *History of North Carolina*, Vol. I, p. 408.
[3] *Ibid.*, p. 411.

tion, and was one of the most truculent opponents of Federalism in his state.   He was a member of the state convention and labored in vain to defeat ratification.   He was an outspoken champion of the agrarian and debtor interests with which he had a practical as well as a theoretical sympathy, for his own fortunes were usually at a low ebb.   He was a loyal Republican until his death, but his loyalty was to his benefactor, Burr, not to Jefferson.

George Mason, of Virginia, remained in the Convention until the completion of the Constitution, but he refused to sign the instrument.   He was also a member of the Virginia convention and there labored to defeat the ratification of the Constitution.   On account of his opposition to the new system he was elected to the first Senate by the Virginia legislature which was practically dominated by Anti-Federalists, but he declined to serve and retired to his estate where he died in 1792.   He took no active part in the great political controversies that began early in Washington's first administration, but it is known that he was opposed to the fiscal policy of the government, for he said to Jefferson a short time before his death that Hamilton had done the country more harm than all the fleets and armies of Great Britain.   This last recorded conversation with Mason shows conclusively that the opponent of the Constitution in 1787 and 1788 must be set down as a Republican in 1792.[1]

John Mercer, of Maryland, like his colleague Luther Martin, refused to sign the Constitution and did his best to prevent ratification by his state.   He was a Representative in the second and third Congresses and was consistently with the opposition.   He was counted among the giants of the Republican party in his state and was chosen governor

---

[1] Rowland, *George Mason*, Vol. II, p. 364.

in 1801. Like Luther Martin, he was a champion of the agrarian and the debtor, and in the Philadelphia Convention, he declared that he was "a friend to paper money," adding that "it was impolitic also to excite the opposition of all those who were friends to paper money. The people of property would be sure to be on the side of the plan, and it was impolitic to purchase their further attachment with the loss of the opposite class of citizens." [1] He seems to have been moved by his sympathy with the paper-money party rather than by any theoretical "cherishment of the people," for in the Convention he had opposed the popular election even of members of the House of Representatives, saying, "the people cannot know and judge of the characters of Candidates. The worst possible choice will be made." [2]

Thomas Mifflin, of Pennsylvania, a signer of the Constitution, was governor of his state for most of the time between the drafting of the Constitution and his death in 1800. On account of his patriotic services during the Revolution he seems to have been able to unite the suffrages of both parties. Nevertheless, it was well known that his leanings were toward the conservative or Federalist party. He was president of the convention which drafted the more conservative constitution for the state in 1790 and was elected first governor under that instrument. He supported the administration during the whiskey rebellion, but not with the zeal which the more ardent Federalists desired. Both parties agreed on him for governor in 1796,[3] but there is no doubt of his sympathy with the important policies of Adams' administration.[4]

Gouverneur Morris, of Pennsylvania, a signer of the Constitution, was a tower of strength for the Federalist party

---

[1] Farrand, *Records*, Vol. II, p. 309.
[2] *Ibid.*, Vol. II, p. 205.
[3] The Aurora, October 11, 1796.
[4] *Pennsylvania Archives, 1785-1717*, p. 403.

until his death in 1816.[1]   He was appointed commissioner to England in 1789, and minister to France in 1792.   He was elected as a Federalist Senator from New York in 1800 and served for three years, waging war on the Republicans at every point.   To him all articles in the "Jacobinical creed" were odious.   He had been in France when the king was executed and the first republic set up, and he thought he had seen with his own eyes the realization of the Utopian vision which the Republicans had beheld from afar.

Robert Morris, of Pennsylvania, a signer of the Constitution, was a member of the first Senate of the United States and was the chief legislative manager for Hamilton in Congress.[2]   After a short service, he retired to private life and labored hard to untangle his private affairs, but in vain, for, in spite of his heroic efforts, he was unable to escape the debtor's cell.[3]   After he left the Senate, Morris did not take an active part in politics, but there can be no doubt that his sympathies lay with the Federalist party.   Notwithstanding this fact, Jefferson would have called him into his cabinet had it not been for the discredit into which Morris had fallen through his financial misfortunes.

William Paterson, of New Jersey, a signer of the Constitution, was a member of the state convention and voted there in favor of ratification.   He was elected to the first Senate and voted in favor of the funding bill.   He resigned, however, in 1790 and was the following year elected governor of his state.   In 1793 he was appointed a Justice of the Supreme Court of the United States by Washington and held that high post until his death in 1806.   Little is known of his personal views on the party controversies that went

[1] Roosevelt, *Gouverneur Morris*, Chaps. XII and XIII.

[2] See below, p. 186.

[3] One of the last measures of the Federalist party was a bankruptcy law under which Morris was released.

on about him, and he may have felt himself precluded by his judicial position from taking too active a part in them. Nevertheless, his sympathies were with the Federalists until the end, and he was set down by the Republicans as a member of the New Jersey Federalist junto in 1800.[1] All of his opinions while on the bench were acceptable to the Federalist party. He took the Federalist view in the case of the United States *vs.* Hylton[2] in which the carriage tax was upheld. Mr. Horace Davis has argued with no little ingenuity to show that Paterson did not accept the Federalist doctrine of judicial control over acts of Congress,[3] but his argument must fall to the ground when it is known that there is a long federal opinion by Paterson in which he distinctly states that it is one of the functions of the Supreme Court to hold null and void acts of Congress which transgress the limits of the Constitution.[4] If this is not sufficient evidence on the point, the fact that Paterson was a member of the Court which decided the celebrated case of Marbury *v.* Madison may be taken as conclusive.

William Pierce, of Georgia, left the Convention long before the Constitution was completed and was not among the signers. It appears, however, that he favored the ratification of the instrument.[5] He took no part in the actual establishment of the new government, for he died in 1789.

Charles Pinckney, of South Carolina, signed the Constitution and gave his support to the ratification of the instrument in his state. He failed to receive any high appointment under the new government and soon became disgruntled with the course of events at the national capital. A very careful and judicious scholar has said of Pinckney:

[1] The Aurora, September 9, 1800.   [2] 3 Dallas, 171.
[3] American Political Science Review, November, 1913.
[4] *Paterson Mss.* (Bancroft Transcripts) New York Public Library.
[5] Farrand, *Records*, Vol. III, p. 100.

"He was, however, a plunger in business affairs and a spoils-man in party politics; and according to tradition he was dishonest in the conduct of trust estates committed to his charge. He launched into Republican leadership partly from a dislike of Adams, but more largely it may be conjectured from a desire for a conspicuous career. In 1795 the South Carolina Republicans were a leaderless party and Charles Pinckney was a talented politician without a following and with no principles in particular. He embraced the opportunity, was elected governor and senator, and in 1800 swung his state to Jefferson and deposed his enemy, Adams, from the presidency." [1] Certainly it cannot be said that "cherishment of the people" was the principle which actuated Charles Pinckney in his political operations, for in the Convention which drafted the Constitution he advocated a property qualification of $100,000 for President, $50,000 for Supreme Court judges, and a proportional sum for members of Congress. [2] Moreover he thought the election of members of the House of Representatives by popular vote was theoretical nonsense which would bring our councils into contempt. [3] Pinckney remained a consistent Jeffersonian until his death in 1824.

Charles Coatesworth Pinckney, of South Carolina, unlike his young and impetuous cousin, Charles, was faithful to the Federalist cause until the end. He signed the Constitution and worked for its ratification by the convention of his state; but he does not seem to have been such a skilled politician or such a shrewd manipulator as his cousin. [4] Professor Phillips informs us that Charles Coatesworth Pinckney was a dignitary and ornament of the Federalist

[1] Professor U. B. Phillips, American Historical Review, Vol. XIV, p. 739.
[2] Farrand, *Records*, Vol. II, p. 248.
[3] *Madison Mss.*, Library of Congress, March 28, 1788.
[4] Professor U. B. Phillips, American Historical Review, Vol. XIV, p. 738.

party in South Carolina rather than a working member. This does not imply, however, that he was by any means an indifferent spectator during the stirring events which followed the establishment of the government, or that his advice and help were not constantly sought by men high in the councils of the Federalist party. When McHenry asked his opinion in the summer of 1800 about political affairs, he showed his deep interest in maintaining the original principles of his party and in avoiding any Jacobinical taint. "If the Federalists will act with decision, energy, and union," he said, "I have no doubt but they will gain a complete victory at the ensuing election over the Jacobinical party, notwithstanding the untoward result of the election at New York and the tergiversation of Mr. A——. Can the accounts I have heard be possibly true that he is endeavoring to coalesce with Jefferson, and that he stigmatizes the Federalists with the odious appellation of a British party, and that he declares that he and Jefferson will convince the federal junto of their joint power? With regard to the conduct of the Southern states at the coming election, I think they are bound fairly and candidly to act up to their agreement entered into by the federal party at Philadelphia, without the Eastern states should be convinced of Mr. A's abandonment of federal principles, his attempt to form a party with Jefferson and his unfitness to be President, and on these accounts or some of them should consent to substitute another candidate in his stead. This event I do not think impossible and his conduct and the critical situation of our country may require it. . . . Marshall with reluctance accepts, but you may rely on his federalism and be certain that he will not unite with Jefferson and the Jacobins." [1] It is perfectly clear from this letter that

[1] Steiner, *The Life and Correspondence of James McHenry*, p. 459.

Pinckney was willing to support Adams in 1800, only on condition that the latter should remain true to Federalist principles and avoid all signs of compromise with the Jeffersonian Democracy. He was, therefore, a Federalist from conviction, not for convenience.

General Pinckney so enjoyed the confidence of his party that he was named as the candidate for Vice-President in 1800 and he then received sixty-four electoral votes as against seventy-three cast for Burr. In 1804 he led the Federalists in a forlorn hope as candidate for President against Jefferson and polled fourteen out of 176 electoral votes. Four years later he again led the Federalists to defeat, this time against Madison, and received fifty-four electoral votes. During this last campaign, he was supported as a genuine and consistent Federalist battling for the Constitution against Madison "the trimmer." "General Pinckney," wrote a Charleston pamphleteer in 1808, "assisted at the formation of our glorious Constitution and afterward employed all of his energies, talents, and influence, *with effect*, in recommending it to the people of this state for *their adoption* in our general convention. And he has from the adoption of that instrument down to the present tempestuous times been its champion and defender and a warm and unceasing advocate for handing it down to posterity unaltered by those mischievous and judiciary-hating demagogues who prefer untried theory to experience and practice. He was at the time of the formation of the Constitution a distinguished and zealous Federal Republican. He is still a Federal Republican. Consequently he is no trimmer [like James Madison]." [1]

Edmund Randolph, of Virginia, did not sign the Consti-

---

[1] *A Letter on the Approaching Election* (1808). By a native of Charleston. Duane Collection, Library of Congress, Vol. 107, No. 4.

tution, but he was a member of the Virginia convention and voted there in favor of its ratification. He was appointed Attorney-General by Washington in 1789 and held that post until 1794 when he was transferred to the office of Secretary of State on Jefferson's resignation. The following year he was asked to withdraw on account of serious charges of corruption made against him by the French minister in despatches to the French government, which were intercepted. From this time forward, his sympathies were with the Anti-Federalist party although he can hardly be said to have joined the democratic faction. On the contrary, he assailed the democratic societies with great vigor.[1] In this, however, there was no inconsistency, because Randolph had taken the position in the Convention that the evils under which the United States had labored were traceable to the "turbulence and follies of democracy."[2] Not even Hamilton had taken a firmer position on the question of providing an adequate check in the Senate against the "demagogues of the popular branch."[3] From his withdrawal to private life in 1795 until his death in 1813, Randolph took no very active part in politics. His feelings toward Jefferson were mixed, to put it mildly; and although by fortune's chance he was thrown into the Republican party, he felt at home there because so many leaders in that group entertained similar views as to "the cherishment of the people" doctrine.

George Read, of Delaware, a signer of the Constitution, was elected to the Senate of the United States in 1789 and voted for the fiscal measures of the Treasury. He left the Senate in 1793 and served as chief justice of the state of Delaware until his death in 1798. In the Senate, he was

---

[1] M. Conway, *Edmund Randolph*, p. 361.
[2] Farrand, *Records*, Vol. I, p. 51. [3] *Ibid.*, Vol. I, p. 218.

regarded by the administration party as a consistent Federalist and his withdrawal was viewed as a decided loss by his colleagues of that group.[1] He supported John Adams for Vice-President in 1792 and remained a firm Federalist until his death.[2]

John Rutledge, of South Carolina, a signer of the Constitution, was appointed by Washington to the office of Associate Justice of the Supreme Court of the United States in 1789 and he held that place two years, resigning to accept the chief justiceship of the supreme court of his state. In 1795, Rutledge was nominated by Washington Chief Justice of the federal Supreme Court, but the Senate refused to confirm the nomination on account of the fact that he had assailed the Jay treaty with great vehemence, describing it as "prostituting the dearest rights of freemen and laying them at the feet of royalty."[3] A mental disorder prevented his taking a further active part in politics, but we may be sure that he would not have allowed his opposition to the treaty to carry him into the extreme democratic group, for he had been one of the stoutest advocates of property qualifications and the rights of property in the Convention.[4] His son, John Rutledge, Jr., although elected to Congress uncommitted in 1796, joined the Federalist party a short time after taking his seat.[5] The elder Rutledge died in 1800.

Roger Sherman, of Connecticut, a signer of the Constitution, was a Representative from his state in the first Congress of the United States, and there gave his warm support to the fiscal measures of the new government. On the ex-

---

[1] W. T. Read, *Life of George Read*, pp. 531, 532, 538.
[2] *Ibid.*, pp. 542, 556, 557, 565, 566.
[3] American Historical Review, Vol. XIV, p. 736.
[4] *Economic Interpretation*, p. 213.
[5] American Historical Review, Vol. XIV, p. 736.

piration of his term he was elevated to the United States Senate where he remained until his death in 1793.   There can be no doubt about the firm Federalism of Sherman.

Richard Spaight, of North Carolina, a signer of the Constitution, was a stanch Federalist during Washington's administration, but went over to the Republicans in the election of John Adams.[1]   Spaight had opposed the doctrine of judicial control in the Convention,[2]   but it does not appear that he was at all in sympathy with the democratic notions associated with Jefferson's name.[3]   Spaight was elected as a Republican to the fifth and sixth Congresses. He was killed in 1802 in a duel which grew out of a political quarrel with his Federalist opponent.[4]

Caleb Strong, of Massachusetts, did not sign the Constitution, but he was a member of the state convention and voted in favor of ratification.   He was a member of the Senate of the United States from 1789 to 1796, and there he supported the fiscal measures of the Treasury Department.   Strong was a Federalist presidential elector in 1809. He served as the Federalist governor of Massachusetts in 1800–1807 and again in 1812–1816.   He remained loyal to that party until his death in 1819.

George Washington, of Virginia, a signer of the Constitution, although not a member of the state convention, materially aided by his extensive correspondence in the work of ratification.   He was elected first President under the Constitution and did more than any one else to reconcile a portion of the opposition to the new order.   Although he sought to smooth away the roughness of the party antagonism by a conciliatory policy, Washington gave his unqualified

---

[1] J. W. Moore, *History of North Carolina*, Vol. I, pp. 436–437.
[2] Beard, *The Supreme Court and the Constitution*, p. 53.
[3] Moore, *op. cit.*, Vol. I, pp. 374, 377.
[4] *Ibid.*, Vol. I, p. 434.

support to every one of the fiscal measures of the new government which were the real source of renewed party strife. Pierce Butler declared that Hamilton bullied others into supporting his policies but won Washington by servility,[1] but this view does not comport with what we know of Washington's character and views. During the struggle over ratification he wrote that it was useless to adopt the Constitution unless provision was made for the faithful discharge of the public debt. He frankly said that they might as well remain under the Articles of Confederation as to accept an instrument that would not permit the government to collect adequate revenues.[2] Inasmuch as Washington entertained such notions as to the purpose of the Constitution, it could hardly have been necessary for Hamilton to "win him by servility." Furthermore, we know that Washington, notwithstanding the great reliance he placed in Hamilton's policies and political skill, worked over the Secretary's plans with care and caution and approved them only after the exercise of his independent judgment. Although he shared Jefferson's dread of the populace of great cities,[3] and seems to have approved privately Jefferson's leanings toward an agricultural rather than an industrial civilization, Washington never faltered in his support of Federalist fiscal and commercial policies. The agitation carried on by the Democratic societies was odious to him,[4] and toward the closing days of his last term he avowed his opinion that no one should be appointed to federal office, who was opposed to the principles of the administration.[5] There is absolutely no doubt that Washington's sympathies

---

[1] *Jefferson Papers* (Library of Congress Mss.), 2d Series, Vol. IV, No. 77.
[2] *Documentary History of the Constitution*, Vol. IV, p. 40.
[3] *Writings* (Sparks ed.), Vol. X, p. 179.
[4] *Ibid.*, Vol. X, p. 429.
[5] *Writings* (Ford ed.), Vol. XII, p. 107.

were with the party that gathered around Hamilton rather than with the Republican party.

Of course, it has been said by many historians that Washington was non-partisan and tried to conciliate all factions by holding an even balance. This is a generalization with which we may not quarrel with great profit. If it is taken to mean that Washington sought to conciliate all sections of the country and to draw to the support of the government all friends of the Constitution, it may be accepted, but such a statement is superficial, to say the least. If it is taken to mean, however, that Washington, in forming the new administration, appointed men without regard to the position which they had taken in the contest over the ratification of the Constitution and placed in high offices opponents and supporters indiscriminately, it is not true in fact. If it means also that Washington, after his administration was well started and the controversies over his policies had arisen, continued to select federal officers without regard to their attitude toward the practical workings of the new system, it is equally untrue.

As is pointed out below, every one of the high officials of the new government, whom Washington selected, was a supporter of the Constitution in the Philadelphia Convention, or in a state convention, or both, or at all events a known advocate of the adoption of that instrument. The apparent exception to this rule is the case of Jefferson who was appointed to the office of Secretary of State. It has been said by many writers that Washington deliberately selected Jefferson because he wanted a well-balanced administration in which the divergent views of Hamilton and Jefferson might be represented. In this connection two facts should be noted. The first is that, although Jefferson was out of the country during the period in which the Constitution was made and ratified and the new administration instituted, he was known to have been, in spite of some misgivings, in favor of its ratification by enough states to set it into operation — the other states to withhold their approval until the bill of rights amendments could be attached. The second fact is that Jefferson's views on the fiscal policies which were to be advanced by Hamilton could not have been known when he was appointed Secretary of State, for they were not yet formulated. Moreover, Jefferson confessed his ignorance of financial questions and was far from being an avowed opponent of all of Hamilton's fiscal policies in the beginning.[1] To say, therefore, that Hamilton and Jefferson entertained in 1789 clearly divergent views which Washington, for non-partisan reasons, desired to have represented in his administration is without foundation.

We may readily admit with Professor Libby [2] that Washington's desire to keep both Jefferson and Hamilton after their serious differences had arisen was an evidence of his desire to "mollify and soften the harshness of factional animosity," but that of course does not mean that Washington took a middle ground between his belligerent Secretaries. In reality, he did not at any time assume a "non-partisan" position with regard to the clashing views of Jefferson and Hamilton. On the contrary he indorsed practically every one of the latter's administrative policies,[3]

---

[1] J. C. Hamilton, *Life of Alexander Hamilton*, Vol. IV, p. 447.

[2] North Dakota Quarterly Journal, Vol. II, p. 219.

[3] Some contemporaries were wont to regard Washington as an old man duped by Hamilton's flattery and therefore willing to accept the Treasury measures without careful examination. In this view Washington was to be exempted from the party attacks made upon the administration. (See Pierce Butler's letter, *Jefferson Mss.*, 2d Series, Vol. IV, No. 77, cited above, p. 63.) The fact is that Washington assumed full responsibility for the measures of his administration.

defended him against the attacks of his enemies, and in the end retained him in office while allowing the disgruntled Secretary of State to retire to the seclusion of his Virginia estate. Therefore, it may be said that as to every one of the great economic measures which the Constitution was designed to effectuate and which were necessary to the establishment of the new system, Washington was never non-partisan — in any sense in which that vague phrase may be reasonably construed.

Actions speak louder than words, but Washington has not left us without guidance as to his formulated views on this question of non-partisanship. Whatever generous conciliatory opinions he may have entertained at the outset of his first administration, he learned by experience the danger of bringing into public office those belonging to the opposition faction. In a letter written to Timothy Pickering on September 25, 1795, he said: "I shall not, whilst I have the honor to administer the government, bring any man into any office of consequence knowingly whose political tenets are adverse to the measures which the general government are pursuing; for this, in my opinion, would be a sort of political suicide." [1] In this declaration, two fundamental principles are implied. One is that the establishment of certain general doctrines of law does not make a government, but that the men who embody those principles in their personal views and con-

He flatly declared to Jefferson, in speaking of the opposition, that "in condemning the administration of government, they condemned him, for if they thought there were measures pursued contrary to his sentiments, they must conceive him too careless to attend to them, or too stupid to understand them." Washington added that "though, indeed, he had signed many acts which he did not approve in all their parts, yet he never put his name to one which he did not think, on the whole, was eligible. That as to the Bank, which had been an act of so much complaint, until there was some infallible criterion of reason, a difference of opinion must be tolerated." Jefferson, *Works* (Washington ed.), Vol. IX, p. 117.

[1] *Writings* (Ford ed.), Vol. XII, p. 107.

duct can alone make the law living and effective. The
second is that Washington must have recognized the existence of a fairly definite body of opposition to the measures
of the federal government — whether those who have a
strict regard for the niceties of language would call it a
party or not.[1]

If it still be contended that Washington took no partisan
position during his administration (and with what justice
the reader may decide for himself), it cannot be denied that
when the admitted division into Federalists and Republicans came, just before the election of Jefferson, the sympathies of the former President were all on the side of the
party of Hamilton. When he heard of Marshall's election
to Congress in the spring of 1799 he congratulated the victorious candidate and said that he received the news "with
infinite pleasure." His only regret was that the majority
had not been greater, but he expressed the hope that as
the tide was turning it would soon run strong in Marshall's
favor.[2] On the same day, he wrote to Bushrod Washington : "The elections of Generals Lee and Marshall are
grateful to my feelings. I wish, however, both of them
had been elected by greater majorities ; but they *are elected*,
and that alone is pleasing. As the tide is turned, I hope it
will come in with a full flow ; but this will not happen, if
there is any relaxation on the part of the Federalists. We
are sure that there will be none on the part of the *Republicans*, as they have very erroneously called themselves. . . .
In point of abilities, I think the superiority [in Congress]
will be greatly on the side of Federalism." [3]

Not only did Washington rejoice in Federalist victories.
He could not bring himself to regard with any esteem the

[1] The enrolled voter in a party under the law of New York merely binds himself
to support the designated party "generally."

[2] *Writings* (Ford ed.), Vol. XIV, p. 180.   [3] *Ibid.*, p. 181, note.

leaders of the Republican faction. In his opinion they had attacked with unwarranted rancor and virulence the policy of the administration with reference to France, they had tortured every act, by unnatural construction, into a design to violate the Constitution, introduce monarchy, and establish an aristocracy; and they had sought to influence the public mind "with art and sophistry, which regard neither truth nor decency; attacking every character without respect to persons, who happens to differ from themselves in politics." [1] In July, 1799, he exclaimed: "Let that [Republican] party set up a broomstick and call it a true son of liberty, — a democrat, — or give it any other epithet that will suit their purpose, and it will command their votes in toto. Will not the Federalists meet, or rather defend their cause, on the opposite ground? Surely they must, or they will discover a want of policy indicative of weakness and pregnant of mischief; which cannot be admitted." [2] In response to Governor Trumbull's request that he become the Federalist candidate for President in 1800, Washington refused, saying: "I am thoroughly convinced I should not draw a single vote from the anti-Federal side, and, of course, should stand upon no other ground than any other Federal character well supported." [3]

There can be no doubt also that Washington shared the alarm of the Federalists generally at the growing strength of the Republican party. In January, 1799, he wrote a confidential letter to Patrick Henry, [4] which, on account

---

[1] *Writings* (Ford ed.), Vol. XIV, p. 142.
[2] *Ibid.*, pp. 190–191.
[3] *Ibid.*, p. 192.
[4] Henry, although he had been a violent opponent of the adoption of the Constitution, had grown rich in land and paper speculations and had become a firm adherent of Federalism. Washington urged Henry in this letter to become a candidate for the Virginia legislature against the Republican opposition.

of its analysis of the opposition and the reasons advanced for Federalist decline, deserves quotation at length: "It would be a waste of time to attempt to bring to the view of a person of your observation and discernment the endeavours of a certain party among us to disquiet the public mind with unfounded alarms; to arraign every act of the administration; to set the people at variance with their government; and to embarrass all of its measures. Equally useless would it be to predict what must be the inevitable consequences of such a policy, if it cannot be arrested.

"Unfortunately, and extremely do I regret it, the state of Virginia, has taken the lead in this opposition. . . . It has been said that the great mass of the citizens of this state are well-affected, notwithstanding, to the general government and the Union; and I am willing to believe it, nay, do believe it; but how is this to be reconciled with their suffrages at the elections of representatives, both to Congress and their state legislature, who are men opposed to the former and by the tendency of their measures would destroy the latter? Some of us have endeavoured to account for this inconsistency, and though convinced themselves of its truth, they are unable to convince others, who are unacquainted with the internal policy of the state.

"One of the reasons assigned is, that the most respectable and best qualified characters among us will not come forward. Easy and happy in their circumstances at home, and believing themselves secure in their liberties and property, they will not forsake their occupations and engage in the turmoil of public business or expose themselves to the calumnies of their opponents, whose weapons are detraction.

"But, at such a crisis as this, when everything dear and valuable to us is assailed; when this party hangs upon the wheels of government as a dead weight, opposing every measure that is calculated for defence and self-preservation, abetting the nefarious views of another nation upon our rights . . . when every act of our government is tortured, by constructions they will not bear, into attempts to infringe and trample upon the constitution with a view to introduce monarchy. . . . When measures are systematically and pertinaciously pursued, which must eventually dissolve the Union or produce coercion; I say, when these things have become so obvious, ought characters who are best able to rescue their country from the pending evil to remain at home? . . .

"Vain will it be to look for peace and happiness, or for the security of liberty or property, if civil discord should ensue. And what else can result from the policy of those among us, who, by all the measures in their power, are driving matters to extremity, if they cannot be counteracted effectually? The views of men can only be known, or guessed at, by their words or actions. Can those of the *leaders* of opposition be mistaken, then, if judged by this rule? That they are followed by numbers, who are unacquainted with their designs, and suspect as little the tendency of their principles, I am fully persuaded. But, if their conduct is viewed with indifference, if there are activity and misrepresentation on one side, and supineness on the other, their numbers accumulated by intriguing and discontented foreigners under proscription, who were at war with their own governments, and the greater part of them with *all* governments, they will increase, and nothing short of Omniscience can foretell the consequences." [1]

Who can doubt, after reviewing the acts of his administrations, his indorsement of, and assumption of responsibility for, Hamilton's policies, his contempt for the agitations

[1] *Writings* (Ford ed.), Vol. XI l, pp. 136 ff.

of the democratical societies, his open espousal of the Federalist party during his last days, that Washington is to be esteemed a Federalist in the most strict partisan interpretation of that term? That he always had the good of the country at heart will be admitted, but he interpreted the good of his country to mean the maintenance of the principles for which his party stood.

Hugh Williamson, of North Carolina, a signer of the Constitution, was elected a Representative to the first and second Congresses, and almost uniformly voted with his colleagues from that state in opposition to the administration measures. Nevertheless, he apparently did not break with his Federalist friends, for in 1796, he warmly congratulated McHenry on his appointment to the office of Secretary of War,[1] and a few months later he sought government employment under Washington.[2] In his letter to McHenry soliciting this favor, Williamson said: "The North Carolina members are, I believe, without exception desirous to do anything that in their opinion would be profitable or acceptable to me, but as they are at present everyone in opposition to the government, I know they would not willingly ask favors. Wherefore I have never intimated to any one of them that I would accept of any employment." [3]

[1] Steiner, *Life and Correspondence of McHenry*, p. 164.

[2] *Ibid.*, p. 178.

[3] The following letter of Williamson to Hamilton in 1794 would indicate decided Federalist leanings: "In travelling through the country I have lately observed a considerable uniformity of sentiment among the people with a great want of consistency of which they do not themselves appear to be conscious. There are frequent complaints of the want of vigorous measures in the executive to resent the insults of the British nation. This they receive from a certain class of politicians and political writers. There is also an observation almost universal among the planters that 15 or 20 years longer peace would make us so rich and powerful that we should despise the attempt of any nation on earth. This opinion is their own and they seem not to suspect until the system is explained that the advocates for vigorous measures are in effect courting a general war in the hope of destroying

James Wilson, of Pennsylvania, a signer of the Constitution, was a member of the state ratifying convention and the leading champion of the new system before that body. He was appointed Associate Justice of the Supreme Court in 1789 by Washington and retained that post until his death in 1798. Of Wilson's Federalism there can be no question, although he was not very actively engaged in politics after his appointment to the bench. Certainly his opinions rendered as Associate Justice were all in accord with Federalist doctrines.

George Wythe, of Virginia, did not sign the Constitution, because he was absent at the close of the Convention, but there is no doubt that he favored its ratification.[1] Wythe was not an active politician. His position as Chancellor of Virginia would have precluded that, had he not been by temper a lover of the study rather than of the forum. He was, however, opposed to the Jay treaty.[2] Moreover, he was a warm and intimate friend of Jefferson and his personal inclinations would have carried him over to the Republican group if there had been no other motives. Wythe was a Republican presidential elector in 1800 and in 1804, and was loyal to his friend Jefferson until his death in 1806.[3]

Robert Yates, of New York, left the Philadelphia convention early, because he thought that body had exceeded its powers in casting aside the Articles of Confederation. He was a stout opponent of the Constitution in New York and as a member of the state convention voted against

public credit and overturning a government to which they have been uniform enemies. I verily believe that this war making project, when well understood, will produce a considerable apostacy from Antifederalism." *Hamilton Mss.*, May 27, 1794.

[1] Madison, *Works* (Hunt ed., 1904), Vol. V, p. 120.
[2] *Ibid.*, Vol. VI, p. 237.
[3] Jefferson, *Works* (Ford ed.), Vol. IX, p. 288; *Jefferson Mss.*, 2d Series, Vol. XXVIII, Nos. 127–130.

ratification. He was a judge of the supreme court in New York from 1777 to 1790 and chief justice of the same tribunal from the latter year until 1798. After the adoption of the Constitution, Yates conciliated the Federalists by charging grand jurors to support and preserve the Constitution, and for this service he was nominated by the Federalists for the office of governor in 1789 against the great opponent of the Constitution, George Clinton. A historian has accounted for this change of front by referring to Yates' deep passion for office,[1] and this may be a correct interpretation of his motives, for it is certain that until the end he was at heart an Anti-Federalist.

With reference to their later political activities, the fifty-five members of the Philadelphia Convention may be divided into seven groups:

1. Members who died before the Federalist-Republican schism was clearly developed: Brearley, Franklin, Houston, of New Jersey, Jenifer, Livingston, and Pierce — 6.

2. Advocates of the Constitution who remained loyal Federalists until the end: Bassett, Bedford, Blair, Clymer, Davie, Dayton, Ellsworth, Fitzsimons, Gorham, Hamilton, Ingersoll, Johnson, King, McHenry, Mifflin, Gouverneur Morris, Robert Morris, Paterson, C. C. Pinckney, Read, Rutledge, Sherman, Strong, Washington, and Wilson — 25.

3. Advocates of the Constitution who went into the opposition early in Washington's administration: Baldwin, Few, Gilman, Madison, and Wythe — 5.

4. Advocates of the Constitution who joined the opposition after the fiscal measures contemplated by the Constitution were firmly established: Butler, Dickinson, Langdon, A. Martin, Charles Pinckney, Randolph, Spaight — 7.

---

[1] D. S. Alexander, *Political History of the State of New York*, Vol. I, p. 41.

5. Advocates of the Constitution unclassified: Blount, Broom, Carroll, Houstoun, of Georgia, McClurg, and Williamson — 6.

6. Opponents of the Constitution who became Republicans: Gerry, Lansing, L. Martin, Mason, Mercer, and Yates — 6.

7. Opponents of the Constitution who became Federalists — 0.

These figures are highly significant. Not a one of the members of the Convention who opposed the Constitution went over finally to the Federalists.[1] They all fought the adoption of the Constitution; they soon went into the opposition; and they remained Republicans until they closed their public careers. Nearly all of the members who lived a few years after the Constitution was adopted may be assigned to one or the other party with a reasonable degree of accuracy. Of the forty-three members of the Convention who supported the Constitution, and who lived several years after its adoption, six cannot be satisfactorily classified, leaving thirty-seven susceptible of classification. Of these thirty-seven, twenty-five became loyal Federalists and twelve became Republicans — seven not until the fiscal measures contemplated by the Constitution were established. Of the advocates of the Constitution who went over to the Republicans, one half, Baldwin, Butler, Dickinson, Madison, Charles Pinckney, and Randolph, were among the most vigorous champions of property rights in the Convention and among the leading opponents of anything approaching simple majority rule under universal manhood suffrage. Among the twelve advocates of the

---

[1] It should be noted, however, that the heavy security holder Gerry voted for all of Hamilton's fiscal measures before he definitely joined the opposition. For personal reasons he supported Adams in 1796.

Constitution who became Republicans, all except three, Gilman, Dickinson, and Langdon, were from the South.

Of course, we are not warranted in assuming that the members of the Philadelphia Convention, in the distribution of their political affiliations, were precisely representative of the country at large. Nevertheless one cannot help surmising that very few of the Anti-Federalists who opposed the adoption of the Constitution in 1787–1788 ever went over to the Federalist party, that the bulk of the Federalist party was composed of those who had supported the formation and adoption of the Constitution, and that most advocates of the Constitution who did become Republicans were not carried over by any theoretical considerations concerning "the cherishment of the people." At all events, the burden of proof would seem to be on those who say that there was no fundamental connection between the parties of the constitutional conflict and the political parties which arose in Washington's administrations.

Certainly there is important contemporary evidence to the effect that the party which rallied around Hamilton's measures — which were in fact the fundamental measures of the first administrations under the new Constitution — was substantially the same as the party that had supported the Constitution. Writers of the period were constantly dwelling on the identity between the opposition to the Constitution and the opposition to Federalist measures. For example, a writer in the Gazette of the United States, on July 11, 1792, declared : "The opposers of the measures which have received the sanction of the Legislature of the United States are *generally* the same persons who opposed the adoption of the new Constitution and were the advocates of *committee systems* and *paper expedients* in the days of our humiliation." A month later, August 15, 1792, a writer in the same paper added: "There are men among us who have always been known as partisans and violent ones too — these say they are opposed to the *measures* of the government only. But let memory do its office. They have been hostile to the Constitution of the United States — and if they now pretend to be converted, their conversion is only a pretense." Hamilton was not indulging in partisan argument when he contended that the two great classes of security holders and men of kindred property interests, who had supported the formation and adoption of the Constitution, also looked to the new government for an adequate provision for public credit.[1]

Throughout his political career, Hamilton consistently regarded the Republican party as the party of opposition to the Constitution and the fiscal measures of the federal government. As late as 1801, he said that the Federalists had justly represented their opponents as hostile to the national Constitution, "because, as a party, and with few exceptions, they were violent opposers of the adoption of the Constitution itself ; . . . because the amendments subsequently made, meeting scarcely any of the important objections which were urged, leaving the structure of the government and the mass and distribution of its powers where they were, are too insignificant to be with any sensible man, a reason for being reconciled to the system if he thought it originally bad ; . . . because they have opposed not *particular plans* of the administration but the general course of it and almost all the measures of material consequence, and this, too, not under one man or set of men, but under all the successions of men ; . . . because, as there have been no alterations of the Constitution sufficient to change the opinion of its merits, and as the practice under it has met

[1] Hamilton, *Works* (Lodge ed.), Vol. VII, pp. 418, 419.

with the severest reprobation of the party, there is no circumstance from which to infer that they can really have been reconciled to it." [1]

Of course the Republicans sometimes denied the charge that their party was made up of former opponents of the Constitution. The measures of the new government furnished them with plenty of political ammunition, and it was not necessary for them to assume the unnecessary burden of overthrowing the Constitution itself. Certainly there was no hope of securing converts to the Republican cause from among the friends of the Constitution, if they continued to pose as the party of opposition to the fundamental law itself. With extraordinary cleverness which can, nevertheless, be quickly penetrated by any one who knows the history of the period, Republican writers claimed the Constitution for themselves and denounced, as open and flagrant violations of that instrument, the very measures which had the support of nearly every member of the constitutional Convention, who found a place in the new government, — as if the unnatural fathers had destroyed their own progeny.

No better illustration could be found of the way in which the Republicans turned the Constitution to their own advantage and declared its original purposes to be their own purposes than in John Taylor's *Inquiry into the Principles and Tendencies of Certain Measures* published in 1794.[2] Throughout this pamphlet, he assumed that the entire fiscal system was contrary to the letter and spirit of the fundamental law drafted in 1787. In other words, Taylor had the moral courage to declare in print that the men who framed the Constitution did not know what their

---

[1] *Works* (Lodge ed.), Vol. VII, p. 185.
[2] See below, p. 197.

intentions were at the time and afterward violated persistently and consistently their own instrument of government when called upon to put it into practical operation.

Speaking of the funding system Taylor said : "It was and is the fashion of thinking that a public debt unequally held gives permanency and weight to government. That is, to use plain terms, it will enable government to control the will of the people, by counterbalancing it with the weight of wealth. The Constitution is compiled upon a principle precisely in opposition to this idea. The sovereignty of the people gave it birth and it acknowledges their parental authority. This is a design of a few individuals, exclusively to appropriate to themselves the management of the national offspring, that they may change its nature and debauch its affections from the great object of its political duty. It is an attempt to transplant the Constitution from democratic ground in which it might flourish to an aristocratical soil in which it must perish. . . . The tone of this instrument also [the funding system] in its several vibrations, harmonizes with the perilous design radically to destroy the Constitution and to erect upon its ruins an usurpation not sanctioned by the national will or acknowledging the fundamental principle that the people are the only legitimate fountain of civil government." In Taylor's opinion it was the mission of the Republicans to restore the Constitution to its "pristine health and proper functions !"

The Federalists were quick to penetrate the assertions of those Republicans who claimed to be the genuine defenders of the principles and purposes of the Constitution. A Connecticut writer in the Litchfield Monitor, in the summer of 1800, levelled his guns against the new "friends of the Constitution," declaring them to be in fact the original enemies unregenerate: "They [the Jeffersonians] profess an attachment to the Constitution and pretend only to dislike *some of the measures of the administration.* Believe me, fellow citizens, they have erected batteries against the *Constitution itself,* batteries too formidable to be held in contempt. They have exerted themselves everywhere to bring into office those influential characters who were *originally opposed to the adoption of the Constitution;* and they have succeeded beyond their most sanguine hopes in New York, Pennsylvania, and the Carolinas. In New York, the former Governor Clinton, Col. Burr, Mr. Osgood, Brockholst Livingston, and a number of others who were bitterly hostile to the Constitution originally are now elected members of the Assembly for the purpose of appointing electors who will vote for Mr. *Jefferson* as President. In Massachusetts, the Democratic candidate for governor last spring was Mr. Gerry who was a member of the Grand Convention that formed the Constitution and *opposed it in all its stages* . . . and now will you believe that *this party* can be *sincerely attached to the Constitution.* Childish credulity itself must stand abashed at the idea. Satan's temptation of our Saviour was not more impudent than such *professions* united with *such* conduct. It is the *Constitution itself* which they abhor ; and they abhor it because it does not establish the reign of *modern philosophy* and *philosophers.*" [1]

There was, in fact, a fatal inconsistency in the Republican contention that the Federalists were threatening, by "aristocratic" measures, to overturn the Constitution, which they had created ; and one extreme champion of democracy, Callender, flatly refused to accept the newly made tradition that the Constitution was the work of the whole people. On the contrary he declared it to have been in a great

[1] Reprinted in the Connecticut Courant, August 18, 1800.

measure established by the very "aristocrats" themselves — the traders in public securities. When in 1798, some officers and soldiers of New Jersey remonstrated with President Adams about his foreign policy, he replied: "Your government is not, I hope, to be called a party; if a government of your own choice is a party, how can you obtain one which will not be so?" This assertion, Callender analyzed with his customary vehemence. The Constitution, he represented, had been adopted by a majority of the people, only after a violent struggle, during which the public had been coerced by threats and misled by false promises. It had been said, ran his argument, that there was grave danger of invasion by foreign powers, that a unified nation would have greater weight in negotiating treaties with other countries, that the national debt should be extinguished, and that the Eastern states might conquer the South; and these contentions induced the people to approve the Constitution. But in spite of the false arguments used in support of the ratification, the battle had been won by a narrow margin.

In very truth, continued Callender, the federal Constitution has been "crammed down the gullet of America. . . . The 'government of your *own choice*' met with long and violent resistance to its adoption. In Virginia it was carried by eighty-nine votes against seventy-nine. From ten to thirty of the majority have long since repented of their vote. . . . In Massachusetts, the federal question was carried by an hundred and eighty-seven votes against an hundred and sixty-eight. Georgia was poor and helpless. . . . In New York, the Constitution was accepted by thirty voices against twenty-five; in Rhode Island by a majority of two. In North Carolina it was at first rejected by a large majority. Hence it follows that the new government was only preferred by a *part* of the people. On this account, Mr. Washington hath since declared that *the federal constitution should not have been adopted.* For, in his farewell letter of September 17, 1796, he remarks that 'the constitution which at any time exists, till exchanged by an explicit act of the *whole* people, is sacredly obligatory upon all.' In Virginia, this Constitution met not only with violent, but with at least equiponderant opposition. In all the other states the people were greatly divided. All the atrocious artifices common at an ordinary election were exerted in support of it. . . . That the federal system had been embraced by the *whole* people never was, nor could be pretended. Yet the first federal Congress met, in defiance of the *constitution then existing* and of the *sacred obligation* referred to by Mr. Washington. They met on the ruins of the old confederation, and sacrificed a variety of rights hitherto held as inviolable. They met when out of the thirteen states eleven only had acceded to the Union. . . . On March 3, 1789, when the first Congress assembled, they bore about them every feature that corresponds with the definition of *traitors*, as just quoted from Mr. Washington himself. . . . The farewell address conveys an explicit censure not only upon the new government, but likewise upon the American revolution ; for that was accomplished by *a part* of the people, in despite of the rest, and in breach of what is called the British constitution. By his own account, therefore, Mr. Washington has been twice a traitor. He first renounced the king of England, and thereafter the old confederation." [1]

This "treasonable" work by a minority, this formation of the Constitution in the teeth of public opinion, Callender declared to have been, in a large part, the wicked deed of the security holders. "The new Constitution," he ex-

---

[1] *The Prospect Before Us,* Vol. I, pp. 9 ff.

claimed, "had been in a great measure established by the influence and activity of the traders in these certificates." [1] And then with extraordinary complacency, in the face of his own attack upon the Constitution, Callender denounced the "six per cent regiment" in Congress as having given to the Constitution, within their twenty-three months' existence, "a blow from which it has almost no chance of recovery," as if the men who had been instrumental in framing and adopting it were planning the destruction of their own handiwork.[2]

Inasmuch as the Republican publicists and pamphleteers were contradicting themselves about the relation of the Federalist party to the party of the Constitution, it is not surprising to find the Federalists ridiculing them. The latter were constantly pointing out the fallacy of the contention that the subversion of the new fundamental law was the purpose of Federalism. Speaking of the Republicans who charged the Federalists with being enemies to the Constitution, a writer in the United States Gazette said: "They chatter about the partizans of kingly power and affect to consider the plan of subverting our republican government and free Constitution as well matured. . . . The certificate men, the stockholders of the bank, the tools of the ministry, the aristocrats, are all conspirators against liberty ; in short all the men who wish *to buoy up the present government.* Strange! that a plan against liberty and the Constitution should be supported by those who are ridiculed for puffing the Constitution and the present happy condition of the Union, and above all, who are for buoying up the government. . . . Is it not plain that all the property created by the bank and funding system depends on preserving the Constitution unchanged? . . . Or will our wise

---

[1] *Sedgwick & Co., or a Key to the Six Percent Cabinet.*   [2] *Ibid.*

ones pretend that men of property are the first to plot revolutions and civil convulsions? But those who delight to cry knave, speculator, aristocrat, and kingly power take both sides of a contradiction, and maintain each with equal good temper and good sense." [1]

In this contest between the friends and enemies of the Constitution, Jefferson occupied a position of peculiar advantage. He had been in Paris when the Constitution was framed and adopted. He had approved parts of the instrument and disapproved other parts so that he could, with some show of justification, be claimed as a friend or an enemy. In fact, Jefferson refused to be classed either as Federalist or an Anti-Federalist in the spring of 1789, declaring that if he could not go to heaven except with a party he would not go at all. "Therefore I protest to you," he wrote to Hopkinson, "I am not of the party of federalists. But I am much further from that of the Antifederalists. I approved from the first moment of the great mass of what is in the new constitution, the consolidation of the government, the organization into executive, legislative, and judiciary, the subdivision of the legislative, the happy compromise of interests between the great and little states by the different manner of voting in the different houses, the voting by persons instead of states, the qualified negative on laws given to the executive, which however I should have liked better if associated with the judiciary as in New York, and the power of taxation. I thought at first that the latter might have been limited. A little reflection soon convinced me that it ought not to be." The points of objection urged by Jefferson were the want of a bill of rights to secure individual liberty "against the legislative as well as the executive, branches of the government," and the perpetual

[1] The Gazette of the United States, June 6, 1792.

reëligibility of the President.[1] The student of political psychology will, therefore, find it extremely interesting to discover that the first President elected by the Republicans could, with equal justice, be claimed as an opponent or a friend of the Constitution at the time of its formation and adoption.

[1] *Documentary History of the Constitution*, Vol. V, p. 159.

CHAPTER III

No one who turns over carefully and patiently the letters and papers of the leaders in the constitutional conflict can accept for a moment the theory that on the morning after the ratification of the Constitution the opposing forces laid down their arms on the pleasing assumption that the battle was over.[1] Statesmen, such as they, were fully aware of the fact that there was no magic in the language of the instrument of government itself that could *ex proprio vigore* call the new system into being. Its champions as well as its opponents knew that its real character was to be determined by the measures of law and administration to be established under it.

[1] *Documentary History of the Constitution*, Vols. IV and V, contains valuable materials on this point. "The progress which had been made [by the time of the inauguration of Washington] in assuaging the bitter animosities engendered in the sharp contest respecting the adoption of the Constitution, and the means which might be used for conciliating the affections of all good men to the new government, without enfeebling its essential principles, were subjects of the most interesting inquiry. The agitation had been too great to be suddenly calmed; and for the active opponents of the system to become suddenly its friends, or even indifferent to its fate, would have been a victory of reason over passion, or a surrender of individual judgement to the decision of the majority, examples of which are rarely given in the progress of human affairs. In some of the states, a disposition to acquiesce in the decision which had been made and to await the issue of a fair experiment of the Constitution, was avowed by the minority. In others, the chagrin of defeat seemed to increase the original hostility to the instrument; and serious fears were entertained by its friends, that a second general convention might pluck from it the most essential of its powers, before their value, and the safety with which they might be confided where they were placed, could be ascertained by experience. . . . In all those states where the opposition was sufficiently formidable to inspire a hope of success, the effort was made to fill the legislature with the declared enemies of the government, and thus commit it, in its infancy, to the custody of its foes." Marshall, *Life of Washington* (2d ed.), Vol. II, p. 150.

The Constitution, when it left the hands of the Convention in the autumn of 1787, was simply a proposition for the conduct of public affairs filled with economic implications which were at once seen, at least in part, by its shrewdest opponents.[1] To make it a mere lawful instrument of government, it was necessary to secure the ratification of at least nine states. Even with ratification, the battle was not half won. All depended upon the character of the men who filled the offices and determined the policies and measures of the new government. The clauses of the Constitution were on their face somewhat uncertain promises of a system to be created. The full potentialities were only understood by the bold spirits in the secret assembly that framed it — those who opposed it on economic grounds only roughly divined the precise powers which could be exercised under the new instrument.

The Constitution did not even go into effect when Washington was inaugurated first President. The wisest men knew that it was only a figment of the imagination then. It did not go into effect until the economic measures which its adoption implied were put upon the statute books and carried into execution — not until the debt was funded and adjusted, finances put on a sound basis, revenue laws put into force, commerce and manufacturing encouraged, a land policy forged out, and a national judicial system established, bringing federal law to the door of every litigant seeking his rights under the Constitution. Only when the President and Congress had been chosen, the corps of judges, marshals, attorneys, collectors, and revenue officers duly installed, the army and navy organized — in fact the whole

---

[1] See particularly the debates in the Virginia ratifying Convention, Elliot, *Debates*, Vol. III. Mason even prophesied an excise tax that would reach the homes of the backwoods farmers. See below, Chap. IX. See also *Economic Interpretation of the Constitution*, Chap. XI.

machine set in motion throughout the length and breadth of the American empire — collecting revenue, paying the national debt, making and enforcing commercial regulations for the benefit of domestic trade and manufactures, determining suits between parties, fighting Indians, laying off Western lands did the Constitution become a real political organism influencing the lives and property of the people. Then it was that the process of government under the Constitution began to be realized. Then it was discovered, as Madison said, who was to govern the country.[1]

Certainly, the most active members of the Philadelphia Convention knew that the general language of the Constitution needed to be filled with concrete meaning in the form of definite statutes and that many of the clauses could only be correctly interpreted by men rightly affected toward the new instrument. They were accordingly doubly anxious about the first elections, about the choice of men to fill the various offices high and low in the new government. They were fully aware of the deep opposition to the Constitution and of the slender character of the "victory" which they had just won, and the most determined plunged at once into politics — manipulation and negotiation — in the hope of securing the election of men who could be trusted to lay the foundations of the federal system firmly in the measures contemplated by the framers. Even Washington whose dignity and reserve precluded his taking part personally in the bitter combats of the forum, wrote voluminous political letters [2] during the campaign that followed the ratification

---

[1] Madison wrote to Jefferson from the seat of government on July 10, 1792: "It pretty clearly appears, also, in what proportions the public debt lies in the country, what sort of hands hold it, and by whom the people of the United States are to be governed." *Writings* (1867 ed.), Vol. I, p. 583.

[2] See *Documentary History of the Constitution*, Vols. IV and V.

of the Constitution, and he was in this manner no less effective than others who took the stump.

In more than one letter sent out from Mt. Vernon, he expressed his anxiety over the approaching elections to the first Congress and warned his correspondents that the battle was not won with the formal ratification of the Constitution, that nearly everything depended on the "federal character" of those who undertook the inauguration of the projected system. After recounting to Major-General Lincoln, on August 28, 1788, the recent rapid strides of federalism he added a caveat "that attempts will be made to procure the election of a number of anti-federal characters to the first Congress in order to embarrass the wheels of government and produce premature alterations in its Constitution. How these hints, which have come through different channels, may be well or ill founded, I know not; but it will be advisable, I should think, for the federalists to be on their guard so far as not to suffer any secret machinations to prevail without taking measures to frustrate them. . . . I wish I may be mistaken in imagining that there are persons, who upon finding that they could not carry their point by an open attack against the Constitution, have some sinister designs to be silently effected, if possible. But I trust in that Providence which has saved us in six troubles, yes in seven, to rescue us again from any imminent, though unseen dangers. Nothing, however, on our part ought to be left undone." [1]

Writing to Lincoln two months later, Washington dwelt at length upon the crucial nature of the impending federal elections: "As the period is now rapidly approaching which must decide the fate of the new Constitution, as to the manner of its being carried into execution and probably as

[1] *Documentary History of the Constitution*, Vol. V, pp. 34, 40.

to its usefulness, it is not wonderful that we should all feel
an unusual degree of anxiety on the occasion. I must
acknowledge that my fears have been greatly alarmed, but
still I am not without hopes. . . . *There will however be no
room for the advocates of the Constitution to relax in their exertions; for if they should be lulled into security, appointments
of antifederal men may probably take place;* and the consequences which you so justly dread be realized." [1]

The tentative character of the gains so far made and the
absolute dependence of the new system upon the continued
active support of those who had been instrumental in launch-
ing it were all made plain in Hamilton's famous letter to
Washington, urging him to accept the presidency: "It
cannot be considered as a compliment to say that on your
acceptance of the office of President the success of the new
government in its commencement may materially depend.
Your agency and influence will be not less important in preserving it from the future attacks of its enemies than they
have been in recommending it in the first instance to the
adoption of the people. Independent of all considerations
drawn from this source, the point of light in which you
stand at home and abroad will make an infinite difference
in the respectability with which the government will begin
its operations in the alternative of your being or not being
at the head of it. I forbear to urge considerations which
might have a more personal application. What I have said
will suffice for the inferences I mean to draw.

"First. In a matter so essential to the well-being of
society as the prosperity of a newly instituted government,
a citizen of so much consequence as yourself to its success
has no option but to lend his services if called for. Permit
me to say that it would be inglorious in such a situation

not to hazard the glory, however great, which he might have previously acquired.

"Secondly. Your signature to the proposed system pledges your judgment for its being such a one as, upon the whole, was worthy of the public approbation. If it should miscarry (as men commonly decide from success, or the want of it), the blame will, in all probability, be laid on the system itself, and the framers of it will have to encounter the disrepute of having brought about a revolution in government, without substituting anything that was worthy of the effort. They pulled down one Utopia, it will be said, to build up another. This view of the subject, if I mistake not, my dear sir, will suggest to your mind greater hazard to that fame, which must and ought to be dear to you, in refusing your future aid to the system than in affording it. I will only add that, in my estimate of the matter, that aid is indispensable." [1]

The very considerations which Hamilton urged upon Washington to induce him to accept the office of President in the first instance were again brought to bear in 1792 to wring from him his consent to serve a second time. The Constitution is not yet securely founded, its enemies are as watchful and energetic as ever, and the federal government has not passed all its crucial tests. Writing on July 30,

[1] Hamilton, *Works* (Lodge ed.), Vol. VIII, p. 196. See also *Documentary History of the Constitution*, Vol. IV, p. 288. Hamilton's sentiments were echoed throughout the country. For example, the Mechanics and Manufacturers Association of Providence presented the following address to Washington in 1790: "Pleased with the establishment of a firm government, we are happy in thus having it within our power to express our sentiments of regard and attachment to the President of the Union, and our determination, as far as in us lies, to support the Constitution and laws of the United States. The Mechanics and Manufacturers of this town feel a confidence in the wisdom and patriotism of the legislature of the United States, — that they will do all in their power to promote the manufactures, as well as agriculture and commerce, of our country; this confidence is greatly strengthened by the consideration that you, Sir, are at the head of it." *Gazette of the United States*, July 28, 1790.

1792, Hamilton declared to Washington: "'Tis clear, says everyone with whom I have conversed, that the affairs of the national government are not yet firmly established — that its enemies, generally speaking, are as inveterate as ever — that their enmity has been sharpened by its success, and by all the resentments which flow from disappointed predictions and mortified vanity — that a general and strenuous effort is making in every state to place the administration of it in the hands of its enemies, as if they were its safest guardians — that the period of the next House of Representatives is likely to prove the crisis of its permanent character — that if you continue in office nothing materially mischievous is to be apprehended, if you quit, much is to be dreaded — that the same motives which induced you to accept originally ought to decide you to continue till matters have assumed a more determined aspect — that indeed it would have been better, as it regards your own character, that you had never consented to come forward than now to leave the business unfinished and in danger of being undone — that in the event of storms arising there would be an imputation either of want of foresight or want of firmness. . . . If a solitary vote or two should appear wanting to perfect unanimity, of what moment can it be? Will not the fewness of the exceptions be a confirmation of the devotion of the community to a character which has so generally united its suffrages after an administration of four years at the head of a new government, opposed in its first establishment by a large proportion of its citizens and obliged to run counter to many prejudices in devising the arduous arrangements requisite to public credit and public order? [1] "

At no time during the period intervening between the ratification of the Constitution and the inauguration of the

<hr>

[1] Hamilton, *Works* (Lodge ed.), Vol. VIII, p. 274.

new government were the leaders in Federalism certain that the agrarian party which had opposed the Constitution might not render the instrument ineffectual by securing possession of Congress. "The murmurs of partial discontent, cloak'd under what is called here antifederalism, seem now greatly to abate," wrote Crèvecœur to Jefferson in October, 1788, "there remains but one wish which is, that those country parties may not preponderate in the choice of federal Senators and Delegates; if a majority of federalists can be obtained in those two bodies everything will go smoothly on. Their first session, which is to begin in March, will put the finishing hand to the great organization: but an amazing task when one considers the extent of all the departments." [1] It was not until January 5, 1789, that Crèvecœur was able to announce his conviction that the nail was clinched and the future of the government assured.[2]

Jefferson himself was very uncertain whether the temper of the people had moderated sufficiently to permit the government under the Constitution to set out on a smooth course. "Our political machine is now pretty well wound up," he wrote to Colonel W. S. Smith, on August, 2, 1788, "but are the spirits of our people sufficiently wound down to let it work glibly?" Indeed, he was not anxious for a too ready acquiescence in the strong government which the new order promised, for he added: "I trust it is too soon for that, and that we have many centuries to come yet before my countrymen cease to bear their government hard in hand." [3]

Opponents of the Constitution were no less anxious about the outcome of the first elections than were the stoutest

[1] *Documentary History of the Constitution*, Vol. V, p. 93.
[2] *Ibid.*, Vol. V, p. 145. [3] *Ibid.*, Vol. V, p. 1.

Federalists. For instance, Clinton in New York and Patrick Henry in Virginia were quite as much concerned about the character of the Senators, Representatives, and federal officers as they had been about the adoption of the Constitution itself. Of course, it was not any longer a question of an outward loyalty to the general system established by the Constitution. It was easy to do lip service. It was a far more fundamental question what measures were to be realized under the Constitution. The Anti-Federalists looked beyond the language of the instrument to the process of government which it implied.

An excellent account of the way in which the opposition read into the phraseology of the Constitution the measures contemplated by its sponsors is afforded by Hamilton's description of the attitude of the Anti-Federalists in New York. "The leaders of the party hostile to the Constitution," wrote Hamilton, on June 8, 1788, "are equally hostile to the Union. They are, however, afraid to reject the Constitution at once, because that step would bring matters to a crisis between this state and the states which had adopted the Constitution, and between parties in the state. A separation of the Southern District from the other parts of the State, it is perceived, would become the object of the Federalists and of the neighboring states. They therefore resolve upon a long adjournment as the safest and most artful course to effect their final purpose. *They suppose that when the government gets into operation, it will be obliged to take some steps in respect to revenue, etc., which will furnish topics of declamation to its enemies in the several states and will strengthen the minorities.* If any considerable discontent should show itself, they stand ready to head the opposition." [1]

It is clear from his letters that the political contest of

[1] *Works* (Lodge ed.), Vol. VIII, p. 187. Italics mine.

1788–1789 must have been regarded by Hamilton as simply a continuation of the fight over ratification. Indeed, he knew from first-hand experience that it was, for he plunged into politics as soon as the call for the federal elections went forth and he met again the old enemies who had fought him and the Constitution at Poughkeepsie. Whoever takes the trouble to examine the newspapers and correspondence of the period of the presidential and congressional elections will find the same partisan flavor that characterized the constitutional struggle.[1] Everywhere the leaders in the campaign treated the conflict as the old battle between Federalists and Anti-Federalists, and in the main the same personalities stand out on both sides of the battle line.[2]

There can be no doubt that the directors of the opposing forces watched the elections with great care and followed the results closely. As early as November 23, 1788, Hamilton had fairly estimated the drift of political sentiment in nearly every state, for on that day he wrote to Madison as follows : "In Massachusetts the Electors will, I understand, be appointed by the legislature and will be all Federal, and

[1] *Economic Interpretation of the Constitution*, Chap. XI.

[2] The following letter written by Tench Cox to Madison (New York, January 27, 1789), for instance, has exactly the same tone as many of the letters written during the struggle over the ratification of the Constitution and shows identically the same political cleavage: "The State of New York still retain their impressions against the Constitution. They still decline to elect Senators upon legislative principles, and I think an absence of two of the Senate is, from Appearances determined on to avoid the precedent of conceding their due legislative independence — They will have two antifdlts, and no Merchant in their Senate. Massachusetts & Pennsa. alone have attended to mercantile character in the Senate, which will assist in obviating the Objections to the commercial powers of that body — This is in favor of the Constitution, but possibly not so favorable to the interests of the Union as if there were five or six merchants. The practice under the Constitution will, in my opinion, be more agreeable to the Opposition in many other particulars than their leaders are aware of. In this particular instance it is fortunate that our Senator is a man of extensive political information, and landed property and, tho a practical Merchant, a friend to a pretty free System of Trade. I do not think the most captious agriculturist in the Senate will find Mr. Morris tenacious of any principle that will be injurious to the landed interest." *Documentary History of the Constitution*, Vol. V, pp. 149–150.

it is probable will be, for the most part, in favor of Adams. It is said the same thing will happen in New Hampshire, and I have reason to believe, it will be the case in Connecticut. In this state it is difficult to form any certain calculation. A large majority of the *Assembly* was doubtless of an Anti-Federal complexion, but the schism in the party, which has been occasioned by the falling off of some of its leaders in the Convention, leaves me not without hope that, if matters are well managed, we may procure a majority for some pretty equal compromise. In the Senate we have the superiority by one. In New Jersey there seems to be no question but that the complexion of the Electors will be Federal, and I suppose, if thought expedient, they may be united in favor of Adams. Pennsylvania you can best judge of. From Delaware, Maryland, and South Carolina, I presume, we may count with tolerable assurance on Federal men ; and I should imagine, if pains are taken, the danger of an Anti-federal Vice-President might itself be rendered the instrument of union. At any rate, their weight will not be thrown into the scale of Clinton, and I do not see from what quarter numbers can be marshalled in his favor equal to those who will advocate Adams, supposing even a division in the Federal votes. On the whole I have concluded to support Adams, though I am not without apprehension on the score we have conversed about. My principal reasons are these : First, he is a declared partisan of deferring to future experience the expediency of amendments in the system, and (although I do not altogether *adopt* this sentiment) it is much nearer my own than certain other doctrines. Secondly, he is certainly a character of importance in the Eastern states ; if he is not Vice-President, one of two worse things will be likely to happen. Either he must be nominated to some important office, for which he is less proper, or will become a malcontent and give additional weight to the opposition to the government."[1]

In no state apparently, except possibly Georgia,[2] did the Anti-Federalists fail to contest with the Federalists for representation in Congress, and in some places the battle was as hot as the conflict over ratification. In the western regions of Massachusetts, several elections were held before any candidate received the requisite majority, Theodore Sedgwick, a Federalist, being victorious at last. In another centre of the Shays' disaffection, the Worcester district, the Anti-Federalists were able to carry the day and return Grout, a former adherent of the agrarian leader.[3] In the Middlesex district, the spectacle of a contest between two former members of the Philadelphia Convention was afforded, Gorham a Federalist, and Gerry an Anti-Federalist. The latter carried the day, but only after having declared his opinion that all citizens of the ratifying states were bound to support the new government and that any opposition to "a due administration of it" would be "unjustifiable and highly criminal." In the Boston region, the Federalists elected Fisher Ames who had been a stout champion of the Constitution in the state ratifying convention — the Anti-Federalists voting for Samuel Adams, who was known to have been lukewarm in his support of the Constitution and strongly in favor of amendments.[4]

In Connecticut, the Representatives were not elected by districts but at large and by a peculiar process. Fifteen candidates were at first selected by popular vote, and then from this list were chosen by popular vote the five Repre-

[1] Hamilton, *Works* (Lodge ed.), Vol. VIII, p. 203.

[2] See Paullin, "The First Elections under the Constitution," *Iowa Journal of History and Politics*, Vol. II, pp. 3 ff.

[3] Grout voted for assumption which took a big burden off the backs of the Massachusetts taxpayers, and true to Shays' principles he voted against the Bank.

[4] Hildreth, *op. cit.*, Vol. I, p. 42.

sentatives to which the state was entitled. The leader of the delegation was Roger Sherman, who had been a member of the Philadelphia Convention and the state ratifying convention. Two other Representatives from Connecticut, Jonathan Sturges and Jeremiah Wadsworth, had also been members of the state convention. The remaining two, Benjamin Huntington and Jonathan Trumbull, were Federalists of high standing.

In New York, the Representatives were chosen by districts and the Federalists carried the three Southern seats, electing John Lawrence, Ebgert Benson, and William Floyd.[1] In other words, they maintained their strength in the regions which had been in favor of the ratification of the Constitution.

In New Jersey, the Representatives were elected at large. There seems to have been a hot contest between the candidates on the "eastern" and the "western" tickets, for the polls were kept open for three or four weeks in some counties and it required the arbitrary intervention of the governor to bring the battle to a finish.[2] The Federalists were victorious, but the opposition threatened to contest the election.

In Pennsylvania, where the Representatives were elected at large, both parties held conventions and nominated candidates.[3] The Federalists carried the day only after a sharp battle. Two of the eight members, Clymer and Fitzsimons, had been members of the Convention which drafted the Constitution. Of the remaining six, four, Thomas Hartley, F. A. Muhlenberg, Thomas Scott, Henry Wynkoop, had been members of the Pennsylvania ratifying convention and had voted in favor of ratification. Six of the eight, there-

---

[1] *Writings of James Madison* (1867 ed.), Vol. I, p. 453.
[2] *Ibid.*, Vol. I, p. 453.
[3] Paullin, *op. cit.*, pp. 5, 6. Pennsylvania was apparently the only state in which the parties held nominating conventions.

fore, had been prominently identified with the formation and adoption of the Constitution.

In Maryland, the Federalists and Anti-Federalists had tickets in the field. The Baltimore Journal of January 13, 1789, speaks of the great exertions put forth by both parties, and it appears that the Federalists barely escaped defeat in Baltimore, their majority over their opponents being only seven votes.[1]

The Virginia Representatives were elected by districts, and out of a delegation of ten, only three had been among the opponents of the Constitution, Bland, Coles, and Parker.[2] Curiously enough, Madison, who was soon destined to become an inveterate Anti-Federalist, had for an opposition candidate Colonel Monroe who had voted against the Constitution in the state convention. The Virginia assembly of 1789–1790 was decidedly Anti-Federalist, and it elected to the United States Senate Richard Henry Lee and William Grayson, the latter a particularly strong opponent of the Constitution in his state.[3]

The back-country regions of South Carolina, true to their principles, sent Anti-Federalist Representatives to the first Congress, including two celebrated opponents of the Constitution, Ædanus Burke and General Sumter.[4] Federalist Charleston returned William L. Smith, a gentleman of wealth who had been in England during the Revolution, and, on that account, was often charged with being a Tory by some of his opponents.

When, at length, in 1790 the North Carolina delegation arrived in Congress, it was found to contain the celebrated Timothy Bloodworth who had been most violent in his

---

[1] Paullin, op. cit., p. 15.
[2] *Writings of James Madison* (1867), Vol. I, p. 458.
[3] Ambler, *Sectionalism in Virginia*, p. 59.
[4] Hildreth, op. cit., Vol. I, p. 45.

opposition to the Constitution in the first convention of his state, as well as Hugh Williamson who had been a member of the Philadelphia Convention, a signer of the Constitution, and a warm advocate of the federal system.

Although it is evident from the newspapers that the rival parties had several sharp skirmishes in some of the states, the elections as a whole do not appear to have elicited very great enthusiasm. On this point Paullin says that "there was little popular interest in the first elections." In Madison's electoral district in Virginia the vote was only 2.7 per cent of the white population. In Maryland, 3.6 per cent of the white population, and in Massachusetts about 3 per cent, participated in the first congressional elections. In Pennsylvania, only about 15,000 voters went to the polls, a number only slightly in excess of that which participated in the ratification elections of 1787. However, it does not appear that this lethargy was any greater than it had been in colonial times. It required the persistent agitation of party leaders to rouse the electorate to action.

Of the fifty-five members of the first House of Representatives, nine or about one-sixth, Gilman, Gerry, Sherman, Clymer, Fitzsimons, Carroll, Madison, Williamson, and Baldwin had been members of the Convention which drafted the Constitution. In striking contrast to this popularly elected branch stood the first Senate, of whose twenty-six members, no less than eleven, Langdon, Strong, Ellsworth, Johnson, King, Paterson, Read, R. Morris, Butler, Bassett, and Few had been members of the Philadelphia Convention. The only opponent of the Constitution at Philadelphia who found his way into the first Congress was Gerry, and he had been elected to the House only after promising no undue opposition to the new administration.

If we examine the political careers of the seventy-eight

members of the first Congress of the United States, omitting Rhode Island which was not represented at Philadelphia and was driven into ratification, we find that the surprisingly large number of forty-four, that is, more than one-half, had been members of the Philadelphia constitutional Convention or of ratifying conventions in their respective states, and many of them of both conventions. The list is impressive. Of the New Hampshire delegation of five in the first Congress, Langdon had been a member of both conventions, Gilman had been at Philadelphia, and Livermore had rendered fine service in the state convention. Massachusetts sent ten members to the first Congress, and only three of these had not acted directly on the adoption of the Constitution; Strong had been a member of the federal and state conventions, Gerry had served in the former, while Dalton, Ames, Partridge, Sedgwick, and Grout had been in the state convention. Connecticut's delegation of five Congressmen included three who had supported the Constitution at the Philadelphia and Hartford conventions, Ellsworth, Johnson, and Sherman, and two, Sturges and Wadsworth, who had been in the state ratifying convention. New York, the state which had been strongly against the Constitution, sent only one member to Congress who had seen convention service — Senator King, who had been a delegate of Massachusetts to Philadelphia. New Jersey, which had ratified unanimously, elected Paterson — a member of the Philadelphia convention — to the Senate, and chose new men for the five additional posts in Congress. Of Delaware's three congressmen, two, Bassett and Read, had been in the federal Convention, and the former had served in the state convention as well. Seven of Pennsylvania's ten had seen convention service : R. Morris, Clymer, and Fitzsimons at Philadelphia, and Hartley, F. A. Muhlenberg, Scott, and

Wynkoop at the state convention. Of Maryland's eight, Daniel Carroll had been in the Federal Convention and Gale and Stone in the state convention. Virginia was entitled to twelve congressmen and of these Madison had been in both conventions and Grayson, Moore, White, and Coles in the state convention. Of North Carolina's seven, Williamson had been in the Philadelphia convention and Steele and Bloodworth in the first state convention. Five of South Carolina's seven members of Congress had acted directly on the Constitution: Butler at Philadelphia and Izard, Smith, Burke, and Sumter in the state convention. Georgia, entitled to five members, sent Few who had been in both conventions, Baldwin who had served at Philadelphia, and Mathews who had voted for the Constitution in the state convention.

Of this long list of forty-four members of Congress who had been instrumental in the formation and adoption of the Constitution, thirty-seven were reckoned as its advocates and champions. It is evident that those who had created the new frame of government were not indifferent as to the measures to be realized under it, but deemed it of high and pressing importance that the new process of government should be continued by the men who had begun it. It is significant also that a very large proportion of the thirty-seven constitutional Federalists gave their hearty support to all or nearly all of Hamilton's measures and remained loyal party Federalists until the end. Of the seven Anti-Federalists of the constitutional conflict — Gerry, Grout, Grayson, Coles, Bloodworth, Burke, and Sumter — all but two were from the South, and with the exception of Gerry, they were generally in the opposition, in the political battles which were waged in Congress, and even Gerry later cast his fortunes unreservedly with the Jeffersonian party.

If we analyze the executive and judicial branches of the government, we find an astoundingly large proportion of the men who had been prominent and active in the formation and adoption of the Constitution. The first President was, of course, Washington who had presided over the Philadelphia Convention and lent the magic of his great name to the cause of ratification. For the most important post in his administration, that of Secretary of the Treasury, he chose Robert Morris, a member of the Convention, and when that gentleman declined the position, he turned to another member of the Convention, that giant of Federalism, Alexander Hamilton. For the office of Attorney-General, Washington selected the spokesman of the Virginia delegation in the Convention, Edmund Randolph. General Knox, of whose stout Federalism there could be no doubt, was continued in the office of Secretary of War. Only one high administrative position went to a man whose views on the new government were, to say the least, somewhat uncertain. Thomas Jefferson, who had been the representative of the United States in France during the formation and ratification of the Constitution, was made Secretary of State, and placed in charge of foreign affairs.

The roll of the first appointments to the Supreme Court of the United States by President Washington shows that it was deemed wise to call to the high function of interpreting the Constitution men who had been instrumental in making it:

Chief Justice, John Jay, of New York, a member of the state ratifying convention, who ably aided Hamilton in wringing a reluctant approval from enough members to carry the day.

Associate Justice, John Rutledge, of South Carolina, a member of the federal Convention and a signer of the Constitution.

Associate Justice, James Wilson, of Pennsylvania, a member

of the federal Convention, a signer of the Constitution, and a leader in the state convention in favor of the ratification.

Associate Justice, John Blair, of Virginia, a member of the federal Convention, a signer of the Constitution, and a valiant worker in the state convention for ratification.

Associate Justice, James Iredell,[1] of North Carolina, one of the most indefatigable champions of the Constitution in that state and a member of the state ratifying convention.

William Cushing, of Massachusetts, chief justice of that state and vice-president of the state ratifying convention.

In organizing the federal district courts under the Judiciary Act, President Washington sought out a large number of members of the state ratifying conventions and commissioned them to serve as judges interpreting federal law and the Constitution, as the following list shows:

New Hampshire district, John Sullivan, president of the state ratifying convention.

Massachusetts, John Lowell, who declined, and was succeeded by John Davis, who had voted for the Constitution in the state ratifying convention.

Connecticut, Richard Law, a supporter of the Constitution in the state ratifying convention.

New York, James Duane, who had labored side by side with Hamilton in the state convention.

New Jersey, David Brearley, a member of the federal Convention, a signer of the Constitution, and a supporter of the new instrument in the state convention.

Delaware, Gunning Bedford, a member of the federal Convention, a signer of the Constitution, and a supporter of the Constitution in the state convention.

Pennsylvania, Francis Hopkinson, one of the most active Federalists in that state, who ably aided the cause by his pen and by negotiations.[2]

---

[1] Iredell was appointed in the place of Harrison, of Maryland, who declined the post.

[2] Simpson, *Eminent Philadelphians*, pp. 544, 545.

Maryland, Thomas Johnson, a member of the state ratifying convention who had voted for the Constitution.

Virginia, Edmund Pendleton, the president of the state ratifying convention who had supported the Constitution.

North Carolina, W. R. Davie, who had supported the Constitution in the federal Convention and in both state conventions, was nominated and declined; John Stokes was then named, but he died shortly; and December 20, 1790, John Sitgreaves, who had voted for the Constitution in the state ratifying convention, was appointed.

South Carolina, William Drayton, who had voted for the Constitution in the state ratifying convention. On June 14, 1790, Thomas Bee was named to succeed Drayton. Bee had voted for the Constitution in the state convention.

Georgia, Nathaniel Pendleton, resigned in 1796 and was followed by William Stephens who had voted for the Constitution in the state convention.

If by way of recapitulation, we call the roll of the men who signed the Constitution, thirty-nine in number, we find that at least twenty-six found a place in the new government, either by election or appointment:

Abraham Baldwin, of Georgia, Representative.

Richard Bassett, Delaware, United States Senator.

Gunning Bedford, Delaware, United States district judge.

John Blair, of Virginia, Associate Justice of the Supreme Court.

William Blount, North Carolina, governor of the Territory South of the Ohio.

David Brearley, New Jersey, judge of the United States district court of his state.

Pierce Butler, South Carolina, Senator.

Daniel Carroll, Maryland, Representative.

George Clymer, Pennsylvania, Representative.

William Few, Georgia, Senator.

Thomas Fitzsimons, Pennsylvania, Representative.

Nicholas Gilman, New Hampshire, Representative.

Nathaniel Gorham, Massachusetts, Supervisor of Federal Excise in Massachusetts.

Alexander Hamilton, New York, Secretary of the Treasury.
William Samuel Johnson, Connecticut, Senator.
Rufus King, of Massachusetts, Senator from New York.
John Langdon, New Hampshire, Senator.
James Madison, Virginia, Representative.
Robert Morris, Pennsylvania, Senator.
William Paterson, New Jersey, Senator, and later Associate Justice of the Supreme Court.
George Read, Delaware, Senator.
John Rutledge, South Carolina, Associate Justice of the Supreme Court.
Roger Sherman, Connecticut, Representative.
George Washington, Virginia, President of the United States.
Hugh Williamson, North Carolina, Representative.
James Wilson, Pennsylvania, Associate Justice of the Supreme Court.

Of the other members who, for one reason or another, did not sign the Constitution, the following were also in the new government, making thirty members of the Philadelphia convention in all :

Oliver Ellsworth of Connecticut, Senator.
Caleb Strong of Massachusetts, Senator.
Edmund Randolph, Virginia, Attorney-General.
Elbridge Gerry, Massachusetts, the only opponent of the Constitution elected to office, Representative.

In other words, over one-half of the members of the Philadelphia Convention entered into the service of the government which they had devised.   It is safe to say that four-fifths of the active, forceful leaders of the Convention helped to realize, as a process of government, the paper Constitution which they had drafted.

Indeed, one may say with a high degree of truth that the constitutional Convention, although it adjourned on September 17, 1787, never dissolved until the great economic measures which were necessary to make the Constitution a living instrument were fully realized. Though separated during the contest over ratification, the leading members were united in the labor of securing the approval of the grand design. When the new government was set up, the great majority of the active spirits met once more as members of Congress, high officers, and judges, and in official capacity gave reality to the words written down at Philadelphia. It is therefore a wholly false notion to regard the constitution-making process as completed with the ratification of the instrument.[1]

The government that began with the inauguration of

[1] Incidentally this throws an important light on a minor point in the *Economic Interpretation of the Constitution* in which it was assumed that a member of the Convention who appeared upon the funding books of the new government was a holder of securities at the time of the Convention, on the theory that very few of them could have been in what Jefferson called the "corrupt squadron" dealing in the funds of the government whose credit depended so much upon their labors. The main point of the chapter in question was that the members of the Convention were of the capitalistic rather than the agrarian interest, and whether they made money out of the adoption of the Constitution was specifically stated to be of no consequence to the main thesis (p. 73). Some superficial critics have imagined the downfall of the whole thesis because it could not be definitely proved that all the security-holding members held their paper *at the time of the Convention*. Such critics have the satisfaction of choosing to believe that the framers who held public funds were men who had risked their money in securities when the fortunes of the government were at a low ebb before 1787, or that most of them were engaged in buying securities while they were serving as legislative, executive, or judicial officers under the government which they had created, and at a time when their influence was determining the value of those securities. Respect for the framers of the Constitution should impel us to choose the former alternative. It is informing to compare the list of security holders in the Convention (p. 150 of the *Economic Interpretation*) with the above list of members of the Convention who took office in the first government under the Constitution. If the members who appear on the funding books of the new government did not hold their securities at the time of the Convention, they must have bought them during those momentous months when the funding measures were being pushed through Congress, and adequate revenues provided and when every officer of the government high and low knew what the effect of the laws would be on securities. The fact that wherever the old treasury records of the Confederation are available the names of the security-holding members of the Convention appear and the high character of the great majority of them induce us to believe that they belonged to that large class of *bona fide* creditors of the United States who had a moral right to expect full payment at the hand of the government.

Washington, on April 30, 1789, was therefore no non-partisan government chosen without regard to the constitutional conflict which had just closed.   It was no indiscriminate group of men untrained in the meaning of that conflict or uncertain as to the general policies that were to be pursued under the Constitution.   Differences of opinion there were, no doubt, for many differences of opinion had been glossed over in the veiled language of the Constitution, but that the new government was to restore public credit, establish adequate revenues, create a nation-wide judicial system, pay the debt, strengthen the defences on land and sea, and afford adequate support to trade and commerce the members of the Convention who met again as members of the federal government must have been reasonably certain.

CHAPTER IV

THE important measures of the new government, composed as it was so largely of leading members from the Philadelphia Convention, may be justly regarded as the first fruits in the fulfilment of the promises of the Constitution. The Senate was, as we have seen, practically controlled by men who had helped to draft that instrument, and a number of significant bills, such as the measure creating the federal judicial system, the Bank act, and the final amendment to the funding bill, originated in that chamber. The executive department, so far as domestic affairs were concerned, was likewise dominated by members of the Convention: Washington, Hamilton, and Randolph. And interestingly enough, the House of Representatives, although it did not embrace a very considerable proportion of former Convention members, was, nevertheless, to a large extent composed of men who held depreciated securities of the old government or purchased them while engaged in placing public credit on a firm foundation, for their names appear on the first funding books of the new government.[1]

In gathering the fruits of the constitutional conflict, it was hardly to be expected that the champions of the new system could escape encountering a strong and vigilant opposition. New fuel was heaped upon the fires of Anti-Federalism. Opposition to the Constitution could now be

---

[1] Below, Chap. VI.

shifted to an antagonism to the measures for which the Constitution stood. It is true that we are told by a careful scholar of our day, Professor Libby, that parties did not develop out of the measures managed in Congress by Hamilton,[1] but over against his opinion we may set the high authority of no less penetrating and competent contemporary observers than John Marshall and Thomas Jefferson, to say nothing of a host of newspaper scribes and pamphleteers, large and small. In his *Life of Washington*, Marshall informs us that "the first regular and systematic opposition to the principles on which the affairs of the union were administered, originated in the measures which were founded" on Hamilton's Report on Public Credit.[2] And speaking of the proposition relative to the Bank, he adds: "This measure made a deep impression on many members of the legislature; and contributed not inconsiderably, to the complete organization of those distinct and visible parties, which, in their long and dubious conflict for power, have since shaken the United States to their centre."[3]

This same view of the origin of parties under the Constitution is revealed in many places in Jefferson's writings. Nevertheless, Professor Libby tells us that the fiscal measures of Hamilton did not produce parties, citing in partial support of his opinion the fact that Jefferson joined the Secretary of the Treasury in securing the passage of the funding bill.[4] This, says Professor Libby, the Secretary of State could not have done if he had been the head of a political party rather than of a mere faction. And it must be confessed that, at first glance, this appears to be a very plausible explanation of the assumption "deal" — for such it truly was if we apply

[1] Libby, *op. cit.*, Vol. II, p. 217.
[2] *Life of Washington* (2d ed.), Vol. II, p. 181.]
[3] *Ibid.*, p. 206.
[4] *Loc. cit.*, Vol. II, p. 217.

to it the language of contemporary politics — but there are several collateral circumstances which should be taken into account before the verdict is rendered.

In the first place, it must be called to mind that Jefferson had been in France during the struggle over the formation and adoption of the Constitution and also during the federal election contests which ensued. He had returned to the country in 1789 after a long absence, and naturally it required some time for him to analyze the political situation and discover the exact nature of the political divisions which were already plaguing the new government. In the second place, Jefferson, on his own confession, knew very little about the implications of the funding bill, and at the time it came up, he was apparently unaware of its relation to the growing agrarian party. As soon as he came to understand Hamilton's capitalistic system, Jefferson regretted his action in the matter of the assumption of state debts, for he wrote to Washington on September 2, 1792, as follows : "I was duped into [helping Hamilton pass the funding bill] by the Secretary of the Treasury, and made a tool for forwarding his schemes, not then sufficiently understood by me ; and of all the errors of my political life, this has occasioned me the deepest regret." [1]

Whether Jefferson became opposed to Hamilton's funding measures on principle, after a more deliberate examination, or merely found it expedient to set himself down as an opponent later when he found out the temper of the country, is of little importance except to the moral philosopher ; but certain it is that he grounded his opposition and that of the Anti-Federalists on the highly exceptionable features of the Treasury program. In the letter to Washington, just quoted, Jefferson continued : "That I have utterly, in my

[1] *Works* (Washington ed.), Vol. III, p. 460.

private conversations, disapproved of the system of the Secretary of the Treasury, I acknowledge and avow ; and this was not merely a speculative difference. His system flowed from principles adverse to liberty, and was calculated to undermine and demolish the Republic, by creating an influence of his department over the members of the Legislature. I saw this influence actually produced, and its first fruits to be the establishment of the great outlines of his project by the votes of the very persons who, having swallowed his bait, were laying themselves out to profit by his plans ; and that had these persons withdrawn, as those interested in a question ever should, the vote of the disinterested majority was clearly the reverse of what they made it. These were no longer the votes then of the representatives of the people, but of deserters from the rights and interests of the people ; and it was impossible to consider their decisions, which had nothing in view but to enrich themselves, as the measures of the fair majority, which ought always to be respected. If what was actually doing begat uneasiness in those who wished for virtuous government, what was further proposed was not less threatening to the friends of the Constitution. For, in a report on the subject of manufactures (still to be acted upon), it was expressly assumed that the general government has a right to exercise all the powers which may be for the *general welfare,* that is to say, all the legitimate powers of government."

In the *Anas,* Jefferson enumerated the funding and Bank measures and the control of the Treasury Department over the members of the legislature as the reasons for his antagonism to the administration. "Here then," he says, "was the real ground of the opposition which was made to the course of administration. Its object was to preserve the legislature pure and independent of the executive, to restrain the administration to republican forms and principles, and not permit the constitution to be construed into a monarchy, and to be warped, in practice, into all the principles and pollutions of their favorite English model. Nor was this an opposition to General Washington. . . . He was not aware of the drift, or of the effect of Hamilton's schemes.[1] Unversed in financial projects and calculations and budgets, his approbation of them was bottomed on his confidence in the man. But Hamilton was not only a monarchist, but for a monarchy bottomed on corruption." [2] Jefferson's remedy for the evils introduced by the Federalists was to establish the supremacy of the agricultural interest over the " stock jobbers." [3]

In that long and confidential letter to Hamilton written by Washington on July 29, 1792, in which are set forth twenty-one propositions constituting the grounds of the Anti-Federalist antagonism to the administration, it is clear that the President was fully aware of the fact that Hamilton's economic policies were the fundamental source of the party cleavage.[4] If Washington had earlier entertained any doubts on that point, he must have been fully satisfied after the conference which he had with Jefferson on July 10, 1792, in which the latter based the complaints of the opposition wholly on the measures which had emanated from the Treasury Department.[5]

In view of the abundant contemporary evidence, it is not to be doubted that Hamilton's fiscal policy was the recognized source of substantially all of the partisan opposition to the government, which arose in Washington's

[1] See above, p. 66, as to the accuracy of this statement.
[2] Jefferson, *Works* (Washington ed.), Vol. IX, p. 95.
[3] *Writings* (Ford ed.), Vol. V, p. 275.
[4] *Writings* (Sparks ed.), Vol. X, p. 249.
[5] Jefferson, *Works* (Washington ed.), Vol. IX, p. 460. See also below, Chaps. VII and VIII, for a more detailed treatment of this proposition.

administrations.[1] At all events, it will be admitted that Hamilton was the intellectual leader of the Federalist party during those administrations, that he had the most systematic and penetrating mind of any one in the first government, that his policies were the foundation of all the important economic legislation of the period, and that all of his proposals were based upon a carefully worked out scheme of economics and politics. In getting at the principles underlying Federalist policies and the partisan conflict which they produced, it is necessary, therefore, to analyze the essential elements of Hamilton's political economy.

Fortunately this is not a difficult task, for the measures which he proposed are known to all and celebrated in the annals of finance, and the economic basis of them all is carefully explained in his famous reports.[2] The measures included:

(1) A funding of the entire debt, principal and interest, at face value instead of on a basis of discrimination between the original subscribers to the debt and the speculators and secondary purchasers.[3]

[1] Some superficial writers deny that there was any connection between Hamilton's fiscal measures and the issues at stake in the constitutional conflict. Some have gone so far as to hold that Hamilton made his program out of whole cloth and that it was not a part of the plans of the members of the Philadelphia Convention. This cannot be admitted. That the details of the fiscal system of the new government were all foreseen at Philadelphia will not be contended by any one, but the untenable character of the view that Hamilton alone funded the debt, or violated the principles of the Constitution by his measures becomes apparent when we count the number of the members of the Philadelphia Convention who were in the first Congress and voted for Hamilton's legislation. We must also remember how many of the same members were loyal Federalists until the end. The framers of the Constitution were indeed traitors to their own cause if they voted for and supported laws that were not contemplated by the Constitution but were in direct conflict with it.

[2] To be found in *Works of Alexander Hamilton* (Lodge ed.), Vols. II and III, and in *American State Papers: Finance*, Vol. I.

[3] A part to draw six per cent at once, another part three per cent, and a third part six per cent after the lapse of ten years.

(2) The assumption of the state debts by the national government, on the basis of funding at face value, thus immensely increasing the national debt.

(3) The establishment of a national bank, three-fourths of whose stock was composed of subscriptions in the recently funded six per cent securities then bearing interest and one-fourth in specie. It appears that only a small part of the specie was actually paid in by the stockholders, and that the bank stock was in fact based almost entirely upon the funded government securities which were thus given an additional value and made the partial basis for an issue of bank notes to be loaned. The note issues were limited to not more than $10,000,000 in excess of the deposits.

(4) The employment of the power to lay customs duties in such a manner as to protect and encourage American manufacture and commerce — those branches of American enterprise most dependent for their activities upon an ample supply of fluid capital. By the protection of American manufacturing and commerce, furthermore, the demand for fluid capital was to be increased and the value of the said capital in the hands of the holders immensely improved.

(5) The disposal of the public lands in large as well as small quantities and the acceptance of public securities bearing six per cent interest in payment therefor, as well as gold or silver.[1]

(6) Sinking fund provisions enabling the federal government to assist the security holders in buoying up the public credit by purchasing securities in the market from time to time. In advocating this plan of partial debt

[1] *State Papers: Public Lands*, Vol. I, p. 8. Land speculators, like Robert Morris, knew very well that a rise in the value of the funds meant a rise in land values, for it released more capital for speculation. See Morris, *Private Letter Book*, Vol. I, p. 258, Library of Congress Mss.

redemption, Hamilton was under no delusion about a debt paying itself. It was not designed to enable the government to buy its debt at the lowest figure but to permit government intervention to sustain the value of the public stock, that is, to sustain the augmentation of fluid capital. This purpose was distinctly avowed by Hamilton in a letter to William Seton, whom he commissioned to buy on behalf of the sinking fund. "A principal object with me," he said, "is to keep the stock from falling too low in case the embarrassments of the dealers should lead to sacrifices; whence you will infer that it is not my wish that the purchases should be made below the prescribed limits, yet if such should unfortunately be the state of the market, it must of course govern." Not only did Hamilton use this powerful engine to help maintain the value of public paper, but he employed it also to help those operators in securities who were "bulling" the market. In the letter to Seton, quoted above, he added a postscript: "If there are any gentlemen who *support* the funds and others who *depress* them, I shall be pleased that your purchases may aid the former, — this in great confidence." [1]

[1] *Works* (Lodge ed.), Vol. VIII, p. 232. That Hamilton used the sinking fund for the benefit of speculators was a common assertion of the opposition (see Taylor's charge, below, p. 204), and it is in connection with this fund that the most substantial indictments of the Secretary were made. At the time Hamilton wrote the above letter, it was known and he himself knew that the leader among those "supporting" the funds was the great speculator, William Duer, one of his closest personal friends. On the next day, August 17, 1791, Hamilton wrote to Duer cautioning him against pushing public securities too high (*Works*, Vol. VIII, p. 233). Two days later, August 19, Seton purchased for the government $14,000 worth of deferred securities from Duer, and on August 27, Seton purchased from him another lot of deferred securities ($38,685 worth) at 12/6 (*State Papers: Finance*, Vol. I, p. 117). On August 6, 1791, deferred stock was at 13/11 and it showed a weakness on the 10th and a further decline on the 13th (*Ibid.*, p. 231). In August, September, and October, 1791, heavy purchases were made for the sinking fund and by October 29, deferred stock was at 13/4. It then continued to rise steadily until it reached 15/8 on January 25, 1792 (*Ibid.*, p. 231). Shortly afterward, Duer failed disastrously and landed in the debtors' prison whence he issued threats to moneyed persons in New York promising unpleasant revelations and violence

In other words, Hamilton's measures provided for underwriting the depreciated and instable public securities at face value by assuring payment of the interest and principal by the federal government, and then for using about one-eighth of them as the capital of a national bank — empowered to issue notes. The bank notes were further underwritten by the promise of the federal government to receive them for all payments due that government. The upshot of the whole procedure, from an economic point of view, was the transformation of well-nigh worthless public paper into substantial fluid capital to be employed in commerce, manufacturing, and the development of Western lands. It was not merely the payment of the debt that Hamilton had in mind; on the contrary the sharp stimulation of capitalism — banking, commerce, and manufactures — was an equally fundamental part of his system. This augmentation of fluid capital by government fiat based upon a promise to pay interest and principal at stipulated periods was exactly the task to which Hamilton set himself, and he constantly employed its advantage to the country as an argument in support of his respective propositions.[1]

in case they refused help. The sinking fund provisions of the funding system were viewed by some of the opposition as mere engines for making fluctuations in securities for the benefit of the speculators. Senator Maclay so regarded them and expressed himself on the subject in the following manner: "It was originated and passed after I left New York, and is certainly the most impudent transaction that I ever knew in the political world. I regret my being absent when it passed. . . . This nominal reduction is a virtual raising of the whole value of the debt. Something of this kind, I have heard, is common in England. When Governments attempt a purchase of any kind of stock, the holders of that kind of stock never fail to raise the residue. Hamilton must have known this well. Our speculators or stockholders knew all this. They have a general communication with each other. They are actuated by one spirit, or I should rather say by Hamilton. Nobody (generally speaking) but them buys; it is easy for them, by preconcert, to settle what proposals they will give in; and these being filed, the commissioners are justified in taking the lowest." Maclay, *Sketches*, p. 271.

[1] Writing sometime afterward in defence of his fiscal policies, Hamilton dwelt at length upon the advantages derived from the augmentation of fluid capital through the proper funding of the debt. He said: "It was true that a large in-

In his very first Report on the Public Credit, Hamilton said: "The advantage to the public creditors, from the increased value of that part of their property which constitutes the public debt, needs no explanation.

"But there is a consequence of this, less obvious, though not less true, in which every other citizen is interested. It is a well known fact, that, in countries in which the national debt is properly funded, and an object of established confidence, it answers most of the purposes of money. Transfers of stock or public debt are there equivalent to payments in specie; or in other words, stock, in the principal transactions of business, passes current as specie. The same thing would, in all probability, happen here, under the like circumstances.

"The benefits of this are various and obvious:

"*First*. Trade is extended by it, because there is a larger capital to carry it on, and the merchant can at the same time, afford to trade for smaller profits; as his stock which, when unemployed, brings him in an interest from the Government, serves him also as money when he has a call for it in his commercial operations.

"*Secondly*. Agriculture and manufactures are also pro-

crease of active capital and augmentation of private fortunes would beget some augmentation of expense among individuals and that a portion of this expense would be laid out on foreign articles of luxury. But the proportion which this employment of the new capital would bear to the part of it which would be employed on useful and profitable objects would be, and has been inconsiderable. Whoever will impartially look around will see that the great body of new capital *created* [italics mine] by the stock has been employed in extending commerce, agriculture, manufactures, and other improvements. Our own *real* navigation has been much increased, our external commerce is carried on much more upon our own capitals than it was; our marine insurances in a much greater proportion are made by ourselves; our manufactures are increased in number and carried on upon a larger scale. Settlements of our waste land are progressing with more vigor than at any former period. Our cities and towns are increasing rapidly by the addition of new and better houses. Canals are opening, bridges are building with more spirit and effect than was ever known at a former period. The value of lands has risen everywhere." *Works* (Lodge ed.), Vol. VII, p. 404.

moted by it, for the like reason, that more capital can be commanded to be employed in both; and because the merchant whose enterprise in foreign trade gives to them activity and extension, has greater means for enterprise.

"*Thirdly.* The interest of money will be lowered by it; for this is always in a ratio to the quantity of money, and to the quickness of circulation. . . ." [1]

In his Report on a National Bank, on December 13, 1790, Hamilton adverted at length to the function of that institution in increasing the fluid capital of the country. First among the advantages of a bank, he placed, "the augmentation of the active or productive capital of a country. Gold and silver, when they are employed merely as the instruments of exchange and alienation, have been not improperly denominated dead stock; but when deposited in banks, to become the basis of a paper circulation, which takes their character and place, as the signs or representatives of value, they then acquire life, or in other words an active and productive quality. . . . It is a well-established fact that banks in good credit can circulate a far greater sum than the actual quantum of their capital in gold and silver. The extent of the possible excess seems indeterminate; though it has been conjecturedly stated at the proportions of two and three to one. . . . The combination of a portion of the public debt in the formation of the capital [of the Bank] is the principal thing of which an explanation is requisite. The chief object of this is to enable the *creation* [italics mine] of a capital sufficiently large to be the basis of an extensive circulation, and an adequate security for it. As has been elsewhere remarked, the original plan of the Bank of North America contemplated a capital of ten millions of dollars which is certainly not too broad a foundation for the extensive operations to which a national bank is destined. But to collect such a sum in this country, in gold and silver, into one depository, may, without hesitation, be pronounced impracticable. Hence the necessity of an auxiliary, which the public debt at once presents.

"This part of the fund will always be ready to come in aid of the specie. . . . The quarter-yearly receipts of interest will also be an actual addition to the specie fund, during the intervals between them and the half-yearly dividends of profits. The objection to combining land with specie, resulting from their not being generally in possession of the same persons, does not apply to the debt, which will always be found in considerable quantity among the moneyed and trading people.

"The debt composing part of the capital, besides its collateral effect in enabling the bank to extend its operations and consequently to enlarge its profits, will produce a direct annual revenue of six per centum from the Government, which will enter into the half-yearly dividends received by the stockholders.

"When the present price of the public debt is considered, and the effect which its conversion into bank stock, incorporated with a specie fund, would, in all probability, have to accelerate its rise to the proper point, it will easily be discovered that the operation presents, in its outset, a very considerable advantage to those who may become subscribers; and from the influence which that rise would have on the general mass of the debt, a proportional benefit to all the public creditors, and in a sense which has been more than once adverted to, to the community at large." [1]

In his Report on Manufactures, in December, 1791, Hamilton likewise discussed at length the place of fluid

[1] *Ibid.*, Vol. I, pp. 67, 75 *passim.*

capital in the development of commerce and industry. One of the objections to a protective tariff, which he thought worthy of considerable attention, was that the scarcity of capital in the United States constituted a decided handicap to American enterprise and made highly improbable a profitable establishment of manufactures, even under government protection. In the mouth of his opponent he put the argument that when "a deficiency of pecuniary capital" is added to a scarcity of hands and the dearness of labor, "the prospect of a successful competition with the manufactures of Europe, must be regarded as little less than desperate." [1]

This argument Hamilton then took into consideration at length, although he believed that "the supposed want of capital for the prosecution of manufactures in the United States is the most indefinite of the objections which are usually opposed to it." [2] With great insight into economic forces, he pointed out the difficulty of ascertaining the real extent of the money capital of the country and the relation of the quantity of money and the velocity of its circulation to its efficiency in commercial operations. But he thought it evident that the United States offered an immense field for the advantageous employment of large masses of capital. Of that there could be no doubt.

The difficulties of securing capital, however, are by no means insuperable: "It does not follow that there will not be found, in one way or another, a sufficient fund for the successful prosecution of any species of industry which is likely to prove truly beneficial." Hamilton then enumerated the sources of this fund: "The introduction of banks . . . has a powerful tendency to extend the active capital of a country. Experience of the utility of these institu-

---

[1] *State Papers: Finance*, Vol. I, p. 123.
[2] *Ibid.*, p. 130.

tions is multiplying them in the United States. . . . The aid of foreign capital may safely, and with considerable latitude, be taken into calculation. . . . The attraction of foreign capital for the direct purpose of manufactures ought not to be deemed a chimerical expectation."

Last but not least of the sources of capital for manufacturing was the national debt properly funded. This was Hamilton's great reliance for the development of capitalistic enterprise. It was more certain than foreign capital or local banking, and, what was no less important, it was in a large measure concentrated in the hands of that very class whose support for the new government Hamilton was most solicitous to obtain. It was a capital fund that was not impersonal, but inhered in definitely ascertainable groups of American society. Hamilton knew and had the closest personal dealings, in public and private matters, with its greatest holders.[1] No wonder his interest in it never flagged.

After citing local banks and foreign countries as sources for the supply of industrial capital, Hamilton concluded with evident pleasure : "It is satisfactory to have good grounds of assurance that there are domestic sources, of themselves adequate to it. It happens that there is a species of capital, actually existing in the United States, which relieves from all inquietude, on the score of the want of capital. This is the funded debt. The effect of a funded debt, as a species of capital, has been noticed upon a former occasion ; but a more particular elucidation of the point seems to be required, by the stress which is here laid upon it. . . . Public funds answer the purpose of capital from the estimation in which they are usually held by moneyed men ; and, consequently, from the ease and dispatch with

---

[1] For example, men like Thomas Willing, Robert Morris, and William Duer.

which they can be turned into money. This capacity of prompt convertibility into money, causes a transfer of stock to be, in a great number of cases, equivalent to a payment in coin. . . . Hence in a sound and settled state of public funds, a man possessed of a sum in them, can embrace any scheme of business which offers, with as much confidence as if he were possessed of an equal sum in coin." [1]

It requires no very subtle analysis to discover that the immediate beneficiaries of these various proposals by the Secretary of the Treasury were the holders of public securities and capitalists generally. A study of the Treasury Books and the records of finance of the period indicates that the great capitalists were also large holders of public securities. Furthermore, in those days, there was not the sharp division between the capitalist and entrepreneur which has since appeared, but the two functions were more often exercised by the same person. The immediate beneficiaries of Hamilton's plans were therefore the security-holding capitalists who were quite generally merchants, traders, shippers, and manufacturers. Incidentally the

[1] *Op. cit.*, pp. 130–131. A fine illustration of Hamilton's plan for turning securities into manufacturing capital is afforded by the National Manufacturing Society of New Jersey whose prospectus quotes his Report on Manufactures almost verbatim. The original incorporators were Elias Boudinot, Nicholas Low, William Constable, William Duer, Philip Livingston, Blair M'Clenachan, Matthew M'Connell and Herman Le Roy, all of whom were large holders of public funds and many of whom were vigorous speculators in public securities. William Duer perhaps the most famous, certainly the boldest operator of all, was chosen governor of the Society in December, 1791. See the Gazette of the United States, September 10, 1791, and December 17, 1791. The following letter from Peter Colt to Hamilton gives an insight into the way in which the industrial concern was financed by public securities: "We have much to fear from the present state of the funds of the [Manufacturing] society [New Jersey]. It is probable that the third payment which falls due the 13th instant will be made wholly in the funded debt of the United States, as well as the last which falls due the 13th July next, and that these payments will be compleated only on *about one half of the original shares*. Should this prove to be the case, it must add greatly to our present embarrassment ; as the debt could not be turned into money without great loss and it will be even difficult to obtain money on the credit of those funds, in the different banks, sufficient for the expenditures of this summer and fall." *Hamilton Mss.*, May 7, 1793.

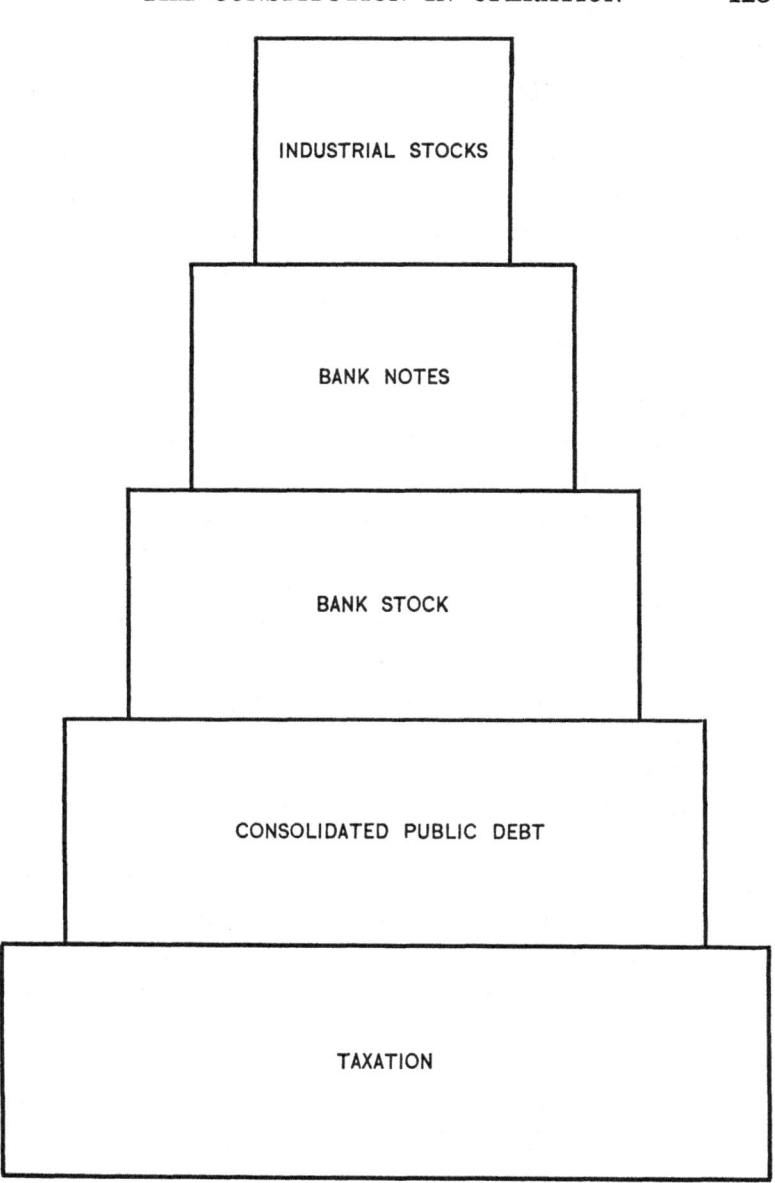

A Diagram of Hamilton's Capitalistic Edifice

entrepreneur benefited by the facility for acquiring capital on more advantageous terms, but inasmuch as the entrepreneur was so commonly a capitalist as well, his benefits were more direct than those of the farmer who likewise derived advantage from the temporary ease which the fiscal system made in the money market. However, the debt-burdened agrarians who had fought the Constitution to the bitter end, would have preferred the augmentation of the fluid capital in the form of state emissions of paper money, but that door was temporarily closed by a constitutional prohibition that was not beaten down until the days of the states rights Supreme Court under Chief Justice Taney.

This is no place to make any fine excursions into economic theory for the purpose of discovering what substantial wealth formed the foundation for this paper augmentation of fluid capital, or of finding out whether the real property owners were correct in their oft-repeated assertions that land and labor paid for it all. The point which concerns the historian is the existence of a widespread belief at the time that fluid capital, in the form of a public debt used to underwrite banking and capitalist enterprise, was a charge upon the production of material commodities, and in the United States, therefore, a charge principally upon agriculture. The existence of this belief is evident from the debates in the House of Representatives over the funding system, and it is finely illustrated in the resolutions of protest to Congress by the legislature of Virginia against the assumption of state debts, passed in December, 1790.[1]

---

[1] *State Papers: Finance*, Vol. I, p. 90; see below, Chap. VII. In this famous set of resolutions, the Virginia legislature declared: "In an agricultural country like this, therefore, to erect and concentrate and perpetuate a large moneyed interest is a measure which your memorialists apprehend must, in the course of human events, produce one or other of two evils; the prostration of agriculture at the feet of commerce, or a change in the present form of Federal Government fatal to the existence of American liberty." Thus early in the contest, the Virginia legislature

Hamilton himself foresaw the rise of the agrarian interest against his proposals. In his first Report on Public Credit, he anticipated this, and sought to parry criticism from that quarter by showing how agriculture was to become an indirect beneficiary from the augmentation of fluid capital. "The effect which the funding of the public debt on right principles would have upon landed property, is one of the circumstances attending such an arrangement which has been least adverted to, though it deserves the most particular attention. The present depreciated state of that species of property is a serious calamity. The value of cultivated lands in most of the states has fallen, since the Revolution, from twenty-five to fifty per cent. In those further south, the decrease is still more considerable. Indeed, if the representations continually received from that quarter may be credited, lands there will command no price which may not be deemed an almost total sacrifice. This decrease in the value of lands ought, in a great measure, to be attributed to the scarcity of money; consequently whatever produces an augmentation of the moneyed capital of the country, must have a proportional effect in raising that value. . . . The proprietors of lands would not only feel the benefit of this increase in the value of their property and of a more prompt and better sale, when they had occasion to sell, but the necessity of selling would be itself greatly diminished. As the same cause would contribute to the facility of loans, there is reason to believe that such of them as are indebted, would be able, through that resource, to satisfy their more urgent creditors." [1]

recognized the battle as one between capitalistic and agricultural interests and frankly protested against the supremacy of the former which Hamilton's fiscal policy promised. Virginia, it will be remembered, ratified the Constitution by a very small majority in a gerrymandered convention. *Economic Interpretation*, p. 235; Ambler, *Sectionalism in Virginia*, p. 58.   [1] *Ibid.*, p. 16.

The antagonism between the landed and manufacturing interests Hamilton sought to soften, on another occasion, by declaring it to be both unfounded and mischievous. In his Report on Manufactures in December, 1791, after the big battle over funding and assumption had been fought and won, he took up this alleged clash of interests. He there adverted to the fact that it was not uncommon to encounter the opinion that the promotion of manufactures redounded to the benefit of the North at the expense of the South. The Northern states had been called manufacturing and the Southern states agricultural, and "a species of opposition is imagined to subsist between the manufacturing and agricultural interests." While quick to admit that the encouragement of some manufactures might be detrimental to agricultural states, Hamilton declared that, taking industries in the aggregate, there was in fact an intimate connection between manufacturing and agricultural prosperity.[1]

The principle upon which he based this mutuality of interests was the ancient maxim that whatever benefits one section of the community is bound in the long run to benefit all sections. "Ideas of a contrariety of interests between the Northern and Southern regions of the Union, are, in the main, as unfounded as they are mischievous. The diversity of circumstances on which such contrariety is usually predicated, authorizes a directly contrary conclusion. Mutual wants constitute one of the strongest links of political connection; and the extent of these bears a natural proportion to the diversity in the means of mutual

---

[1] Hamilton did not rely upon mere anticipatory arguments to parry such thrusts as that which came from the Virginia legislature. When the resolutions in question reached him, he transmitted copies to Chief Justice Jay with the pertinent query: "Ought not the collective weight of the different parts of the Government be employed in exploding the principles they contain?" *Correspondence and Public Papers of Jay*, Vol. III, p. 405. This is an interesting passage in the history of "the separation of powers."

supply. Suggestions of an opposite complexion are ever to
be deplored, as unfriendly to the steady pursuit of one great
common cause, and to the perfect harmony of all the parts.
In proportion as the mind is accustomed to trace the intimate connexion of interest which subsists between all
the parts of a society, united under the same government,
the infinite variety of channels which serve to circulate the
prosperity of each, to and through the rest — in that proportion will it be little apt to be disturbed by solicitudes
and apprehensions, which originate in local discriminations."[1]

There was still another source of antagonism between
the capitalistic and agrarian interests which Hamilton
thought worthy of consideration ; that was the competition
between them for labor supply. "A scarcity of hands for
manufacturing occupation and a dearness of labor generally," were cited by him as being among the objections
urged against the development of industries in the United
States. The force of this argument compelled him to seek
new sources of labor supply not in competition with
that already drawn upon by agriculture. One new source
would be persons now idle and disqualified and indisposed
for the toils of the country ; and another source would be
women and also children "of a tender age," if the example
of Great Britain was followed. But the chief source of the
new labor supply was to be foreign immigration. "Whoever inspects with a careful eye, the composition of our
towns will be made sensible to what an extent this resource
may be relied upon. This exhibits a large proportion of
ingenious and valuable workmen, in different arts and
trades, who, by expatriating from Europe, have improved
their own condition and added to the industry and wealth
of the United States." The natural inference is, he con-

_____
[1] *State Papers: Finance*, Vol. I, p. 134.

cluded, that with the increasing demand in industries, a bountiful supply of immigrants will follow.[1]

Without questioning the validity of the claim that all sections of the country and all classes of society participated in the benefits of that augmentation of fluid capital which Hamilton's measures secured, it cannot be gainsaid that the immediate beneficiaries of his fiscal policy were the security holders and the capitalistic-entrepreneurs. This Hamilton frankly acknowledged in the Reports just cited, although, of course, he declined to put them in antagonism to the agrarian sections of the population. It seems correct, therefore, to place the beneficiaries of the new fiscal system in the following order:

1. Direct beneficiaries: security-holding capitalists.

2. Indirect beneficiaries: trading, commercial, and manufacturing entrepreneurs in need of capital.

3. Incidental beneficiaries: land-owning farmers.

As to Hamilton's solicitude for the first group there can be no doubt. The justice of their claims he eloquently pleaded on all appropriate occasions, and the necessity of drawing their support to the new government was ever present in the foreground or the background of his arguments. His first great Report dealt, of course, with their interests and the ways and means of meeting them. In establishing the national bank he planned for such an extensive use of the public debt that a decided advantage was certain to accrue to the holders of securities; and in his Report on Manufactures he explained at length how the development of industries would create a demand for the employment of the debt for the double purpose of capital and securities. To his belief in the justice of their claims, he added the knowledge that they had "had a considerable

[1] *State Papers: Finance,* Vol. I, pp. 126 ff.

agency in promoting the adoption of the new Constitution," and could be counted upon as pillars of the new system.[1] That Hamilton was equally concerned with the development of manufacturing in the United States there can likewise be no doubt. On account of his connections, his sympathies, his interests, and his notions of political economy he looked upon the advancement of industries as a necessary part of national greatness. This was no academic theory with him. He put his convictions to practical test by becoming a leading adviser and director in the Paterson manufacturing concerns which were built upon capital derived from the public debt. In public and in private life he consistently favored the encouragement and protection of American industrial interests.[2]

Yet it would be a mistake to assume that Hamilton's

[1] *Works* (Lodge ed.), Vol. VII, p. 418.

[2] See *Hamilton Mss.*, Library of Congress, under date of October 3, 1792, and *passim*, correspondence relative to his manufacturing connections. In preparing his Report on Manufactures, Hamilton was not dealing with abstractions. He had carefully consulted his friends in all parts of the country and had received reports on the nature and location of the various industries which needed protection and encouragement. These reports, which are of high economic and political significance, are preserved in the *Hamilton Mss.*, Library of Congress. For the reports on Killingworth, Connecticut, see September 14, 1791; on New London, September 14, 1791; Southington, September 14 and 21, 1791; Stonington, September 15, 1791; Winsor, September 16, 1791; Stamford, September 16, 1791; Farmington, September 27, 1791; Lebanon, September 29, 1791; Montville, September 6, 1791; Suffield, September 12, 1791; Danbury, September 12, 1791. It is not without significance that all these Connecticut towns needing protection, except Suffield and Lebanon, were Federalist towns at the time of the ratification of the Constitution (*Economic Interpretation*, p. 265). For the report from Charleston, South Carolina, October 3, 1791; Wilmington, Delaware, November 28, 1791; Norfolk, Virginia, September 28, 1791; Richmond, October 4 and 8, 1791; Beverly, Massachusetts, September 6, 1791. Consult *Hamilton Mss.* for the summer and autumn of 1791. The way Hamilton's agents scoured the country for manufactures to protect is illustrated by the following letter to him from D. Stevens of South Carolina: "Agreeable to your request have wrote a circular letter to the most leading characters throughout the state relative to the manufactures that may be carried on in the several counties, — as yet have only two letters on the subject, one contains some small sample of the cotton and linen manufacture carried on in families for their own wear — as any others come to hand I will transmit them to you, and shall shortly give you some account of what manufactures are carried on in Charleston." *Hamilton Mss.*, September 3, 1791.

interest was in economics rather than in political economy. In all his public and private papers it is abundantly evident that he was deeply aware of the relation between the beneficiaries of his fiscal system and the stability, credit, and permanence of the federal government. In his first Report on Public Credit, he declared that one of the purposes of a properly established fiscal system was "to cement more closely the union of the States." In support of the proposal to assume state debts he said: "If all the public creditors receive their dues from one source, distributed with an equal hand, their interests will be the same. And, having the same interests, they will unite in support of the fiscal arrangements of the Government. . . . These circumstances combined, will ensure to the revenue laws a more ready and more satisfactory execution." [1] In his elaborate defence of the funding system which he prepared but did not publish, Hamilton explained that the improper adjustment of the debt would have been "a severe blow to the security of property," and have alienated from the federal government both the public creditors who had so ardently aided in its establishment, and also allied property interests which formed a no less secure bulwark for the national system.[2]

[1] *State Papers: Finance*, Vol. I, p. 18.

[2] *Works* (Lodge ed.), Vol. VII, pp. 417–419. This was the accepted view of the best informed Federalists. Writing from New York, on March 27, 1790, to his father in Litchfield, Connecticut, Oliver Wolcott, Jr., voicing what was doubtless the sentiment of the Secretary of the Treasury, said: "I can consider the funding system as important, in no other respect than as an engine of government. The only question is what that engine shall be. The influence of a clergy, nobility and armies, are and ought to be out of the question in this country; but unless some active principle of the human mind can be interested in the support of the government, no civil establishments can be formed, which will not appear like useless and expensive pageants, and by their unpopularity weaken the government which they are intended to support. . . . Duties on most of the articles imported, ought to be imposed from political considerations, even though the money were to be buried. If the money is paid in such a manner as to interest the people in the government, and at the same time not corrupt their integrity, the circulation of the revenue

Surely no further evidence is required to prove that Hamilton's measures were primarily capitalistic in character as opposed to agrarian and that they constituted a distinct bid to the financial, commercial, and manufacturing classes to give their confidence and support to the government in return for a policy well calculated to advance their interests. He knew that the government could not stand if its sole basis was the platonic support of genial well-wishers. He knew that it had been created in response to interested demands and not out of any fine-spun theories of political science. Therein he displayed that penetrating wisdom which placed him among the great statesmen of all time.

answers a good purpose. . . . For these reasons, I think the state debts ought to be assumed, as without assumption, the political purposes which I have enumerated, cannot be attained." Gibbs, *op. cit.*, Vol. I, p. 43. On February 10, 1790, James Jarvis wrote to Hamilton: "In your report of the 9th January last, there appear two great and predominant principles — namely the preservation of the public faith inviolate and the creation to the community of the United States of America, of a powerful and active representation of their agriculture, commerce and manufactures. . . . It becomes good policy to strengthen the executive arm and which cannot be effected by any means so certain and gently diffusive as that of collecting sufficient revenue. Hence the impolicy of paying the principal of the national debts, beyond that certain point, which, not burthensome, becomes a stimulant to industry and commerce, and a gentle compulsion to the citizens of a country to pay that homage and respect to government which is really necessary to its existence." *Hamilton Mss.*, February 10, 1790.

CHAPTER V

HAMILTON'S SYSTEM BEFORE CONGRESS

THE first session of the Congress of the United States under the Constitution was devoted principally to the problems of immediate revenues and administrative and judicial organization. When the Representatives assembled for the second session on January 4, 1790, Hamilton's first Report on the Public Credit was about ready for publication, and five days later the Secretary announced that he would present it whenever the House was prepared to receive it. Hamilton was anxious to appear in person before that honorable body to read his Report and defend it, but to his great disappointment he was compelled to communicate it in writing. On January 14, the document was laid before the House, and after a fortnight's delay it was taken up for consideration.

On that day there was outstanding against the United States and the several commonwealths within the Union a total domestic debt of something like $60,000,000 [1] — an amount equal in many states to the total value of all the money on hand and at interest.[2] The holders of this paper, particularly of the continental securities, were anxiously looking to the new government for a funding arrangement that would meet all public obligations at their nominal or

---

[1] And a foreign debt of about $10,000,000.

[2] For Mercer's comparative estimate, see below, p. 220 ; *Economic Interpretation of the Constitution*, p. 36.

face value. A considerable portion of this paper — in some
states certainly from one-half to three-fourths — had passed
from the hands of the original possessors at rates ranging
from one-twentieth to one-sixth of its face value. The
demand of those who had originally risked their money and
of the speculators for immediate action on the part of the
federal government was so great that the funding operation
could not be long postponed.

When the members of Congress took up Hamilton's
Report on Public Credit, they found proposed no mere
device for the payment of the debts of the United States,
but a complete funding system, contemplating a certain
degree of permanency in the debt, and above all the utiliza-
tion of it to increase the fluid capital of the country for the
purpose of promoting trade, manufactures, operations in
finance, and agriculture. Those representing the financial,
commercial, and industrial interests looked upon the proposal with favor at once, and the representatives of the
agricultural interest as quickly came to view the whole
scheme as a burden thrown upon land and labor. The
latter saw that actual capital could not be increased by a
fiat of the government and they believed that the fluid
capital which Hamilton's fiscal system was to call into being
was merely a claim to the fruits of toil on the land, vested
by legal action in the hands of the capitalistic classes and
realized through taxation.

The opposition, led by Jackson, of Georgia, sought at
once to secure delay. The members of this group believed
that the people would repudiate the plan if it was laid
before them and full opportunity given to discuss it in the
regions away from the great cities. The champions of immediate action were, in fact, afraid that a serious delay in
funding the debt might end in complete failure, so great

was the ill-temper in the country against it.[1] The speculators in New York City filled the galleries, and Sedgwick, a
Representative and a security holder from Massachusetts,
exclaimed that "the ardent expectations of the people on
this subject want no other demonstration than the numerous body of citizens assembled within these walls."[2] The
party of quick and decisive action carried the day, and the
debates on public credit proceeded with great vigor and
prolixity.

In order to ascertain the economic principles upon which
the opposition in Congress was based it is necessary to examine these debates in the House of Representatives on
the various aspects of the funding measures.[3] The pages

[1] Fisher Ames, a Massachusetts Representative and a security holder, was
specially anxious about the funding process. He evidently thought that if it was
delayed, the popular feeling against it would defeat assumption altogether, and he
believed that the government would not last long unless the public credit was
properly established. In a letter dated May 20, 1790, he wrote: "The success of
it [assumption] would be certain if the Pennsylvania creditors were well disposed
towards it. . . . I am surprised that men, who are to depend on government
should be careless as to arguments, which seem to prove how much its strength will
be impaired by a divided revenue system. They seem to be secure as to the permanency of the government, and mindful of nothing but the property of the debt.
I hope we shall not finish the session without funding the whole debt; if not the
whole, then as much as we can. *For if we should not fund at all, I am apprehensive
that the popular torrent, at a future session, would be found to be strong against funding. . . . Without a firm basis for public credit, I can scarcely expect the government
will last long."* The Life and Works of Fisher Ames, Vol. I, p. 78. Izard of South
Carolina somewhat sharply informed Jefferson in the spring of 1789, shortly before he set out for New York to take his place in the first Senate that he hoped no
time would be wasted discussing amendments. "By whatever appellation therefore
Gentlemen may choose to be distinguished, whether by federal or anti-federal, I
hope we shall not be wasting time with idle discussions about amendments of the
Constitution; but that we shall go to work immediately about the finances, and
endeavour to extricate ourselves from our present embarrassed and disgraceful
situation." Documentary History of the Constitution, Vol. V, p. 170.

[2] Annals of Congress, Vol. I, p. 1135. The reporter notes that the galleries were
unusually crowded.

[3] The Senate, as is well known, sat behind closed doors and we therefore have no
official record of the debates in that body. The Republicans attacked the Federalists for the secrecy with which the latter surrounded their proceedings, especially
in the Senate. One of the best ways of establishing popular control over the government, said John Taylor, the belligerent pamphleteer from Virginia, was to open

which follow are devoted to an outline of the reasoning employed, particularly by the opposition, so far as it relates to the underlying economic doctrines thrown into relief by the conflict. To tell again the general history of the period is no part of the purpose of this study ; that has been done often and well. We are here concerned only with the economic motives which were avowedly brought into play in the political struggle.

The Report of the Secretary of the Treasury came before the House for consideration in the committee of the whole on Monday, February 8, and the battle royal was on at once. Mr. Smith, a large security holder from Charleston, South Carolina, brought the general policy of the administration group to a concrete form in the shape of a series of resolutions to the effect that Congress ought not to adjourn without making adequate provision for the public debt, that no discrimination should be made between the original holders and the assignees, that the state debts incurred during the war should be assumed by the general government, that the arrearages of interest on the state and continental debt ought to be funded and consolidated with the principal, and that a certain rate of interest, to be decided upon, should be paid for the time being. Another set of resolutions, in the same tenor, but embodying more specifically Hamilton's propositions, was shortly afterward brought forward by Mr. Fitzsimons, of Philadelphia, a

their doors, "to subject their legislative discussions to the free and common audience of every citizen, and to promote the free and rapid circulation of the newspapers. But has this been done? On the contrary, have we not seen with amazement, one branch of the legislature, withdraw itself into a sequestered chamber, and shut its doors upon its constituents, still guarding them with obstinate perseverance, although more than one half of the union have required that they be opened? Have we not likewise seen the free circulation of the newspapers clogged with taxes which amount almost to a prohibition? Are these things the mere effect of accident, or are they the results of cool deliberation? contemplating objects dreadful to this country." John Taylor, *An Examination of the Late Proceedings in Congress, etc.* (1793).

security holder and former member of the constitutional Convention.[1]

It is perfectly clear from the debates which ensued that those who favored funding at face value and the assumption of state debts by the national government understood that not only would the security holders benefit by the direct appreciation of their paper, but that the fluid capital of the country would be immensely augmented to the advantage of all industrial and commercial enterprises. Gerry adverted to this fact early in the debates over the public credit, saying "It has been thought, that a public debt is a source of great emolument to a nation, by extending its capital, and enlarging the operations of productive industry. . . . In the contest [with France], Great Britain increased her national debt to an astonishing degree; and when all Europe expected to see her sink beneath the burthen, she stood firm and fixed as ever, with an increase of strength. The influx of specie, after the peace, to purchase into her funds, furnished the means for the expansion of her commerce and manufactures, and rather made the revolution an advantage than a disadvantage to her." [2]

The debate had not gone far before Hamilton's whole theory that a large funded debt, an extensive augmentation of fluid capital, and the stimulation of industries, meant a diffusion of prosperity throughout the nation was warmly attacked by his opponents. Jackson, of Georgia, who seems to have held no securities himself and represented a state whose citizens held little of the public funds,[3] took the view that a large national debt simply implied the purchase of prosperity at the expense of the taxpayer and future generations. "Gentlemen may come forward, perhaps, and tell

---

[1] *Annals of Congress*, Vol. I, pp. 1170 and 1178.
[2] *Ibid.*, Vol. I, p. 1137.   [3] See below, p. 193.

me," he said, "that funding the public debt will increase the circulating medium of the country, by means of its transferable quality; but this is denied by the best informed men. The funding of the debt will occasion enormous taxes for the payment of the interest. These taxes will bear heavily both on agriculture and commerce. It will be charging the active and industrious citizen, who pays his share of the taxes, to pay the indolent and idle creditor who receives them, to be spent and wasted in the course of the year, without any hope of future reproduction; for the new capital which they acquire must have existed in the country before, and must have been employed, as all capitals are, in maintaining productive labor. Thus the honest, hard working part of the community will promote the ease and luxury of men of wealth; such a system may benefit large cities, like Philadelphia and New York, but the remote parts of the continent will not feel the invigorating warmth of the American treasury; in the proportion that it benefits one, it will depress another. . . . Let us endeavor to discover whether there is an absolute necessity for adopting a funding system or not. If there is no such necessity, a short time will make it apparent; and let it be remembered what funds the United States possess in the Western Territory. The disposal of those lands may perhaps supersede the necessity of establishing a permanent system of taxation." [1]

Later in the debate, Jackson denied that a funded debt could be of great advantage to a nation and cited the example of England. "Government stock," he said, "can never be considered as cash. The stock employed in agriculture, commerce, and manufactures may, by great prospects of advantage, be diverted into the hands of brokers,

[1] *Annals of Congress*, Vol. I, p. 1181.

for the purpose of speculating further in the funds; *but no real addition will be made to the means of productive industry,* nor was anything of this kind contemplated at the time funding was first introduced into England." [1] This was the main point of the opposition; namely, that, while claims to property might be augmented in the hands of individuals by the inflation of capital, real wealth, which was the product of land and labor, could not be increased thereby.

Hamilton's theory that the support of the public creditors was necessary to the strength of the new government was also brought up and contested by Jackson. "We learn from Blackstone," he said, "that the reason for establishing a national debt, was in order to support a system of foreign politics, and to establish the new succession at the Revolution; because it was deemed expedient to create a new interest, called the moneyed interest, in favor of the Prince of Orange, in opposition to the landed interest, which was supposed to be generally in favor of the King, who had abdicated the throne. I hope there is no such reason existing here; our Government, I trust, is firmly established without the assistance of stockjobbers. We ought to reign universally in the hearts of our fellow citizens, on account of the salutary tendency of our measures to promote the general welfare, and not depend upon the support of a party, who have no other cause to esteem us but because we realize their golden dreams of unlooked for success." [2]

In attacking the whole process of capitalistic inflation and expansion, the opponents of Hamilton's system contended that a very large proportion of the debt which he proposed to fund at face value was represented no value received by the government from the holders of the certifi-

[1] *Annals of Congress,* Vol. I, p. 1214.   [2] *Ibid.,* Vol. I, p. 1214.

cates and was so understood by the holders as well as the public. From this point of view, the Federalists were inflating paper that was largely fictitious when issued, and thus increasing gratuitously the burden laid on "land and labor."

The case of those who contended that the continental debt was largely fictitious was put most effectively and succinctly, perhaps, by Livermore, of New Hampshire, in the House of Representatives, on February 9, 1790. He opened by pointing out the grave injustice which would be done by funding the foreign loans, from which the United States had received hard money, on the same basis as the domestic debt which represented a little real money and much depreciated paper. "There is a great difference," he said, "between the merits of that debt which was lent the United States in real coin, by disinterested persons, not concerned or benefited by the revolution, and at a low rate of interest, and those debts which have been accumulating upon the United States, at the rate of six per cent interest, and which were not incurred for efficient money lent, but for depreciated paper, or services done at exorbitant rates, or for goods or provisions supplied at more than their real worth, by those who received all the benefits arising from our change of condition. . . . It is very well known, — that those who sold goods or provisions for this circulating medium [loan office certificates], raised their prices from six to ten shillings at least. . . . There is as much reason that we should now consider these public securities in a depreciated state, as every holder of them has considered them from that time to this. There was a period at which they were considered of no greater value than three or four shillings in the pound; at this day they are not at more than eight or ten. If this, then, is the case, why should Congress put it upon the same footing as the foreign debt, for which they have received a hard dollar for every dollar they engaged to pay? Could any possible wrong be done to those who hold the domestic debt, by estimating it at its current value?" [1]

But it had been argued that some part of the domestic debt had been incurred by loans of hard money. "There might be a small part lent in this way," the speaker conceded, "but it was very small indeed, comparable with the whole of the domestic debt. It is in the memory of every gentleman, that, before the beginning of the revolution, every state issued paper money; it answered the exigencies of government in a considerable degree. The United States issued a currency of the same nature, which answered their purposes, except in some particular cases, and these were effected by loans of certain sums of hard money. If any distinctions are to be made among the domestic creditors, it ought to be made in favor of such only, and that in consequence of the origin of the debt; while the great mass given for the depreciated paper, or provisions sold at double prices, ought to be liquidated at its real value. . . . It is well known, that a large proportion of this domestic debt was incurred for paper-money lent. To be sure Congress acknowledged its value equal to its name; but this was done on a principle of policy, in order to prevent the rapid depreciation that was taking place. But money lent in this depreciated and depreciating state, can hardly be said to be lent from a spirit of patriotism; it was a mere speculation in public securities. They hoped, by putting their money in the loan office, though in a

---

[1] Livermore, however, called attention to the special position held by the regular continental certificates which Congress had put on a different footing and made transferable. These, the speaker admitted, were hardly susceptible of discrimination.

depreciated state, to receive hard money for it by and by. I flatter myself this prediction will never be effected." [1]

It is unfair to assume that any considerable portion of the Anti-Federalists who resisted the establishment of Hamilton's fiscal system desired a repudiation of the debt.[2] The most radical merely proposed to scale down the debt to something like its real value and thus materially reduce the burden of the taxpayers. The majority of them were just as anxious as the Secretary of the Treasury to do "exact justice" to the public creditors. Their notion of exact justice was not, however, to pay the existing security holders at face value and leave unrecognized the claims of those who, through a necessity created by the negligence of the government, had been compelled to part with their original certificates. In other words, they were looking primarily toward the just discharge of the debt, not the augmentation of the fluid capital in the hands of the existing holders who were largely concentrated in the cities. They, therefore, proposed a "discrimination" between the original holders and the secondary or speculative purchasers, little knowing, probably, how many of the latter there were in Congress.

[1] *Annals of Congress*, Vol. I, p. 1185.

[2] The two proposals of those who opposed funding at face value the certificates in the hands of all holders are thus summed up by Callender: "When the business came originally before the Congress of 1789, three different plans were suggested. The first proposed a new settlement of accounts, and aimed to annihilate the largest part of the debt. But the new constitution had been, in a great measure, established by the influence and activity of traders in these certificates. They and their friends were superior in the legislature, and this scheme was rejected by a numerous majority. A second proposal went on the ground of paying to the purchasers only the real value which they had given for the certificates, and to give the difference between the half crown which they had disbursed and the twenty shillings which they claimed to the original holders. Thus when William Smith [M. C.] demanded five hundred dollars as the arrears due to an old sergeant the reply might have run : 'You gave fifty dollars of money for these five hundred of paper. Here take your fifty silver dollars back again. We shall reserve the remaining four hundred and fifty for the man who shed his blood earning them.' The plan, also, was negatived." Callender, *Sedgwick & Co., or a Key to the Six Per Cent Cabinet* (1798).

The most reasoned and effective argument for discrimination was made by James Madison, who did not hold any securities himself and was able to take a dispassionate view of the merits of the several claims against the United States. He freely admitted the sacredness of the duty laid upon the government to pay the value which it had received with lawful interest, but he held that there was one point at issue which they could with propriety discuss, namely, to whom the payment should be made. For the purpose of examining this question he classified the creditors into four groups : original creditors who had never sold their paper, original creditors who had alienated their securities, present holders of alienated securities, and intermediate holders through whose hand securities had passed. The merits of these respective claimants he then analyzed at length.

As to the first group, the original holders who had not alienated, he said, "there can be no difficulty. Justice is in their favor, for they have advanced the value which they claim ; public faith is in their favor, for the written promise is in their hands ; respect for public credit is in their favor, for if claims so sacred are violated, all confidence must be at an end ; public opinion is in their favor, for every honest citizen cannot but be their advocate. With respect to the last class, the intermediate holders, their pretensions, if they have any, would lead us into a labyrinth, for which it is impossible to find a clue. This will be the less complained of, because this class were perfectly free, both in becoming and ceasing to be creditors ; and because, in general, they must have gained by their speculations." [1]

For the two remaining groups of creditors, original holders who had alienated and the present holders who had purchased, much might be said. The former might well

[1] *Annals of Congress*, Vol. I, p. 1235.

appeal to justice and public faith, for they had furnished values to the government and had been compelled by the policy of the government to sacrifice their property. Moreover the soldiers might appeal on grounds of humanity, "for the sufferings of the military part of the creditors can never be forgotten, while sympathy is an American virtue. To say nothing of the singular hardship, in so many mouths, of requiring those who have lost four-fifths or seven-eighths of their due, to contribute the remainder in favor of those who have gained in the contrary proportion."

On the other hand, continued Madison, the holders who had purchased securities had claims which could not be denied. The gains which they might make were the due rewards of the risks they had taken; they held the government's solemn obligation to pay; and they could point with reason to the truth of the statement that the literal fulfilment of engagements is the best foundation of public credit. Justice required that the original holders who had sacrificed their securities should be paid for the loss which the policy of the government had entailed upon them; and public credit required the discharge of the debt whose evidences lay in the hands of those who had purchased for speculation. To pay both was beyond the ability of the government, and, moreover, that would be in excess of the value actually received by the public treasury.

In this dilemma, Madison came to the conclusion that "a composition, then, is the only expedient that remains; let it be a liberal one in favor of the present holders, let them have the highest price which has prevailed in the market; and let the residue belong to the original sufferers. This will not do perfect justice; but it will do more real justice, and perform more of the public faith, than any other expedient proposed. The present holders, where they have purchased at the lowest price of the securities, will have a profit that cannot be reasonably complained of ; where they have purchased at a higher price, the profit will be considerable ; and even the few who have purchased at the highest price cannot well be losers, with a well-funded interest of 6 per cent. The original sufferers will not be fully indemnified ; but they will receive, from their country, a tribute due to their merits, which, if it does not entirely heal their wounds, will assuage the pain of them."

The most effective reply to Madison's proposals was made by Boudinot, of New Jersey, a security holder, who said by way of preface that he felt disinterested in the matter.[1] The speaker refused to concede that there was a fundamental difference between the original creditors and those who had acquired alienated securities. "I am willing to risk my reputation," he said, "that you will find the greatest part of the debt in the hands of those who never were real creditors of the United States. The original creditors, I take it, are those who actually loaned the money, furnished the supplies, or rendered the service; the contract was made with them. . . . Congress, in order to benefit those persons, whom they could not immediately pay off, gave to them an evidence of the debt, to which was annexed a negotiable quality. Hence the contract was formed upon the idea of the transferable quality of the certificate to be issued. The original creditor having, then, alienated his debt, under these circumstances, conveyed all his right and title thereto, under the sanction of the government; the transferee is, therefore, *ipso facto*, the original creditor. This will be set in a clear light, by a reference to the face of the certificate itself, where the

[1] *Annals of Congress*, Vol. I, pp. 1286 ff. See below, p. 184.

promise is not to the original holder alone, there is an alternative to A B, or bearer, either one or the other. Will any one say, the bearer is not concerned in the contract? How can you say to the assignee, that you have nothing to do with him in this business, when the resolutions of Congress, and the express words of the evidence acknowledged him a party in the contract, at least equal to the original creditor? . . . Considering this in every point of view, I am free to declare that public justice requires the bearer to be considered as the original creditor."

The original holder, Boudinot placed in the position of those unfortunate persons whose property was destroyed by British soldiers during the revolution, "with this difference, that the loss of one was voluntary, on the principle of yielding a part to save a part." The speaker then inquired what justice would say in the matter: "Suppose the case to be that of a private person before a court of equity, or even that of a nation before that Supreme Tribunal which forces the most potent to do right. A is bound to B in an express contract; A fails in the performance, which reduces B to distress; B, with the assent of A, sells to C (by which he is considerably relieved), though at an under rate, and therefore suffers fifty per cent loss; C calls for payment from A, of his principal and simple interest; B calls for damages suffered by the breach of A's promise. Where is the court of law or equity in the world; nay, where is the court in more pure regions, which would not give the debt to C, and damages to B, and both against A? There is no room for a decree against C. . . . I well know the worth, the honor, and integrity of the gentleman who brought this proposition forward, and I would appeal to these qualities to answer me. Suppose, as an original holder, he was to have given him, by the United States, ten shillings out of every twenty he had assigned, at the expense of the assignee, would he not, on a principle of honor, return it?"

Madison's proposition to discriminate between original holders and assignees was defeated on February 22 by a large majority, thirty-six to thirteen. Thus was settled the not inconsiderable question of whether the bonds of the new government and the augmented fluid capital were to be widely distributed among original holders or concentrated in the cities where most of the assignees and speculative purchasers lived. It is an interesting commentary, perhaps not without significance, that of the sixty-four members of the House at that time nearly one-half, twenty-nine, appeared on the funding books of the government as security holders under the law of August 4, 1790. How the security holders were divided on Madison's proposition we do not know, for no roll-call occurred on that occasion.[1]

After the attempt to discriminate between original holders and assignees was defeated, the proposition to augment the national debt by about fifty per cent, through the assumption of the state debts came before Congress for consideration. Here, as in the preceding discussion, the economics and politics of the debt were brought under review. A

[1] *Annals of Congress*, Vol. II, p. 1344. While the contest over Madison's proposition to discriminate between original holders and purchasers of securities was being waged, the Senators, as well as private citizens, followed the debates with keen interest. Maclay records in his *Journal* under the date of February 15: "Adjourned and went to hear the debates in the lower house. Sedgwick, Lawrence, Smith, and Ames took the whole day. They seemed to aim at one point, to make Madison ridiculous. Ames delivered a long string of studied sentences, but he did not use a single argument that seemed to leave an impression. He had public faith, public credit, honor, and, above all, justice, as often over as an Indian would the Great Spirit, and, if possible, with less meaning, and to as little purpose. Hamilton, at the head of the speculators, with all the courtiers, are on one side. These I call the party who are actuated by interest. The opposition are governed by principle. But I fear in this case interest will outweigh principle." *Sketches of Debate in the First Senate of the United States* (Harrisburg ed.), p. 169.

Federalist champion, Fisher Ames, explained the advantages of the fiscal system in an astounding argument to the effect that the people were adding capital to their own possessions by self-denying taxation. "The debt," he said, "is to be considered, when funded, as an increase of active capital. We have been often told that a public debt is not a blessing, but an evil. We are not to compare a debt with no debt for it is a desirable thing to be free from debt; but the debt is already contracted, and we are to compare an unfunded fluctuating debt with a funded debt. Such a debt as the latter may be comparatively a blessing, for it makes the capital transferable as well as the income. We have but a small share of personal property; but this will make the very land and houses circulate. It is true it is an artificial capital formed by a charge upon every other capital, but it is also true, that it is formed by small savings in expense, and if the taxes were not to be laid, there would not be an increase of wealth at the end of a year equal to the debt or the interest of it. A single cent in the price of an article cannot be said to impoverish the people, or to restrain them from enjoying their usual habits of living. Indeed, it may tend in some degree to prevent excess, and to promote frugality, which will enrich the people. But at the end of the year these almost imperceptible sums, by their union into one mass, acquire a new power. The whole may be said to have properties which did not belong to the separate parts. The active circulation promoted by the debt will, in a considerable degree, compensate the burthen of paying taxes. Those whose property is increased by possessing the debt will become greater consumers in proportion, and contribute largely to the revenue." [1]

The Anti-Federalist leader, Jackson, of Georgia, was un-

[1] *Ibid.*, Vol. II, p. 1483.

able to see exactly how the people, by taxing themselves to maintain a large funded debt, were themselves to derive the advantage. To him it seemed like taxing one section of the community to benefit another, and furthermore, in his opinion, it was the agricultural section that would have to bear the brunt of the burden. In discussing the public sentiment of the state of South Carolina, he said : "I believe I speak with justice, when I advance, that three-fourths of the back inhabitants of that state are opposed to the measure. Sir, they are republicans, who have fought and bled for the cause of liberty, and know the value of it. I know and regard them as such, and although I wish not to wound the feelings of any gentleman present, I assert that they will see through this thin veiled artifice to take a portion of their state power from them, and they will feel that continual drain of specie which must take place to satisfy the appetites of basking speculators at the seat of Government. . . . Connecticut manufactures a great deal, and she imports little. Georgia manufactures nothing, and imports everything. Therefore Georgia, although her population is not near so large, contributes more to the public treasury by impost. . . . Let us not rear a monument to mankind of the impossibility of preserving republican manners, by aping European nations and laying the foundation of our government in immense debts. Sir, our terms of service, happily I believe for the country, are near expiring. We shall return to the mass of the people, and participate in the burdens we impose. When the cool hour of investigation arrives, happy indeed will it be for us if, amidst the murmurs of an oppressed people, we have not to say, in self-condemnation, I too have been guilty of bringing this load of sin on the nation, and this load of fetters on the people. America, sir, will not always think as is the fashion of the present day; and when the iron hand of tyranny is felt, denunciations will fall on those who, by imposing this enormous and iniquitous debt, will beggar the people and bind them in chains." [1]

The politics of assumption, namely the firmer establishment of the Constitution and the federal government, was not overlooked in the debate. On May 25, 1790, Ames took this point up at the close of a long speech, saying: "Little notice has been taken of the argument for assumption, which, if just, is entitled to a great deal. I mean that which has been urged to show that it will strengthen the Government. The answer given is, that instead of pecuniary influence, new powers are wanting to the Constitution. . . . Before we ask for new powers on paper, let us exercise those which are actually vested in Congress. What will the new powers avail us, if we suffer the Constitution to become a dead letter? . . . Little topics of objection sink to nothing when it is allowed that the assumption will strengthen the Government. . . . Shall we make the union less strong than the people have intended to make it, by adopting the Constitution? And

---

[1] *Annals of Congress*, Vol. II, pp. 1748–1752. The Southern position on assumption was concisely summed up in a letter written by Oliver Wolcott, of the Treasury Department, in February, 1790: "Congress are proceeding in their deliberations on the Secretary's report. The Northern states seem generally to favor the plan. In Virginia and some other states, there is a determined and stubborn opposition. They fear a consolidation of the government; and also that if their state debts are assumed all the securities will be purchased by foreigners and by their neighbors. They say that the system of raising revenues by imposts operates unequally, they being the greatest consumers; that to remedy this inequality by a land tax, will make such establishments necessary as will render the general government formidable; that though the assumption will be a temporary relief by causing the revenues to be expended where they are collected, yet in the end it will operate to them like a foreign debt, as they know the disposition of their people will be to sell everything which will produce money. . . . The worst circumstances attending our affairs, arise from the great variety of prejudices and manners in the United States. If they shall not be shortly assimilated, I fear that disagreeable consequences will ensue." Gibbs, *op. cit.*, Vol. I, p. 39.

do not all agree that the assumption is not a neutral measure? If its adoption will give strength to the union, its rejection will have a contrary effect. . . . At this late period of the debate, it is hardly possible for gentlemen to exercise impartiality. . . . They [the opposition] love their country, and mean to serve it; and I am sure they would shrink from the spectre of its misery which haunts us; they would not consent to *undo the Constitution in practice*, to realize the evils which were only apprehended under the Confederation, and which were prevented [from being remedied] by the total want of power in Congress." [1]

This use of the public debt and the public creditors to underwrite the Constitution and the federal government was by no means overlooked by the opposition. Stone of Maryland saw it very clearly. "A strong binding force, exterior or interior," he said, "is supposed essentially necessary to keep together a government like ours; and of all the bands of political connexion, perhaps there is none stronger than that which is formed by a uniform, compact, and efficacious chain or system of revenue. A greater thought could not have been conceived by man; and its effect, I venture to predict, if adopted by us, and carried into execution, will prove to the Federal government walls of adamant, impregnable to any attempt upon its fabric or operations. I have viewed it with some degree of attention, and I see the subject rise into gigantic height. . . . I think, sir, wherever the property is, there will be the power. And if the general government has the payment of all the debts, it must, of course, have all the revenue; and if it possesses the whole revenue, it is equal, in other words, to the whole power." [2]

The same theme was also taken up by Jackson in his final

<hr>

[1] *Annals of Congress*, Vol. II, p. 1668.   [2] *Ibid.*, Vol. II, p. 1359.

assault on assumption : "The object certainly was the absorbing of the whole of the state powers within the vortex of the all-devouring General Government ; seven years were we fighting to establish props for liberty, and in less than two years since the adoption of the Constitution are we trying to kick them all away, and he is the ablest politician, and the best man of the day, who can do most to destroy the child of liberty of his own raising. . . . So far will it be from producing the harmony the gentleman has supposed, that I think I can venture to prophesy it will occasion discord, and generate rancor against the Union. For if it benefits one part of the United States, it oppresses another. If it lulls the Shays of the North it will rouse the Sullivans of the South." [1]

Speaking on the same point on an earlier occasion, Jackson had warned the Federalists that the debt could not in fact help bind the Southern states to the Union because the state and continental securities in the South were already gone from the hands of the original holders into the hands of the speculators in the commercial cities.[2] He also declared his belief, doubtless with some exaggeration, that there were not twenty original holders in the state of Georgia.[3] The general truth of Jackson's contention that the public funds in the South had been bought up is adequately demonstrated by the records of the Treasury Department,[4] and his prophecy that discord would be stirred up in the sections where there were few security holders was strangely fulfilled by the growth of Anti-Federalism in North Carolina, Georgia, and the western parts of Virginia and South Carolina.

[1] *Ibid.*, Vol. II, p. 1749.
[2] *Ibid.*, Vol. II, p. 1429.
[3] *Ibid.*, Vol. II, p. 1551.
[4] See *Economic Interpretation of the Constitution,* p. 36.

When at last the advocates of assumption were victorious by the dint of skilful negotiation,[1] Congress adjourned for a brief respite ; and then finally, in the third and last session, it took up the third of Hamilton's great fiscal measures, the Bank bill. The managers who were in charge of this bill evidently thought it wise to start the measure in the Senate where the proportion of heavy investors in public funds was larger than in the House of Representatives.[2] The measure appears to have been pressed with singular zeal, for the Report of the Secretary of the Treasury was not made public until December 14, 1790, and, notwithstanding the intervening Holidays, an act to incorporate the Bank passed the Senate on January 20, 1791. The fact that we have no records of the discussions in the Senate for that period prevents our following the arguments on the bill, but the progress of the measure in the lower house may be easily traced.

The debate opened in the House of Representatives on the Bank bill on February 1, 1791, and it had hardly got under way before the old antagonism of the agricultural to the capitalistic interests, which had dogged the steps of every fiscal measure proposed by the Secretary of the Treasury, made its appearance. After Smith of Charleston, South Carolina, made a few desultory remarks in favor of the bill, the famous champion of agrarianism, Jackson, of Georgia,

[1] See below, Chap. V.

[2] "It is known that the Bank bill originated not in the House of Representatives, but in the close and mysterious House of Senators, clothed by the weight of whose sanction it was sent to the other House, when it was hurried through with immense speed. . . . It is acknowledged that the bill has been greatly applauded by some proprietors in the public funds amongst us, who thought they saw their interest concerned in promoting it — and hence the most powerful class of orators I have met with in favor of it are of this number. As to the general yeomanry of America, they have given themselves no trouble in this business, and will probably concern themselves little about it." Gazette of the United States, May 11, 1791. See below, p. 202.

where there were few security holders to take advantage of the opportunity for gain opened by the measure, announced that he resolutely was opposed to the bill on principle.

He declared that the bill in question was a piece of class legislation : "This plan of a National Bank is calculated to benefit a small part of the United States, the mercantile interest only; the farmers, the yeomanry, will derive no advantage from it ; as the bank bills will not circulate to the extremities of the Union. He said, he had never seen a bank bill in the state of Georgia, nor will they ever benefit the farmers of that state, or of New Hampshire. . . . He urged the unconstitutionality of the plan ; called it a monopoly ; such a one as contravenes the spirit of the Constitution ; a monopoly of a very extraordinary nature ; a monopoly of the public moneys for the benefit of the corporation to be created. He then read several passages from the Federalist, which he said were directly contrary to the assumption of the power proposed by the bill." [1]

Stone, of Maryland, came to the support of Jackson : "He observed, that upon the present occasion, the opinions respecting the Constitution seem to be divided by a geographical line, dividing the continent. Hence it might be inferred, that other considerations mixed with the question ; and it had been insinuated that it was warped by the future seat of Government. But other causes may be assigned for the diversity of sentiment — the people to the Eastward began earliest in favor of liberty. They pursued freedom into anarchy — starting at the precipice of confusion, they are now vibrating far the other way. He said, that all our taxes are paid by the consumers of manufactures ; those taxes are all bounties upon home manufactures. The people to the Eastward are the manufacturers of this country ; it

[1] *Annals of Congress*, Vol. II, p. 1941.

was no wonder that they should endeavor to strengthen the hands of a Government by which they are so peculiarly benefited. It is a fact, that the greatest part of the Continental debt has travelled Eastward of the Potomac. This law is to raise the value of the continental paper. Here, then, is the strong impulse of immediate interest in favor of the bank. He took notice of the distinction made by the plan of the bill, between continental and state paper. The state paper, on account of the partial payments of interest, still remained in the respective states. But this could not, by the present system, be subscribed ; so that the Southern states were deprived of the advantage that might have been given to the only paper they have. . . . He proceeded. I say there is no necessity, there is no occasion, for this Bank. The states will institute banks which will answer every purpose. But a distrust of the states is shown in every movement of Congress. . . . By this bill, a few stockholders may institute banks in particular states, to their aggrandizement and the oppression of others. This bank will swallow up the state banks ; it will raise in this country a moneyed interest at the devotion of the government ; it may bribe both states and individuals. . . . He said it is one of those sly and subtle movements which marched silently to its object ; the vices of it were at first not palpable or obvious ; but when the people saw a distinction of banks created — when they viewed with astonishment the train of wealth which followed individuals, whose sudden exaltation surprised even the possessors — they would inquire how all this came about. . . . But, Gentlemen will say, upon emergencies the Bank will loan money [to the government]. We differ in opinion. I think when we want it most the bank will be most unable and unwilling to lend. If we are in prosperity, we can borrow money almost anywhere ; but in adversity, stockholders will avoid us with as much caution as any other capitalists." [1]

While Southern Representatives were laying stress upon the undue advantages offered by the measure to Northern capitalistic interests, Representatives from the North adverted to those advantages as among the merits of the bill. Ames, of Massachusetts, said, "It seems to be conceded within doors and without, that a public bank would be useful to trade, that it is almost essential to revenue, and that it is little short of indispensably necessary in times of public emergency. . . . This new capital will invigorate trade and manufactures with new energy. It will furnish a medium for the collection of the revenues ; and if Government should be pressed by a sudden necessity, it will afford seasonable and effectual aid. . . . It is of the first utility to trade. Indeed, the intercourse from state to state can never be on a good footing without a bank, whose paper will circulate more extensively than that of any state bank." [2]

Sedgwick, of Massachusetts, took the same view as his colleague, Ames. He had little patience with theoretical objections. "If we attempt to proceed in one direction," he complained, "our ears are assailed with the exclamation of 'the Constitution is in danger ;' if we attempt to obtain our objects by pursuing a different course, we are told the pass is guarded by the stern spirit of democracy." Having expressed his slight regard for such arguments against the measure, he proceeded to consider the utility of banks. "There were two circumstances," he said, "which would render banks of more importance in this country than in any other country where they are at present in use : the first, the commercial enterprise of our merchants compared with the smallness of their capitals, which, as we had no

[1] *Annals of Congress*, Vol. II, pp. 1981 ff.   [2] *Ibid.*, Vol. II, pp. 1953 ff.

large manufacturing capitals, whereby the precious metals could be retained in circulation, would frequently, by their exportation, greatly distress the people; the other originated from a measure of the Government. . . . Gentlemen had been pleased to consider the proposed terms as giving an undue advantage to the stockholders. He would leave this part of the subject to gentlemen who better understood it; only observing, that as Government must rely principally on merchants to obtain the proposed stock, it would be necessary to afford to them sufficient motives to withdraw from their commercial pursuits a part of their capitals." [1]

Gerry, also of Massachusetts, as usual came to the aid of the holders of public securities, for whose advantage he was especially solicitous, notwithstanding his oft-repeated assertions of disinterestedness. "The plan proposed by the Secretary of the Treasury, which is now the subject of discussion," he said, "does honor, like all his other measures, to his head and heart; it will be mutually beneficial to the stockholders and to Government, and consequently so to the people. The stockholders by this plan will be deeply interested in supporting Government; because three-quarters of their capital, consisting of funded certificates, depend on the existence of Government, which therefore is the prop of their capital, the main pillar that supports the bank. Again, the credit of Government, which is immaterial to the other banks, is essential to the National Bank, for the annual interest of three-quarters of its capital, which must form a great share of its profits, will depend altogether on the credit of Government, and produce, on the part of the stockholders, the strongest attachment to it." [2]

It is useless to pursue further the contest which turned on

[1] *Annals of Congress*, Vol. II, pp. 1961 ff.
[2] *Ibid.*, Vol. II, p. 2001.

the question as to whether the fluid capital of the country should be augmented and additional advantages offered to the holder of public funds, particularly continental funds, to secure their adherence and devotion to the new government. That this was the essence of the matter appeared again and again in the discussion in Congress and outside, and that the country was divided on this proposition according to the intensity of the direct economic interests of the several sections was evidenced by the vote in Congress on propositions connected with the Bank bill.

Having shown the economic character of the real issue between the parties, it would seem a work of supererogation to examine the discussion of the constitutionality of the Bank bill; but this first great war of the dialecticians about the powers of Congress occupies such a prominent place in the history of our constitutional law, that it deserves the respectful attention, even of those who believe with Mr. Justice Holmes, that "general propositions do not decide concrete cases," and that every constitutional decision "depends on a judgment or intuition more subtle than any articulate major premise."

It is true that questions of constitutionality had arisen in connection with the assumption of state debts, the removal power of the President, and many other matters,[1] but it was the Bank bill which first summoned to the political battle that high talent for analysis, deduction, reticulation, and

[1] "We have near twenty *antis*, dragons watching the tree of liberty, and who consider every strong measure, and almost every ordinary one, as an attempt to rob the tree of its fair fruit. We hear, incessantly, from the old foes of the Constitution, 'this is unconstitutional, and that is;' and indeed, what is not. I scarce know a point which has not produced this cry, not excepting a motion for adjourning. If the Constitution is what they affect to think it, their former opposition to such a nonentity was improper. . . . The fishery bill was unconstitutional; is it unconstitutional to receive plans of finance from the Secretary; to give bounties; to make the militia worth having; order is unconstitutional; credit is ten fold worse." *Life and Works of Fisher Ames*, Vol. I, p. 114

speculative imagination which has characterized American constitutional conflicts from that day to this.

In the House of Representatives the opposition to the constitutionality of the Bank was led by James Madison, of Virginia. Those who are inclined to bring against the "father of the Constitution," a charge of inconsistency in thus opposing a measure so eminently calculated to bring powerful support to the new government will do well to consider two facts. In the first place, Madison, although he was anxious to see the federal government strong at home and respectable abroad, from the beginning of the constitutional movement, looked upon the necessity for restrictions on the state legislatures as the fundamental reason in favor of the framing and adoption of the Constitution.[1] In the second place, the speculations and culpable conduct of so many members of the first federal Congress so outraged Madison's sense of propriety that he was unwilling to lend any countenance to a movement calculated to afford another opportunity for gambling in public paper on a magnificent scale.[2] Madison had none of the securities himself, and was a somewhat disinterested observer of the course of events under Washington's administration. He therefore had many reasons for attacking the constitutionality of the law which put such large sums in the hands of Northern speculators.

Although some of the Federalists in the House deemed the question of constitutionality worthy of extended discussion, it appears that Smith, of South Carolina, was inclined to dismiss it on the practical ground that "constitutionality grows out of expediency."[3] In fact, as long as they were in power the Federalists had no doubt about the "constitutionality" of their own measures. The great Marshall was under no de-

---

[1] *Economic Interpretation*, p. 178.   [2] *Ibid.*, p. 125.
[3] *Annals of Congress*, Vol. II, p. 1994.

lusion about constitutional law as an exact science, and in a sentence which anticipated Mr. Justice Holmes' famous dictum that subtle intuitions rather than articulate major premises decide concrete cases, he spoke of the controversy over the constitutionality of the Bank as follows : "The judgment is so much influenced by the wishes, the affections, and the general theories of those by whom any political proposition is decided that a contrariety of opinion on this great constitutional question ought to excite no surprise." [1]

The question of constitutionality which was so ardently discussed by members of Congress was no less earnestly considered by members of Washington's cabinet, before whom it was laid for consideration and report.   Hamilton, naturally enough, thought the Bank constitutional and wrote his opinion in a document which has justly passed into history as one of the greatest of American state papers. Jefferson and Randolph, both from Virginia and both later to be identified with the great agrarian party that was destined to sweep the Federalists out of power, took a firm stand against the constitutionality of the Bank.   The Secretary of State elaborated his views in a state paper which is fairly comparable in acumen and skilful arrangement to the brief which emanated from the Treasury.   As Marshall remarked, the "wishes, the affections, and the general theories" of the contestants in logic had a "decided" influence on their judgment.   Washington was convinced by Hamilton with whose economic policy he agreed in the main, and on February 25, 1791, he signed the act to incorporate the subscribers to the Bank of the United States.   The last of Hamilton's great fiscal devices was completed.

It remains now to consider that other pillar of Hamilton's capitalistic edifice, the protective tariff designed to develop

[1] *Life of Washington* (2d ed.), Vol. II, p. 205.

American industry, give more extensive employment to the
fluid capital created by the funding and Bank schemes, and
to draw another allied group of interests to the aid of the
security and bank-stock holders in maintaining the new
government. Hamilton's Report on Manufactures was not
communicated to the House of Representatives until December 5, 1791. However, the debate which had already
taken place on the first revenue bill, in 1789, indicated that
the group who supported the Secretary's fiscal policies were
quite as warmly attached to the principle of protection for
American commerce and manufactures, although often
divided on questions of ways and means.

Efforts have been made to represent the Fathers as free-
traders, and Democrats of a later time even went so far as to
declare protective tariffs "unconstitutional." All this is
without historical warrant. There can be no doubt that
the first revenue measure under the Constitution was designed for protection as well as for income. Its preamble
declares as much : "Whereas it is necessary for the support
of the government, for the discharge of the debts of the
United States, and the encouragement and protection of
manufactures." And a careful study of the debates and
contemporary sources supports that view.[1]

The voice of the manufacturing interests of Pennsylvania
was heard at the very beginning in the House of Representatives in favor of a system of protective tariff. It was
on Wednesday, April 1, 1789, that a quorum was secured ;
the rules of the new assembly were adopted on the 7th ; the
following day Madison laid before the committee of the
whole his proposals for duties on imposts. The next day,
Hartley (who had been a member of the Pennsylvania con-

---

[1] W. Hill, *Early Stages of the Tariff Policy* (Publications of the American Economic Association, Vol. VIII, pp. 107 ff.) ; Journal of Political Economy, Vol. II,
pp. 54 ff.

vention and voted in favor of the Constitution) served notice
that the revenue system was to be viewed as an instrument
of protection. "I have observed, sir," he said, "from the
conversation of the members, that it is in the contemplation
of some to enter on this business in a limited and partial
manner, as it relates to revenue alone; but, for my own part,
I wish to do it on as broad a bottom as is at this time practicable. . . . If we consult the history of the ancient
world, we shall see that they have thought proper, for a
long time past, to give great encouragement to the establishment of manufactures, by laying such partial duties on
the importation of foreign goods, as to give the home manufactures a considerable advantage in the price when brought
to market. . . . I think it both politic and just that the
fostering hand of the General Government should extend
to all those manufactures which will tend to national utility.
. . . Our stock of materials is, in many instances, equal to
the greatest demand and our artisans sufficient to work
them up even for exportation. In these cases, I take it to
be the policy of every enlightened nation to give their
manufactures that degree of encouragement necessary to
perfect them, without oppressing the other parts of the community; and under this encouragement the industry of the
manufacturer will be employed to add to the wealth of the
nation." [1]

The importance of securing a revenue at once to pay the
current expenses of the government and sustain its credit,
prevented a full discussion of the principle of protection
which Hartley suggested, but Madison took advantage of
the occasion to announce his doctrines on the subject. "I
own myself the friend," he said, "to a very free system of
commerce, and hold it as a truth, that commercial shackles

are generally unjust, oppressive, and impolitic ; it is also a truth, that if industry and labor are left to take their own course, they will generally be directed to those objects which are the most productive, and this in a more certain and direct manner than the wisdom of the most enlightened legislature could point out." Having stated this broad principle, Madison proceeded, however, to enumerate certain exceptions wherein commerce might be regulated and manufactures protected within the limits of sound policy.[1]

After these somewhat desultory remarks on the general principle of protection, the House proceeded with the consideration of particular schedules and the debates which ensued showed that the tariff was then, as ever, a "local issue." Nevertheless, in the contest over the rates of duty to be imposed on separate articles, the antagonism between agriculture and manufacturing came out very clearly.[2]

We may illustrate the nature of this antagonism by reference to the debate over the duty on unwrought steel. On April 15, Lee, of Virginia, moved to strike that item from the schedule, observing that "the consumption of steel was very great, and essentially necessary to agricultural improvements. He did not believe any gentleman would contend,

---

[1] *Annals of Congress*, Vol. I, p. 116.

[2] "The North advocated a high duty on rum, a prosperous manufacture which ought to be protected against Jamaica distilleries ; while it objected to a high duty upon molasses, which was largely consumed as an article of food in New England and was also the raw material for the famous rum of that section. On the other hand, New England opposed high duties on hemp, because it would increase the cost of cordage, which was an essential material in shipbuilding, while those interested in western lands wished to develop the growth of hemp. New England representatives were willing to encourage the manufacture of nails by a protective duty, and Pennsylvania championed the special needs of steel ; but a southern representative feared that agriculture would be depressed by high prices of farming tools. . . . In general, the South strongly protested against the immense increase in rates proposed in protective amendments, and animadverted on the sectional character of a tariff which was designed to assist the producing manufactures rather than the purchasing agriculturalists." Dewey. *Financial History of the United States*, p. 81.

that enough of this article to answer consumption could be fabricated in any part of the Union : *hence it would operate as an oppressive, though indirect tax upon agriculture, and any tax whether direct or indirect, upon this interest, at this juncture, would be unwise and impolitic.*" [1] Tucker, of South Carolina, joined in this opinion. Madison, of Virginia, also agreed, and suggested that the article in question be transferred to the non-enumerated list where it would be subject only to five per cent. The South Carolina Representatives, said he, "considered the smallest tax on this article to be a burthen on agriculture, which ought to be considered an interest most deserving protection and encouragement." [2]

Unwrought steel found its defenders in the Pennsylvania delegation. Clymer, who had been a member of the Convention which drafted the Constitution, declared, "that the manufacture of steel in America was rather in its infancy ; but as all the materials necessary to make it were the produce of almost every state in the Union, and as the manufacture was already established, and attended with considerable success, he deemed it prudent to emancipate our country from the manacles in which she was held by foreign manufactures. A furnace in Philadelphia, with a very small

---

[1] *Annals of Congress*, Vol. I, pp. 153 ff. ; italics mine.

[2] That the Constitution would bring about a subjection of the landed to the commercial interests was prophesied by George Mason, a member of the Philadelphia Convention from Virginia, and in fact assigned as one of his reasons for opposing the adoption of the system. Among his objections forwarded to Washington in a letter of October 7, 1787, he said : "By requiring only a majority to make all commercial and navigation laws, the five southern states (whose produce and circumstances are totally different from that of the eight northern and eastern states) will be ruined ; for such rigid and premature regulations may be made, as will enable the merchants of the northern and eastern states not only to demand an exorbitant freight, but to monopolize the purchase of the commodities at their own price, for many years : to the great injury of the landed interest and impoverishment of the people : and the danger is the greater, as the gain on one side will be in proportion to the loss on the other." *Documentary History of the Constitution*, Vol. IV, p. 318.

aid from the legislature of Pennsylvania, made three hundred tons in two years, and now makes at the rate of two hundred and thirty tons annually, and with a little further encouragement would supply enough for the consumption of the Union. He hoped, therefore, gentlemen would be disposed, under these considerations, to extend a degree of patronage to a manufacture which a moment's reflection would convince them was highly deserving protection." Fitzsimons, likewise of Pennsylvania and a former member of the constitutional Convention of 1787, warmly supported Clymer, and begged his colleagues to get rid of local considerations and to remember the concessions which his state had made on other points.

It is abundantly evident from the debates and contemporary discussions that the revenue measure, like the funding and Bank measures, was designed to encourage capitalistic interests. Of course, it was said at the time that the whole country was to benefit from the tariff as well as from the augmentation of capital which the Federalist scheme contemplated; but the representatives of the agrarian regions were unconvinced. They regarded the protective tariff as a burden laid upon the consumers, of whom the major portion were farmers, for the benefit of the manufacturing or capitalistic classes. The tariff, therefore, added to the antagonism between the two dominant economic interests in the country, and helped to sharpen the division between North and South.

CHAPTER VI

THE first Congress of the United States had scarcely adjourned before the political storm burst. The ineluctable and truculent opponents of the Constitution, who had seen in its adoption the triumph of "the rich and well born," were now convinced that their worst fears had been well founded. In their opinion, it had been no mere victory of talents and numbers, but the conquest of the people through chicanery. Dark hints of corruption soon sprang into circulation, and after the controversy was well under way John Taylor startled the country with his *Examination of the Late Proceedings in Congress Respecting the Official Conduct of the Secretary of the Treasury*,[2] a remarkable pamphlet in which he distinctly charged the members of Congress with being personally interested in the operations of the Treasury Department, and therefore not representatives of the people at all.[3]

Although Jefferson derived considerable information concerning the operations of Congress from Taylor's pamphlet, he had come to similar conclusions at least two years before its publication. As early as February 4, 1791, that is, about six months after the passage of the funding bill and before the enactment of the Bank bill, he wrote to

[1] This chapter is largely a reprint of an article published in The American Historical Review for January, 1914.

[2] For an examination of this pamphlet, see below, p. 197.

[3] Though this pamphlet dealt particularly with the second Congress, a large number of the members of that Congress had served in the first Congress which laid the foundations of Hamilton's system.

George Mason: "What is said in our country of the fiscal arrangements now going on? I really fear their effect when I consider the present temper of the Southern states. Whether these measures be right or wrong abstractedly, more attention should be paid to the general opinion. . . . The only corrective of what is corrupt in our present form of government will be the augmentation of the numbers in the lower house, so as to be a more agricultural representation, which may put that interest above that of the stockjobbers." [1]

A year later Jefferson became more specific. He declared that the great outlines of Hamilton's system had been carried "by the votes of the very persons who, having swallowed his bait, were laying themselves out to profit by his plans"; and he added that "had these persons withdrawn, as those interested in a question ever should, the vote of the disinterested majority was clearly the reverse of what they made it. These were no longer the votes then of the representatives of the people . . . and it was impossible to consider their decisions, which had nothing in view but to enrich themselves, as the measures of the fair majority, which ought always to be respected." [2]

It seems that as Jefferson watched the progress of Hamilton's measures in Congress, he became more and more convinced that the members who supported them represented their own personal interests rather than the mass of the voters — particularly, the agrarian interests. At all events, he took the trouble to compile a roll of the "paper men" in Congress in March, 1793, and this list he incorporated in the *Anas*. This list of stockholders in the Bank embraces the following men who were in the first Congress; Gilman,

---

[1] *Writings* (Ford ed.), Vol. V, p. 275.

[2] *Ibid.*, Vol. VI, pp. 102–103. For this and several other references, I am indebted to Professor Max Farrand.

Gerry, Sedgwick, Ames, Goodhue, Trumbull, Wadsworth, Benson, Lawrence, Boudinot, Fitzsimons, Heister, Williamson, W. L. Smith, Sherman, Ellsworth, King, Robert Morris, W. S. Johnson, and Izard. After this enumeration of the paper men, Jefferson places a table showing the composition of Congress at that time:

	H.-REPR.	SENATE
Stockholders (Bank)	16	5
Other paper	3	2
	19	7
Suspected	2	4

It is not apparent how Jefferson secured this information, but it would seem from the foot-notes which he adds that he derived it from personal inquiry and through the inquiries of his friends. Whether he had access to the Treasury and Bank books through a clerk or a partisan is a matter for conjecture.[1]

Jefferson was not alone in characterizing the Federalist party in Congress as a group held together by private economic interests. All through Maclay's querulous sketches of the debates in the first Senate there runs a plaint that some of his colleagues were busily engrossed in augmenting their personal fortunes as the prices of securities mounted upward during the battle over the funding process. Maclay even went so far as to say that the whole funding scheme was simply a speculator's device. "Pay the debt," he declared, "or even put it in a train of payment, and you no longer furnish food for speculation. The great object is by funding, and so forth, to raise the certificates to par; thus the speculators, who now have them nearly all engrossed, will clear above three hundred per cent."[2] Maclay not only charged many of his colleagues with speculation, but denounced the

[1] *Writings* (Ford ed.), Vol. I, p. 223.   [2] Maclay, *op. cit.*, p. 171.

whole funding process as a gambler's device. He reported rumors to the effect that Vining of Delaware was offered a thousand guineas for his vote in favor of the assumption of state debts; but he confessed that he did not know whether pecuniary influence was actually used although he was "certain that every other kind of management has been practiced and every tool at work that could be thought of." [1]

Madison also discovered the weight of personal interest in the Congress when he sought to bring about a discrimination between the original holders of public paper and the speculators and purchasers, and was defeated by a vote of thirteen to thirty-six. [2] Writing a year later to Jefferson, he described the subscriptions to the Bank as nothing but a scramble for public plunder and added that "of all the shameful circumstances of this business, it is among the greatest to see the members of the Legislature who were most active in pushing this job openly grasping its emoluments."

Long afterward, in the calm evening of his life, Jefferson reduced to order some notes which he had made at the time on the funding process and prepared a systematic account of the affair and his part in them. [3] This account runs as follows: "Hamilton's financial system . . . had two objects; 1st, as a puzzle, to exclude popular understanding and inquiry; 2d, as a machine for the corruption of the legislature; for he avowed the opinion, that man could be governed by one of two motives only, force or interest; force, he observed, in this country, was out of the question, and the interests, therefore, of the members must be laid hold of, to keep the legislative in unison with the executive. And with grief and

---

[1] Maclay, op. cit., p. 209.   [2] Above, p. 146.

[3] "At this day, after the lapse of twenty-five years or more from their dates, I have given the whole a calm revisal, when the passions of the times are passed away and the reasons of the transactions alone act upon the judgment." The Anas in Works (Washington ed.), Vol. IX, p. 87.

shame it must be acknowledged that his machine was not without effect; that even in this, the birth of our government, some members were found sordid enough to bend their duty to their interests, and to look after personal rather than public good.

"It is well known that during the war the greatest difficulty we encountered was the want of money or means to pay our soldiers who fought, or our farmers, manufacturers, and merchants who furnished the necessary supplies of food and clothing for them. After the expedient of paper money had exhausted itself, certificates of debt were given to individual creditors, with assurance of payment so soon as the United States should be able. But the distresses of these people often obliged them to part with these for the half, the fifth, or even a tenth of their value; and speculators had made a trade of cozening them from the holders by the most fraudulent practices, and persuasions that they never would be paid. In the bill for funding and paying these, Hamilton made no difference between the original holders and the fraudulent purchasers of this paper. Great and just repugnance arose at putting these two classes of creditors on the same footing, and great exertions were used to pay the former the full value, and to the latter, the price only which they had paid, with interest. But this would have prevented the game which was to be played, and for which the minds of greedy members were already tutored and prepared. When the trial of strength on these several efforts had indicated the form in which the bill would finally pass, this being known within doors sooner than without, and especially, than to those who were in distant parts of the union, the base scramble began. Couriers and relay horses by land, and swift sailing pilot boats by sea, were flying in all directions. Active partners and agents were associated and employed in every state, town, and country neighborhood, and this paper was bought up at five shillings, and even as low as two shillings in the pound, before the holder knew that Congress had already provided for its redemption at par. Immense sums were thus filched from the poor and ignorant, and fortunes accumulated by those who had themselves been poor enough before. Men thus enriched by the dexterity of a leader, would follow, of course, the chief who was leading them to fortune, and become the zealous instruments of all his enterprises.

"This game was over,[1] and another was on the carpet at the moment of my arrival ; and to this I was most ignorantly and innocently made to hold the candle. This fiscal manœuvre is well known by the name of the assumption. Independently of the debts of Congress, the States had during the War contracted separate and heavy debts ; and Massachusetts particularly, in an absurd attempt, absurdly conducted, on the British post of Penobscott ; and the more debt Hamilton could rake up, the more plunder for his mercenaries. This money, whether wisely or foolishly spent, was pretended to have been spent for general purposes, and ought, therefore, to be paid from the general purse. But it was objected, that nobody knew what these debts were, what their amount or what their proofs. No matter, we will guess them to be twenty millions. But of these twenty millions, we do not know how much should be reimbursed to one state, or how much to another. No matter ; we will guess. And so another scramble was set on foot among the several states and some got much, some little, some nothing. But the main object was obtained, the phalanx of the Treasury was reinforced by additional re-

---

[1] Jefferson must here refer to the defeat of Madison's proposal for a discrimina-tion. See above, p. 146.

cruits. This measure produced the most bitter and angry contest ever known in Congress, before or since the union of the states. I arrived in the midst of it. But a stranger to the ground, a stranger to the actors in it, so long absent as to have lost all familiarity with the subject, and as yet unaware of its object, I took no concern in it. The great and trying question, however, was lost in the House of Representatives. So high were the feuds excited by this subject, that on its rejection business was suspended. Congress met and adjourned from day to day without doing anything, the parties being too much out of temper to do business together. The eastern members particularly, who, with Smith from South Carolina, were the principal gamblers in these scenes, threatened a secession and a dissolution. Hamilton was in despair. As I was going to the President's one day, I met him in the street. He walked me backwards and forwards before the President's door for half an hour. He painted pathetically the temper into which the legislature had been wrought; the disgust of those who were called the creditor states; the danger of the *secession* of their members, and the separation of the states. He observed that the members of the administration ought to act in concert; that although this question was not of my department, yet a common duty should make it a common concern; that the President was the centre on which all administrative questions ultimately rested, and that all of us should rally around him, and support, with joint efforts, measures approved by him; and that the question having been lost by a small majority only, it was probable that an appeal from me to the judgment and discretion of some of my friends, might effect a change in the vote, and the machine of government, now suspended, might be again set into motion. I told him that I was really a stranger to the whole subject; that not having yet informed myself of the system of finances adopted, I knew not how far this was a necessary sequence; that undoubtedly, if its rejection endangered a dissolution of our Union at this incipient stage, I should deem that the most unfortunate of all consequences, to avert which all partial and temporary evils should be yielded. I proposed to him, however, to dine with me the next day, and I would invite another friend or two, bring them into conference together, and I thought it impossible that reasonable men, consulting together coolly, could fail, by some mutual sacrifices of opinion, to form a compromise which was to save the Union. The discussion took place. I could take no part in it but an exhortatory one, because I was a stranger to the circumstances which should govern it. But it was finally agreed that whatever importance had been attached to the rejection of this proposition, the preservation of the Union and of concord among the states was more important, and that therefore it would be better that the vote of rejection should be rescinded, to effect which, some members should change their votes. But it was observed that this pill would be particularly bitter to the southern states, and that some concomitant measure should be adopted to sweeten it a little to them. There had been before propositions to fix the seat of government either at Philadelphia or at Georgetown on the Potomac; and it was thought that by giving it to Philadelphia for ten years and to Georgetown permanently afterwards, this might, as an anodyne, calm in some degree the ferment which might be excited by the other measure alone. So two of the Potomac members (White and Lee, but White with a revulsion of stomach almost convulsive) agreed to change their votes, and Hamilton undertook to carry the other point. In doing this, the influence he had established over the eastern members, with the agency of Robert Morris with those of the middle states, effected his side of the engagement; and so the Assumption was passed, and twenty millions of stock divided among favored states and thrown in as a pabulum to the stock-jobbing herd. This added to the number of votaries to the Treasury, and made its chief the master of every vote in the legislature, which might give to the government the direction suited to his political views.

"I know well, and so must be understood, that nothing like a majority in Congress had yielded to this corruption. Far from it. But a division, not very unequal, had already taken place in the honest part of that body, between the parties styled republican and federal. The latter being monarchists in principle, adhered to Hamilton of course, as their leader in that principle, and this mercenary phalanx added to them, insured him always a majority in both Houses : so that the whole action of the legislature was now under the direction of the Treasury. Still the machine was not complete. The effect of the funding system, and of the Assumption, would be temporary ; it would be lost with the loss of the individual members whom it has enriched, and some engine of influence more permanent must be contrived, while these myrmidons were yet in place to carry it through all opposition. This engine was the Bank of the United States. All that history is known, so I shall say nothing about it. While the government remained at Philadelphia, a selection of members of both houses were constantly kept as directors who, on every question interesting to that institution, or to the views of the federal head, voted at the will of that head ; and, together with the stock-holding members, could always make the federal vote that of the majority. By this combination, legislative expositions were given to the Constitution, and all the administrative laws were shaped on the model of England and so passed." [1]

Although this full account of the affair was not written until long after the events related, it must not be thought that Jefferson kept his opinion concerning the methods of the funding group to himself during the transaction. On the contrary he was at great pains to impress his view upon the President. "I said [to Washington]," wrote Jefferson, in 1792, "that the two great complaints were, that the national debt was unnecessarily increased, and that it had furnished the means of corrupting both branches of the legislature; that he must know and everybody knew, there was a considerable squadron in both, whose votes were devoted to the paper and stock jobbing interest, that the names of a weighty number were known, and several others suspected on good grounds. That on examining the votes of these men, they would be found uniformly for every Treasury measure and that as most of these measures had been carried by small majorities, they were carried by these very votes. That, therefore, it was a cause of just uneasiness when we saw a legislature legislating for their own interests, in opposition of those of the people. He said not a word on the corruption of the legislature, but took up the other point, defended the Assumption, and argued that it had not increased the debt, for that all of it was honest debt." [2]

At a later date, Jefferson again brought up the matter in a private conversation with President Washington and of this conference, he wrote: "I confirmed him [Washington] in the fact of the great discontents to the South, that they were grounded on seeing that their judgments and interests

---

[1] *Works* (Washington ed.), Vol. IX, pp. 91 ff.
[2] Jefferson, *Works* (Washington ed.), Vol. IX, p. 117.

were sacrificed to those of the Eastern states on every occn. and their belief that it was the effect of a corrupt squadron of voters in Congress at the command of the Treasury, and they see that if the votes of those members who had an interest distinct from and contrary to the general interest of their constts. had been withdrawn, as in decency and honesty they should have been, the laws would have been the reverse of what they are in all the great questions." [1]

From Jefferson's day to this, students of history have wondered how much credence should be given to the rumors of Maclay and the allegations of Jefferson and his partisans concerning the "paper men." [2] Writers have given weight to them or discounted them according to their predilections, but no one seems to have taken the trouble to attempt a verification or refutation of them from the records of the Treasury Department, where, for nearly a hundred years, the books of the early fiscal administration have lain covered with accumulating dust.

As every one knows, under the funding system set up by the new government, nearly all holders of old paper brought their securities to the Treasury or to the loan offices of their respective states to be transformed into new certificates of

---

[1] *Writings* (Ford ed.), Vol. I, p. 215.

[2] Although the critics of the Federalist administration usually refrained from bringing charges of personal interest against Washington himself, the boldest of them seem to have hazarded the suggestion that the President himself was not above the private operations with which members of the legislature were all too commonly associated. Jonathan Dayton, whose speculations in lands and securities were notorious throughout the country, in a letter of September 15, 1796, to Oliver Wolcott, Secretary of the Treasury, urging him to make speedy provision for the survey and location of lands selected for military donations according to an act of Congress passed at the preceding session, observed concerning the critics of the government: "I hear some of them remark with pain, that the President and members have lands of their own to sell, or they would not be so neglectful in providing for the location of the military warrants, which then might come in competition with them. The fact as to many of us holding such lands being undeniable, the imputation becomes from that circumstance more plausible, and enforces the necessity on the part of our government to defeat, as soon as possible, the charge of neglect." Gibbs, *op. cit.*, Vol. I, p. 384.

indebtedness. If the Treasury records at Washington were complete (unfortunately they are not) it would be possible to discover the names of all those who funded public securities under the law of August 4, 1790, except perhaps those represented by attorneys.

The incompleteness of the records makes it impossible, however, to discover positively what members of Congress did *not* have securities; but the mass of material which remains enables us to find a large number who did hold public paper at the time of the funding of the debt. The exact number cannot be ascertained; but the evidence concerning those who did hold securities is indisputable, unless we are to assume that the members of Congress who appear on the ledgers were attorneys for other parties.

The method of search by which the data below were secured was as follows. The names of all the Senators and Representatives of the first Congress were taken in alphabetical order and a search for each name was made among all the old books in the Treasury Department. When the search was finished, the names of all security holders were starred. *Not until this was done was an inquiry made into the way in which the several members voted on Hamilton's fiscal measures.* Thus an attempt was made to eliminate all bias which might have led to oversights in particular cases. When a member of Congress is put down as *not* holding securities, it is to be understood, therefore, that this may be an error due to the incompleteness of the records or to an oversight by the present writer.

That the percentage of error is not high, however, seems to be probable, in view of the geographical distribution of the members not holding securities. They appear principally from the South, where, it can be shown from the Treasury Books, the amount of public securities in the hands of residents was far smaller than in the Northern and Eastern states.

The amount held by each member who appears on the books is not set down here and the assumption is not made that all security holders in Congress were at the same time speculators. A number of them, particularly the Senators, were vigorous speculators, but that is not the point. The question at issue is the number of members of Congress who were "disinterested" parties in the contest over the fiscal measures of the new government.

The proposition to assume the state debts was taken up in the House of Representatives in February, 1790, immediately after the defeat of Madison's scheme for discriminating between original holders and purchasers.[1] In March, it was carried in the committee of the whole house. Maclay thus records the event: "Officers of Government, clergy, citizens, (Order of) Cincinnati, and every person under the influence of the Treasury; Bland and Huger carried to the chamber of Representatives — the one lame, the other sick; Clymer stopped from going away, though he had leave, and at length they risked the question, and carried it, thirty-one votes to twenty-six. And all this after having tampered with the members since the 22d of last month (February), and this only in committee, with many doubts that some will fly off and great fears that the North Carolina members will be in before a bill can be matured or the report gone through."[2]

As Maclay predicted, the North Carolina members shortly afterward put in their appearance. On April 12 the assumption plan was defeated in the House by a vote of thirty-one to twenty-nine. Maclay was in great glee over the outcome of the struggle, and he recites how Fitzsimons "endeavored

---

[1] *Annals of Congress*, Vol. II, p. 1355.　　　　　　　[2] *Op. cit.*, p. 176.

to rally the discomfited and disheartened heroes" and expressed the belief that reconsideration and adoption were not yet out of the question. At this, says the Pennsylvania Senator, "the Secretary's group pricked up their ears and Speculation wiped the tear from either eye. Goddess of description, paint the gallery; here's the paper, find fancy quills, or crayons yourself." [1]

Those whose tears were wiped away set to work to bring over enough Southern representatives to carry the assumption measure, in spite of the gloomy outlook. The way in which the "innocent" Jefferson was undone by the "wily" Hamilton and unwittingly used to bring about the exchange of the capital for the assumption of state debts, on July 7, is told in the account by the former cited above.[2] Jefferson informs us that "two of the Potomac members (White and Lee, but White with a revulsion of stomach almost convulsive) agreed to change their votes and Hamilton undertook to carry the other point." Daniel Carroll, a large property holder in the region where the new capital was to be located, also considerately changed his vote. Thus the bargain

---

[1] *Op. cit.*, p. 194. The reporter of the debates over the public credit notes that "the galleries were unusually crowded" on January 28, 1790, and doubtless there was a crowd on April 12. A gentleman in New York in a letter to a friend in Virginia, dated April 14, 1790, gave the following humorous description of the defeat of assumption: "Last Monday Mr. Sedgwick delivered a funeral oration on the death of Miss Assumption. . . . Her death was much lamented by her parents who were from New England. Mr. Sedgwick being the most celebrated preacher was requested to deliver her funeral eulogium. It was done with puritanic gravity. . . . Sixty-one of the political fathers of the nation were present and a crowded audience of weepers and rejoicers. Mrs. Speculator was the chief mourner, and acted her part to admiration: she being mother of Miss Assumption who was the hope of her family, the picture of herself, and her youngest child. Twenty-nine of the political fathers cried aloud — Thirty-one bore the loss with fortitude, being in full hope of a glorious resurrection. . . . Mrs. Excise may have cause to rejoice, because she will be screened from much drudgery — as she must have been the principal support of Miss Assumption, as well as of her mother and all her relations. Mrs. Direct Tax may rest more easy in Virginia as she will not be called into foreign service." Gazette of the United States, June 2, 1790.

[2] Above, p. 168.

whereby the capital was to be built on the Potomac and the debts of the states were assumed by the federal government was brought to a conclusion at a private dinner given by Jefferson. The funding bill with the assumption amendment was carried in the Senate on July 21, where the Treasury had its most dependable vote.[1] Three days later the motion of Jackson, of Georgia, to disagree with the Senate amendment, was defeated by a vote of thirty-two to twenty-nine.[2] It is this vote which is analyzed below.

The vote on the bill as passed by the Senate,[3] in its amended form, on July 21 was as follows:

Yeas: Langdon, New Hampshire
Strong and Dalton, Massachusetts
Ellsworth and Johnson, Connecticut
King and Schuyler, New York
Paterson and Elmer, New Jersey
Read, Delaware
Morris, Pennsylvania
Carroll, Maryland
Butler and Izard, South Carolina [14]

Nays: Wingate, New Hampshire
Foster and Stanton, Rhode Island
Bassett, Delaware
Maclay, Pennsylvania
Henry, Maryland
Johnston and Hawkins, North Carolina
Lee and Walker, Virginia
Few and Gunn, Georgia [12]

Of the fourteen Senators who voted in favor of the funding bill, with the assumption amendment, on July 21, 1790, at least ten, Langdon, Strong, Ellsworth, Johnson, King, Schuyler, Read, Morris, Charles Carroll, and Izard, appear upon the Treasury records as holders of public securities at the time of the funding process.[4] To this list Pierce

[1] *Annals of Congress*, Vol. I, p. 1055.   [2] *Ibid.*, Vol. II, p. 1753.
[3] *Ibid.*, Vol. I, pp. 1054–1055.
[4] For the holdings of Langdon, Strong, Ellsworth, King, Johnson, Schuyler, Read, Morris, and Carroll, see Beard, *Economic Interpretation of the Constitution*,

Butler doubtless should be added.[1] Those not found on the records are Dalton, of Massachusetts, and Elmer and Paterson, of New Jersey.[2]

Of the twelve who voted against the funding bill on July 21, 1790, at least five, Maclay, Bassett, Johnston, Few, and R. H. Lee, were holders of public debt, but the holdings of Maclay, Bassett, and Few were trivial in amount.[3] The names of seven Senators who voted against funding, Wingate, Stanton, Foster, Henry, Hawkins, Walker, and Gunn, were not found on the Treasury records.

A table built upon this data would run as follows :

	Security holders	Non-holders
For the funding bill	11	3
Against the bill	5	7
Total, 26	16	10

A study of the Treasury records shows that the Senators who held securities and voted for the funding bill were, with one or two exceptions, among the large holders of public paper, and that the Senators of the same class who voted against the bill (with the possible exception of Johnston of North Carolina) were among the minor holders.

Even a superficial examination of the vote in the Senate is interesting in view of the party divisions which soon ensued. The "Eastern" states were almost solid for the bill. New Hampshire was divided ; but Massachusetts, Connecticut,

Chap. V.; for Izard, see "Loan Office : S. C., 1790," p. 17. Ellsworth moved assumption in the Senate saying that "the influence of every class of creditors should be united." *Paterson Papers*, Bancroft Mss., New York Public Library.

[1] *Economic Interpretation*, p. 82. After the publication of this work I found Pierce Butler's name on the "Index to the Registered Debt," which I believe was the debt at the Treasury itself, the records of which are largely missing.

[2] The name of William Paterson appears on the New Jersey records for a small amount, but it is not possible to identify this security holder with the Senator.

[3] For Few and Bassett, see *Economic Interpretation*, Chap. V.; R. H. Lee, "Virginia : Index to Loans" ; Maclay, "Loan Office : Penna., 1790-1791," pp. 117, 118; Johnston, "Loan Office : N.C., 1791-1797," pp. 1, 40.

New York, and New Jersey were unanimous. The financial centres of Portsmouth, Boston, Hartford, New York, Philadelphia, and Charleston were correctly represented.

Equally significant is the vote against the bill. Seven of the twelve votes in opposition came from Southern states. Virginia, North Carolina, and Georgia were solid against it. These were the states (particularly Georgia and North Carolina) in which the debt had been so largely bought up by speculators.[1] Only one of the votes against the bill came from north of Pennsylvania: Wingate of New Hampshire refused to join his colleague, Langdon, in support of the measure.

The vote in the House of Representatives, on July 24, on the proposition to disagree with the Senate amendment to the funding bill providing for the assumption of state debts stood twenty-nine to thirty-two. A study of this vote in the light of the Treasury records is informing and it seems best to take members up *seriatim*, beginning with New Hampshire.

The delegation of *New Hampshire* was divided on assumption. Nicholas Gilman and Samuel Livermore were against it, and Foster (of Rockingham county) voted in favor of it. As measured by the interest disbursements in 1795,[2] New Hampshire stood tenth in the amount of federal securities held by her citizens, and there was a strong opposition to assumption in that commonwealth. Livermore, in voting against it, said that he would only approve the proposition in case it was agreed merely "to assume the balances found to be due to the creditor States, upon the final adjustment and liquidation of the accounts between the United States and the individual States."[3]   Of the three New Hampshire

[1] See below, pp. 191, 193.
[2] *An Account of the Receipts and Expenditures of the United States for the Year 1795*, p. 65.   [3] *Annals of Congress*, Vol. II, p. 1412.

Representatives, one, Nicholas Gilman,[1] was found among the holders of public paper, and he voted against assumption.

The eight Representatives of *Massachusetts* in the House voted solidly in favor of assumption. Of these, Ames, Gerry, Grout, Leonard, Partridge, and Sedgwick, at least six, appear as security holders on the loan office books of Massachusetts.[2] As measured in the interest disbursements of 1795, that state stood second in the amount of securities held by her citizens, and the weight of the state debt which was transferred to the federal government was so great that Massachusetts taxpayers, as well as security holders, felt a great relief when the burden was shifted. Mr. Sedgwick doubtless expressed the sentiments of all his colleagues when he said, on February 24, that assumption "will terminate in the suppression of direct taxes; it will abolish invidious distinctions between States and their citizens; it will fix the value of State securities, and bring them into operation as a circulating medium."[3]

Connecticut cast her five votes solidly in favor of assumption. Of her five members in the House, at least four, Sherman, Sturges, Trumbull, and Wadsworth, appear among the holders of public securities on the loan office books

[1] Beard, *Economic Interpretation*, p. 93.

[2] Consult indexes to the 6 per cent deferred stock and the 3 per cent stocks in Massachusetts collection in the Treasury Department; for Gerry, see *Economic Interpretation*, p. 95.

[3] *Annals of Congress*, Vol. II, p. 1386. Fisher Ames was anxious to relieve Massachusetts. On January 13, 1790, he wrote: "I think the assumption will be a serious article of our business in Congress. I wish, from our state, co-operation, not resistance. Our people pay great taxes. In this [New York] and every other state, they are more moderate. They have not raised twenty-five thousand pounds in this state these three years. Their dry taxes are very trifling. Why should our industrious people be crushed, to pay taxes to maintain state credit, and without maintaining it, too, when the United States by excises, &c. equally imposed, can do it effectually? Will they love their fetters so well as to contend against the hand that would set them at liberty?" *The Life and Works of Fisher Ames*, Vol. I, p. 72.

of Connecticut.[1] That state, though reckoned among the smaller commonwealths, stood fifth in the amount of securities held by her citizens, as measured by the interest disbursements of 1795. Not only was the amount of the state debt considerable; but it was widely distributed among the various towns. This fact is proved by the records in the Treasury Department.[2] Moreover, Sherman confirms this, for during the debates in the House on March 1, he said: "The circulation of the revenue would be very agreeable to the greater proportion of the inhabitants; because the evidences of the State debts were generally in the hands of the original holders. He had made particular inquiry into this circumstance, and so far as it respected Connecticut, he was led to believe it was true of nineteen-twentieths. There were one hundred thousand dollars in specie in the hands of the original holders in the very town in which he lived. He believed very little besides the army debt had been transferred in that State; and even of the army debt, it was only that portion which fell into the hands of the soldiers." [3]

New York was evenly divided on assumption. Benson and Lawrence, who "ably represented the southern districts of New York," [4] voted in favor of the proposition, and to their votes was added the vote of an up-state Representative, Peter Sylvester. Of the three, Lawrence was a security holder, and among the large operators in public stocks in New York.[5] He was also deeply interested in the first United States Bank and was on the first board of directors.[6]

---

[1] Consult Indexes to the Loan Office Books of Connecticut in the Treasury Department. For Sherman, see *Economic Interpretation*, p. 143.

[2] See map in *Economic Interpretation*, p. 265.

[3] *Annals of Congress*, Vol. II, pp. 1440–1441.

[4] Hildreth, *History of the United States* (Second Series), Vol. I, p. 43.

[5] New York Loan Office Books in the Treasury Department, and *State Papers: Finance*, Vol. I, p. 165.

[6] Dunlap's Daily Advertiser, October 22, 1791.

Jefferson records Benson in his list of paper men on hearsay,[1] but an examination of the records in the Treasury Department failed to reveal his name. Sylvester does not seem to have been interested in public paper on his own account. Of the three New York Representatives who voted against assumption, two, Floyd and Hathorn, were not found among the security holders; but Van Rensselaer appears on the New York loan office records.[2]

New Jersey had four Representatives in the House and all of them voted in favor of assumption. Of this group, at least three, Boudinot, Schureman, and Sinnickson, were security holders.[3] Boudinot seems to have been the spokesman of the New Jersey delegation, but he did not participate extensively in the debate on assumption. He was warmly moved by Madison's proposition to discriminate between original holders and speculators and pleaded with his fellow-members to come to the support of the public credit in the following passionate strain: "Humanity, as well as justice, makes this demand upon you; the complaints of ruined widows, and the cries of fatherless children, whose whole support has been placed in your hands, and melted away, have doubtless reached you. Rouse, therefore; strive who shall do most for his country; rekindle that flame of patriotism which, at the mention of disgrace and slavery, blazed throughout America, and animated all her citizens."[4]

The single vote of *Delaware* is recorded in favor of assumption; but Representative Vining does not seem to have been a security holder and citizens of that state held only a

---

[1] *Writings* (Ford ed.), Vol. I, p. 223, note 1.
[2] "Loan Office: New York, Ledger" (no. 32), fol. 104.
[3] For Boudinot, see "Penna. Loan Office, 6% Stock, Ledger A," fol. 24, and Jefferson, *Writings* (Ford ed.), Vol. I, p. 223. For Schureman, "N. J. Loan Office, 3% Stock, Ledger C," fols. 84, 122; for Sinnickson, *ibid.*, fol. 91; Rebecca Cadwalader appears on *ibid.*, fols. 83, 127.
[4] *Annals of Congress*, Vol. I, p. 1176.

small amount of paper from the local loan office. Maclay records, as we have seen, among his rumors a statement to the effect that Senator Butler heard a man say that he would give Vining one thousand guineas for his vote on assumption, but such rumors, unsubstantiated by other evidence, deserve little or no credence.[1]

Three members of the House from *Pennsylvania*, George Clymer, Thomas Fitzsimons, and Henry Wynkoop, voted in favor of assumption, and the first two were among the largest speculators and operators in securities in Philadelphia.[2] Wynkoop was not found among the security holders, and he seems to have hesitated awhile before casting his vote with the Philadelphia members. Maclay records, April 1, 1790 : "I took an opportunity of speaking to Mr. Wynkoop. I was pointing out some inconveniences of the assumption. I found he seemed much embarrassed. Lawrence and Benson[3] had got him away from his usual seat to near where they commonly sat. He paused a little; got up rather hastily; said, 'God bless you!' went out of the chamber, and actually took his wife and proceeded home to Philadelphia."[4] He returned in time however to cast his vote with Benson and Lawrence for assumption.

Four Pennsylvania Representatives voted against assumption, Hartley, Heister, Peter Muhlenberg, and Thomas Scott — the last being "from the settlements beyond the Alleghanies." Of this group, Daniel Heister appears to be the only security holder on the books.[5]

The manager of the Pennsylvania delegation in the House

[1] The collection of the Delaware Loan Office in the Treasury is meagre indeed. Maclay, *Sketches*, p. 176 (date of March 9, 1790). Vining married the daughter of Seton, Hamilton's public and private agent in New York.

[2] *Economic Interpretation*, pp. 83, 91.

[3] See above, p. 183.

[4] *Journal*, p. 228.

[5] "Index to Pa. Loan Office Books, Loan of 1790."

was Robert Morris, then in the Senate.[1] In that remarkable group of pen pictures of the negotiations over the funding of the debt drawn for us by Maclay we find always in the foreground the portly figure of this distinguished Senator, the mighty speculator and manipulator. Maclay records that on June 9, 1790, Morris "blazed away for six per cent on the nominal amount of all public securities. Ellsworth answered want of ability. Mr. Morris made nothing of the whole of it. The broadside of American was able enough for it all. We had property enough, and he was for a land tax; and if a land tax were laid, there would be money enough."[2] When the committee of the Senate reported in favor of a rate of only four per cent on the debt, "Mr. Morris rose against the report. His choler fairly choked him. He apologized to the House that his agitation had deprived him of his recollection on the subject, and he sat down. He rose again some little time before the Senate adjourned; mentioned his late confusion, but declared it did not arise from the personal interest he had in public securities; that although he was possessed of some, he was no speculator, &c., &c."[3]

[1] "We hear no more about the injustice of the assumption. . . . This looks like coming over. Besides, consequences are feared. The New England states demand it as a debt of justice, with a tone so loud and threatening, that they fear the convulsions which would probably ensue. Further, they are going to fix the residence permanently on the Potomac, and by the apostacy of Pennsylvania will do it, removing, however, immediately to Philadelphia, and staying there ten years. Two such injuries would be too much. They dare not, I trust, carry Congress so far South and leave the debts upon us. R. Morris, too, is really warm for the assumption, and as he is the *factotum* in the business, he will not fail to insist upon the original friends of it, and who have ever been a majority, voting for it. With five Pennsylvanians, our former aid from that delegation, we can carry it, or at least obtain four-fifths of the debts to be assumed. Accordingly they begin to say, these violent feuds must be composed; too much is hazarded to break up in this temper. Maryland is the most alarmed as well as, next to Virginia, most anxious for the Potomac. I am beginning to be sanguine in the hope of success." *Life and Works of Fisher Ames*, Vol. I, p. 84 (June 27, 1790).

[2] Maclay, *Sketches*, p. 222; Maclay's statement is corroborated by Paterson, *Paterson Papers* (Bancroft Transcripts, New York Public Library), p. 409.

[3] *Ibid.*, p. 228.

Notwithstanding this discomfiture, it seems that Morris continued to fight valiantly for funding the whole debt at the rate of six per cent interest. According to Maclay, Morris, on July 13, "said openly, before the Senate was formed, *I am for a six per cent fund on the whole; and if gentlemen will not vote for that, I will vote against the assumption.* I thought him only in sport then. But he three times in Senate, openly avowed the same thing, declaring he was, in judgment, for the assumption; but if gentlemen would not vote for six per cent, he would vote against the assumption and the whole funding bill. . . . Izard got up and attacked him with asperity." [1] It was apparently only with great difficulty that Morris could bring himself to accept the funding bill on any other basis, but he yielded at length on July 20. Of his surrender, Maclay says: "Mr. Morris having often threatened that he would vote against the bill, at last made this remarkable speech: *Half a loaf is better than no bread. I will consent to the bill on behalf of the public creditors, for whom I am interested* (I looked up at him, and he added), *as well as for the rest of the Union.* This last shed some palliation over his expressions." [2]

[1] Maclay, *Sketches*, p. 247.

[2] *Ibid.*, p. 256; see also Paterson's notes on the debates in the Senate, Bancroft Transcripts, New York Public Library. Morris was personally interested in every important economic operation of the Federal government. He was a large security holder; he was a large holder of Bank stock; and he engaged vigorously in speculation in Washington lots when the location of the capitol was decided upon. The following letter gives some idea of his Washington interests, but unhappily for him they did not turn out so well as he expected: "Our interest there [Washington, D.C.] is a deep and promising affair. We have lately sold 500 lotts for five pence currency per square foot, each lot 5265 feet, and for ready money which we have received, and further we have just concluded another sale to the amount of £20,000 Cy at the same price . . . and we are in treaty for lotts to the amount of £40,000 more, which I think, will succeed at 6*d.* or 7*d.* per square foot. Single lotts sell at 8*d.*, 9*d.*, 10*d.*, and 12*d.* per foot according to circumstances and position so that you see we shall wind up well, especially as the purchasers are obliged to build a house on every third lott." *Private Letter Book*, Vol. I, p. 89. Letter to Willink, March 16, 1795. From 1790 until his failure, Morris had large financial connections with members of Congress and prominent politicians all over the

As we move southward we find the opposition to assumption and the funding system steadily increasing (if we except South Carolina, where the security operations were considerable, particularly among the Charleston Federalists). The *Maryland* delegation was seriously divided. Only two Representatives from that state voted in favor of assumption when the test vote was taken on July 24 — Daniel Carroll and George Gale, both of whom were security holders.[1] Carroll voted against assumption at first, but was induced to change his view during the negotiations over the location of the capital.[2] He was of the inner circle which traded assumption for the capital; he was somewhat interested in public paper; and he had the satisfaction of helping to engineer the laying out of the city of Washington in such a manner as to give an immense appreciation to the value of his farm lands in the vicinity.[3]

Of the four Maryland Representatives who voted against assumption, Stone and William Smith appear

United States. He owed Lambert Cadwalader's sister money and Cadwalader carried on the negotiations (*Private Letter Book*, Mss. in the Library of Congress, Vol. I, pp. 172, 773). Morris tried to get Tristram Dalton, Senator, of Massachusetts to go his security on two notes of $16,000 and $17,000 (*ibid.*, Vol. II, p. 134). Philemon Dickinson, of New Jersey, tried to sell lands to Morris but the latter was not able to buy at the time (*ibid.*, Vol. I, p. 67). John Drayton, of Charleston, tried to sell land to Morris (*ibid.*, Vol. I, p. 302). Morris was engaged in land negotiations with Thomas Hartley, a Representative from Pennsylvania (*ibid.*, Vol. I, p. 459). Morris was engaged in extensive operations with Thomas Fitzsimons, member of the Convention and of the House of Representatives (see indexes to *Private Letter Books*). Morris had 165 shares of Columbia Bank stock (*ibid.*, Vol. I, p. 49). He also had one block of 330 shares of United States Bank stock (*ibid.*, Vol. I, p. 57). Gouverneur Morris, diplomatic representative of the United States at Paris, carried on European operations for Robert Morris (*ibid.*, Vol. I, p. 15). Robert Morris had considerable business dealings with Richard Bland Lee (*ibid.*, Vol. I, pp. 31, 59). Morris bought and sold bank stock for John Marshall, of Virginia (*ibid.*, indexes under John Marshall). Marshall's brother, James, married Morris' daughter. Wade Hampton, of South Carolina, had connections with Morris (*ibid.*, Vol. I, p. 95.)

[1] *Economic Interpretation*, p. 82; "Alphabet Dividend Book" in the Loan Office records of Maryland in the Treasury Department.

[2] Jefferson, *Writings* (Ford ed.), Vol. I, p. 164, note 1.

[3] H. Crew, *History of Washington*, p. 168.

among the security holders,[1] but Seney and Contee were not found.

The weight of the *Virginia* delegation in Congress was thrown against assumption from the beginning of the contest, and apparently the vote would have been solid against it at the end had it not been for the famous bargain whereby Alexander White and Richard Bland Lee changed their votes and bought the capital at the cost of assumption.[2] The "Index to the Virginia Loans," preserved in the Treasury Department, shows only John Brown of Richmond among the security holders, and Brown was among the seven Virginia Representatives who voted against assumption. The two members who at last gave their reluctant consent to the scheme do not seem to have been holders of public paper.

As measured by interest disbursements in 1795 Virginia, in proportion to her population, stood surprisingly low in the amount of securities held by her citizens. Massachusetts citizens received from the federal government in that year $309,500 and Virginia citizens received only $62,300. In fact, Massachusetts, Connecticut, New York, Pennsylvania, Maryland, and South Carolina stood above Virginia in the list. The "Loan Office: Register of Subscriptions" (for 1791) now in the Treasury Department shows that of the total £500,307 15s. 10d. worth of Virginia certificates presented for funding only a small amount was in the hands of the original holders. The major portion had been bought up by brokers and speculators in Virginia towns and in Baltimore, New York, Philadelphia, and other financial centres. Among the larger operators in Virginia paper were Thomas Willing (the partner and agent for Robert

---

[1] "Alphabet Dividend Book," as above cited.

[2] Jefferson, *Writings* (Ford ed.), Vol. I, p. 164. Theodorick Bland, of the Virginia delegation, died before the final vote.

Morris and first president of the first United States Bank) and LeRoy and Bayard of New York City. This large folio volume would repay detailed examination by any one attempting to penetrate into the origins of high finance in the United States.

The entire delegation from *North Carolina* in the House of Representatives voted against assumption. Maclay informs us that on March 26 the Pennsylvania group had induced Williamson and Ashe from North Carolina to change their minds,[1] but for one reason or another they reverted to their first view. Of the five members from that state on record against assumption, only one, Williamson, seems to be entered among the security holders.[2] It would appear that he was inclined to support assumption, but yielded to the great pressure of his constituents and colleagues.

North Carolina stood third from the bottom of the list in the amount of securities held by her citizens, as measured by the interest disbursements of 1795 ($3200). The books of the North Carolina loan office preserved in the Treasury Department explain how this result had been brought about. Speculators from Northern cities appear on nearly every page of the ledgers as purchasers of the certificates from original holders. Thus it happened that North Carolina paper was not only taken out of the hands of widely scattered holders, who might otherwise have given their weight to the funding system, but it was concentrated in the hands of brokers in cities in other states.[3]

In fact, it was the action of Northern brokers (particularly from New York City) in buying up the securities of North Carolina, as well as those of Georgia and South Carolina,

[1] *Journal*, p. 224.
[2] *Economic Interpretation*, p. 146.
[3] See particularly the "Journal of Assumed Debt." Richard Platt, of New York, for example, had $192,723.14 worth.

which made many Southern opponents of assumption so
bitter in their denunciation of Hamilton's proposals. Very
early in the debate on the report of the Secretary of the
Treasury, Mr. Jackson, of Georgia, exclaimed with evident
feeling: "Since this report has been read in this House, a
spirit of havoc, speculation, and ruin, has arisen, and been
cherished by people who had an access to the information
the report contained, that would have made a Hastings
blush to have been connected with, though long inured to
preying on the vitals of his fellow men. Three vessels, sir,
have sailed within a fortnight, from this port, freighted for
speculation; they are intended to purchase up the State and
other securities in the hands of the uninformed, though
honest citizens of North Carolina, South Carolina, and
Georgia. My soul rises indignant at the avaricious and immoral turpitude which so vile a conduct displays." [1]

One of the features of the federal Constitution which the
North Carolina delegates to the Philadelphia Convention of
1787 had pointed out as an inducement to their fellow-citizens to ratify that instrument was the provision requiring
the apportionment of land and capitation taxes which that
state, whose wealth was in real property and slaves rather
than personalty in general, had reason to fear. And this
very danger of a direct tax, which the assumption process
might involve, caused a leading representative from that
commonwealth, Mr. Williamson, to speak of that matter in
the House while the assumption was under discussion: "He
observed that his fellow-citizens in North Carolina were not
in general rich, few of them so provident as to lay up money;
for this reason, while he was entrusted with their concerns,
he should oppose every measure that looked towards direct
taxation. He wished never to see the day, when to satisfy

---

[1] *Annals of Congress*, Vol. I, p. 1132.

a land tax, or a capitation tax, a poor man's cow or horse might be taken from him, on which he depended for the support of helpless children. Let the State debts be once assumed and you must proceed, if your calculations are bad . . . and the impost and excise does not come up to your expectations, the national honor must be preserved. . . . People would not readily be reconciled to the new creed, ' that the debts lately paid are State debts, but all the debts not paid are National debts,' *especially as this discovery is made after most of the certificates have changed their original holders, and have passed for a trifle into the hands of moneyed men.* . . . One obvious benefit will arise from this sudden adoption [of assumption]. A few men who chanced to be near the seat of Government, and first possessed of the scheme, flew to Carolina, and there bought up securities at 3*s.* in the pound ; those men will be liberally rewarded, while his unfortunate fellow-citizens are left to pay a second tax for the same object, and to complain of the injustice of Government." [1]

South Carolina was divided on assumption. For it voted Burke, William Smith, and Tucker, all of whom appear on the records of the loan office of that state as holders of public paper.[2] Only Thomas Sumter voted against assumption, according to the *Annals of Congress;* the name of Huger, the other South Carolina member, does not appear there. A search in the Treasury records fails to reveal either Sumter or Huger among the holders of public paper. South Carolina stood third from the top of the list in the amount

---

[1] *Annals of Congress*, Vol. II, pp. 1539 ff. Italics mine.

[2] For Burke, see Treasury Department, "Loan Office, S.C., 1791–1797," p. 266 ; for Smith, *ibid.*, p. 45 ($11,910.70 worth) ; and for Tucker, *ibid.*, volume for 1790, p. 167. Jefferson wrote in the margin of the *Anas* (but struck it out later), "I do not know any member from South Carolina engaged in this infamous business, except William Smith, whom I think it a duty to name therefore, to relieve the others from the imputation." *Writings* (Ford ed.), Vol. I, p. 162, note.

of federal debt held by her citizens, with only New York and Massachusetts ahead.

The *Georgia* Representatives went solidly against assumption. Of the three members composing the delegation, Baldwin, Jackson, and Matthews, only the first appears to have been a holder of public paper. A part of Baldwin's holdings was in the state paper of Connecticut, and it seems that he also held some continental paper.[1]

The amount of securities held in Georgia by the original owners was almost negligible. Mr. Jackson, in one of his vehement speeches against assumption, declared, "I do not believe that there are twenty original holders in Georgia; the original holders received no interest, nor did they expect any; they parted with the certificates as they stood, without interest; the speculators now hold them, and contrary to the tenor of the certificates, the intention of the State, and the contract they made, they will be allowed interest."[2] In the interest disbursements of 1795 Georgia received only $6800 as contrasted with $367,600 for New York. The Treasury records of the Georgia loan office also show that Jackson's statement was fairly accurate.

A collective view of the data here presented yields the table[3] shown on page 194.

The temptation to draw too many conclusions from the data here presented and from the table below should be resisted. The one conclusion which is indisputable, however, is that almost one-half of the members of the first House were security holders. This may account partially for the defeat which overwhelmed Madison's proposal to

---

[1] *Economic Interpretation*, p. 75.   [2] *Annals of Congress*, Vol. II, p. 1751.

[3] The Constitution made provision for 65 members of the House of Representatives. Sixty-one votes were cast on the assumption proposition. The four not recorded were Speaker Muhlenberg, Bland, of Virginia, Huger, of South Carolina, and the Rhode Island representative.

STATES	NUMBER OF MEMBERS IN THE HOUSE	FOR ASSUMPTION	AGAINST ASSUMPTION	SECURITY HOLDERS FOR ASSUMPTION	SECURITY-HOLDERS VS. ASSUMPTION
New Hampshire	3	1	2		1
Massachusetts .	8	8		6	
Connecticut . .	5	5		4	
New York . . .	6	3	3	1	1
New Jersey . .	4	4		3	
Delaware . . .	1	1			
Pennsylvania . .	8	3	4	2	1
Maryland . . .	6	2	4	2	2
Virginia . . .	10	2	7		1
North Carolina .	5		5		1
South Carolina .	5	3	1	3	
Georgia . . .	3		3		1
	64	32	29	21	8

discriminate between original holders and the speculative purchasers — thirty-six to thirteen.[1] This certainly justifies Jefferson's assertion that had those actually interested in the outcome of the funding process withdrawn from voting on Hamilton's proposals not a single one of them would have been carried.

But it should be observed that had the security holders abstained from voting on assumption, the decision of the matter would have been left to what Jefferson called "the agricultural representation," speaking for the taxpayers on whom the burden of taxation for the support of public credit principally fell. The great financial centres would have been left without any representation. Whether this would have been intrusting the delicate matter of public credit to purely "disinterested" representatives may be left to the imagination of the reader.

[1] Above, p. 146.

Finally, it should be noted that quite a number of security holders voted *against* assumption and contrary to their personal interest; and an examination of the vote with reference to the geographical distribution of the public securities would seem to show beyond question that nearly all of the members, security holders and non-security holders alike, represented the dominant economic interests of their respective constituencies rather than their personal interests. In many instances there was, it is evident, a singular coincidence between public service, as the members conceived it, and private advantage; but the charge of mere corruption must fall to the ground. It was a clear case of a collision of economic interests: fluid capital versus agrarianism. The representation of one interest was as legitimate as the other, and there is no more ground for denouncing the members of Congress who held securities and voted to sustain the public credit than there is for denouncing the slave-owners who voted against the Quaker memorials against slavery on March 23, 1790.[1]

By way of conclusion, one is moved to conjecture what kind of government could have been established under the Constitution, if there had been excluded from voting on the great fiscal measures all "interested" representatives, and the decision of such momentous issues had been left to those highly etherealized persons who "cherished the people" — and nothing more.

[1] *Annals of Congress*, Vol. II, p. 1523.

CHAPTER VII

ONE does not have to examine many newspapers and
pamphlets of the period between the inauguration of Washington and the election of Jefferson to discover that contemporary writers entertained very decided notions as to the
economic character of the issues which divided the country
into two parties. Of course, there was a great deal of
calumny employed on both sides, and religious and theoretical questions were brought into play, but the more temper-
ate and thoughtful of the combatants were unusually pains-
taking in their efforts to point out the economic lines along
which the contest was waged. Indeed, so many writers
dwelt upon the economic aspects of the conflict that the
student is embarrassed with the riches at his command.[1]

---

[1] For important Anti-Federalist pamphlets see J. T. Callender, *Sedgwick & Co.,
or a Key to the Six Per Cent Cabinet* (1798), and by the same author, *The Prospect
Before Us* (1800–1801) ; *The Honorable Mr. Sedgwick's Political Last Will and
Testament* (1800) in the New York Public Library ; William Findley, *Review of the
Revenue System Adopted by the First Congress under the Federal Constitution* (1794),
in the Library of Congress ; *Definition of Parties or the Political Effects of the Paper
System Considered* (Philadelphia, April 5, 1794), in the New York Public Library ;
Abraham Bishop, *Connecticut Republicanism* (New Haven, 1800), in the Columbia
University Library ; Charles Pinckney, *Speeches* (1800), in the Library of Congress ;
W. Duane, *Politics for American Farmers* (Philadelphia, 1807) ; B. Austin, *Consti-
tutional Republicanism in Opposition to Fallacious Federalism* (Boston, 1803) ;
for some of John Taylor's letters see *Miscellaneous Pamphlets* in the Library of
Congress, Vol. 731, Number 10. See, of course, the great Republican newspaper,
The Aurora. The newspapers in the rural regions were the chief support of the
Republicans. "The greatest evil which pervades our country," wrote David Lord,
of Morristown, New Jersey, to Hamilton in 1798, "is the country press — these
have been, many of them, set up and supported by the Democratic party in different places, and those not actually raised by their private collections of money,

The pamphlet literature is very large and the newspapers are filled with letters and articles discussing the economic features of the conflict between the Federalists and Republicans. Perhaps, the most vigorous and systematic presentation of the lines of the Republican attack on the administration is to be found in John Taylor's *An Examination of the Late Proceedings in Congress Respecting the Official Conduct of the Secretary of the Treasury*, printed in 1793, and in his *Inquiry into the Principles and Tendencies of Certain Public Measures*, printed the following year.[1]

In the first of these pamphlets, Taylor opened with a commentary on the natural tendency of federal governments to escape from public responsibility and of the several departments of government, designed to check one another, to fuse into one sovereignty. But the real source of the consolidation of the administration party under Washington's first term was the public debt. "A charm has been formed," he said, "of sufficient strength to draw them [the executive and legislature] together, if the repulsive power had been naturally ten times greater than the attractive one really is. An immense debt has been accumulated, from every region of the union and of every possible description, constituted into funds of almost perpetual duration, and subject from its nature upon the slightest incidents to constant fluctuation, with a power in the Secretary of the Treasury, through the medium of the sinking fund to raise

---

have been as it were seized or hired by the party to retail scandal against the government so that 9 tenths of the Presses out of the great towns in America south of the Hudson are Democratic and most of them by direct pay or by influence. While the opposers of the government are doing all this and ten times as much by misrepresentation, the wealth, information and abilities of our country are not excited at all or very little indeed." *Hamilton Mss.*, April 11, 1798. See also Freneau's writings and S. E. Forman's valuable essay on Freneau, in the Johns Hopkins Studies.

[1] Copies of both of these pamphlets may be found in the New York Public Library.

it at pleasure. [It has depended upon the Secretary to say when money could or could not be furnished for the sinking fund, out of the funds appropriated for the purpose, and even out of monies borrowed for and legally applicable to no other purpose. And under his direction has ultimately fallen the execution of the purchases.][1] And upon the basis of this debt, a bank of discount has been formed, allied by its charter to the government itself, and in a great measure subjected to the direction of the same officer."

The holders of public debt were naturally and easily consolidated into a party based upon identical interests. "The experience of other countries has shewn," continued Taylor, "that the dealers in the public funds, and especially those whose fortunes consist principally in that line have no interest and of course feel but little concern in all those questions of fiscal policy which particularly affect the landholder, the merchant, and the artist [artisan.] Although these classes should groan under the burdens of government, yet the public creditor will be no otherwise affected by the pressure, than as he receives what has been gleaned from their industry. . . They are the tenants of the farm, he the landlord and the man of revenue. The disparity of their interests, and the difference of their sensations, respecting the objects to which they point, in a great measure separate them in society."

Taylor then analyzed the psychology of the security holders and found why they were such a readily consolidated group. "Knowing that they live upon the labour of the other classes, the public creditors behold them with jealousy, suspect a thousand visionary schemes against their welfare, and are always alarmed and agitated with every [sic] the most trifling incident which happens. And having one

---

[1] Footnote in the original; see above, p. 114.

common interest, which consists simply in the imposition of high taxes and their rigid collection, they form a compact body and move always in concert. Whilst the administration finds the means to satisfy their claims, they are always devoted to it, and support all its measures. They therefore may be considered in every country, where substantial funds are established and their demands are punctually paid, as a ministerial corps, leagued together upon principles to a certain degree hostile to the rest of the community."

There were, however, in the United States exceptional circumstances which made the security-holding party all the more jealous of its interests and fearful of the populace. "The trifling consideration given for the debt by the present holders, with the comparative merit of their characters with that of the officers and soldiers of the late army, and the well known sense which the community entertain on that subject, must inspire a distrust that will disquiet their peace for a time. The claims of justice although from motives of policy, they may be suppressed, yet the cries which they raise are terrible to those who live on the usurpation. . . . This throws them blindly into the hands of those who patronize their interests. In addition to which, the policy and operation of the sinking fund, by which the rise of stocks is in a great measure regulated, must contribute greatly to subject the party interested to the control of those who direct its application."

Having demonstrated to his satisfaction that the security-holding group constituted a class separate from the landholder, merchant, and artisan, and fully conscious of its interests, Taylor proceeded to an analysis of the political aspects of the banking and credit system. "The proprietors of bank stock are still more subservient to this policy than any other class of public creditors. The institution itself being founded on the same paper system must communicate the same interest to those within its sphere. And in other respects, it possesses a strength and energy to which the common members of the fiscal corps are strangers. The superiority of its gains invigorates the principle common to them all ; but the constitutional subordination to the head of that department sanctifies under the cloak of authority, that degree of subservience which a sense of shame, among independent men, might occasionally forbid. The bank, however, should not be considered simply in the light of an institution, uniting together with greater force, the members of the fiscal corps. As an engine of influence, capable under management authorized by its principles, of polluting every operation of the government, it is entitled to particular attention."

That certificate holders, dealers in funds, bank stockholders, and borrowers from the bank should become attached to the Treasury administration was serious enough, Taylor thought; but what was to be said about members of Congress who became personally interested in the fiscal operations of the government whose policy they were determining? Could they be expected to retain their character as "representatives of the people"? "Being on the great theatre of speculation and gain and possessed of more correct information, with the means of turning it to better account, will they abandon their occupation and slight the opportunity offered of becoming thrifty? In what condition would the landholder, the merchant, and the artist find themselves, if they should be represented in the national legislature by persons of this description only? Might they not count at least upon high taxes and their rigid collection?"

Moreover, what about members of Congress involved in transactions at the bank? Can they be regarded as the representatives of the landholders, merchants, and artisans?

"In this view a concise illustration may not be deemed improper. The stocks are low, and the command of money for a short term only would enable the holder to clear with certainty such a sum. A question of moment is depending and a member of Congress may obtain a discount with the bank for that sum. He makes the purchase. The party aiding in this operation with the bank has likewise the direction of the sinking fund : its monies are *seasonably* and *publicly* exhibited at the market and the stocks rise. The gain has been made and the demands of the bank may likewise be answered. Or perhaps he is indigent, pressed by difficulties and seeks thus to be relieved : or his note has already been deposited in the bank and to some amount and the day for repayment approaches, has he the means? and if he has not, how shall he be relieved from this painful dilemma? Shall the indulgence be extended again and again and by the intercession of this person? Have the members of the legislature sufficient independence, virtue, and firmness, to withstand these temptations?"

Such an expectation would be illusory. The fact that members of Congress were security holders and owners of bank stock simply increased the power of the fiscal corps. "In all operations upon the legislature, whether for the particular emolument of the bank, the fiscal corps in general, or any other purposes, in which the views of the party are interested, the prospect of success is greatly improved. And in all inquiries relative to the conduct of the officer, in the management of the public monies, these members of Congress, *bank directors*, and the bank itself, give him their firm and uniform support. In *their eyes* his conduct will appear *immaculate, angelic,* and partaking of something still more divine." [1]

---

[1] Here Taylor remarks in a footnote : "See the speech of William Smith, of South Carolina, where he says, 'That the Secretary would in the issue rise above

In Taylor's opinion, conclusive evidence that the ruling financial interests dominated Congress was afforded by the vote on the resolutions growing out of the investigation of the Treasury Department in March, 1793,[1] when Hamilton was exonerated. The resolution to censure the Secretary was defeated by a vote of thirty-four to seven. "Of the thirty-five," [2] said Taylor, "twenty-one were stockholders or dealers in the funds, and three of these latter bank directors and whose degree of zeal was obviously in the ratio above stated, as their relative profits; the bank directors being considerably more active and zealous than the other members of the corps. That the fact of this number being stock-holders, is true, can, it is believed, be satisfactorily shewn."

Thereupon, Taylor brought forth a list of the security and bank stockholders in Congress, saying, "The books of transfer at the Treasury and the books at the bank are held secret under the obligation of an oath on all persons who use or inspect them not to reveal the names or amount of the stockholders.[3] But from information obtained through

every calumny as fair as the purest angel in heaven.' Mr. S ——, it *is well known* holds between three and four hundred shares in the bank of the United States and has obtained discounts, *ad libitum.*"

[1] *Annals of Congress* (2d Congress), pp. 899 ff.

[2] Taylor was mistaken. The vote was thirty-four. *Ibid.*, p. 963.

[3] The secrecy which surrounded the Treasury Department prevented the Republicans from getting possession of the records to prove their charge that a large number of members of Congress were involved in paper operations or were security holders. The Treasury Records which have come down to us are principally those of the loan offices in the several states which were later concentrated at Washington. The books of the central Treasury Department have nearly all disappeared and they were the books which contained most of the holders of stock at the seat of the government. There was a fire in the Treasury just before Jefferson's inauguration during the last days of the Federalist administration, and the Republicans declared that it was a design not an accident. Among Hamilton's miscellaneous papers is a printed circular which insinuates that the Federalists had some records which they did not want to pass on to the Republicans. The following passage occurs in this circular: "A few days before the meeting of Congress, a fire broke out in the War Office which consumed many valuable records and works of a rare kind not to be replaced; about the 20th of January a fire broke out in the federal

other sources, the following members of C–g–ss are known to be stockholders in the bank of the United States or in the public funds :

N-w-H-pshire [1]

Mr. G–m-n *
  L–gd-n *

M-ssa—s—tts

Mr. C-b-t *
  St—g
  A—s *
  G—y *
  G–d–e
  S-dg—k

Rh— Isl–d

Mr. B——n *
  F-st-r

Conn—t—t

Mr. T—b-ll *
  S–rm-n *
  E-sw–th *
  W–sw–th *
  H-llh–se *
  L-n-d *

N-w-Y–k

Mr. L–r–ce *
  K–g *

N-w J-r—y

Mr. B–di–t
  D-yt-n *
  R–hf–d

P—ns—v—a

Mr. M-rr-s *
  F—zs——s *
  H–st-r

D-la—re

Mr. R–d

M—yl–d

Mr. M-rr-y *
  K-y

manufactory of arms at Springfield (Massachusetts) by which all the implements and materials to an immense value were consumed. About the same period the treasury office in this place was also set on fire. Three fires thus succeeding each other at a period, when patronage and the secrets of office were about to be transferred to different hands could not but excite the worst suspicions; after much inquiry on the subject the only thing discovered is that nobody knows anything about the origin of the fires!" A printed circular, dated, Washington, March 6, 1801. *Hamilton Mss.*, March 6, 1801. Marked "A Southern Circular" [in Hamilton's hand]; signature cut out.

[1] "Those marked thus * are believed to be stockholders in the bank."

N–th C—l–a	*S–th C—l–a*
Mr. J–ns–n *	Mr. Iz–d *
W——ms-n	S–th *
St–le	T–k-r
	G—g-a
	Mr. F-w *"

Taylor did not regard these fiscal operations by members of Congress as an incidental part of the work of the government under Washington's first administration. On the contrary, he said: "If we take an impartial review of the measures of the government from its adoption to the present time [1793], we shall find that its practice has corresponded, in every respect, with this theory. The demonstration strikes us in every page of the law, that a faction of monarchic speculators seized upon its legislative functions in the commencement and have directed all its operations since. We shall find that to the views of this faction, an apt instrument has been obtained in the Secretary of the Treasury. . . . If the public debt has been accumulated by every possible contrivance, buoyed up by means of the sinking fund, made in a great measure perpetual, and formed into a powerful monied machine, dependent on the fiscal administration, to this combination it is due. If by means of this sudden elevation of fortune, a dangerous inequality of rank has been created among the citizens of these states, thereby laying the foundation for the subversion of the government itself, by undermining its true principles, to this combination it is due. If those sound and genuine principles of responsibility which belong to representative government and constitute its bulwark and preserve its harmony, have been annulled or weakened; if a practicable means of influence, whereby the members of the legislature may be debauched from the duty they owe their constituents has been formed; if, by implication and construction, the obvious sense of the constitution has been perverted and its powers enlarged, so as to pave the way for the conversion of the government from a limited into an unlimited one, to this combination they are due."

It would be difficult to imagine a more concise, pointed, and unequivocal arraignment, on economic grounds, of the ruling party during Washington's first administration. There is nothing about "democracy" or "equality" in it. The epithet "monarchical" is applied to the enemy, but that was simply a common term of reproach continually used by the Republican opposition from the beginning. The whole indictment may be summed up as follows:

1. The financial interests gathering around the funding of the debt and the bank took possession of the government and constituted the dominant directing party.

2. This financial group constituted a separate class thriving at the expense of other classes composed of the landholders, the merchants, and the artisans who paid the taxes and suffered from the inflation of capital.

3. Every measure of the federal government from 1789 to 1793 was an expression of the will of this financial class operating through the Treasury and the security and bank stockholding members of Congress.

4. The federal government was in 1793 a class government in which the landowners, merchants, and artisans were not truly represented.

The remedy which Taylor advanced for this evil condition of affairs may be stated in his own words:

1. "Let the public creditors stand apart, not as a class of men to be branded with reproach and infamy, but as constituting an interest, which, without due restraint, may en-

danger the general welfare; and if admissible at all into that branch [the legislature], let them be inhibited under the severest penalties from a profanation of its functions afterwards, by any traffic in the public funds."

2. "Let the law establishing the bank, as a violation of the principles of the Constitution, be declared null and void, or at least the establishment be repudiated from its present impure connection with the government."

3. "Let the whole system of the treasury department undergo a thorough reform."

4. "Let us return to the Constitution," is Taylor's last plea. "Renovations of this sort will not violate public credit, but establish it in the public confidence; will not impair the energy of the Constitution, but restore it to its pristine health and proper functions; will not stain our national character, but exhibit it in its legitimate features, of a dignified simplicity and genuine republicanism." [1]

Taylor's second great pamphlet against the fiscal party in control of the federal administration, *An Enquiry into the Principles and Tendency of Certain Public Measures* (1794),

---

[1] By no means all of the opponents of Federalism were against the funding and revenue systems as such. Many moderate critics directed their attacks against the particular policy for which Hamilton was sponsor and which Congress accepted. "A citizen of Philadelphia" voiced this type of opposition in a letter published in Fenno's Gazette on October 10, 1792, in which he said: "My greatest objection is more to the disposal of the money when it is collected, than to the existing mode of assessing or collecting it — the money when collected from the labors of the people is given by the funding system, not to the men who *originally earned it*, not to the men to whom the *public faith* was plighted over and over again, not to the men who *contributing their substance and services* SAVED *our country*, saved us all in the time of deepest distress — but by this fatal system a title is given and payments actually made of an immense treasure — the *dear earnings* of the forementioned Patriots, *not to them*, I say, but to a parcel of *speculators*, who never earned a shilling of it, or paid *any adequate compensation* for it, or even set up any kind of title to it grounded either on their *merit, earnings, services*, or any purchase for valuable considerations paid, but they claim and receive it under a most extravagant construction of an old rule of law, *strained and stretched* far beyond every reason on which the law ever was or is grounded."

was prefaced by an open letter to the President of the United States directed to him "in the spirit of truth, and not of adulation." His first point of attack was the Bank and he devoted many pages to an analysis of the political economy of the fiscal system and its relation to productive labor. He declared that "a design for erecting aristocracy and a monarchy is subsisting — that a *money impulse,* and not the *public good,* is operating on Congress; and that taxes are imposed upon motives other than the general welfare."

In the operations of the Bank, Taylor saw arising a conflict between capitalism and labor. "A portion of the rich class of citizens are the proprietors of the device, whilst labour supports it. An annuity to a great amount is suddenly conjured up by law, which is received exclusively by the rich, that is the aristocracy. Will it not make them richer? It is paid out of labour, and labour in all countries falls on the poor. Will it not make this class poorer? . . . Banking in its *best* view is only a fraud whereby labour suffers the imposition of paying an interest upon the circulating medium; whereas if specie only were circulated, the medium would, in passing among the rich, often lie in the pockets of the aristocracy without gaining an interest. But the aristocracy, as cunning as rapacious, have contrived this device to inflict upon labour a tax, constantly working for their emolument. . . . Labour is deprived of its hard earned fruits. A portion of these is gotten from it and bestowed upon ease and affluence. The loss is the same, whether a daring robber extorts your property with his pistol at your breast or whether a midnight thief secretly filches it away."

By the robbery of labor an aristocracy is being erected in the United States. It is true, the Constitution forbids titles of nobility, but a "money-ocracy" is far more to be feared than any "shadow titles." "Which is most to be dreaded; titles without wealth, or exorbitant wealth without titles? Have the words *prince, lord, highness,* or *protector,* a magical influence upon our minds, or can they lay a spell upon our exertions? . . . Who are most to be dreaded, the *nominal* or *real* lords of America? It is evident that exorbitant wealth constitutes the substance and danger of aristocracy. Money in a state of civilization is power. If we execrate the shadow, what epithet is too hard for an administration, which is labouring to introduce the substance. . . . A democratic republic is endangered by an immense disproportion in wealth. In a state of nature, enormous strength possessed by one or several individuals would constitute a monarchy or an aristocracy — in a state of civilization similar consequences will result from enormous wealth. . . . The acquisitions of *honest industry* can seldom become dangerous to public or private happiness whereas the accumulations of *fraud* and *violence* constantly diminish both." [1]

The development of an aristocracy of wealth was not the purpose of the Constitution. "Did labour intend to place

[1] J. F. Mercer, of Maryland, joined with Taylor in looking upon the public debt as a charge upon labor. In a speech made in Congress in 1792, he said : "All public revenue or private income is a contribution, mediate or immediate, of the labour of the industrious farmer or mechanic. If the rich pay anything, it is only mediate — a part of what they first receive from these classes. . . . All public burdens fall, in a great measure, on the land, so as to diminish its value and price, as I shall observe; but then, to the men who lend to government, lands have no value but from the hands that are to work it. . . . Every atom of funded debt is so much taken from the value of the land in the hand of the landholders, and so much diminished from the value of labor to the laborer. . . . A love and veneration of equality is the vital principle of free Governments. It dies when the general wealth is thrown into a few hands. The effect of stocks is to transfer the fruits of the labor of the many, who are able to appreciate its value by the difficulty of acquirement, and would convert it into useful improvement, into the hands of the opulent few, who exchange them for foreign luxuries and consume in an hour the labor of industrious families for years. It prevents a general diffusion of wealth by drawing it to a centre, and saps the foundation of a Republican Government." *Annals of Congress,* 1791–1793, pp. 506 ff.

itself under the whip of an avaricious, insatiable, and luxurious aristocracy? Labour, in the erection of a government, after deducting the necessary expence of supporting it, designed to secure safety to itself in the enjoyment of its own fruits. The stimulating system [applied by Hamilton] frustrates this object and changes government into its master, brandishing the lash of legislation and leaving to labour what measure of sustenance it pleases. . . . A beast of burthen is more remarkable for its patience than its spirit. An aristocracy, therefore, have good reason to exclaim 'a national debt is a national blessing,' and in pursuance of their maxim, to create one that is fictitious, payable to themselves out of the hard-earned fruits of labour. To them it is a mine, yielding gold without work. . . . The plebians of this age are too wise to be individually cozened by patricians, so that the latter are obliged to create a fictitious debt, by the help of law, imposing generally upon the former, both an usurious and compound interest."

The aristocracy thus established at the expense of land and labor tended to weaken the sovereignty of the states by drawing powerful interests to the support of the federal government. "A recurrence to direct taxation by Congress will swallow up the little sovereignty, now left to the once sovereign individual states; and every accumulation of the debts of the Union is an impulse toward that end. Hence all assumptions and hence the enormous loans which have been negociated. In the power of money is the confidence of administration placed; by assuming all money negociacions, a face of business and activity will be bestowed on the Federal government. The exclusive payment of debts and imposition of taxes will exhibit it as the only political object to interest the attention of individuals; whilst the state governments will become only speculative commonwealths to be read for amusement, like Harrington's *Oceana* or Moore's *Utopia*. . . . The funding system was intended to effect what the bank was contrived to accelerate:

"1. Accumulation of great wealth in a few hands.

"2. A political moneyed engine.

"3. A suppression of republican state assemblies, by depriving them of the political importance resulting from the imposition and dispensation of taxes."

Therefore, said Taylor, the federal Constitution was flagrantly violated by the Federalists. From the system flowed "the following infractions of the clearest constitutional principles":

"1. Members of Congress may vote for the erection of a *gainful* project and be the *receivers* of the gain.

"2. They may impose a tax on the community or a part of it, and instead of sharing in the burthen share in the plunder.

"3. The higher and more unnecessary the taxes and loans are, the more public money will be deposited in the bank and the greater will be the profit of the bank-members of Congress, who nevertheless vote for taxes and loans.

"4. A member of Congress, debauched by a profitable banking interest ceases to be a *citizen* of the Union or an *inhabitant* of the state which chooses him, *as to the purposes* of the Constitution. He becomes a citizen and inhabitant of Carpenters Hall. . . .

"6. The Constitution aims at a real representation of the states in proportion to numbers, making no provision for members from corporations; and yet if the members of this corporation keep their seats in Congress, it is moderate to state that it will be better represented than any state. . . .

"7 . . . . It would be better to allow the bank, members [in Congress] than to permit it to plunder the states of their several quotas.

"8. It was evidently designed, that the senate as judges of impeachments should be *constitutionally* preserved in a state of impartiality. Impeachments originate in the house of representatives, and the crimes to be restrained by this process will mostly be comprised in a misapplication of public money. But if those who are to inquire into such misapplications, to impeach, and to decide upon impeachments, may in consequence of banking and paper systems, be gainers by the misapplications, it is obvious that the check provided by this article of the Constitution upon a species of criminality, so dangerous as to have attracted the particular attention of a general convention is entirely defeated. If accomplices are to set enquiries on foot — to accuse and to decide, no prophetical spirit is necessary to foresee the decision. . . . Bank directors, stock holders and a paper interest may be more likely by their judgments to disqualify honest patriots from holding 'any office of honour, trust, or profit under the United States' who shall obstruct peculations from public labour in any shape, than to remedy frauds favouring a moneyed interest in general, and accruing to their own emolument in particular." [1]

Taylor's attack upon the fiscal system as a capitalist device was warmly seconded by the notorious Callender's clever and bitter pamphlets. In his *Sedgwick & Co. or a*

---

[1] It is not to be supposed that attacks on the security-holding interests were confined to the somewhat mild-mannered pamphleteers of Anti-Federalism. It is not often that such hot political controversies are carried on entirely in language appropriate for the drawing room. The Anti-Federalists assembled in convention in Alleghany county, Pennsylvania, in April, 1794, suggested more violent methods for rescuing the Federal Government from the hands of "the aristocracy of wealth" than those proposed by Taylor, of Virginia. By a resolution they declared: "We have observed with great pain, that our councils want the integrity or spirit of Republicans. This we attribute to the pernicious influence of the stockholders or their subordinates; and our minds feel this with so much indignacy, that we are almost ready to wish for a state of revolution, and the guillotine of France for a short space, in order to inflict punishment on the miscreants that enervate and disgrace our Government." *Annals of Congress,* 1794–1795, p. 929.

Key to the Six Per Cent Cabinet, published in 1798, Callender fell upon the Federalist party, charging its leaders with having corrupted the country and cloaked their proceedings in ostentatious patriotism and unctuous piety. He carried the argument to its extreme length and declared the funding process to be nothing but a scheme for enriching those who were, as members of Congress, actually creating the system. He also referred to the immense concentration of the public securities which had taken place, holding that "if divided among the original holders, the debt would have fostered a substantial and republican yeomanry." In the place of this wide distribution of the debt among these holders a sharp concentration in the hands of speculators had actually occurred and it was largely through the influence of interested members of Congress, acting under Hamilton's skilled leadership, that the debt was generously funded. "An act of Congress of September 2d, 1789," he said, "prohibits all persons holding an office from being 'concerned in the purchase or disposal of any public securities of any state, or of the United States.' Disqualification and a penalty of three thousand dollars are to be the consequence of detection. But if the injunction was requisite upon officers of the Treasury, it seemed yet more wanted for Congress members. They moved in a higher sphere. By purchasing certificates by one hand and making laws with the other, they could accumulate, as William Smith actually did, an enormous fortune. Their statute book has no prohibition against themselves. . . . If Dr. William Smith and forty other members of the two houses were entitled to trade in paper, they had no right of hindering any one else. Speculation was not to be hedged in for them. . . . Much noise has been made and much indignation excited with respect to democratic infidelity. Compare it with the performances of six per cent *piety*. While our legislative majorities continue to serve an apprenticeship in the Hamiltonian academy of morals, it is of very small consequence whether they are atheists, anabaptists, profess any religion or none. . . . The reproach of free thinking branched into a million modifications has been repeated and with some effect for a prodigious number of times. But on tracing the treasury faction up to the fountain head, it is clear that the first bond of union among their leaders was a conspiracy for paper jobbing. To enrich perhaps fifty members of Congress, the whole continent was converted into an immense gaming table, and the wheels of government were clogged and the industry of the country was oppressed with forty millions of domestic debt, instead of ten or fifteen millions. Of their *religion*, the six per cent heroes have given many practical proofs. . . . This is a bird's eye landscape of the *truly federal* system ; and of the precepts and projects of its godly and sanctified conductors." [1]

Minor pamphleteers appeared to be no less certain of their ground than Taylor and Callender. In an anonymous tract bearing the title *Five Letters Addressed to the Yeomanry of the United States,* issued at Philadelphia in 1792, "A Farmer" made a long argument for a bill of rights, citing the example of the French Declaration of the Rights of Man. "Had the Constitution of the United States a foundation equally firm and equitable," he held, "we should not at this day witness the laws of the Union stained with,

---

[1] Callender, *Sedgwick & Co. or a Key to the Six Per Cent Cabinet.* Boudinot (see above, p. 184) was president of the American Bible Society, and Hamilton proposed in 1802 to link religion with the Federalist Party by founding the "Christian Constitutional Society," whose objects were to be "the support of the Christian Religion," and "the support of the Constitution of the United States." *Works* (Lodge ed.), Vol. VIII, p. 598.

"1st. Mercantile regulations impolitic in themselves and highly injurious to the agricultural interests of our country.

"2. With funding systems, by which the property and rights of poor but meritorious citizens are sacrificed to wealthy gamesters and speculators.

"3. With the establishment of Banks authorizing a few men to create fictitious money, by which they may acquire rapid fortunes without industry.

"4. With excise laws which violate the tranquillity of domestic retirement and which prevent the Farmer from enjoying the fruits of his care and industry." The farmers, he added, constitute nine-tenths of the population, and yet ask for no "partial privileges" such as manufacturers demand for themselves.

In another Philadelphia pamphlet of 1793 bearing a similar title, *Letters Addressed to the Yeomanry of the United States* by "An American Farmer," the antagonism between agrarian and capitalist interests was sharply brought out. The author declared that the property of the "farmers and soldiers" had been taken away from them for the benefit of "undeserving speculators," and he then savagely attacked Hamilton's entire system for the following reasons: "First. It is certain that national debts cause a mighty confluence of people and riches to the capital, by the great sums levied in the provinces to pay the interest of these debts. Secondly. Public stocks being a kind of paper money have all the disadvantages attending that species of property. . . . Thirdly. The taxes which are levied to pay the interest of the debts are apt either to heighten the price of labor or to be an oppression on the poorer sort. . . . Fifthly. The greatest part of the public stock being always in the hands of idle people who live on their revenue our funds give great encouragement to an useless and inactive life."

To the southward, popular writers, in attacking the fiscal system, constantly referred to the burden which it had laid upon the agrarian and planting interests. To them, as it seemed to Calhoun and McDuffie long afterward, the burden of capitalism was borne almost entirely by the South alone. Charles Pinckney in the City Gazette of Charleston, on October 3, 1800, for example, not only criticised Hamilton's policy as an avowed discrimination in favor of the moneyed as against the planting interest, but held up Jefferson, the planter, as the true representative of the Republicans against John Adams, a probable "stockholder" and the spokesman of the moneyed group. In order to conciliate those planters who might have been frightened at Jefferson's theoretical views against slavery, Pinckney assured his readers with high confidence that no practical application of those views would be attempted by the sage of Monticello. "How then does it happen," he inquired, "that in laying a direct tax the whole of it is laid on *lands and slaves only*, and on no other species of property? Why is the whole of it laid on the agricultural interest and the landholder? . . . Wise governments have invariably considered the landed and agricultural interest as the most valuable of their citizens . . . whereas our government has placed the landholder and the planter in an oppressive and degrading predicament. And what is this done for? Why, clearly to exempt all the *monied interest*, which is by far the largest in the Northern states." [1]

It was not merely in pamphlets and newspapers of uncertain importance or slight circulation that the protest of agriculture against the Federalist fiscal system was voiced. As early as December 16, 1790, about four months after the passage of the funding bill, the legislature of Virginia, in

[1] For more of Pinckney's reflections in a similar vein, see below, p. 373.

regular session adopted, as we have noted above, a solemn protest against that measure and everything implied in it.[1] "Your memorialists," runs this historic document, "discern a striking resemblance between this system and that which was introduced in England at the Revolution — a system which has perpetuated upon that nation an enormous debt, and has, moreover, insinuated into the hands of the Executive an unbounded influence which, pervading every branch of the government, bears down all opposition and daily threatens the destruction of everything that appertains to English liberty. The same causes produce the same effects. In an agricultural country like this, therefore, to erect and concentrate and perpetuate a large moneyed interest is a measure which your memorialists apprehend must, in the course of human events, produce one or other of two evils: the prostration of agriculture at the feet of commerce, or a change in the present form of Federal Government, fatal to the existence of American liberty." . . .

This protest of agriculture against capital is then transformed into a fundamental doctrine of constitutional law. "Your memorialists turn away from the impolicy and injustice of the said act and view it in another light, in which to them it appears still more odious and deformed. During the whole discussion of the federal Constitution, by the convention of Virginia, your memorialists were taught to believe, 'that every power not granted was retained'; under this impression and upon this positive condition, declared in the instrument of ratification, the said Government was adopted by the people of this commonwealth; but your memorialists can find no clause in the Constitution, authorizing Congress to assume debts of the states!

[1] *American State Papers: Finance*, Vol. I, p. 90.

As guardians then of the rights and interests of their constituents; as sentinels placed by them over the ministers of the Federal Government, to shield it from their incroachments or at least to sound the alarm when it is threatened with invasion; they can never reconcile it to their consciences silently to acquiesce in a measure which violates that hallowed maxim — a maxim on the truth and sacredness of which the Federal Government depended for its adoption in this Commonwealth." Thus economics becomes politics, and politics in turn becomes constitutional law. Yet a little while and Virginia and Kentucky shall protest again; and yet a while longer and the guns of Sumter shall be heard throughout the land.

The Republican economic analysis thus expressed in pamphlets, newspapers, and resolutions was accepted by the acute agents of France in the United States, Ternant, Genet, and Fauchet, and employed in their despatches to their home government as the chief explanation for the partisan division in this country.[1] In his famous paper of October 31, 1794, Fauchet represented the party contest as a conflict between the landed and capitalistic interests. After calling attention to the primitive differences of opinion with respect to the political form of the state and to the ingenious way in which the party of consolidation had seized upon the states' rights term, "Federalism," Fauchet remarked that these early dissensions would have disappeared if the system of finance that originated with the Constitution had not given them renewed vigor under different forms. "The manner of organizing the national credit, the consolidation of the government, the funding of the public debt . . . imperceptibly created a financial class

[1] Edited by Professor Turner in the *Report of the American Historical Association* for 1903, Vol. II, see pp. 51, 52, 54, 71, 107, 138, 139, 154, 167, 248, 340, 342, 343, for examples of the economic analysis.

which threatens to become the aristocratic order of the state. Many citizens, and among them, those who have aided in the establishment of independence either by their purses or their arms, have felt themselves injured by these financial arrangements. Whence arises a declared opposition between the agricultural and the moneyed interests. . . . The proprietors of a barren coast fear that if the Mississippi is once opened and its numerous branches devoted to navigation, their fields will be deserted, and in short commerce dreads to see in the back country a people who will become rivals as soon as they have ceased to be subjects. ⁤ The last supposition is well founded. Mr. Izard, an influential member of the Senate, in conversing with me one day, avowed it without disguise. I shall not dwell as much upon the grumbling excited by the methods pursued in the sale of lands. It is found to be unjust that those vast and fruitful domains should be sold in whole provinces to capitalists who enrich themselves with great profits by parcelling out to the cultivators lands which they never saw themselves. . . . Why reserve to be sold or distributed to favorites of the government, to a class of flatterers and courtiers, lands which belong to the state and should be sold to the greatest possible profit of all its members?" . . .[1]

[1] Le mode d'organization du Crédit National, la consolidation, la fondation de la dette publique; l'introduction dans l'économie politique de la méthode des Etats qui ne prolongent leur existence ou ne diffèrent leur chute que par des expédiens, créerent imperceptiblement une classe Financière qui menace de devenir l'ordre aristocratique de l'Etat. Plusieurs Citoyens, et entr' autres ceux qui avoient aidé à l'indépendance ou de leurs bourses ou de leurs bras se sont prétendus lésés par les arrangemens Fiscaux. *Delà une opposition qui se déclare entre l'intéret foncier ou agricole, et l'intéret fiscal:* le Fédéralisme et son contraire qui se fondent sous ces dénominations nouvelles à mesure que le Fisc usurpe la prépondérance dans le Gouvernement et la Législation : delà enfin l'Etat divisé en partisans et en ennemis du Trésorier et de ses théories. . . . Nous atteignons le principal grief des occidentaux et le motif ostensible de leurs mouvements. Républicains par principes, indépendans par caractère et par situation ils doivent accèder avec enthousiasme aux criminations que nous avons esquissées. Mais *l'Excise* surtout les affecte. . . . Ne peut-on supposer que Madrid et Philadelphie se donnent

In levelling their heaviest batteries against the holders of public funds and bank stock, the Republicans were really attacking the very citadel of capitalistic interests. This point must be strongly emphasized. The power of the public creditors in the politics of the period is easily underestimated by the superficial observer who compares the public debt of to-day with the remainder of the fluid capital of the country. Such a comparison is of course utterly meaningless. It is the amount of the public debt of 1795 contrasted with the value of the landed property at the time which must be taken into consideration. In Massachusetts, the public securities more than equalled the amount of money loaned at interest, and this was doubtless true of many other states. The situation would be more analogous to affairs to-day if we should put all of the railway and industrial securities in a single mass and make their value and their increment depend largely upon the measures enacted into law at Washington. What a mighty army of interested private persons would be speedily transformed into active politicians may be readily imagined.

Anti-Federalists in Washington's administration had carefully gauged the relative weight of the public debt and landed property in the scale of wealth and in the scale of politics as well. Speaking in 1792, on a proposition, ad-

la main pour prolonger l'esclavage du Fleuve [Mississippi]; que les propriétaires d'une côté infeconde craignent que le Mississippi une fois ouverte, et ses nombreuses ramifications rendue à l'activité, leurs campagnes ne deviennent désertes, et enfin que le Commerce redoute d'avoir sur ces derrières des rivaux dès que leurs habitans cesseront d'être sujets? Cette dernière supposition n'est que trop fondée; Un membre influent dans le Senat, M. Izard l'a énoncée un jour en conversant avec moi sans déguisement. Je ne m'entendrai pas autant sur les murmures qu'excite ⸱e système qui préside à la Vente des Terres. On trouve injuste que ces païs Vastes et Féconds se vendent par provinces à des Capitalistes qui s'enrichissent ainsi et détaillent avec d'immenses bénéfices au Cultivateur, des possessions qu'ils n'ont jamais vues. . . . Pourquoi se reserver de vendre ou distribuer à des favoris, à une classe de flatteurs et de Courtisans ce qui appartient à l'Etat et devrait être vendu au plus grand profit possible de tous ses membres." *Report of the American Historical Association for 1903*, Vol. II, pp. 444 ff.

vanced by Fitzsimons, for extending the period for subscriptions to the public debt, J. F. Mercer, of Maryland,
said: "It [the debt] will in the aggregate form a mass of
seventy millions of dollars. The property of the United
States is worth what it will sell for at an ordinary market.
Although it cannot be precisely ascertained what the amount
would be, we are still furnished with sufficient data to form
a tolerable estimate. In the state I have the honor to
represent . . . property was assessed, soon after the war
was raised, to an ideal height, to twelve millions their
money. From the fall of price, I do not believe that the
whole or any proportion of it would now bring at a fair
market, the money. From this we must deduct four millions for the negro property, which cannot be included in a
relative comparison with other countries, where the laborers,
although equally and more valuable, are not considered as
property; there would then remain eight millions. Maryland is at least one-twelfth of the United States; she has,
indeed, always been rated at a higher proportion; this would
fix the property of the United States at two hundred and
sixty millions of dollars. The debt, then, is more than one-
fourth of the whole value of the property." [1] It would
seem that this estimate of the value of the other property
in the United States is low, for the survey for direct taxes
in 1798 put the value of the land alone at $479,293,263.13.[2]
Nevertheless, it is apparent from the evidence massed in
this chapter, the Anti-Federalists correctly understood the
enormous weight of the debt in politics and did their best
to exaggerate it in the eyes of their followers. It is equally
apparent that they appealed to the agrarian interests to
wage war on the "moneyed aristocracy."

[1] *Annals of Congress*, 1791–1793, p. 508.
[2] Beard, *Economic Interpretation of the Constitution*, p. 36.

CHAPTER VIII

THE FEDERALIST ANALYSIS OF THE PARTY CONFLICT

The vehement assaults of the Republicans upon the capitalistic policies of Washington's administration forced the Federalists to exhaust the entire armory of their argument.[1] Being on the defensive, however, they did not always maintain in their polemical literature that sharpness of class distinction which marked the writings of the Republicans. The wisest of them were, of course, too shrewd to add bitterness to the conflict by unnecessary attacks upon the agrarians as such, and they often employed the good tactics of blurring the economic antagonism by denying its existence or referring to the essential identity of interest between capitalism and agriculture. Yet they could not altogether

---

[1] The chief sources for the Federalist view of politics are the writings of eminent Federalists, like Hamilton, Wolcott, Ames, Cabot, King, and H. G. Otis. The most valuable popular discussions are to be found in the great Federalist newspaper, the Gazette of the United States. See, for example, "A ¡Friend to the Union," in the Gazette of April 21, 1790, where Congress is threatened for delaying assumption, and attention is called to the dangers from the Indians, Spanish, and British in case of the continued divisions at home. The Gazette for June 23, 1790, contains an article showing that the funding of all debts is a guarantee of the permanence of the Constitution. See also "Defense of the Government and the Funding System," by "A Farmer," The Gazette, February 18, 1792. An attack on Freneau's glorification of husbandry in prose and poetry and a defence of mechanics and manufacturers is printed in the Gazette of August 4, 1792. Among the pamphlets are: *An Address from William Smith of South Carolina to His Constituents* (1794), in the New York Public Library. J. Fenno, *Desultory Reflections on the New Political Aspects of Public Affairs in the United States . . . since . . . 1799* (1800), in the New York Public Library. For the conflict in South Carolina between the landed and capitalistic interests, see T. Ford, *The Constitutionalist*, published in 1794, New York Public Library. Henry W. Dessausure, *Answer to a Dialogue between a Federalist and a Republican* (1800), Wolcott Pamphlets, Library of Congress.

escape the necessity of recognizing the economic nature of the party division when it became necessary to rally specific groups to the support of Hamilton's measures. Consequently we find in Federalist literature frank appeals to certain economic groups for political support, denials of the existence of class divisions, assertions that the interests of all classes were identical, and condemnation of the agrarians for their assaults on capitalistic enterprises.

When the battle over assumption was on, the newspapers fairly teemed with letters and addresses directed to the financial elements. This was particularly true when there was grave danger that assumption would be defeated. One polemical writer went so far as to threaten Congress with a special convention of public creditors at New York or Philadelphia to "facilitate" the progress of the measure through that body and added a warning that the number of "respectable men" who were holders of the public debt was too large to be treated with indifference. This advocate evidently thought also that the capitalistic element was the very substance of the new government, for he declared emphatically that it would be nothing but a shadow without "a prosperous funding system" — meaning one which would consolidate the state and continental debt and place the holders thereof on a secure basis.[1]

---

[1] "I am persuaded Congress are not so ignorant of the circumstances of the United States as to imagine a partial system of finance is practicable. Unless the state debts are assumed, no funding system will operate prosperously, and *without a prosperous funding system our national government will be but a shadow.* In short I dare not predict the consequences of having the public debts long neglected, or partially provided for. The creditors of the United States and of the several states have not yet lost their patience, or their confidence. I hope they will never lose either, but I imagine, if nothing is done for their relief within a few weeks, they will unite in some measures to express their sentiments to Congress in very unequivocal, but respectful language. Perhaps a Convention of Delegates from the public creditors to meet at New York or Philadelphia could make some representations to Congress that would facilitate their determinations. The opposers of the funding system, and in this light, I view all anti-assumptionists, are not sen-

While this writer was endeavoring to frighten Congress by suggesting the possibility of a concerted effort on the part of the financial interests, another Federalist was rallying the security holders to the support of the administration by showing them that the Constitution, so full of promise, might be undone by a failure to consolidate the debt and properly fund it. It was possible for them to serve both God and mammon — strengthen the party in possession of the government and protect their own pecuniary interests. "Is there a prudent man among you," insinuated this shrewd political psychologist, "who, comparing the funding system without assumption, with the conduct of other nations, and judging of the interests and passions of the state creditors and legislatures, will say gravely and upon reflection, the revenue will be more safe and productive without assumption than with it? . . . Judge then whether the interest of your own paper does not require the assumption. You cannot be safe without it. Patronize justice and practice a magnanimity which will cost you nothing, but do you honor, by insisting that the provision shall comprehend the kindred claims of state creditors. . . . Remember that as the adoption of the constitution raised your hopes, the undoing it in practice may blast them." [1]

That which cropped out in polemical literature, namely, that the security holders were supporting the administration party as they had the Constitution, appeared in private correspondence as well as in the newspapers. Indeed, a competent observer of contemporary politics, Chauncey Goodrich, of Connecticut, went so far as to declare that the successful continuance of the government depended upon the cordial support of the creditors without whose active

sible how large a number of respectable men are holders of the public debt." United States Gazette, April 17, 1790. Italics mine.

[1] The Gazette of the United States, May 15, 1790.

influence the very Constitution itself probably would not have been established. Writing on February 3, 1790, to Oliver Wolcott, Jr., Auditor of the Treasury under Hamilton, Goodrich said: "I have received your letter enclosing the secretary's Report [on public credit], which I have forwarded to your father. . . . The report has been reprinted in this town [Hartford] and is sought for with much avidity.[1] . . . So far as I can collect the sentiments of your acquaintance, they are favourable to the system. We hope the government will improve the present season of its popularity to establish a more permanent foundation than what it now rests on. *Its only stable support will be a well-regulated treasury,* and I am sure that the best friends of the government will not only be disappointed but dissatisfied, if the present session of Congress passes without a good arrangement of the finances. The public creditors will esteem themselves honorably used, in case the Secretary's ideas be carried into effect; and even if they are not so advantageous, I do not imagine it will occasion any discontent to be regarded. *Perhaps, without the active influence of the creditors, the government could not have been formed, and any well grounded dissatisfaction on their part will certainly make its movements dull and languid, if not worse. . . .*"[2]

A similar view of the situation was entertained by Oliver Wolcott, Sr., president of the Connecticut convention that ratified the federal Constitution and father of Oliver Wolcott. In a letter dated at Litchfield on January 28, 1790, the senior Wolcott said: "This much I will venture upon that the efficiency of this government will essentially depend upon the system of their finances and the regulation of their militia, both of which therefore, I suppose, they

---

[1] Hartford had more assumed debt holders than any of the other Connecticut towns. *Economic Interpretation of the Constitution*, p. 265.

[2] Gibbs, *op. cit.*, Vol. I, p. 37. Italics mine.

will extend as far as the principles of the Constitution will admit, and consequently endeavour to include ultimately the state debts in the system, and render the militia as dependent as the case will admit, upon the general Executive." [1] On a later date, April 23, 1790, Wolcott wrote to a correspondent, evidently his son in the Treasury Department: "Your observations respecting the public debts as essential to the existence of the national government are undoubtedly just, — *there certainly cannot at present exist any other cement.* The assumption of state debts is as necessary, and indeed more so, for the existence of the national government than those of any other description; if the state governments are to provide for their payment, these creditors will forever oppose all national provisions as inconsistent with their interest; which circumstances, together with the habits and pride of the local jurisdictions, will render the states very refractory. A rejection to provide for the state debts, which it seems has been done by a committee of Congress, if persisted in, *I consider as an overthrow of the national government.*" [2]

Powerful as the security holders were, it was not to them alone that the Federalist leaders made their appeal. All through their writings there ran the firm opinion that "respectable men" of "wealth" and "talents" were inevitably on the side of Hamilton in the partisan conflict. For example, John Steele wrote to the Secretary of the Treasury, on March 17, 1793, that "to support a constitution which cost the best people of the Union so much pains to establish, to counteract the nefarious designs of its enemies, and to rally around the Federal Government as a standard where our most precious interests are well secured is the duty of

[1] *Ibid*, p. 36.
[2] *Ibid.*, p. 45. Italics mine. See Fisher Ames' view to the same effect, above, p. 134.

men who possess talents, property, reputation or influence." [1] A year later Francis Corbin, of Buckingham, Middlesex, Virginia, wrote to Hamilton that "War is waged by this faction [Anti-Federalists] against every Candidate who possesses the union of requisites. Independent fortune, independent principles, talents and integrity are denounced as badges of aristocracy; but if you add to these good manners and a decent appearance, his political death is decreed without the benefit of a hearing. In short, with a few exceptions, everything that appertains to the character of a gentleman is ostracised. That yourself and Mr. Jay should be no favorites in Virginia then is not to be wondered at." [2]

While representing the Constitution as the chief hope of the financial interests and the successful execution of Hamilton's policies as the culmination of their labors, Federalist writers naturally completed the picture of class antagonism by portraying Jefferson as the enemy of "sound finance" and his followers as propertyless levellers, the spiritual heirs of Jack Cade and Daniel Shays. A keen Federalist, under the pen name of "Catullus" declared, in the Gazette of the United States, that it was all very well for Jefferson to have opposed the funding bills while they were pending before the country, but that the continuance of his opposition after the measures had become the deliberate and solemn acts of the legislature was highly reprehensible. In his opinion, this revealed a clear purpose to render the fiscal measures odious to the people and to undermine public confidence in the constituted authorities. Jefferson's poli-

---

[1] *Hamilton Mss.* (Library of Congress), March 17, 1793. See Manlius, *Letters to the Columbian Centinel* (1794) in which it is represented that the "anarchists" had tried to stir up opposition to the government in New England but were outwitted by "the merchants, the tradesmen, and the friends to order and our excellent Constitution."   [2] *Ibid.*, July 20, 1794.

tics, he concluded, "tend to national disunion, insignificance, disorder, and discredit. . . . Disunion would not long lag behind. Sober minded and virtuous men in every state would lose all confidence in and all respect for a government which had betrayed so much levity and inconstancy, so profligate a disregard to the *rights of property*, and to the obligations of good faith. . . . *The invasion of sixty millions of property could not be perpetrated without violent concussions.* The States whose citizens, both as *original* creditors and *purchasers* own the largest portions of the debt (and several such there are) would not long remain bound in the trammels of a party which has so grossly violated their rights." [1]

If Jefferson was an enemy of wealth and respectability, his agrarian followers were more than worthy of their leader. Federalist champions never wearied of representing them as the foes of property and order. One declared that the Republicans were a horde of levellers bent on dividing the savings of the thrifty. Another vented his anger upon the opposition by formulating their philosophy in a "Sample Oration" purported to have been delivered by a leveller at a "Volunteer State Convention," such as had been popular in the days of the Revolution. In this ironical partisan document, the Republican apostle put himself forward as the champion of the landed as against the "moneyed" interest and declared his principles in the following extravagant strain: "As to property, I have none; thank heaven, I have divested myself of all yellow dirt, all filthy lucre, in those blest days when I was a committee-man and watched night and day, in public houses for the public good. Property . . . is the mother of aristocracy. . . . A Numarian law would be a rich blessing. Oh, how it would gladden

[1] The Gazette of the United States, September 29, 1792.

the hearts and gild with pleasure the faces of the true disciples, to serve once more on committees, whose business it should be, at least once in three years, to inspect the chests and coffers of the overgrown purse-proud man or the paltry muck worm, who toiled with the dirty view of 'laying up pelf against a rainy day,' and divide their ungodly spoil amongst the pure lovers of liberty.

"A Numarian law is not an object to be dispaired of. In order to gain the land holders it is only necessary to convince them that it is their interest to pare commerce to the quick. . . . That the landed interest is one thing, and the monied is another, is very plain. . . . I have heard it reported that there is one state in the Union of no mean size, that would not suffer land to be touched by that harpy the law. If this is true, it is a glorious example, a noble policy. A new made landed-man laughs his monied dupe creditor in the face, with virtuous scorn. . . . View the American Court and tremble. The head of the system and all coadjutors ought speedily to be ostracised and banished. . . . For a beginning I would remove the Secretary of the Treasury and appoint some young Broker in his place. . . . For Secretary of War I would chuse their worthy re-inflated fellow citizen, Daniel Shays, Esq." [1]

This capitalistic-agrarian antagonism which was brought out by those Federalists who frankly loved the lust of battle and sought neither compromise nor conciliation was quite as definitely set forth by those milder, and perhaps shrewder, writers who contented themselves with filing a demur to the allegations of the Republicans, that is, admitted a divergence of economic activity but denied the necessity of an inherent conflict. As early as September 23, 1789, some months before Hamilton announced this economic theory in his

[1] Gazette of the United States, October 22, 1791.

Report on Manufactures, a writer in the Gazette of the United States adopted the tactics of "harmonizing the interests" rather than sharpening them, by saying: "It is asserted that there is, at this day, so great a diversity between the different states in point of religion, manners, habits, and interests as to render the administration of a general government inconvenient and perhaps impracticable. . . . Many appeal to the supposed fact that the eastern and southern states have opposite interests. Undoubtedly a diversity of interests is one of the most fruitful sources of contention and hatred. Too much stress, however, is generally laid upon it. For such interests, tho *different* are not always *repugnant*. . . . It is very certain that the employments of the southern and eastern states are different: But it is denied that their interests are incompatible. . . . The eastern and southern states are necessary to one another. And nature has interposed to forbid their becoming commercial rivals. What one raises, the other wants, and when one prospers the other will partake. . . . Without violent evidence, a patriot should not admit that the interests of the southern and eastern parts of the Union are opposite. It will require some reflection to suppress his wonder, that not only without evidence, but against the most palpable, it has ever been the creed of the country. It is time to think more justly and more *rationally*, which is the same thing." [1]

[1] *Ibid.*, September 23, 1789. A friend of the Federalist administration is represented as saying to an "honest husbandman" in Massachusetts: "Be not discouraged; let not the most frightful suggestions of the discontented scare you from your industry, [for the debt will be repaid in due time]. Taxes in this country, never have been and, we confidently believe, they never will be the means of imprisoning the industrious man. The case of the farmer has in some respects been hard, too small a comparative value has been set on the produce of his farm, when made the consideration of money. Too free a use of foreign commodities was the reason, the purchase of which made large and constant draughts on our specie. But against this evil we are daily strengthen-

Other Federalists were even more enthusiastic about harmony. They were not satisfied with merely showing the natural reciprocity which existed between the agricultural and trading regions, but they also undertook to prove that the augmentation of fluid capital which was contemplated by Hamilton's fiscal system would benefit all members of the community whether they held securities or not. This was, of course, the burden of the Report on Public Credit, and popular writers thought it an argument sufficiently self-evident to lay before the readers of newspapers. The Gazette of the United States declared, within four months of the passage of the funding act, that "Every citizen of the United States is interested in the rise of public paper — whether a proprietor or not ; for in proportion as its value approaches to that of specie, an additional medium is introduced, by which every person who has anything to do with trade, commerce, agriculture, or manufactures is benefited. It is undoubtedly a fact that this country has never been in possession of a sufficient quantity of the precious metal to constitute a competent circulating medium without the auxiliary of paper money. . . . An addition to the present medium of the United States, bank paper, bottomed on substantial funds, such as through the favor of heaven are now within our reach, will most undoubtedly invigorate every spring of industry and enterprise that can be set in motion." [1]

ing ourselves. Progress in preparation for supplying our demands from among ourselves is successfully made: the interests of the mechanic, husbandman, and artisan are anxiously blended with the first objects of our legislators. Under their watchful protection all the means within reach for promoting them will be hunted up. Thus will industry be encouraged and our money made more plenty.'; Gazette of the United States, April 10, 1790. (From the Massachusetts Spy.)

[1] Gazette of the United States, December 29, 1790. One Federalist pamphleteer in his enthusiasm for the administration policies even suggested that the wizard Hamilton had devised a plan whereby the debt would pay itself. "The safety, dignity, and prosperity of the United States," wrote Daniel Leonard in 1792,

For those who took this view the prosperity of the country was ample proof of the general beneficence of the fiscal system. Before the new government was established unemployment was widespread, industry languished, and the farmers were discouraged. But shortly after the Federalist policy went into operation, the land began to flow with milk and honey : "To what physical, moral, or political energy shall this flourishing state of things be ascribed ? There is but one answer to these inquiries : *Public credit is restored and* ESTABLISHED. The general government, by uniting and calling into action the pecuniary resources of the states, has created a new capital stock of several millions of dollars, which, with that before existing, is directed into every branch of business, giving life and vigor to industry in its infinitely diversified operations. The enemies of the general government, the funding act and the National Bank may bellow *tyranny, aristocracy,* and *speculators* through the Union and repeat the clamorous din as long as they please ; but the actual state of agriculture and commerce, the peace, the contentment and satisfaction of the great mass of people, give the lie to their assertions and stamp on them in capitals : *Vox et praeterea nihil.*" [1]

"have grown out of the systems he has proposed. It is this important character who has taught us and brought it home to the sense of the people at large that public credit is an inestimable jewel. It is he who has taught us to derive an advantage from the public debt by creating the means, out of the debt itself, to discharge it. . . . The establishment of the national bank to facilitate the operations of the government and to provide against all hazards from a want of punctuality in the regular discharge of the interest of the debt at stated periods, is equally an act of judgment as of policy." Daniel Leonard, *Strictures and Observations upon the Three Executive Departments* (1792), New York Public Library.

[1] The Gazette of the United States, September 5, 1792. While instructing grand jurors in the principles of the new constitutional system, federal judges did not overlook directing attention to the economic advantages to be derived from it. For example, Judge Grimke, in a charge to the grand jury of the Camden district in 1791, called their attention to the fact that assumption had relieved South Carolina of a burden of about $4,000,000, enhanced the value of securities in the hands of holders, and would "augment the price of property to a very considerable

This plea that agrarian and capitalistic interests were reciprocal and that the general prosperity diffused throughout the country by the fiscal system was an evidence of the fact did not, however, meet all of the Republicans' objections. It left unanswered the contention of the latter that a long continuance of the economic policy of the government would end in the prostration of the agricultural class at the feet of the financial and commercial classes. In attacking this assertion, Federalist apologists admitted the class division but flatly denied that capitalism would conquer agriculture. The very idea was, in their opinion, preposterous. The great majority of the people were farmers and lived outside of the cities. The amount of capitalist property was relatively small when compared with the value of the lands. "On an impartial view of the United States, no man will deny," wrote "The Republican" in Fenno's Gazette, "that the landed interest maintains its ancient preponderance; nor will he pretend that the value to which the public stocks have risen will diminish it. The debt is not increasing, but is diminishing daily, and the time of its extinguishment need not be far removed. The amount of the bank stock is also fixed and it is to the landed property as a drop in the ocean. The landed interest, on the contrary, has thousands of hands yearly imported to increase its importance. Some hundred thousand acres are added every year to the cultivation of our country. Look at the late enumeration, and see how few live in cities compared with those in the country; and while the cities increase ten, the country gains a thousand. On this general view of the subject, a man may be convinced that there is no overruling monied influence raised up to govern the landed,

degree." This happy outcome, the judge thought, would reconcile to the federal union the minds of those honest citizens who were at first opposed to the Constitution. The Gazette of the United States, February 19, 1791.

as those writers have insinuated, whose purpose it is to set one part of the people against another. . . . If the title to a horse or a barrel of corn be in dispute, it is a noble privilege that the whole power of our government cannot destroy a man's right. But when fifty or sixty millions of property are depending before Congress, these republicans, as they dare to call themselves would make a sport of the acknowledged right of the possessors." [1]

It surely does not require additional testimony to show that the agrarian-capitalistic antagonism, whether real or imaginary, was, in the minds of many Federalist champions, at the very centre of the partisan conflict. But it may be objected that the sources cited thus far in this chapter are fugitive pieces of polemical literature and do not represent any serious or systematic thinking on the part of the authors. Without admitting the validity of this contention, it seems worth while to inquire whether in the more orderly and pretentious writings of the time or in the statements of men of larger authority than those just quoted the same economic considerations appear to have been at the heart of the political controversy.

One of the most effective and widely known of the smaller Federalist works was a pamphlet by "Marcellus" bearing the title *Letters from the Virginia Gazette*, published in 1794. In its way, it deserves to rank with the essays of John Taylor, of Caroline. The author of this ingenious tract opens cleverly by insinuating that the farmers have been deceived by the demagogue, not because their intentions are evil but because they have been improperly informed on the subject of the fiscal system and the policy of the Federal administration. Thus at the outset, "Marcellus" admits that the enemy is the farmer, and he shrewdly introduces his attack

[1] The Gazette of the United States, October 10, 1792.

by saying that, "Men devoted to the laborious and honorable occupations of agriculture, at a distance from the seat of information, without the means of inquiring or the leisure to make deep researches and to investigate complex principles and obscure facts — however virtuous (and in all nations they are to be regarded as the most virtuous part of the society) — are liable from these circumstances to be imposed on and misled by the artifices of the wicked and ambitious." [1]

After having thus sought to engage the interest of the farmer, "Marcellus" endeavors to destroy the idea of an "aristocracy" in America which had been employed so assiduously by the Republicans to stir up the populace. "What is aristocracy?" he asks. . . . "If aristocracy in this meaning [hereditary] does not exist [in America] let those who so frequently use the terms *aristocrat* and *democrat,* define them. . . . Do they mean by the term *aristocrat* a *rich man,* contradistinguished from a *poor man?* If by the term *aristocrat,* they mean the rich and by the term *democrat,* the poor; by villifying the first and exalting the last do they mean to censure industry by which wealth is acquired and commend idleness which is the cause of poverty and the fruitful source of every vice. If they make it a crime to be rich, men will cease to make any efforts to better their condition, to provide for the education and comforts of their families, and add to their own wealth as well as the riches of their country by honest industry, and from a civilized society we shall become a horde of savages. To this deplorable condition would their system gradually reduce us. But it cannot be expected that such haughty dictators would wait for the slow operation of time. They may attempt to reduce all property at once to a level; abo-

1 Copy in the New York Public Library.

lition of debt, agrarian laws and emancipation of slaves may be expected among their first *coups de main*. For, if by the term *democrat* they mean the poor, who so poor as our slaves, who therefore so fit to participate in the spoils of the rich and to direct the affairs of the nation?"

With the assertion of the Republicans that an aristocracy is being built up through the operations of the fiscal system "Marcellus" has no patience. "I ask again," he says, "whence proceeds the danger of the growth of aristocratic orders amongst us? Certainly not from the accumulations of landed property. I may be answered from the funding system. I may be told in the same cant, indefinite, and unintelligible language of the existence of a *paper nobility*. . . . It will be sufficient to say that we owed the debt — that if we were honest we were bound to pay it."

The charge that much money had been made by the appreciation of securities, "Marcellus" meets with the counter charge that land owners had been making money through the increase of land values and that one form of accumulation of riches was no more reprehensible than the other. "That much speculation existed at the commencement of the system is true; and perhaps much property acquired by fraud, but are not all other negotiations also subject to fraud? Has not land risen almost as rapidly in value as stock in the funds? If a man makes a fortunate purchase of land is he censured for it? If he buys the bond of an individual for half its nominal value is he censured for it? Why then load with opprobrious epithets those . . . who have purchased the obligations of the public?"

If those who espouse the cause of "democracy" do not mean thereby the cause of the poor, but direct government [1] by the voters, "Marcellus" is equally ready to combat

[1] For Jefferson's view of simple, direct government, see below, p. 459.

their views. "If instead of meaning the poor by the term democrat, they denominate a friend to that kind of government in which each person in his individual capacity exercises those functions which in our society are delegated to representatives, such as were some of the petty tumultous commonwealths of old, this would be a government so hostile to the happiness of our citizens and so counter to the habits and practice of the American people that no man would deem it honorable to assume the name, as in this sense it would be regarded as another term for anarchist."

Before dismissing the subject of democracy, "Marcellus" remarks in a cutting tone that the apostles of that new order would find it difficult to reconcile their system of "liberty" with slavery and the disfranchisement of the white non-freeholders in Virginia. "I could wish," he says, "that the doctrines of the times and justice to the subject would permit me to draw a veil over certain peculiarities. But when we hear so much about *Liberty* and *Equality* we are obliged to consider how far the application of these principles in their *most extensive meaning* to our situation would be promotive of our happiness and consistent with our peace. . . . It can hardly be necessary to tell a Virginian that two-fifths of the inhabitants of our state are slaves: and that even part of the freemen have no share in the management of public affairs. What do those who preach *liberty* and *equality* mean? Do they mean to raise the blacks to equal social rights with the whites? Do they mean to remove the existing discriminations amongst the whites themselves? . . . Perhaps nothing is meant but frothy declamation." "Marcellus" then adds a final stab by suggesting that the apostles of democracy might find in New England, which was charged with being the home of the new aristocracy, those very conditions that seemed most compatible with democratic ideals : no slavery and small land holdings. Such a "nursery of purest republican principles" could hardly be a source of danger to the country.[1]

Again it may be objected that "Marcellus" is a pamphleteer and that his tract directed to the instant needs of politics does not represent a reasoned view of the merits of the party controversy. If this is true, there is still a higher authority whose knowledge of the period and whose powers of judgment and exposition will hardly be denied by the most critical, John Marshall, who, in his *Life of Washington*, expounded in a few passages of that remarkable clarity and precision which characterized his opinions from the bench, the economic nature of the grievances on which the Republicans thrived. The specific charges brought by them against Washington's administration, which formed the source of antagonism between the two parties, Marshall summarized as follows : "It was alleged [by Republicans] that the public debt was too great to be paid before other causes of adding to it would occur. This accumulation of debt had been artificially produced by the assumption of what was due from the states. . . . The banishment of coin would be completed by ten millions of paper money in the form of

[1] The scorn which "Marcellus" had for Virginia democrats who "prated" about equality and liberty while holding two-fifths of the population in chattel slavery and disfranchising all the non-freeholders was frequently expressed at a safer range in New England. "Manlius," a Massachusetts pamphleteer, attacked the southerners for inconsistency — talking about equality while enjoying a representation in Congress for three-fifths of the slaves held in bondage whereas "the people of New England are equally represented whether rich or poor and their representatives are the representatives of men equally free and possessing equal rights" (a statement which was wanting in historical accuracy in view of the property qualifications on voting then imposed in New England). "Where," he exclaimed, "are the rights of equal liberty more truly represented? From a land where a great proportion of the inhabitants are slaves and till the ground of their lordly masters, where education at public expense is unknown, where the poverty of the poor is their curse, for they are necessarily bred up in ignorance and absolute idleness or condemned to the severest drudgery?" Manlius, *The Columbian Centinel* (1794). New York Public Library. The copy in the Library of Congress is ascribed to Christopher Gore.

bank bills, which were then issuing into circulation. Nor would this be the only mischief resulting from the institution of the bank. The ten or twelve per cent annual profit paid to the lenders of this paper medium would take out of the pockets of the people, who would have had, without interest, the coin it was banishing. *That all the capital employed in paper speculation is barren and useless, producing like that on a gaming table, no accession to itself, and is withdrawn from commerce and agriculture, where it would have produced addition to the common mass.* The wealth therefore heaped upon individuals by the funding and banking systems, would be productive of general poverty and distress. That in addition to the encouragement these measures gave to vice and idleness, they had furnished effectual means of corrupting such a portion of the legislature as turned the balance between the honest voters. This corrupt squad, deciding the voice of the legislature, had manifested their disposition to get rid of the limitations imposed by the Constitution; limitations on the faith of which the states acceded to that instrument. They were proceeding rapidly in their plan of absorbing all power, invading the rights of the states, and conver;ing the federal into a consolidated government.

"That the ultimate object of all this was to prepare the way for a change from the present Republican form of government to that of a monarchy, of which the English constitution was to be the model. So many of the friends of monarchy were in the legislature, that, aided by the corrupt squad of paper dealers who were at their devotion, they made a majority in both houses.[1] The Republican

---

[1] The charge of the Republicans that "a paper nobility" in Congress was actually interested in the public securities through their personal holdings, the Federalists indignantly denied. They demanded certain proof. Blandly overlooking the fact that the Treasury Records were under the seal of the profoundest secrecy,

party, even when united with the anti-federalists, continued a minority. . . .

"These strictures on the conduct of administration were principally directed against measures which had originated with the secretary of the treasury, and had afterwards received the sanction of the legislature. In the southern division of the continent, that officer was unknown, except to a few military friends, and to those who had engaged in the legislative or executive departments of the former or present government. His systems of revenues having been generally opposed by the southern members, and the original opposition to the Constitution having been particularly great in Virginia and North Carolina, the aspersions on his views, and the views of the eastern members by whom his plans had been generally supported, were seldom controverted." [1]

they called upon the Republicans to prove their assertions. The latter, they contended, had stirred up the hatred of the populace by slanderous allegations and then had shrunk from the test of naming the members of "the corrupt squadron." The whole attack upon the paper nobility in Congress, the Federalists declared to be a sinister move to discredit a system whose merits were sufficient to commend it to men who had the honor to desire that the government discharge its just debts. Fisher Ames of Massachusetts was especially vehement in repudiating the charge that members of Congress were themselves interested in securities to any considerable extent or were influenced in their policies by private considerations. In a long and impassioned address attacking the activities of the "Jacobinical clubs," he referred to the allegations of the Anti-Federalists as follows: "The other slander which has contributed to kindle a civil war, is the *paper nobility* in Congress ; that the taxes are voted for the sake, and carried solely by the strength of those who put the proceeds in their pockets. Is there a word of truth in this? On the contrary, there are probably not ten members who have *any* interest in the funds, and that interest very inconsiderable. Citizens have thus been led by calumny and lies to despise their Government and its Ministers, to dread and hate it, and all concerned in it, so that the [whiskey] insurrection is chiefly owing to the men and the societies, who have invented, or confirmed, and diffused these slanders." It would thus seem that Ames' acquaintance with security holders in Congress extended little beyond the Massachusetts delegation, or he would not have been as loose in his generalization as to the number interested in public funds. *Annals of Congress*, 1793–1795, p. 929. Ames declared that the interest on the public funds held by members of Congress would no more than pay for the oats for their horses. Gerry alone had $3500 a year from that source so that the Federalist stables must have been very large.

[1] *Life of Washington* (2d ed.), Vol. II, pp. 227 ff.

Although the Republican grievances were, in Marshall's opinion, chiefly directed against the capitalistic features of the Federalist system, he did not emphasize economic divisions alone. He called attention to the political aspects of the early conflict over the rights and powers of the states and the federal government, and then continued : "To this great and radical division of opinion, which would necessarily affect every question of the authority of the national legislature, other motives were added, which were believed to possess considerable influence on all measures connected with the finances."

These other motives were economic in character. "As an inevitable effect of the state of society," continued Marshall, "the public debt had greatly accumulated in the middle and northern states, whose inhabitants had derived from its rapid appreciation, a proportional augmentation of their wealth. This circumstance could not fail to contribute to the complacency with which the plans of the secretary [of the treasury] were viewed by those who had felt their benefit, nor to the irritation with which they were contemplated by others who had parted with their claims on the nation. It is not impossible, that personal considerations also mingled themselves with those which were merely political." [1]

Notwithstanding this apparent subordination of economic to political considerations, Marshall in fact declared emphatically (as we have already seen) that "the first regular and systematic opposition to the principles on which the affairs of the union were administered, originated in the measures " which were founded on Hamilton's Report on Public Credit. [2] And he added that the Bank act "contributed, not inconsiderably, to the complete organization

of those distinct and visible parties, which, in their long
and dubious conflict for power, have since shaken the United
States to their centre." [1] Marshall was even more specific.
He said that the effect of Hamilton's funding measure "was
great and rapid. The public paper suddenly rose, and was
for a short time above par. The immense wealth which
individuals acquired by this unexpected appreciation,
could not be viewed with indifference. Those who participated in its advantages, regarded the author of a system
to which they were so greatly indebted, with an enthusiasm
of attachment to which scarcely any limits were assigned.[2]
To many others, this adventitious collection of wealth in
particular hands, was a subject rather of chagrin than of
pleasure. . . . Its being funded was ascribed by many,
not to a sense of justice, and to a liberal and enlightened
policy, but to a desire of bestowing on the government an
artificial strength, by the creation of a moneyed interest
which would be subservient to its will. The effects produced by giving the debt a permanent value, justified the
predictions of those whose anticipations had been most
favorable. The sudden increase of moneyed capital derived
from it invigorated commerce and gave a new stimulus to

[1] *Ibid.*, p. 206.
[2] The rising tide of business prosperity which had begun before the drafting of
the Constitution and continued through Washington's first administration was
naturally attributed to the Federalist policies, and particularly Hamilton's fiscal
measures. The man who is able, declared Oliver Wolcott, Sr., "to establish a
system of public credit after it was by abuse of all public faith and confidence nearly
annihilated, so as within the short term of four years fully to restore and establish
it upon a stable basis, and by his provident care to guard against all contingencies
which might do it injury, and by the same operation raise a people from the most
torpid indolence and despondency to a state of the most vigorous enterprise, industry, and cheerfulness, and increase the value of property within the same period
one third more than it was before (which I believe has been the case within this
state, notwithstanding our vast emigrations) ; he who can effect all of this without imposing a sensible burden upon any one, or deranging one useful occupation
or business, must possess talents and industry and a species of intuition.". Gibbs,
op. cit., Vol. I, p. 101.

agriculture. About this time, there was a great and visible improvement in the circumstances of the people. Although the funding system was certainly not inoperative in producing this improvement, it cannot be justly ascribed to any single cause. Progressive industry had gradually repaired the losses sustained by the war, and the influence of the Constitution on the habits of thinking and acting, though silent, was considerable. In depriving the states of the power to impair the obligation of contracts, or to make anything but gold and silver a tender in payment of debts, the conviction was impressed on that portion of society which had looked to the government for relief from embarrassment, that personal exertions alone could free them from difficulties." [1]

That Marshall's great work from which these citations are taken was dominated by a political motive cannot be denied. Nevertheless the accuracy of his analysis of the causes of party dissension will hardly be disputed, and its implications are so clear as to need no further comment. They may be strengthened and elucidated, however, by reference to an authority scarcely less weighty, Fisher Ames, of Massachusetts, whose experience and standing entitle him to special respect. In a letter, written on November 30, 1791, from Philadelphia, where he was serving in Congress, this statesman, for such he truly was, made an examination of the economic forces and the accompanying class psychology which then divided the North and the South — a section of capitalistic processes and a section controlled by agriculturalists. In this letter he said that the causes which brought about differences of opinion in the two portions of the country were "equally lasting and

[1] Gibbs, *op. cit.*, Vol. I, p. 191. Marshall seems unaware of the fact that it was government aid that had helped the Federalists out of their difficulties.

unpleasant. To the northward, we see how necessary it is to defend property by steady laws. Shays confirmed our habits and opinions. The men of sense and property, even a little above the multitude, wish to keep the government in force enough to govern. We have trade, money, credit, and industry, which is at once cause and effect of the others. At the southward, a few gentlemen govern; the law is their coat of mail; it keeps off the weapons of the foreigners, their creditors, and at the same time it governs the multitude, secures negroes, etc., which is of double use to them. It is both government and anarchy, and in each case is better than any possible change, especially in favor of an exterior (or federal) government of any strength; for that would be losing the property, the usufruct of a government, by the state, which is light to bear and convenient to manage. Therefore, and for other causes, the men of weight in the four Southern states (Charleston city excepted) were more generally *antis*, and are now far more turbulent than they are with us. Many were federal among them at first, because they needed some remedy to evils which they saw and felt, but mistook, in their view of it, the remedy. A debt-compelling government is no remedy to men who have land and negroes, and debts and luxury, but neither trade nor credit, nor cash, nor the habits of industry, nor of submission to a rigid execution of law. My friend, you will agree with me, that, ultimately, the same system of strict law, which has done wonders for us, would promote their advantage. But that relief is speculative and remote. Enormous debts required something better and speedier! I am told, that to this day, no British debt is recovered in North Carolina. . . . Patrick Henry, and some others of eminent talents, and influence, have continued *antis* and have assiduously nursed the embryos of faction, which the adoption of ᵢ the Constitution did not destroy. It soon gave popularity to the *antis* with a grumbling multitude. It made two parties.

"Most of the measures of Congress have been opposed by the southern members. . . . The funding system, they say, is in favor of the moneyed interest — oppressive to the land; that is, favorable to us, hard on them. They pay tribute, they say, and the middle and eastern people, holders of seven-eighths of the debt, receive it. And here is the burden of the song, almost all the little that they had and which cost them twenty shilling for supplies or services, has been bought up, at a low rate, and now they pay more tax towards the interest than they received for the paper. This *tribute* they say, is aggravating, for all the reasons before given; they add, had the state debts not been assumed, they would have wiped it off among themselves very speedily and easily. Being assumed, it has become a great debt; and now an excise, that abhorrence of free states. . . . Faction glows within [the southern states] like a coal pit. The President lives — is a southern man, is venerated as a demigod, he is chosen by unanimous vote, etc., etc. Change the key and —— You can fill up the blank. But, while he lives, a steady prudent system by Congress may guard against the danger. . . . Yet, circumstanced as they are, I think other subjects of uneasiness will be found. For it is impossible to administer the government according to their ideas. We must have a revenue; of course, an excise. The debt must be kept sacred; the rights of property must be held inviolate. We must, to be safe, have some regular force, and an efficient militia. . . . In fine, those three states are circumstanced not unlike our state in 1786. . . . I will confess my belief that if, now, a vote was to be taken, 'Shall the Constitution be adopted,' and the people of Virginia, and the other more southern states (the city of Charleston excepted), should answer instantly according to their present feelings and opinions, it would be in the negative." [1]

Finally, we may say again that the great Federalist colleague of Marshall and Ames, Hamilton, waged his political battle on the assumption that the Jeffersonian party was the party of opposition to his fiscal measures. As early as 1792, he had announced the two cardinal reasons why the friends of the Constitution and public credit should unite against Jefferson. In his famous papers signed "An American," he declared: "1st. That while the Constitution of the United States was depending before the people of this country for their consideration and decision, Mr. Jefferson, being in France, was opposed to it in some of its most important features, and wrote his objections to some of his friends in Virginia. That he at first went so far as to discountenance its adoption, though he afterwards recommended it, on the ground of expediency in certain contingencies. 2d. That he is the declared opponent of almost all the important measures which have been devised by the government, more especially the provision which has been made for the public debt, the institution of the Bank of the United States, and such other measures as relate to the public credit, and the finances of the United States." [2]

[1] *Life and Works of Fisher Ames*, Vol. I, pp. 103 ff. That the debts due in the South to the British were one of the chief sources of strength to the Republican opposition was also the opinion of Oliver Ellsworth. Writing to Oliver Wolcott, Sr., from Philadelphia, on April 4, 1794, he said: "The debts of the South, which were doubtless among the causes of the late Revolution, have ever since operated to obstruct its benefits, by opposing compulsive energy of government, generating mist and irritation between this country and Great Britain, and of course giving a baleful ascendance to French influence. Under these auspices, an extensive combination of the wicked and the weak has been arranged for some time past, and will probably continue its efforts to disturb the peace of this country so long as the European contest continues in its present state of dubiety." Gibbs, *op. cit.*, Vol. I, p. 134. [2] *Works* (Lodge ed.), Vol. VI, p. 317.

It was this affiliation of Jefferson with the party of opposition to the Constitution and the entire capitalistic system that led Hamilton to engage in bitter personal controversy. He declared that he had remained silent and suffered many indignities until he saw the real nature of the opposing party. Then and only then had he taken up arms. "When I no longer doubted," he said, "that there was a formed party deliberately bent upon the subversion of measures, which in its consequences would subvert the government; when I saw that the undoing of the funding system in particular (which, whatever may be the original merits of that system, would prostrate the credit and the honor of the nation, and *bring the government into contempt with that description of men which are in every society the only firm supporters of government*) was an avowed object of the party, and that all possible pains were taken to produce the effect, by rendering it odious to the body of the people, I considered it as a duty to endeavor to resist the torrent, and, as an effectual means to this end, to draw aside the veil from the principal actors." [1]

NOTE TO CHAPTER VIII

One striking feature of this partisan conflict was the absence of any considerable appeal to the working classes or "mechanics" in the towns. Of course, the Republicans, in attacking the "aristocracy of wealth," naturally struck a responsive chord in the breasts of the poor, but neither the Republicans nor the Federalists seem to have paid much attention to capturing the vote of the mechanics. Even Hamilton, who was so deeply concerned in the growth of manufactures, does not appear to have given that consideration to the labor vote which its importance demanded. Nevertheless, he did not overlook the matter, for among the various fragments preserved in his manuscripts, there appears the following passage: "They [the Anti-Federalists] pretend to hate great men and to love and protect the common people. Yet abused and insulted citizens, this very faction has never ceased to resist every protection or encouragement to arts and manufactures. The body of useful mechanics now rising into a well-earned importance in society well know that this faction have done all they could to throw them back again into the forlorn condi-

[1] *Works* (Lodge ed.), Vol. VI. p. 386. Italics mine. See above for Hamilton's view as to the character of the "firm supporters of government," p. 5.

tion where the weakness of the old government left them to struggle." (*Hamilton Mss.*, 1794; last sheet in Vol. XV.)

The widespread conviction, which had high authority in Jefferson's *Notes on Virginia* (see below, p. 422), published in 1786, to the effect that a working class was servile in character, depraved in manners and morals and, therefore, not to be desired in the United States, was the subject of occasional discussion.   The Federalists, of course, refused to admit the doctrine of innate depravity ascribed to capitalism by the Republicans, and as a last resort they pointed out that the menial working man could escape at will from his thraldom by taking up lands in the west.   "It has been insinuated," says a writer in the Gazette of the United States, "that the establishment of manufactures will tend to make menials of our citizens while they are immured in the factories constructed for carrying on the works.   But let it be remembered that we are all under just and equal laws, that every man is free to chuse what occupation he pleases and that our boundless western territories will forever afford a retreat from domestic impositions. . . .   It is highly probable that much higher wages can be afforded to manufacturers and artists than are usually paid to those descriptions of persons in Europe, particularly in Great Britain — for it is evident that while the great body of manufacturers continue poor and dependent, the proprietors amass immense fortunes.   The establishment of manufactures in this country has long been a very desirable event. — This will afford a new source of employment for the poor which will be constantly increasing." (The Gazette of the United States, September 7, 1791.)

An illuminating article on slavery and labor in the Gazette of the United States for May 6, 1789, contains the following penetrating passage in economics: "It must be allowed that in all societies, subordination and servitude are in some degree necessary — these naturally imply superiority and power: Power, therefore cannot be supposed in itself unjust, but only the abuse of that power: A frequent change or rotation of property, occasioned by the introduction of *commerce* into many of the European states has greatly checked this wanton exercise or abuse of power; and in many of those states has by degrees, totally abolished that villanage which existed in the primitive ages.   Yet, as in all civilized states, an excess of poverty will be the inevitable lot of some, it may therefore naturally be expected that the poor in general will experience a certain degree of dependence and servility. . . .   If the state of the poor may be supposed in some respects preferable to that of the African slaves, yet I am of opinion, that in other respects it may sometimes be less eligible, unless we should allow an equal degree of sensibility to mankind in every state and condition. . . .   Be that as it may, all Europe evinces that where there are no Black men, there must be white men to do the menial, and other servile offices requisite in society; or in other words, where there are no *black slaves*, there must be *white slaves*."

CHAPTER IX

So violent was the opposition to Hamilton's funding system that it required only another irritant to transform the popular anger into open defiance of the law and the government. This irritant was supplied by the Excise Act, which passed the House of Representatives on January 25, 1791, and was approved by the President on March 3 of that year. That measure had been a part of Hamilton's original scheme as outlined in his first Report on the Public Credit and had grown directly out of another report communicated to the House on December 13, 1790. At the latter date, the assumption of state debts had been carried and the Secretary of the Treasury estimated that $826,624.73 was necessary to meet the new charges and the slight estimated deficit in the funds already established.[1] In recommending an excise on spirits Hamilton seems to have been anxious, for many reasons, to avoid a direct tax on lands. "It has become an acknowledged truth," he said, "that, in the operation of those [excise] taxes, every species of capital and industry contribute their proportion to the revenue, and consequently, that, as far as they can be made substitutes for taxes on lands, they serve to exempt them from an undue share of the public burden."

As soon as the excise measure was taken up in the House, Jackson, of Georgia, the leader of the opposition to the funding bills, renewed his assaults on the fiscal system and bitterly attacked the excise as an auxiliary to it. He

[1] *State Papers: Finance*, Vol. I, p. 64.

set out to show that the tax was odious, unequal, unpopular, and oppressive, particularly in the Southern states, where spiritous liquors had become necessary articles and where breweries and orchards furnished no substitutes. Jackson then sketched the history of excises in England: "He said that they had always been considered by the people of that country as an odious tax, from the time of *Oliver Cromwell* to the present day; even *Blackstone*, a high prerogative lawyer, had reprobated them. He said, he hoped this country would take warning by the experience of the people of Great Britain, and not sacrifice their liberties by wantonly contracting debts which would render it necessary to burthen the people by such taxes as would swallow up their privileges; . . . and by an indication of several particulars he showed its unequal operation in the southern states. It will deprive the mass of the people of almost the only luxury they enjoy, that of distilled spirits." Parker, of Virginia, warmly seconded Jackson and warned his colleagues that the excise tax would "convulse the government." [1]

In spite of the opposition from the Southern delegates particularly, the bill passed the House on January 25, by a large majority. It appeared to be necessary to sustain the public credit, for without the additional revenue the interest on the debt could not be paid. It is probable that it was with unmixed feelings that the "old guard" of security holders, Ames, Benson, Boudinot, Carroll, Clymer, Fitzsimons, Gerry, Gilman, Goodhue, Lawrence, Sedgwick, Sherman, Sturges, and Wadsworth, voted to impose the excise on spirits distilled in the United States. Madison [2]

---

[1] *Annals of Congress*, Vol. II, pp. 1890 ff.

[2] Madison declared that he was opposed to an excise tax, but that money must be forthcoming to sustain the government and that it was evident that the House was not prepared to lay a tax on land. *Annals of Congress*, Vol. II, p. 1894.

voted with them, but the South furnished most of the opposition vote. Hathorn and Van Rensselaer from New York, Hartley, Heister, and P. Muhlenberg, from Pennsylvania, joined their Southern colleagues in resisting the tax.

This opposition from the South and from Pennsylvania is explicable on purely economic grounds. The excise law, as finally passed, imposed a certain duty on imported spirits, a graded excise on spirits made from molasses and other imported products, and a small graded excise on those distilled from grain. It would thus appear that there was some discrimination against New England, where most of the spirits distilled from molasses were made. On examination, however, it will be found that the New England spirits were made in distilleries of considerable size and that the manufacturers, without much difficulty, could shift the tax to the consumer, thus making it almost impalpable. In the country districts of New England, where spirits could not be afforded, the farmers relied upon hard cider as a strong drink. To the southward, on the other hand, particularly in Pennsylvania, Maryland, Virginia, and North Carolina, where spirits were distilled from grain, the manufacture of liquor was not concentrated in large plants, but widely distributed among the farmers. The state of Pennsylvania alone was estimated to have at least five thousand distilleries.[1] A great deal of this liquor was made for

[1] Hildreth, *op. cit.*, Vol. I, p. 256. The economic situation in western Pennsylvania is thus described by a descendant of one of the participants in the events connected with the insurrection: "The four western counties, at the time of the Western Insurrection, or riots (Westmoreland, Fayette, Washington, and Alleghany), contained about seventy thousand inhabitants, scattered over an extent of country nearly as great as that of Scotland or Ireland. Except Pittsburgh, which contained about twelve hundred souls, there were no towns except a few places appointed for holding the courts cf justice in each county. There were scarcely any roads, the population had to find their way as they could through paths or woods, while the mountains formed a barrier which could only be passed on foot or on horseback. The only trade with the East was by packhorse; while the navigation of the Ohio was closed by Indian wars, even if a market could have been found by

domestic or at least local use, although not a little was transported to the cities for trade, that being one of the most economical forms in which grain could be carried to market. In Pennsylvania and the Southern states, therefore, the excise duty fell as a sort of direct tax on the farmers and set thousands of backwoods communities in turmoil.[1]

The effect of the measure was instantaneous. In fact, while it was under consideration, the legislature of Pennsylvania, then sitting in Philadelphia, where Congress was holding its sessions, passed resolutions denouncing the bill, and shortly afterward the Virginia, Maryland, and North Carolina legislatures joined in the protest. Before long Washington learned that revolt was brewing in the regions adversely affected by the tax, but he could not bring himself to believe that the opposition was serious. Indeed, he wrote to Lafayette in July: "On the 6th of this month I returned from a tour through the southern states, which had employed me for more than three months. In the course of the journey, I have been highly gratified in observing the flourishing state of the country and the good dispositions of the people. . . . The attachment of all

descending its current. The farmers having no markets for their produce, were from necessity compelled to reduce its bulk by converting their grain into whiskey ; a horse could carry two kegs of eight gallons each, worth about fifty cents per gallon on this [western], and one dollar on the other side of the mountains, while he returned with a little iron or salt, worth at Pittsburgh, the former fifteen to twenty cents a pound the latter five dollars per bushel. The still was therefore the necessary appendage of every farm, where the farmer was able to procure it ; if not, he was compelled to carry his grain to the more wealthy to be distilled. In fact, some of these distilleries on a large scale, were friendly to the excise laws, as it rendered the poorer farmers dependent upon them. . . . This tax created a numerous host of petty officers, scattered over the country as spies on the industry of the people, and practically authorized at any moment to inflict domiciliary visits on them, to make arbitrary seizures and to commit other vexatious acts ; the tax was thus brought to bear on almost each individual cultivator of the soil." H. M. Brackenridge, *History of the Western Insurrection*, p. 17.

[1] *Ibid.*

classes of citizens to the general government seems to be a pleasing presage of their future happiness and respectability." [1]

However, the President was not permitted long to enjoy this tranquil assurance of obedience to the excise law. Protest meetings began to appear here and there in the disaffected regions and committees similar to those which had engineered the Revolution were organized in many counties preparatory to resisting the enforcement of the law. The unrest was not confined to obscure farmers. Prominent leaders, many of whom had been open opponents of the Constitution a few years earlier, began to assume control of the movement, and at length Congress, evidently somewhat frightened, abolished the tax on the smaller stills, by a law approved May 8, 1792, thus averting a crisis in Virginia and North Carolina.

In the debate on this revision of the law, the antagonism of the small farmers to the capitalistic policy of the government again became clearly apparent. Steele, of North Carolina, declared that the law had been opposed because "it operates, and is in fact, a tax upon this occupation [distilling] and agriculture, as they stand connected in one part of the union, while manufactures in other parts are not only rewarded by high protecting duties, but in some instances even by specified bounties. The agricultural interest has experienced the unfavorable influence of this law likewise, and it operates most oppressively too upon that class of farmers whose estates are situated in the interior country, and whose interests have thus far passed almost unnoticed in the policy of the general government. That class of citizens, though they have not been most solicitous, are nevertheless not insensible of their burdens,

[1] *Writings* (Sparks ed.), Vol. X, p. 180.

and the neglect with which their interest has been treated. The value of our lands has been stationary for some time; its produce not in demand, and, where it is, at depreciated prices; and notwithstanding this, taxes are imposed, evidently calculated in their operation to render agriculture tributary to the more favored branches of business. . . . If a farmer is possessed of a given quantity of rye for sale, money cannot be obtained for it at any price — he sends it to a distillery, where one-half of it is given in the first instance for manufacturing the other. The duty is then to be paid out of the farmer's part, which reduces the balance to less than one-third of the original quantity. If this is not an oppressive tax, I am at loss to describe what is so; and if a proposition had been made to lay a similar tax upon American porter, nails, paper, shoes, or any other article of this kind, we should not shortly hear the last of it. And here let me ask, what is in the nature of these manufactories which entitles them to such priorities and preferences? It may fairly be answered that they are nearer to perfection, that they are aided by more capital, that they are therefore better able to bear taxation, and that the advantages which they now enjoy have been derived from the generosity of members representing the agricultural parts of the country. It is most sincerely to be wished that the manufacturing states would fix some bounds to their expectations. . . . The tendency of this law has been, and, if not modified differently, will continue to be, to build up the rum distilleries upon the ruins of those employed by farmers for domestic uses." [1]

Even the modification of the law, which seems to have fairly satisfied the farmers of North Carolina and Virginia, did not allay the discontent in the frontier counties of

[1] *Annals of Congress* (2d Cong.), p. 586.

Pennsylvania. On September 1, 1792, Hamilton wrote to Washington that the continued opposition to the law in the western survey district of that state gave the affair a more serious aspect than it had hitherto worn and called for vigorous and decisive measures on the part of the government. He declared that enough moderation had been shown and that it was time to assume a different tone, for otherwise the well-disposed part of the community would think the executive wanting in decision and vigor. From that time forward the opposition grew in organization and determination.

The administration shortly afterward decided upon the sharp prosecution of the distillers who refused to register and pay the tax. Indictments were found against a considerable number and an attempt of the United States marshal to serve the warrants in the summer of 1794 led to an armed resistance in which several were killed and wounded. The militia of the western counties was summoned by the revolutionary leaders and threats were made to the effect that they would not only defend themselves but also establish an independent state. At first, the insurrectionists confined their operations to what they called "legal measures designed to obstruct the operation of the law," that is, to meetings, resolutions, and protests; and their leaders disclaimed any intention of resorting to violence. In the spirit of the American Revolution, they proposed non-intercourse and passive resistance.

Who provoked open violence and how far the resistance to the law would have gone if the armed forces of the federal government had not been called out have always been matters of controversy. Washington's cabinet was divided at first as to the seriousness of the outbreak, and writers of Republican sympathies have consistently held that

Hamilton's report to the President on the situation in the western counties was inaccurate, unfair, and deliberately designed to bring about a show of force that would strengthen the government and the party in control.[1] They also declare that Justice Wilson's certificate to the effect that the execution of the law by civil processes or by the federal marshal was so far obstructed as to call for the use of armed force, was issued "without sufficient evidence or without a careful investigation deliberately made." [2]

Whether the circumstances actually required a military display on a large scale or not, Washington, in August, 1794, called upon the governors of Pennsylvania, New Jersey, Maryland, and Virginia for several thousand men to quell the uprising, and the forces headed by Washington and Hamilton set out for the scene of disturbance. Before the army had gone far on the journey, it was met by delegates from the disaffected regions, who assured Washington that the sentiments of the people were now entirely pacific, "that the riotous indications had subsided as rapidly as they had arisen; that the courts of justice were in full operation, and that not a single individual could be found in opposition to the law." [3] Although Washington received the delegates with respectful civility, he was firmly convinced that it was inexpedient to turn back. Consequently the troops were ordered forward, and on their arrival at the scene of trouble, they were broken into detachments and sent into the several districts to secure complete submission. A small number of

---

[1] Brackenridge says: "The growing disposition to submit to the law, the peaceful service of all the writs except the last, in the immediate neighborhood of the Inspector, and the sudden outbreak which followed, which had all the characteristics of a common riot, without preconcerted design to resist, much less to overturn the government, were passed over by the Secretary." *Op. cit.*, p. 263.

[2] *Ibid.*, p. 264.

[3] *Ibid.*, p. 269.

the insurgents were arrested and Hamilton advised severe measures as a lesson to those who had resisted the enforcement of the law; but milder counsels prevailed because it was discovered that the gravity of the offences had been exaggerated. A few were tried, and two convicted, only to be pardoned by the President.

A study of the personnel of the rebellious movement and of the districts disaffected shows that a very considerable portion of the opposition to the excise tax in Pennsylvania was identical with the opposition to the ratification of the Constitution a few years before. It was in the old Anti-Federal regions around Pittsburg[1] that the revolt broke out openly when attempts were made to arrest those who refused to obey the law. The leader of the more moderate faction opposed to the excise law was Albert Gallatin, who had been a member of the Anti-Federalist convention assembled at Harrisburg after the adoption of the Constitution to demand the calling of a new convention — the same Gallatin, interestingly and significantly enough, whom Jefferson elevated to the post of Secretary of the Treasury when he was elected President. Three other leaders more or less involved in the uprising were Findley, Smilie, and Marshel, who had been members of the Pennsylvania convention and had voted against the ratification of the Constitution. It may be confidently asserted that the whiskey party of 1792–1794 was in leadership and rank and file largely composed of the opponents of the Constitution, who had become, and remained, consistent Republicans.

During the resistance to the excise, denunciation of the "stock-jobbing" party was coupled with the criticism of the obnoxious law. In fact, the leaders of the movement

[1] Pittsburg had been Federal in 1787.

flatly declared that the tax would not have been necessary at all, if the Federalists had not funded, at face value, millions of depreciated paper from which the government had originally secured very little return in the form of supplies and services. It was the fiscal system that heaped an enormous burden upon the taxpayer and afforded the occasion for the inquisitorial excise law. Thus men like Findley and Gallatin were able to denounce the excise law as "a base offspring of the funding system." [1]

Some color was given to the claim that the struggle over the excise law was a part of the old contest over the Constitution and the funding of the debt by the fact that the federal authorities selected as excise inspector for the four counties of Pennsylvania west of the Alleghanies and Bedford on the east, General John Neville. This high

[1] At a meeting in Pittsburg in 1791, the following resolution was passed : "Resolved, that having considered the laws of the late Congress, it is our opinion that in a very short time hasty strides have been made to all that is unjust and oppressive. We note particularly the exorbitant salaries of officers, the unreasonable interest of the public debt, and the making of no discrimination between the original holders of public securities and the transferees, contrary to the ideas of natural justice in sanctioning an advantage which was not in the contemplation of the party himself to receive and contrary to the municipal law of most nations and ours particularly, the carrying into effect an unconscionable bargain, where an undue advantage has been taken of the ignorance and necessities of another ; and also contrary to the interest and happiness of these states, being subversive of industry by common means, where men seem to make fortunes by the fortuitous concurrence of circumstances, rather than by economic, virtuous, and useful employment. What is an evil still greater, the constituting a capital of nearly eighty millions of dollars in the hands of a few persons who may influence those occasionally in power to evade the Constitution. As an instance of this already taken place, we note the act establishing a National Bank on the doctrine of implication, but more especially, we bear testimony to what is a base offspring of the funding system, the excise law of Congress, entitled, "An Act laying duties upon distilled spirits within the United States, passed the 3d of March, 1791. . . . It is a bad precedent, tending to introduce the excise laws of Great Britain and of countries where the liberty, property, and even the morals of the people are sported with, to gratify particular men in their ambitions and interested measures. . . . That in the opinion of this committee, the duties imposed by the said act upon spirits distilled from the produce of the soil of the United States, will eventually discourage agriculture, and a manufacture highly beneficial in the present state of the country." H. M. Brackenridge, *History of the Western Insurrection*, p. 36.

officer, who was described as "a man of great wealth for those days," [1] had been a member of the state convention of 1787 and had there voted for the ratification of the Constitution. It appears that at the time of the insurrection Neville was a holder of certificates of the funded debt, because his son, in an advertisement published after the sack of the General's house, declared that some of the certificates of registered debt had been stolen. [2] With a champion of the federal Constitution and a security holder on the one side as a federal officer and opponents of the Constitution on the other as enemies of the excise law, it looks quite like the antagonism of 1787 over again.

Although the insurrection, if such it may be justly called, was confined to the western counties of Pennsylvania, other sections of the country were known to have been in undisguised sympathy with resistance to the law, if not with open rebellion. The Democratic societies in many towns rejoiced in "the return of the spirit of 1776." The Philadelphia Democratic society, in particular, denounced the excise law in very violent language. Washington and Hamilton, therefore, had some reason for fearing that it was no local uprising with which they had to deal, but a widespread disaffection which seriously threatened the stability of the federal government. The administration naturally felt that there was no slight cause for congratulation when the soldiers returned triumphantly, and it could be announced that there was no interruption in the

---

[1] Brackenridge, *op. cit.*, p. 31.

[2] *Ibid.*, p. 51. Speaking of Neville's acceptance of the office of excise inspector, Brackenridge says: "The claim for disinterested patriotism, in taking the office under the circumstances, was not universally admitted; on the contrary, some said, that in accepting, he was influenced by its emoluments, which would not have been the case if he had pursued the course of declining and then recommending someone of equal respectability and capacity, and at the same time exerting his influence as a citizen to aid him in the execution of its duties. As it was, the course pursued by him tended greatly to increase the unpopularity of the excise." P. 21.

enforcement of Federal law throughout the American empire.

Even after order was restored, Washington did not regard the incident as entirely closed. The insurrection had made a profound impression on him and had moved him to unwonted anger at every form of opposition which had been stirred up against his administration. He refused to think of the affair as a mere revolt in western Pennsylvania against the excise tax. The seriousness of the outbreak was due, in his mind, to the growth of democracy as manifested in the formation of Democratic societies which were attacking the policies of the government and, by systematic political organization, preparing to get possession of the federal system. "The insurrection," he wrote on September 25, 1794, "may be considered as the first ripe fruits of the Democratic Societies. I did not, I must confess, expect it would come to maturity so soon, though I never had a doubt that such conduct would produce some such issue, if it did not meet the frowns of those, who were well-disposed to order and good government; for can anything be more absurd, more arrogant, or more pernicious to the peace of society, than for self-created bodies, forming themselves into permanent censors, and under the shade of night in a conclave resolving that acts of Congress, which have undergone the most deliberate and solemn discussion by the representatives of the people, chosen for the express purpose and bringing with them from the different parts of the Union the sense of their constituents, endeavoring as far as the nature of the thing will admit, to form *their will* into laws for the government of the whole; I say, under these circumstances, for a self-created *permanent* body (for no one denies the right of the people to meet occasionally to petition for, or remonstrate against, any act of the legislature) to declare that *this* *act* is unconstitutional, and *that* *act* pregnant with mischiefs, and that all, who vote contrary to their dogmas, are actuated by selfish motives or under foreign influence, nay, are traitors to their country? Is such a stretch of arrogant presumption to be reconciled with laudable motives, especially when we see the same set of men endeavoring to destroy all confidence in the administration by arraigning all its acts, without knowing on what ground or with what information it proceeds." [1]

It is evident from Washington's correspondence at this time that he became more and more convinced of the necessity of destroying or at least discountenancing the Democratic societies which, by their attacks on the policies of his administration, were undermining the foundations of the federal government. He turned the matter over in his mind carefully, consulted the members of his cabinet and his closest friends about it, and in his message to Congress in November, 1794, he discussed at length the insurrection in Pennsylvania, resistance to law, the self-created societies, and criticism of the government, leaving it to the people to determine whether the late rebellion had "not been fomented by combinations of men, who, careless of consequences, and disregarding the unerring truth that those who rouse cannot always appease a civil convulsion, have disseminated, from an ignorance or perversion of facts, suspicions, jealousies, and accusations of the whole government."

In the Senate the President's sentiments about the Democratic societies were warmly supported and the proceedings of those associations were attacked as founded in political error and calculated to disorganize the government by misleading the citizens. In the House, however, the message did not find the same approval. It appears that the members were at first inclined to overlook the reference to the self-created societies, but that staunch Federalist, Fitzsimons, of Pennsylvania, could not restrain his feelings and, remarking that it would be somewhat incongruous for the House to present an address to the President and neglect such an important part of his message, he proposed an amendment to the address as follows: "As a part of this subject, we cannot withhold our reprobation of the self-created societies, which have risen up in some parts of the Union, misrepresenting the conduct of the Government, and disturbing the operation of the laws, and which, by deceiving and inflaming the ignorant and the weak, may naturally be supposed to have stimulated and urged the insurrection." [1]

This action stirred the Republicans in the House. They had not openly sympathized with the insurrection, of course, but many of them, particularly those who had fought the enactment of the excise law, must have secretly rejoiced in the fulfilment of their prophecies. Moreover, they were not prepared to go on record as denouncing the "self-created societies" whose agitations were daily adding strength to the Republican party. The Republican leader, Giles, after passing a high encomium upon the public services and personal character of Washington, rather sharply criticised the language employed by the President in his message. He mildly suggested: "If the House are to censure the Democratic societies, they might do the same by the Cincinnati society," which, it was well known, had by numerous resolutions supported the fiscal system of the Treasury Department. "If the House undertake to censure particular classes of men," Giles continued, "who can

[1] *Annals of Congress* (3d Cong.), p. 899.

tell where they will stop? Perhaps it may be advisable to commence moral philosophers, and compose a new system of ethics for the citizens of America. In that case, there would be many other subjects for censure, as well as the self-created societies. Land-jobbing, for example, has been in various instances brought to such a pass that it might be defined swindling on a broad scale.[1] . . . Gentlemen were interfering with a delicate right, and they would be much wiser to let the Democratic societies alone." [2]

Another Republican, McDowell, exclaimed, "Your wanton laws, begotten in darkness, first, raised the insurrection"; and added that the Democratic societies had done only what other people had done, namely, denounced "the assumption business and the system of funding." Chrystie declared that the "Republican society of Baltimore was composed of a band of patriots, not the fair weather patriots of the present day, but the patriots of seventy-five, the men who were not afraid to rally around the American standard when that station was almost concluded to be a forlorn hope." A Revolutionary soldier, who had served under Washington, Rutherford, praised the President, but objected to his attack upon societies formed by his fellow-citizens for political purposes. "By the turn which the debate has now taken," he said, "if any man is in favor of these societies, *the President is drawn across his face.* . . . These societies contain many valuable and excellent characters. It answers no purpose then to pass votes of this kind. Perhaps Democratic societies sometimes have done wrong, but this was not a proper foundation for condemning them in whole. Every government under heaven hath a tendency to degenerate into tyranny. Let the people then speak out. *Why not let them speak out?* What oc-

---

[1] See above, p. 218.   [2] *Annals of Congress* (3d Cong.), p. 900.

casion is there for all this alarm among the stockholders? A man falls from his horse, and, while stunned by the blow he says to his neighbor, is not the universe fallen? Just so the paper holders have got a small alarm about their stock on account of this war, and in their fright imagine that the Continent is ready for an insurrection." [1]

This reference to the alarm of the stockjobbers must have stung the security holders in the House. Dayton, the most notorious land and security speculator in the country, had been hot in his support of the President's criticism of the Democratic societies, and Ames of Massachusetts, shortly after Rutherford's sarcastic outbreak, exclaimed that the talk about "a paper nobility in Congress" was false, adding: "There are probably not ten members who have *any* interest in the funds, and that interest very inconsiderable." [2] Other security holders, William Smith, of South Carolina, Sedgwick, of Massachusetts, and Boudinot, of New Jersey, were among those who spoke in favor of Fitzsimons' resolution; but in vain, for it did not command a majority of the House.

The division over the resolution to approve the President's reference to the self-created societies was very close, the House dividing evenly on some of the minor details of the amendment to the address. [3] At length, however, the Republicans succeeded in expunging the irritating word "self-created" and the implication that the Democratic societies had been responsible directly for stirring up the public sentiment which culminated in the insurrection. The Federalists were able, nevertheless, to secure the insertion of a regret "that any misrepresentations whatever, of the government and its proceedings, either by individuals or combinations of men, should have been made and so far

[1] *Ibid.*, p. 915.　　　　[2] *Ibid.*, p. 929.　　　　[3] *Ibid.*, p. 947.

credited as to foment the flagrant outrage which has been committed on the laws." Taking it all in all, the victory was with the Republicans.

The general effect of the Pennsylvania insurrection and its aftermath was not altogether favorable to the administration party. True, the strength of the Federal Government — its capacity to enforce the law — had been manifested in a striking manner and the Federalists rejoiced in what they deemed to be a newly demonstrated security. Thought of armed resistance was at an end, but the resort to political agitation by the Republicans was all the more vigorous. Certainly none of the leaders in the resistance to the excise, like Smilie, Findley, or Gallatin, were converted to Federalism. The concessions which had been made to the North Carolinians had not diminished their political disaffection. And the standing afforded to the Democratic societies by the embroglio in the House of Representatives increased for a time the activities of organizations which the Federalists openly designated as contemptible, pernicious, and vile.[1]

Jefferson looked upon the whole affair as hastening the Nemesis that was bound to come to the Federalists and as one more illustration of the inevitable conflict between the popular and aristocratic elements. On December 28, 1794, he wrote to Madison, who had stood consistently against the administration during the contest in the House, saying: "The denunciation of the democratic societies is one of the extraordinary acts of boldness of which we have seen so many from the faction of monocrats. It is wonderful indeed, that the President should have permitted himself to be the organ of such an attack on the freedom of discussion, the freedom of writing, printing, and publishing.

[1] Marshall, *Life of Washington* (2d ed.), Vol. II, p. 353.

It must be a matter of rare curiosity to get at the modifications of these rights proposed by them, and to see what line their ingenuity would draw between democratical societies, whose avowed object is the nourishment of the republican principles of our Constitution, and the society of the Cincinnati, a *self-created* one, carving out for itself hereditary distinctions, lowering over our Constitution eternally, meeting together in all parts of the Union, periodically, with closed doors, accumulating a capital in their separate treasury, corresponding secretly and regularly, and of which society the very persons denouncing the democrats are themselves the fathers, founders and high officers." [1]

Not only did the attack on the popular societies help to strengthen the opposition to the fiscal party, but it increased the widespread feeling that the extensive employment of troops against the insurgents was a piece of unnecessary bravado, calculated to bolster up the declining prestige of the Federalists.[2] In the letter to Madison, just quoted, Jefferson added: "With respect to the transactions against the excise law, it appears to me that you are all swept away in the torrent of governmental opinions, or that we do not know what these transactions have been. We know of none which, according to the definitions of the law, have been anything more than riotous. There was indeed a meeting to consult about a separation. But to consult on a question does not amount to a determination of that question in the affirmative, still less to the acting on such a determination. . . . The excise law is an infernal one. The first error was to admit it by the Constitution;

---

[1] *Works* (Washington ed.), Vol. IV, p. 111; *Economic Interpretation*, p. 38. The Societies and their members appear frequently among the holders of the securities of the federal government.

[2] B. W. Bond, "The Whiskey Insurrection in Pennsylvania," *The Randolph-Macon Historical Papers*, Vol. I, p. 78.

the second, to act on that admission; the third and last will be, to make it the instrument of dismembering the Union, and setting us all afloat to choose what part of it we will adhere to. The information of our militia, returned from the westward, is uniform that though the people there let them pass quietly, they were the objects of their laughter, not of their fear; that one thousand men could have cut off their whole force in a thousand places of the Alleghany; that their detestation of the excise law is universal, and has now associated to it a detestation of the government; and that a separation which was perhaps a very distant and problematical event is now near, and certain, and determined in the mind of every man. I expected to have seen some justification of arming one part of the society against another; of declaring a civil war the moment before the meeting of that body which has the sole right of declaring war; of being so patient of the kicks and scoffs of our enemies, and rising at a feather against our friends; of adding a million to the public debt and deriding us with recommendations to pay it if we can, &c., &c. . . . However, the time is coming when we shall fetch up the leeway of our vessel. The changes in your House, I see, are going on for the better, and even the Augean herd over your heads [the Senate] are slowly purging off their impurities."

Whether Jefferson accurately described the situation in this letter, it is certain that he reflected the sentiment of many Republicans. They did not openly praise the violence of those who resisted, with arms, a tax which they had resisted by argument in the sphere of politics. Formally, they approved the action of the government in enforcing the law, but they made great political capital out of the conflict. Western Pennsylvania avenged herself by sending Republican Representatives to Congress down until the great revolution of 1800 and beyond. Everywhere those who had fought the economic measures of the federal government only redoubled their efforts to get possession of that government at the ballot box. The sage of Monticello, in retirement, was biding his time.

CHAPTER X

On November 19, 1794, about a week before the House of Representatives began its long and acrimonious debate over the President's reference to the self-created Democratic societies, there was signed a treaty between England and the United States which was destined to aggravate, as much as any other measure of the administration except the funding of the debt, the partisan bitterness then permeating the country. It afforded a peculiar opportunity for agitation to Jefferson and his followers, because it enabled them to detach from the Federalist cause some of the mercantile interest and a considerable number of the large planters of the South. It did more. It enabled them to connect Federalism with subserviency to the hated monarchy against which independence had been declared less than twenty years before, and to identify Republicanism with that patriotic pride and heroic valor which had sustained the declaration on the battle field. It permitted them to bring out, even more emphatically than ever, that antagonism between capitalism and agrarianism which had been the source of the troubles of the new federal government.

It is no part of the purpose of this work to trace all of the intricate details of the contest between the United States and Great Britain which brought them to the verge of war in 1794. However, a few of the economic aspects of that conflict which bear upon the party contests at home must be pointed out. One important feature of the struggle was the injury inflicted upon Northern commercial interests by the policy of the mother country. When war broke out between England and France in 1793 the latter nation, which had hitherto shown as little regard for American interests as the former, opened to neutrals the trade with the French West Indies. This action, though dictated by economic necessity, afforded the Republicans a pretext for claiming the special friendship of the country which had just embarked upon the paths of revolution. At first, the prospect seemed highly gratifying to the commercial interests of the United States, but this hope was short lived. The British government, as a war measure, declared all ships of neutrals engaged in this trade with the French West Indies liable to seizure, and hundreds of American vessels and thousands of seamen soon fell into the hands of the British. This irritating order was scarcely in effect before it was followed by a decree condemning all ships carrying goods belonging to French citizens, — another deadly blow to American commercial interests.

It is useless to discuss here the fine points in international law involved in this action on the part of Great Britain. Its effect on the people of the United States may well be imagined. The newspapers printed horrifying stories of the seizure of fine merchant vessels, the cruel treatment of American sailors who had been thrown into prison, if accounts may be believed, more than half naked, and other outrages against the nationals of the United States. The commercial interests, North and South, which had quite uniformly been Federalist in sympathy, began to incline a more kindly ear toward the Republicans who frankly avowed their hatred for Britain and their affiliations with the French revolutionists. Ship building suffered grave losses and unemployment spread throughout that and allied trades, giving the working classes involved a practical illustration of what was represented as the folly of supporting a party evidently British in sympathy.

There were special economic reasons which made the controversy with Great Britain highly acceptable to some of the larger planting interests of the South.[1] It afforded just the desired opportunity to postpone or perhaps defeat altogether the enforcement of Article IV of the treaty of peace of 1783 (which closed the War of Independence) to the following effect: "It is agreed that creditors on either side shall meet with no lawful impediment to the recovery of the full value in sterling money of all bona fide debts heretofore contracted." As is generally known, the debts due to British merchants and other private citizens constituted one of the powerful causes leading to the Revolution, particularly among the better classes; and during the War various schemes of confiscation and sequestration had been employed to "sponge off the slate." After peace was established, attempts were made by British creditors to collect their just debts, with little success, especially in the South. In the North, the debtors were more prompt, as the newspapers would have it, on account of their superior sense of business honor; but it would seem that they made a virtue of necessity. Being commercial and mercantile in their interests and dependent upon Great Britain for credit and capital, they found it expedient to settle the old scores.

[1] "The affairs of this country appear to be verging to some important crisis. The opposition to the measures which have been adopted, conduct as if they were influenced by something more than rivalry and personal ambition. . . . The best solution which I can give of this disquiet is the pressure of the foreign debts due from the Virginia planters; these, they imagined had been thrown off. The effect of the treaty and of the Constitution is to make them responsible; at least, this is believed, though no decision of this question has been made by the national judiciary. The prospect of poverty and dependence to the Scotch merchants is what they cannot view with patience. They seem determined to weaken the public force, so as to render the recovery of these debts impossible." Oliver Wolcott, Jr., February 8, 1793; Gibbs, *op. cit.*, Vol. I, p. 86.

From the British point of view, the situation in the
United States with regard to the collection of these debts
is well summed up in a pamphlet bearing the title of *A
Review of the Laws of the United States of North America,*
published in London, in 1790. The writer makes the following discrimination among the states : "Property is best
secured and more easily attainable in the state of New York
than in any other and the practice of the courts here and in
New Jersey bears the nearest resemblance to that of West-
minster Hall. In Georgia, South and North Carolina,
British debts are recovered with infinite difficulty, such
actions being discountenanced by the bench and where not
denied by the laws are the same in effect by the delays and
other impediments thrown in the way of them. Where the
demand is prior to the treaty of peace, the judges assume a
discretionary power and the first generally falls to the ground
while later claims are so much impeded and procrastinated
that they are seldom recovered till the end of two or three
years and then the debtor easily finds a way of making over
his effects and going into gaol for a few days, from whence
he is altogether liberated and exonerated. In Maryland
the creditors are fettered with an installment bill. In Virginia, Delaware, Pennsylvania, and New Jersey, the means
of liberation are equally easy to the debtor and though in
more northern states debts are better secured and there is
somewhat less opening for fraud and evasion, yet even there,
if a man who goes to law for a British debt has the good luck
to get over the frowns of the bench and the unpopularity
which is sure to be stamped upon his character, he may be
considered fortunate in recovering his property at the end
of three years. . . . In Virginia no alien can hold lands nor
alien enemy maintain an action for money or other personalty. The lands of the aliens are forfeitures to the state and

to an action brought by an alien defendant may plead 'that he is an alien enemy' which extinguishes his right in the hands of the debtor."[1]

It would seem that the greatest offender in this matter of resistance to the collection of debts was appropriately enough the greatest debtor, Virginia. We have Jefferson's testimony to the effect that his state was the most heavily in debt. "Virginia," he wrote, "certainly owed two millions sterling to Great Britain at the conclusion of the war. Some have conjectured the debt as high as three millions. I think that state owed near as much as all the rest put together. This is to be ascribed to peculiarities in the tobacco trade. The advantages made by the British merchants, on the tobacco consigned them, were so enormous, that they spared no means of increasing those consignments. A powerful engine for this purpose, was the giving good prices and credit to the planter, till they got him more immersed in debt than he could pay, without selling his lands or slaves. They then reduced the prices given for his tobacco, so that let his shipments be ever so great, and his demand of necessaries ever so economical, they never permitted him to clear off his debt. These debts had become hereditary from father to son, for many generations, so that the planters were a species of property, annexed to certain mercantile houses in London."[2]

In addition to the debts owed to the British, there was another factor which helped to drive the slave-owning planters of the Southern states into closer sympathy with the Republicans in the back regions — that was the refusal

[1] Copy in the New York Public Library. By questioning Republican members of Congress, Jefferson found that there was in fact "no obstruction" to the collection of debts in the South. *Works* (Washington ed.), Vol. III, p. 409.

[2] Jefferson, *Works* (Washington ed.), Vol. IX, p. 250. See Wolcott's estimate, below, p. 298.

of the British to pay for several thousand slaves who had
been carried off at the conclusion of the Revolutionary War
without compensation to the owners.[1] The Treaty of
peace of 1783 had provided that his Britannic Majesty
should withdraw his troops with all convenient speed and
"without causing any destruction or carrying away any
negroes or other property of the American inhabitants."
Notwithstanding the clear provision of the treaty, it was
claimed that thousands of slaves had been taken out of the
country by the British soldiers and set free. The owners
of the slaves had demanded the return of their property or
compensation and had failed to secure either. This griev-
ance afforded justification, in the states most deeply concerned, to those who resisted the payment of the private
debts to British creditors.[2]

Here was, therefore, a mass of economic discontent
which the Republicans could use to the greatest advantage
in augmenting the agrarian dissatisfaction over the fiscal
system of the Treasury Department.[3] Obviously, from the
point of view of practical politics, it was good tactics for the
opposition party to throw the blame for commercial difficulties on the administration and to delay still further the
payment of the debts due to British creditors. Another
way of embarrassing the Federalists was to force a war, or
at least drive the government to the verge of war with Great

---

[1] Jefferson estimated the number of slaves taken off by the British during a
single campaign at one-fifth of the entire negro population of Virginia. Grigsby,
History of the Virginia Federal Convention, Vol. I, p. 8 n.

[2] Edward Carrington, in a letter to Hamilton, put the "Democratic societies,
British debtors, and other factions" in the Anti-Federalist party. *Hamilton
Mss.*, August 25, 1794.

[3] For further information on the contests over debts in Maryland, see J. F.
Mercer, *An Introductory Discourse to an Argument in Support of the Payments made
of the British Debts into the Treasury of Maryland during the late War*, and *Strictures
on Mercer's Introductory Discourse relative to the Payments made of the British Debts*
(London, 1790 ; New York Public Library).

Britain, thus depreciating securities and deranging the financial system by disorganizing the revenues. That such was the object of so conservative a Republican as Madison can hardly be imagined. In fact, he distinctly disavowed the motive, but he thereby admitted its existence in the minds of some of his partisan colleagues.

The method pursued steadily by the Republicans, with some support from Federalists of uncertain faith, like Jonathan Dayton, brought out very clearly in Congress the economic issues at stake in the controversy with Great Britain. On January 3, 1794, Madison, acting upon a report on commerce prepared by Jefferson, proposed a series of resolutions providing for restrictions and retaliations aimed at Great Britain; later Jonathan Dayton proposed sequestration of British debts; still later the House passed a non-importation bill only to meet defeat in the Senate by a close margin, the Vice-President casting the vote which saved the day for the Federalists.[1]

In the debates on these measures, the economic character of the antagonism between the party of negotiation and the party of aggression was definitely set forth. The representatives of the former declared that an interruption of trading relations with Great Britain meant irreparable loss to American merchants, a diminution of revenues which would lead to the impairment of public credit and a fall in stocks, and a destruction of that private credit with British capitalists which was so essential to the advancement of kindred interests in the United States. Some Federalist speakers stressed one factor and some another, but none of them strayed very far from the main issues at stake. The Republicans, on the other hand, being the agrarian opponents of capitalism, thought these were the very reasons why a

---

[1] *Annals of Congress* (3d Cong.), pp. 155, 535.

bold and defiant attitude should be taken toward Great Britain. In their hatred for the "stock jobbing and banking" group they were willing to go to great lengths, particularly in view of the fact that chaos in foreign relations meant at least a temporary relief for Southern creditors and no serious difficulties for the farmers anywhere.

In unfolding their programme, the champions of peace and negotiation devoted no little time to demonstrating the enormous importance of the British trade as compared with the trade of other countries, particularly France. They showed very clearly the fallacy of those who contended that the United States received larger and more generous commercial privileges at the hands of France than of Great Britain. "Accustomed as our ears have been," said William Smith, speaking from data furnished to him by Hamilton, "to a constant panegyric on the generous policy of France towards this country in commercial relations, and to as constant a philippic on the unfriendly, illiberal, and persecuting policy of Great Britain towards us in the same relations, we naturally expect to find in a table which exhibits their respective systems, numerous discriminations in that of France in our favor, and many valuable privileges granted to us, which are refused to other foreign countries; in that of Great Britain frequent discriminations to our prejudice, and a variety of privileges refused to us which are granted to other foreign nations. But an inspection of the table will satisfy every candid mind, that the reverse of what has been supposed is truly the case." [1] This assertion he amply supports in an extended review of the commercial relations of the United States with England and France.

Having proved from the exports and imports that the overwhelming preponderance of American trade abroad was

[1] *Ibid.*, p. 176.

with England rather than France, Smith went carefully into the relation of credit to the volume of capital and showed that American merchants could obtain far more credit, and therefore a greater augmentation of their working capital, from British than from French merchants. In other words, trade with the mother country, in addition to affording ordinary economic advantages, fitted into the scheme for expanding the fluid capital in the hands of the merchants, which Hamilton had so ingeniously worked out in his Report on the Public Credit. In short, it was the same battle over again, or rather another battle in the long campaign begun with the adoption of the Constitution, and Smith was speaking on the authority of Hamilton and employing facts and arguments devised by him. Indeed the following passage in Smith's speech may very well have been written by the Secretary of the Treasury: "It has been said, that France can supply us with many articles better than Great Britain. This expression, *better*, ought to include credit, as well as price and quality; for, if we stand in need of credit, that country which cannot give it to us, cannot supply us on as good terms as the country which can. Now, it is known that the merchants of France are unwilling or unable to give competent credit to our merchants. . . . Among the contrivances used to depreciate the value of our commercial connexion with Great Britain, is this, that the credit which she gives us is pernicious, by inducing us to run in debt. As well might it be said, that the credit which a settler of new land obtains, upon the land which he has purchased, or that which a tailor gets upon the cloth which he works up, in the course of his trade, is prejudicial. *The truth is that credit, though liable to abuse, is the substitute for capital in all trades*, and that it serves to foster them, and increase the mass of industry, though the slothful and extravagant suffer by it. In a young country, like ours, it is an essential nutriment." [1]

It was the reduction of credit, the serious limitation on the quantity of fluid capital,[2] which Smith emphasized in attacking the later proposal of Dayton to sequester British debts. "If in contempt of the law of nations," he said, "we seize on private debts, we shall forever forfeit all credit; no trust can be reposed in our citizens, and no faith in our government. No foreign merchants will ever deal on credit with our citizens, from a well guarded apprehension that, in case of a war between the countries, the sacred nature of private contracts will not protect them against the hand of a Government which has exhibited the example of a deliberate violation of the laws of nations. When we consider the immense advantages that can be derived from private credit and national honor, it will be easy to imagine the infinite mischief that must result from a disregard of those principles." [3]

The question of sustaining the national credit by keeping peace with England was taken up by Hartley, who called the attention of the House to the great pains at which Congress had been, under the Constitution, to provide for the Revolutionary debt. "Adequate funds were established," he said, "and the legislature, by the same law, solemnly engaged that those funds should be applied accordingly. The legislature was not to invade or alter those funds without regular and adequate substitutes. By the resolutions [of retaliation] offered, the funds will most assuredly (in my mind) be endangered. We are going upon speculations, the con-

---

[1] *Annals of Congress* (3d Cong.), p. 190. Italics mine.

[2] See R. Morris' view that a treaty with Great Britain would help land speculation and other capitalist ventures. Mss. *Private Letter Book*, Vol. I, p. 80 (March 16, 1795). Morris sold a million acres of land in England in 1791 for $75,000. *Private Letter Book*, Vol. I, p. 113.   [3] *Annals of Congress* (3d Cong.), p. 554.

sequences of which we know not; and which may shake the fundamental principles of public credit, which has been so solemnly guaranteed. We ought not to act like mere colonies, in proposing or entering into non-importation agreements. We are a nation; we ought to conduct ourselves in such a manner as not to endanger the faith, credit, and reputation of America. . . . We are, in this business, not barely waging a commercial war against Britain, for many citizens of this country have their all depending upon public faith." [1]

Although Hartley thus admitted that the importance of protecting the public creditors weighed with him in considering all propositions affecting the revenues, Swift thought too much influence had been assigned to the funded debt. He "remarked that a popular opinion in some parts of the Union had been prevailing, that many of the Representatives in Congress were under such an influence arising from the funding system that they dared not adopt measures necessary for the public defence, for fear the interest of the national debt should remain unpaid. He said that a most unreasonable and unfounded jealousy respecting the funding system existed among the people; that he was satisfied, during the time he had held his present office, that no measure had been influenced by an exclusive regard to the public debt; that he had never owned a farthing in the public funds." Swift believed that the proposition to sequester the British debts should be considered as a war measure and that such a measure should be only the last resort of Congress after the failure of negotiations.[2]

Whatever may have been the view of the Federalists in Congress, it is certain that Hamilton looked upon war with Great Britain as a blow to public credit and calculated

---

[1] *Annals of Congress* (3d Cong.), p. 293.　　　　[2] *Ibid.*, p. 581.

to alienate the public creditors. In a letter to Washington on the situation, he said : "We are but just recovering from the effects of a long, arduous, and exhausting war. The people but just begin to realize the sweets of repose. We are vulnerable both by water and land ; without either fleet or army. We have a considerable debt in proportion to the resources which the state of things permits the government to command. Measures have been recently entered upon for the restoration of credit which a war could hardly fail to disconcert, and which, if disturbed, would be fatal to the means of prosecuting it. Our national government is in its infancy. The habits and dispositions of our people are ill-suited to those liberal contributions to the treasury which a war would necessarily exact. . . . There is a general disinclination to it in all classes. The theories of the speculative, and the feelings of all are opposed to it." [1]

In addition to the obvious economic reasons of the capitalistic party for maintaining peace with Great Britain and securing a pacific settlement of disputed issues there was another important, although somewhat more remote, economic support for that policy. Since the close of the Revolutionary war, the English by maintaining garrisons in several strong posts had held a large portion of the western territory of the United States, and they informed the administration that they would not relinquish their grip until the debts were paid according to the terms of the treaty of 1783. By this action the Indians were kept in a state of hostility that checked the advance of the settlements on the frontier, thus irritating the land speculators. At the same time the British trappers and merchants were able to snatch away from the Americans a rich fur trade worth about £100,000 a year, a trade that would have flowed through the eastern

[1] *Works* (Lodge ed.), Vol. IV, p. 39.

ports if it had not been diverted to Canada.[1] These were items which the party of peace and negotiation could not ignore and no doubt the fur traders were willing to see Virginians forced to pay their debts, even if it did look like "truckling to a monarchy," for it was the price of shaking off the British grip in the West.

The Republicans frankly accepted the declaration that the foreign policy of the hour turned upon economic antagonisms at home. In opposing the Federalist position, Nicholas admitted the dependence of the United States on British credit, but apparently he thought that a cause for a new kind of Declaration of Independence. He pointed out how, before the Revolution, British factors had granted credit to the farmers and attached them to their stores, in this manner precluding competition with the merchants of other countries. "Since the Revolution, the business has been conducted by persons in the habit of dependence on Great Britain, and who had no other capital than the manufactures of that country furnished on credit. The business is still almost wholly conducted by the same means. In no stage of its growth then, does there appear to have been a power in the consumer to have compared the productions of Great Britain with those of any other country, as to their quality or price, and therefore there is no propriety in calling the course of trade the course of its choice."[2]

When the mercantile interests pointed out that three-fourths of the revenue of the United States would be seriously affected by the drastic action against Great Britain, Giles, the persistent Republican warrior of Virginia, begged the opposition to "divulge the pleasing secret, when the nation may make an exertion for the restoration of violated rights

---

[1] McLaughlin, "Western Posts and British Debts," *American Historical Association Report*, 1894, pp. 413, 428.   [2] *Annals of Congress* (3d Cong.), p. 236.

without alarms to revenue! It has been emphatically remarked by a gentleman from New Jersey [Mr. Clark], who
has had great experience in American affairs, that this was
not the language of America at the time of the non-importation associations. This was not the language of America
at the time of the Declaration of Independence. Whence,
then, this change of American sentiment? Has America
less ability than she then had? Is she less prepared for a
national trial than she then was? This cannot be pretended.
There has been, it is true, one great change in her political
situation. America now has a funded debt; she had no
funded debt at those glorious epochs. May not this change
of sentiment, therefore, be looked for in her change of
situation in this respect? May it not be looked for in the
imitative sympathetic organization of our funds with the
British funds? May it not be looked for in the indiscriminate participation of citizens and foreigners in the emoluments
of the funds? May it not be looked for in the wishes of
some to assimilate the Government of the United States to
that of Great Britain, or at least in wishes for a more intimate connexion? If these causes exist, it is not difficult to
find the source of the national debility. It is not difficult
to see that the interests of the few who receive and disburse
the public contributions, are more respected than the interests of the great majority of the society who furnish the
contributions. It is not difficult to see that the Government, instead of legislating for a few millions, is legislating
for a few thousands, and that the sacredness of their rights
is the great obstacle to a great national exertion." [1]

In the long contest over retaliatory measures which
threatened to bring on war with Great Britain the party of

---

[1] *Ibid.*, p. 288.

peace, powerfully supported by Washington, prevailed. A temporary embargo was laid, it is true, but it was short lived. Military precautions were taken but they were regarded as in support of negotiations. As every one knows, Washington sent Chief Justice Jay as an envoy extraordinary to conclude with Great Britain a treaty that would secure a redress of grievances, indemnity for American losses, and remove the conditions which impeded the peaceful commercial relations of the two countries. And as every one knows also, Jay succeeded in negotiating a treaty which gained several concessions favorable to the mercantile interests of the North, though falling far short of their reasonable expectations, and at the same time afforded no consolation to the South at all.

It is not within the scope of this work to analyze the details of Jay's negotiations and the results, but it is pertinent to point out the features which bear directly upon the partisan contest in the country, for it may be said with safety that the Jay treaty detached a large number of Federalists from their old allegiance. In the first place, the trade concessions which Jay obtained were by no means as liberal as the commercial interests expected and believed could be obtained by a bolder show of firmness. Certainly Washington was far from satisfied with them and he accepted the treaty with reluctance, only because he felt that its rejection meant war. The owners of American shipping were especially discontented with the meagre rights obtained for them.

If the Northern merchants had reason to be disgruntled over the terms of the treaty, the Southern planters were warranted in displaying an unwonted temper. In the first place, not a word was said about compensation for the slaves that the British army had carried off.[1] In the

---

[1] Professor Ogg says that the slaveholders of the South, knowing the abolitionist propensities of Jay, were not slow to conclude that he had willingly betrayed their

second place, Article VI of the Treaty provided that debts, contracted by citizens of the United States with British merchants prior to the peace and whose collection was impeded by various lawful devices should be paid by the United States on the basis of a determination by a joint commission. This commission, which was to sit in London, was authorized to take into consideration the interest as well as the principal of such debts and its awards were to be final — the United States binding itself to pay the awards in specie. Article XII put British trade in America on the most favored nation footing, thus precluding such retaliatory and discriminatory measures as the Republicans had been proposing. Finally, the treaty was a direct slap at France and thus indirectly at the French sympathizers in the Republican party. In short, it was, through necessity or design or a mixture of both, a thoroughly partisan document, tender to Northern commercial interests, as far as it wrung any concessions at all from Great Britain. The very best that could be said for its hard terms was that they prevented war and gave the new government longer time to put the public credit and the fiscal system on a firm foundation.

The treaty reached the United States in March, 1795, and Washington at once called a special session of the Senate to pass upon the results of Jay's labors. On June 24, the treaty with the Twelfth Article suspended was approved by the Senate, but only after the most adroit and skilful negotiations on the part of the Federalists. When the news of the terms of the treaty leaked out, popular and partisan fury began to rage. Mass meetings were held to oppose the " nefarious plot against the liberties of the people " ; Hamilton was stoned while attempting to defend it ; the British

interests by trading their slavery claims for commercial privileges for New England. "Jay's Treaty and the Slavery Interests of the United States," *American Historical Association Report*, 1901, pp. 275 ff.

minister was openly insulted; and Jay was burned in effigy in cities, towns, and villages, amid the howls of mobs. Far to the South good Federalists, like John Rutledge, to whom Washington had offered the post of Chief Justice of the Supreme Court, denounced the whole affair in the most violent language; and far to the North another good Federalist, John Langdon, who had supported the administration in all of its fiscal policies and rejoiced with the speculators in the appreciation of public funds[1] execrated the treaty as the sum of villanies and was thanked by his fellow-citizens for his courage.

On July 22, 1795, Hamilton began that truly famous series of papers under the pen name of "Camillus," which are to be classed first among his masterful defences of the Federalist administration and its policies. With that trenchant clarity, that full knowledge of all the details of the controversy, that stinging criticism of his adversaries, which made him so formidable that Jefferson thought Madison the only man capable of standing up under his pitiless fire, Hamilton brought out the favorable points of the treaty, found reasons which made the objectionable clauses seem less unpalatable, and dissected the arguments of the opponents.

With his customary directness, he went at once to the heart of the controversy, by showing that the opposition to the Jay treaty was born of that conflict of economic interests which began with the adoption of the Constitution and that it was a part of the very same battle between capitalism and agrarianism. The Jay treaty was not the real cause of the trouble; it was rather an occasion which the Republicans had seized in order to make another assault upon the party of public and private credit. In his first sentence he launches into the fray. "It was to have been foreseen, that the treaty

---

[1] See *Economic Interpretation*, p. 120; and above, p. 179.

which Mr. Jay was charged to negotiate with Great Britain, whenever it should appear, would have to contend with many perverse dispositions and some honest prejudices; that there was no measure in which the government could engage, so little likely to be viewed according to its intrinsic merits — so very likely to encounter misconception, jealousy, and unreasonable dislike. For this, many reasons may be assigned. It is only to know the vanity and vindictiveness of human nature, to be convinced, that while this generation lasts there will always exist among us men irreconcilable to our present national Constitution; embittered in their animosity in proportion to the success of its operations, and the disappointment of their inauspicious predictions. It is a material inference from this, that such men will watch, with lynx's eyes, for opportunities of discrediting the proceedings of the government, and will display a hostile and malignant zeal upon every occasion, where they think there are any prepossessions of the community to favor their enterprises. A treaty with Great Britain was too fruitful an occasion not to call forth all their activity." [1]

With the economic objections advanced by Southern interests, Hamilton was particularly severe. Writing on the point of Great Britain's refusal to return the slaves as stipulated by the Treaty of 1783, he said: "In the interpretation of treaties, things *odious* and *immoral* are not to be presumed. The abandonment of negroes, who had been induced to quit their masters on the faith of official proclamation, promising them liberty, to fall again under the yoke of their masters, and into slavery, is as *odious* and *immoral* a thing as can be conceived. It is odious, not only as it imposes an act of perfidy on one of the contracting parties, but as it tends to bring back to servitude men once made free. The general

---

[1] *Works* (Lodge ed.), Vol. IV, pp. 371 ff.

interests of humanity conspire with the obligation which
Great Britain had contracted towards the negroes, to repel
this construction of the treaty [1783], if another can be found.
. . . It has been shown, as I trust, to the conviction of dispassionate men, that the claim of compensation for the
negroes is, in point of right, a very doubtful one; in point of
interest, it certainly falls under the description of partial
and inconsiderable; affecting in no respect the honor or
security of the nation, and incapable of having a sensible
influence upon its prosperity." [1]

That opposition which was based on the clause of the
treaty providing compensation for uncollectible debts due
British merchants, Hamilton met in the following language :
"To a man who has a due sense of the sacred obligation of
a just debt, a proper conception of the pernicious influence
of laws which infringe the rights of creditors, upon morals,
upon the general security of property, upon public as well as
private credit, upon the spirit and principles of good government; who has an adequate idea of the sanctity of the
national faith, explicitly pledged — of the ignominy attend-
ant upon a violation of it in so delicate a particular as that
of private pecuniary contracts — of the evil tendency of a
precedent of this kind to the political and commercial
interests of the nation generally — every law which has
existed in this country; interfering with the recovery of the
debts in question, must have afforded matter of serious regret and real affliction. To such a man, it must be among
the most welcome features of the present treaty, that it
stipulates reparation for the injuries which laws of that
description may have occasioned to individuals, and that,
as far as is now practicable, it wipes away from the national
reputation the stain which they have cast upon it. He will

---

[1] *Works*, (Lodge ed.), Vol IV, pp. 398, 419.

regard it as a precious tribute to justice, and as a valuable
pledge for the more strict future observance of our public
engagements; and he would deplore as an ill-omened symp-
tom of the depravation of public opinion, the success of the
attempts which are making to render the article unacceptable
to the people of the United States. But of this there can
be no danger. . . . Let those men who have manifested
by their actions a willing disregard of their own obligations
as debtors — those who secretly hoard, or openly or un-
blushingly riot on the spoils of plundered creditors, let such
men enjoy the exclusive and undivided satisfaction of
arraigning and condemning an act of national justice, in
which they may read the severest reproach of their iniquitous principles and guilty acquisitions. But let not the
people of America tarnish their honor by participating in
that condemnation, or by shielding with their favorable
opinion, the meretricious apologies which are offered for
the measures that produce the necessity of reparation." [1]

After disposing of the Southern objections to the treaty
which were based on the clear provision for the payment
of private debts and the failure to settle the question of the
confiscated slaves, Hamilton showed in great detail why all
the capitalistic interests should rally to the support of the
government in the execution of the agreement with Great
Britain. In the first place commercial interests would
suffer grievously if a war should break out. "Their want of
a marine in particular to protect their commerce would
render war in an extreme degree a calamity." The country
would be thrown back into the condition existing under the
Articles of Confederation. "Our trade, navigation, and
mercantile capital would be essentially destroyed." As a
result "every branch of industry would suffer." This ap-

[1] *Ibid.*, Vol. V, pp. 3, 4.

peal went directly home to that large and influential group which only a few years before had rallied to the support of the movement to overthrow the Articles and substitute the Constitution. A second appeal went to those interested in western land speculation and the fur trade : "Spain being an officiate with Great Britain, a general Indian war might be expected to desolate the whole exterior of our frontier." The third appeal went to those concerned in the state of the national funds : "Our public debt instead of a gradual diminution would sustain a great augmentation and draw with it a large increase of taxes and burthens on the people." It was obvious to all what that meant : for almost every taxable source that could be touched with safety was already reached, and an increase in the debt would bring a serious reduction in the value of stocks. Finally Hamilton warned the agrarians that even "agriculture would of course languish," as business in general was reduced in volume.

Having finished with the economic issues, Hamilton, with great penetration, divined the growing fear of the conservative propertied classes as the French revolution advanced. Shays' rebellion was hardly a decade off. The direct and obvious economic evils, however great, "were perhaps not the worst to be apprehended. It was to be feared that the war would be conducted in a spirit which would render it more than ordinarily calamitous. There are too many proofs that a considerable party among us is deeply infected with those horrid principles of Jacobinism which, proceeding from one excess to another, have made France a theatre of blood. . . . It was too probable [when the Jay negotiations were begun] that the direction of the war, if commenced, would have fallen into the hands of men of this description. The consequences of this, even in imagination, are such as to make any virtuous man shudder." It is small wonder that merchants and shippers who were at first inclined to revolt against the Jay treaty began to swing around to the support of the administration, when Hamilton thus made it clear that war not only meant a destruction of capitalistic enterprises and interests, but a possible social war at home which would make Shays' rebellion appear trivial in comparison.

On July 22, 1795, the very day that Hamilton began his powerful papers in support of the treaty, the New York chamber of commerce passed resolutions indorsing its terms. Among these resolutions was a declaration to the effect that "if the treaty should fail to be ratified, we should apprehend a state of things which might lead to hostilities; in which event our navigation (now dispersed in all quarters of the globe) may be intercepted, our underwriters injured, our commerce abridged, our produce reduced to little value, our artisans, mechanics, and laborers deprived of employment, our revenue diminished, and the lives of our fellow citizens sacrificed." [1]

A small minority of the chamber of commerce voted against the resolutions of indorsement and shortly afterward addressed a letter to Washington protesting that the majority of those members of the chamber who approved the treaty "were either inimical to this country in the late war or have emigrated to America since that period." The protestants went on to give particulars, saying that of the fifty-nine who had voted in the affirmative, only eighteen had resided out of the British lines during the late war, eight were refugees, i.e., had joined the British, seventeen resided within the British lines during the whole war, six emigrated to this country from Great Britain during the war and resided in towns held by the British, and ten had

[1] The Aurora, July 28, 1795.

emigrated to America since the peace. That these allegations are well founded would appear from the fact that the persons concerned were mentioned by name.[1]

In the private correspondence of the time also, we catch some of the flavor of the old partisan controversy. George Cabot, in letters to Oliver Wolcott, wrote that the chamber of commerce of Boston was unanimous in favor of the treaty, that at Salem "the respectable people are all acquiescent and many of them approve," that at Newburyport "the principal merchants were well satisfied," and that "on the whole it may be safely pronounced that the sober and discreet part of even our seaports and still more of our country towns feel a great anxiety lest the treaty should by any means miscarry."[2] A few days later, on August 14, 1795, Cabot wrote to King: "Since my last, I have been at Newburyport, where the merchants are perfectly well united, and have by this time probably made a formal declaration of their opinions. . . . The Boston Chamber of Commerce have held a meeting. The number attending was, as usual, about forty. They were of the most reputable class, and with only a single dissentient approbated the treaty, and reprobated the attempts everywhere made to excite discontent and tumult among the people. . . . The members of the Chamber of Commerce who did not attend are to be invited to concur in writing; and it is expected that three-fourths, including nineteen-twentieths of the real respectability, will concur."[3]

It may be safely asserted that in general the support for the treaty came from the same sources as the earlier support for the ratification of the Constitution. Chambers of commerce indorsed it, meetings of merchants and business

---

[1] The Aurora, August 10, 1795.
[2] Lodge, *Life and Letters of George Cabot*, p. 84.   [3] *Op. cit.*, p. 85.

men in the seaboard towns approved it, and petitions from men prominent in commercial and financial operations were laid before Congress praying for its ratification. Speaking of the Philadelphia contingent which came to the support of the treaty, the Aurora declared : [1] "In looking over the list of subscribers to that address [of Philadelphians who favored the treaty] the names of many may be distinguished who are opposed to the treaty ; but who have been seduced by the influence of certain bank directors who were most active on the occasion. The earnestness and persuasion which the bank directors used to obtain signatures is truly extraordinary. They seemed to make an appeal to the interests of those whose signatures they have solicited, not as related to the treaty, but as connected with the banks. . . . Were we to say that bank directors, stock-holders and stock-jobbers are more interested in the treaty than other citizens, it would be a truth ; but a truth of that sort, which ought to make the President spurn their opinions."

That the capitalist interests generally were upholding the hands of the administration in the negotiation of the treaty was also the conclusion which Madison reached and communicated in a letter to Monroe, dated at Philadelphia, December 20, 1795 : "As soon as it was known that the Pres. had yielded his ratification the Br. party were reinforced by those who bowed to the name of constituted authority, and those who are implicitly devoted to the Pres. Principal merchants of Phila., with others amounting to about 400, took the lead in an address of approbation. There is good reason to believe that many subscriptions were obtained by the Banks, whose directors solicited them, and by the influence of Br. capitalists. In Balt., Charleston, and other commercial towns, except Phila., New York, and Boston,

[1] The Aurora, August 27, 1795.

no similar proceeding has been attainable. Acquiescence has been inculcated with the more success by exaggerated pictures of the public prosperity, an appeal to the popular feeling for the Pres., and the bugbear of war; still however, there is little doubt that the real sentiment of the mass of the community is hostile to the Treaty." [1]

From the agrarians came plaintive criticisms of the treaty, based on the assumption that it was a victory for the capitalistic interests. Even before Jay's mission, while the proposed negotiations were under advisement, "A Farmer of the Back Settlements" wrote to the General Advertiser at Philadelphia that the whole conduct of the federal administration was little more than an attempt to copy the British model and that closer treaty relations merely meant the triumph of the British party in the United States. In a letter of January 2, 1794, the writer complained that our agents abroad and at home had been influenced by a propensity to aristocracy and by a bias for British interests and that Hamilton was a faithful copyist of the British ministry "who by his inverted politics has continued to create a monied aristocracy, give individuals an opportunity of accumulating immense fortunes, which it would have been more expedient and more conformable to republican principles to have divided among the many, who has formed our system of finance on the odious model of that of England, with loans, banks, excises."

Opponents of the treaty were never tired of asserting that the attempts at an accommodation between the United States and Great Britain proceeded from the desire of the financial and commercial interests to form profitable connections with identical interests in England and that this meant coming to terms with the very Tories against whom the

---

[1] *Writings of Madison* (Hunt ed.), Vol. VI, p. 259.

"embattled farmers" had fought in the war of the Revolution. For example, "Cato," in the General Advertiser of Philadelphia, so represented the affair in letters written early in 1794:[1] "The same timid language, which distinguished a party prior to the late revolution is again heard, and is doubtless thought the real language of America by the Minister of Britain, who only judges by the atmosphere of cities tainted with the breath of tories and foreign emissaries, without having the least knowledge of the pure and elastic air which dilates the lungs of the American yeomanry— Our cities are unfortified— Our funds will be shaken— The Indians are upon our backs &c. &c. &c. — As if the experience of the last war, an established government, and the duplication of our numbers had enfeebled us, and rendered us less capable than we were in 1776 of resisting a nation evidently fallen from her former greatness."

"Peace, commerce with Britain, and the lenity of the states. . .," he continued, "give an influence to two classes of people, whose voices were not heard in the hour of danger, British merchants and American loyalists. They possessed wealth and resources which were unknown to the war-worn soldiers and the impoverished patriot. These had seen their fortunes exhausted by the length of the war, and years which are usually employed in acquiring the means of supporting a family [had been] devoted to securing the freedom of their country.

"Artful politicians among us saw that power would follow property, and that this new phalanx, [British merchants and loyalists] disciplined to habits of submission, and attached to the monarchy, would afford the firmest support to those who secured their confidence, and gave them reason to hope for establishments, in which wealth rather

[1] The General Advertiser, January 8 and February 6, 1794.

than public virtue, should be the test of merit. They were invited to come from their lurking places; to assume a loftier tone; to declare their contempt of the populace; to share in the honors of our own government, while they possessed their veneration for that which we had shaken off. As these people and their patrons gave the tone in polite societies, it is not to be wondered that the British government should be admired, that its measures, however unjust and violent with respect to us, should be palliated, . . . and above all a hatred of the French nation inculcated. . . . The reasoning of those who could give good dinners was irresistible, and it was generally adopted in our capitals."

After the fashion of the day, the Republicans attempted some crude satire at the expense of the champions of the treaty by setting forth their principles in the form of a set of mock resolutions. For example, "Alexander Pacificus" is supposed to have reported the following declaration of faith at an imaginary convention held while the British controversy was going on during the winter of 1794 :[1] "At a meeting of the paper noblemen of the U. S. and the emissaries of the British Gov't, to take into consideration the resolves of the Democratic Society, irredeemable public debt in the Chair, the following resolutions were unanimously adopted :

"That it is the unalienable right of stock-holders, stock-jobbers, bank-directors, and speculators to discuss with freedom, all subjects of public concern, and, that as no other person or persons are seized of this right, as they [the stock-holders &c.] alone have the genuine interest of the public debt at heart, it being the paramount interest of America, to which all other interests ought to submit.

"That the high professions of disinterested patriotism held out by those persons who are not within the vortex of

[1] The General Advertiser, February 12, 1794.

the funding system, are very equivocal proofs of their public virtue." . . .

[That to keep our engagements with France is] "a breach of the funding interest."

"That the determination expressed by the Democratic Society to abide by our national engagements and preserve our national friendships is a flagrant instance of inconsistency; for 'Pacificus' asserts that interest and not honor or gratitude ought to be the bond of nations, and he is our Bible. . . .

"That the trade of America has been the means of prostrating her at the feet of some of the tyrants of Europe, and that this trade having been greater with Great Britain and her colonies than with all the rest of Europe, its interruption at this time would overwhelm the British and the treasury influence here in unspeakable distress. . . .

"That the despotism of the people is as tremendous an evil as that of a Monarch, for the people always tyrannize over themselves; and that to encourage this despotism, is to incur the execration of mankind."

It is impossible for any one who runs through the debates in Congress, the public papers of the statesmen of the period, the newspapers, the pamphlets, and the private correspondence to escape the conclusion that the Jay treaty originated in the economic interests of the Federalist party and that the maintenance of the stability of the fiscal system through the continued regularity of the revenues was among the first considerations that appealed to them. Rather than risk war, they were ready to accept terms which were highly unsatisfactory to many commercial and shipping interests and thus alienate some of the support which they had received from those groups. When the latter began their furious protests against the treaty, the Federalist leaders had little difficulty in showing them the very subtle connections which united all the fiscal, capitalist, commercial, and shipping groups — credit and fluid capital. Nevertheless, a great number of Federalists of the trading centres evidently did not return to their old allegiance after the agitation subsided. Moreover, the Republicans were recruited by hundreds of Southern planters who were disgruntled over the terms of the treaty, the settlement of the private debts due British creditors, and the failure to take up the question of the stolen slaves.

By no means one of the least significant results of the contest over the Jay treaty was the temporary depreciation of Washington's influence with the nation at large. Hitherto, pamphleteers and writers of partisan screeds had almost altogether uniformly spoken of him in terms of the highest respect, as a person above all ordinary party considerations. After the storm over the treaty arose, he was commonly referred to as a tool of the Federalist party, doing its work under the guise of his splendid patriotism. This new spirit of unlimited abuse was expressed forcibly in the Republican organ, Aurora, on March 4, 1797, when Washington gladly laid down the heavy burdens of his office: "If there ever was a period for rejoicing, this is the moment — every heart in unison with the freedom and happiness of the people, ought to beat high with exultation that the name of WASHINGTON from this day ceases to give a currency to political iniquity, and to legalize corruption. A new æra is now opening upon us, an æra which promises much to the people; for public measures must now stand on their own merits."

NOTE TO CHAPTER X

A convention for the payment of the British debts as provided by the Jay treaty was negotiated during Jefferson's administration and thus by a sort of poetic justice the Virginia debts were shifted to the nation under the administration of a

Virginia President.   Oliver Wolcott, the former Federalist Secretary of the Treasury, attacked Jefferson's policy in a savage pamphlet from which the following extracts are taken: "To those who are incapable of discovering the secret motives which govern Mr. Jefferson and his associates of the Virginia party, it has appeared surprising that the convention negotiated by Mr. King, in pursuance of instructions from the federal administration should have attracted so little attention. By this convention, the sum of £600,000 sterling or nearly *three million dollars* is payable at the treasury of the United States, for losses sustained by British subjects, in consequence of the non-execution of the 4th article of the Treaty of Peace. . . .

"The payment of so considerable a sum as *three millions of dollars*, for any purpose whatever except for the reduction of the funded debt, or the purchase of *new lands*, for the purpose of extending the 'blessings of freedom,' must appear to be a strange departure from the economical maxims of the present administration. But that such a sum should be paid to *British subjects*, for losses in the recovery of *private debts;* that a convention should be made in support of the 4th article of the *Treaty of Peace*, which for twenty years had been the cause of the most vehement controversies ; that it should contain an *express* recognition of a stipulation in Mr. Jay's Treaty which had been repeatedly recognized as a degrading surrender of the judicial honor of this country ; that the obligation should be ratified by democratic Senators, though formed by Mr. King, a gentleman highly esteemed and revered by the federal party ; these are indeed most astonishing phenomena.   They are, however, susceptible of explanation ; and when this paper is perused with attention, it is believed that all candid men will concur with the poet, that,

"'The clue once given, unravels all the rest,
The prospect cleared, *Virginia* stands confest.'

It is a firmly established opinion of men well versed in the history of our revolution, that the *whiggism* of Virginia was chiefly owing to the *debts of the planters.* It is certain that their *creditors* were among the *first objects* of a severe and impolitic hostility, which occasioned great dissatisfaction among reflecting men in this country and deeply injured the popularity of the American cause in Great Britain.   It is also certain that measures of a very extraordinary nature were adopted during the War, for the purpose of extinguishing the debts of individuals; and that the 4th article of the Treaty of Peace, which stipulated that there should be no lawful impediments to the recovery of the full value of all bona fide debts was received with the utmost disgust in Virginia."

Wolcott now cites the acts of the Virginia assembly designed to frustrate the enforcement of the provision of the treaty of 1783 relative to debts, and calls attention to the fact that while the adoption of the Constitution was under debate in the Virginia convention efforts were made to secure an amendment to the judiciary section which would deprive the federal courts of jurisdiction over suits between citizens and foreign states, citizens, and subjects.   "It has been asserted," Wolcott then continues, "that the opposition of Virginia to the National Constitution, and particularly to the powers vested in the *judicial department*, originated in sinister and local interests."   In support of this allegation reference is now made to the papers of the Commissioners appointed in pursuance of the 6th article of the treaty of 1794, by which it will appear that "the claims exhibited against the *United States* exceeded *eighteen millions of dollars*.   It will not be pretended that these claims are of themselves evidence of just demands ; though on the contrary it is deemed fair to infer that the proceedings of those states were just and equitable where the claims were comparatively inconsiderable, in proportion to their relative commerce with Great Britain.

STERLING

The claims exhibited against the New England states amounted to .   £   23,000
The states of New York and New Jersey   180,000
The states of Pennsylvania and Delaware   15,000
The whole amount of the claims against the states north of Maryland
    amounted therefore to no more than   218,000
While those against the five southern states amounted to   3,869,000
of which 8,500,000 dollars or one half of the whole amount was claimed of the single state of *Virginia*.

"An analysis of the individual claims would exhibit the disproportion in a more striking point of view, and more fully explain the real motives of the Virginia party. Such an investigation would show that the claims upon *Virginia* were for debts due to *commercial houses*, while those against the states north of *Maryland* were almost exclusively on behalf of American loyalists who were not entitled to compensation under the Treaty. . . . According to the best estimate which can now be formed, four-fifths of the sum payable in pursuance of the convention negotiated by Mr. King will be awarded to the creditors of Virginians." *British Influence on the Affairs of the United States Proved and Explained*, Boston, 1804. Anonymous [by Oliver Wolcott]. Duane Collection of Pamphlets (Library of Congress), Vol. 89, No. 6.

CHAPTER XI

THE POLITICAL ECONOMY OF JOHN ADAMS [1]

DURING the election of Washington's successor it became apparent that the country was sharply divided and that the dissatisfaction with Federalist policies was deep and fervent. It is true, a sturdy Federalist, John Adams, carried the day, but his victory over Jefferson was won by a margin of three electoral votes — a fact which stung him like a nettle. Moreover, he knew that many who voted for him, including no less an important person than Hamilton, had accepted his candidature with reluctance as a lesser evil. Yet, unpropitious as were the signs, the election of 1796 was a victory for the party that had framed the Constitution and carried it into effect.

Whatever may have been the objections brought against Adams on personal grounds, it could not be said that his system of politics was unknown to those who had occasion to vote for presidential electors in the autumn of 1796. On the contrary, Adams, unlike Jefferson and Washington, had published a large work in which he had elaborated with great pains and with copious details his theories of government, politics, economics, and democracy : *A Defence of the Constitutions of Government of the United States of America against the attack of M. Turgot in His Letter to Dr. Price,* first

---

[1] See A. D. Morse, "The Politics of John Adams," American Historical Review, Vol. IV, p. 292. A classified list of materials on Adams' politics is given in a note on p. 302 of the same. C. M. Walsh, *The Political Science of John Adams.* (This valuable work appeared after this chapter was written.)

issued in 1786.[1] This work, although too laborious and too prolix for popular interest, was nevertheless widely read and still more widely commented upon in American newspapers. Large sections, particularly those considered in this chapter, had been reprinted in full in several papers and had been the subject of friendly and adverse criticism by those interested in politics. It was an unlettered voter who was not able to discover in 1796 John Adams' system of political economy.

For the purposes of American politics, the most important part of Adams' long treatise is the Sixth Letter, entitled, "The Right Constitution of a Commonwealth Examined," in which he subjects to searching scrutiny Marchamont Nedham's *The Excellency of a Free State or the Right Constitution of a Commonwealth*, published in the middle of the seventeenth century. Adams built his entire system upon an economic foundation, upon the material needs of human nature. In fact, he bluntly declared : "That the first want of every man is his dinner and the second want his girl were truths well known to every democrat and aristocrat, long before the great philosopher Malthus arose to think he enlightened the world by his discovery." [2] Out of these elemental passions to preserve and continue the species sprang the struggle for economic goods. "Indolence," he says, "is the natural character of man, to such a degree, that nothing but the necessities of hunger, thirst, and other wants equally pressing, can stimulate him to action, until education is introduced in civilized societies, and the strongest motives of ambition to excel in arts, trades, and professions, are established in the minds of all men : until this emulation is introduced, the lazy savage holds property in

[1] Volume III of the London edition of 1794 is used here.

[2] John Adams, *Life and Works*, Vol. VI, p. 516. Unless otherwise stated, quotations are from the Sixth Letter above cited.

too little estimation to give himself trouble for the preservation or acquisition of it."

In spite of the powerful incentives of hunger and thirst and "other wants equally pressing," natural indolence and other causes prevent a large majority of the people from acquiring any property. "There is in every nation and people under heaven a large proportion of persons who take no rational and prudent precautions to preserve what they have, much less to acquire more." Hence there ensues a division of every society into two broad groups : a propertied class and a propertyless class. "Suppose," says Adams, "a nation, rich and poor, high and low, ten millions in numbers, all assembled together; not more than one or two millions will have lands, houses, or any personal property: if we take into account the women and children, or even if we leave them out of the question, a great majority of every nation is wholly destitute of property, except a small quantity of clothes, and a few trifles of other moveables."

The broad division of society into "gentlemen" and "common people" which apparently rests upon cultural distinctions is, in fact, only the outward sign of the economic division into rich and poor. "The people, in all nations," remarks Adams, "are naturally divided into two sorts, the gentlemen and the simplemen, a word which is here chosen to signify the common people. By gentlemen are not meant the rich or the poor, the high or the low born, the industrious or the idle, but all those who have received a liberal education, an ordinary degree of erudition in liberal arts and sciences, whether by birth they be descended from magistrates and officers of government, or from husbandmen, merchants, mechanics, or laborers; or whether they be rich or poor." While thus making the distinction between gentlemen and common people rest upon cultural differences, Adams is quick to add that "*generally* those who are rich and descended from families in public life will have the best education in arts and sciences, and therefore the gentlemen will ordinarily, notwithstanding some exceptions to the rule, be the richer, and born of more noted families. By the common people we mean laborers, husbandmen, mechanics, and merchants in general, who pursue their occupations and industry without any knowledge in liberal arts or sciences, or in anything but their own trades and pursuits; though there may be exceptions to this rule, and individuals may be found in each of these classes who may really be gentlemen."

The economic divisions in society not only manifest themselves in social classes; they form the basis of those "canons of Reputability," such as emulation in conspicuous consumption, which are the outward and visible signs of social superiority. "Consideration," says Adams, "is attainable by appearance and ever will be; and it may be depended on that rich men in general will not suffer others to be considered more than themselves, or as much, if they can prevent it by their riches. The poor and the middle ranks, then, have it in their power to diminish luxury as much as the great and rich have. . . . The higher ranks will never exceed their inferiors but in a certain proportion; but *the distinction* they are absolutely obliged to keep up or fall into contempt and ridicule. It may gratify vulgar malignity and popular envy, to declaim eternally against the rich and the great, the noble and the high; but generally and philosophically speaking, the manners and character of a nation are all alike; the lowest and the middling people, in general, grow vicious, vain, and luxurious, exactly in proportion. As to appearance, the higher sort are obliged to raise theirs in

proportion as the stories below ascend. A free people are
the most addicted to luxury of any ; that equality which they
enjoy and in which they glory, inspires them with sentiments
which hurry them into luxury. A citizen perceives his fellow
citizen, whom he holds his equal, have a better coat or hat,
a better house or horse, than himself, and sees his neighbors
are struck with it, talk of it, and respect him for it : he
cannot bear it ; he must and will be upon a level with him."

Thus, according to Adams, the whole system of modern
culture rests upon economic foundations laid in the impera-
tive necessities of human nature. Cultural badges are but
the outward signs of economic distinctions. The gentleman
and the boor are pretty much of the same clay, but the
possession of worldly goods divides them. A considerable
number of persons may pass from the lower to the upper
class or drop from the upper to the bottom stratum, but the
social categories, the class divisions, remain. Private property is their basis.

These economic divisions, which produce social classes
and cultural distinctions, are likewise the basis of politics —
the conflict of parties. "In every society where property
exists," says Adams, "there will ever be a struggle between
rich and poor." The rich will employ all of the arts and
chicane of civilization to augment their possessions, and unless they are checked a battle will go on until nearly all property is concentrated in the hands of the few and the masses
sink into poverty : "The gentlemen are more intelligent
and skilful, as well as generally richer and better connected,
and therefore have more influence and power than an equal
number of common people : there is a constant effort and
energy in the minds of the former to increase the advantages
they possess over the latter, and to augment their wealth
and influence at their expense. This effort produces re-

sentments and jealousies, contempt, hatred, and fear between the one sort and the other. Individuals among the common people endeavour to make friends, patrons, and protectors among the gentlemen. This produces parties, divisions, tumults and war : but as the former have most address and capacity, they gain more and more continually, until they become exorbitantly rich and the others miserably poor."

While the rich organize to despoil the poor, the latter unite to protect themselves and this class contest usually ends in monarchy. In the progress of great riches accompanied by great poverty, says Adams, "the common people are continually looking up for a protector among the gentlemen, and he who is most able and willing to protect them acquires their confidence. They unite together by their feelings, more than their reflections, in augmenting his power, because the more power he has and the less the gentlemen have, the safer they are. This is a short sketch of the history of that progress of passions and feeling which has produced every simple monarchy in the world; and if nature and its feelings have their course without reflection, they will produce a simple monarchy forever."

But it must not be thought that the conflict has but one side. The poor are equally anxious to despoil the rich. "Perhaps, at first, prejudice, habit, shame, or fear, principle or religion would restrain the poor from attacking the rich, and the idle from usurping on the industrious." But to rely on these as the real safeguards of property would be to rely on broken reeds. "The time would not be long before courage and enterprise would come, and pretexts be invented by degrees, to countenance the majority in dividing all the property among them, or at least in sharing it equally with its present possessors. Debts would be abolished first;

taxes laid heavy on the rich, and not at all on the others; and at last a downright equal division of everything be demanded and voted. What would be the consequence of this? The idle, the vicious, the intemperate would rush into the utmost extravagance of debauchery, sell and spend all their share, and then demand a new division of those who purchased from them. The moment the idea is admitted into society, that property is not as sacred as the laws of God and that there is not a force of law and public justice to protect it, anarchy and tyranny commence."

We may confidently appeal to history for proof of the fact that the majority will attack the property rights of the minority if given the opportunity. It is all very well to flatter the democratical portion of society by saying that they are not as the monarchical and the aristocratical, "but flattery is as base an artifice and as pernicious a vice when offered to the people as when given to others. There is no reason to believe the one much honester or wiser than the other; they are all of the same clay, their minds and bodies are alike. The two latter have more knowledge and sagacity, derived from education, and more advantages for acquiring wisdom and virtue. As to usurping others' rights, they are all three equally guilty when unlimited in power: no wise man will trust either with an opportunity; and every judicious legislator will set all three to watch and control each other. We may appeal to every page of history we have hitherto turned over, for proofs irrefragable that the people, when they have been unchecked, have been as unjust, tyrannical, brutal, barbarous, and cruel as any king or senate possessed of uncontrollable power: the majority has eternally, and without one exception, usurped over the rights of the minority."

While placing a high value on moral sentiments, Adams

is unwilling to rely upon them as a real check upon this sway of private interests. "Moral and Christian, and political, virtue cannot be too much beloved, practised, or rewarded ; but to place liberty on that foundation only would not be safe : but it may be well questioned whether love of the body politic is, precisely, moral or Christian virtue, which requires justice and benevolence to enemies as well as friends, and to other nations as well as our own. It is not true, in fact, that any people ever existed who loved the public better than themselves, their private friends, neighbours, &c. and therefore this kind of virtue, this sort of love, is as precarious a foundation for liberty as honour or fear." This is a fact which we cannot ignore. "If we should extend our candor so far as to own that the majority of men are under the dominion of benevolent and good intentions, yet it must be confessed that a vast majority frequently transgress."

This inevitable battle of rich and poor in politics is, by the force of circumstances, all the more bitter in a democracy than in a simple monarchy where the status of the classes is fairly well established and there is less economic and "cultural" rivalry. In a democracy where the badges of class distinction are not so firmly fixed, the lust for the object of riches knows no bounds : "In proportion as a government is democratical, in a degree beyond a proportional prevalence of monarchy and aristocracy, the wealth, means, and opportunities being the same, does luxury prevail. Its progress is instantaneous. There can be no subordination. One citizen cannot bear that another should live better than himself ; a universal emulation in luxury instantly commences."

If the political system in which this war of the classes is carried on permits simple majority rule, the laws will inevitably bear the stamp of the class interest which dictates them. "In every society where property exists, there will ever be a struggle between rich and poor. Mixed in one assembly, equal laws can never be expected : they will either be made by numbers, to plunder the few who are rich, or by influence, to fleece the many who are poor. Both rich and poor, then, must be made independent, that equal justice may be done, and equal liberty enjoyed by all. To expect that in a single sovereign assembly no load shall be laid upon any but what is common to all, nor to gratify the passions of any, but only to supply the necessities of their country, is altogether chimerical."

To suppose that frequent elections, rotation in office, single-chambered assemblies, and democratic devices generally will check the propensities of the majority to devour the rights of the minority is to fly in the face of all human experience. The pages of Roman history are replete with examples which warn us against indulging in any such fond hopes. "Each scene of election [in England or the United States] will have two or more candidates, and two or more parties, each of which will study its sleights and projects, disguise its designs, draw tools, and worm out enemies. We must remember that every party, and every individual, is now struggling for a share in the executive and judicial power as well as legislative, for a share in the distribution of all honors, offices, rewards, and profits. Every passion and prejudice of every voter will be applied to, every flattery and menace, every trick and bribe that can be bestowed and will be accepted will be used. . . . When vice, folly, and impudence and knavery have carried an election one year, they will acquire, in the course of it, fresh influence and power to succeed the next. In the course of the year, the delegate in an assembly that disposes of all commissions, contracts, and pensions has many opportunities to reward his friends among his own constituents and to punish his enemies."

Far from placing a check on avarice and self-interest — the two predominating motives in the human breast — the single democratic assembly annually elected is the best calculated to facilitate the gratification of self-love and the pursuit of the private interest by a few individuals. "A few eminent conspicuous characters will be continued in their seats in the sovereign assembly, from one election to another, whatever changes are made in the seats around them; by superior art, address, and opulence, by more splendid birth, reputation, and connection, they will be able to intrigue with the people and their leaders out of doors until they worm out most of their opposers, and introduce their friends : to this end they will bestow all office, contracts, privileges in commerce, and other emoluments, and throw every vexation and disappointment in the way of the former until they establish such a system of hopes and fear throughout the state as shall enable them to carry a majority in every fresh election of the house."

The political system thus built up by "the cohesive power of public plunder" will dominate all society. "No favors will be attainable but by those who court the ruling demagogues in the house, by voting for their friends and instruments; and pensions and pecuniary rewards and gratifications, as well as honors and offices of every kind, will be voted to friends and partisans. The leading minds and most influential characters among the clergy will be courted, and the views of the youth in this department will be turned upon those men, and the road to promotion and employment in the church will be obstructed against such as will not worship the general idol. Capital characters among the physicians will not be forgotten, and the means of acquiring reputation and practice in the healing art will be to get the state trumpeters on the side of youth. The bar too will be made so subservient that a young gentleman will have no chance to obtain a character or clients, but by falling in with the views of the judges and their creators. Even the theatres, and actors and actresses, must become politicians and convert the public pleasure into engines of popularity for the governing members of the house. The press, that great barrier and bulwark of the rights of mankind when it is protected in its freedom by law, can now no longer be free: if the authors, writers, and printers will not accept of the hire that will be offered them, they must submit to the ruin that will be denounced against them. The presses with much secrecy and concealment will be made the vehicles of calumny against the minority and of panegyric and empirical applauses of the leaders of the majority; and no remedy can possibly be maintained. In a word, the whole system of affairs and every conceivable motive or hope and fear will be employed to promote the private interest of a few and their obsequious majority; and there is no remedy but in arms."

Inasmuch as simple, popular sovereignty leads at once to demagogy and the spoliation of the rich, "to give the people, uncontrolled, all the prerogatives and rights of supremacy, meaning the whole executive and judicial power, or even the whole undivided legislative, is not the way to preserve liberty. In such a government it is often as great a crime to oppose or decry a popular demagogue, or any of his principal friends, as in a simple monarchy to oppose a king, or in a simple aristocracy, the senators: the people will not bear a contemptuous look or disrespectful word; nay, if the style of your homage, flattery, and adoration is not as hyperbolical as the popular enthusiasm dictates, it is construed into disaffection; the popular cry of envy, jealousy, suspicious temper, vanity, arrogance, pride, ambition, impatience of a superior, is set up against a man, and the rage and fury of an ungoverned rabble, stimulated underhand by the demagogic despots, breaks out into every kind of insult, obliquy, and outrage."

Under the circumstances, those who are called upon to form the constitution of a commonwealth must take into account the divisions of society which are engendered by the unequal distribution of property and must provide ample safeguards for the rights of those who have acquired property as well as the rights of the propertyless.   "It must be remembered, that the rich are *people* as well as the poor; that they have rights as well as others; that they have as clear and as *sacred* a right to their large property as others have to theirs which is smaller; that oppression to them is as possible, and as wicked, as to others; that stealing, robbing, cheating, are the same crimes and sins, whether committed against them or others. The rich, therefore, ought to have an effectual barrier in the constitution against being robbed, plundered, and murdered, as well as the poor; and this can never be without an independent senate.. The poor should have a bulwark against the same dangers and oppressions; and this can never be without a house of representatives of the people.   But neither the rich nor the poor can be defended by their respective guardians in the constitution without any executive power, vested with a negative, equal to either, to hold the balance even between them, and to decide when they cannot agree."

In this balanced government, it is necessary to keep the executive power entirely out of the people's hands, "and give the property and liberty of the rich a security in the senate, against the encroachments of the poor in a popular assembly. Without this, the rich will never enjoy any liberty, property, reputation, or life, in security. The rich have as clear a right to their liberty and property as the poor: it is essential to liberty that the rights of the rich be secured; if they are not, they will soon be robbed and become poor, and in their turn rob their robbers, and thus neither the liberty or property of any will be regarded. . . . If debts are once abolished, and goods are divided, there will be the same reason for a fresh abolition and division every month and every day; and thus the idle, vicious, and abandoned will live in constant riot on the spoils of the industrious, virtuous, and deserving. 'Powerful and crafty underminers have nowhere such rare sport' as in a simple democracy or single popular assembly. Nowhere, not in the completest despotisms, does human nature show itself so completely depraved, so nearly approaching an equal mixture of brutality and devilism, as in the last stages of such a democracy, and in the beginning of that despotism that always succeeds it."

Not only must the executive power be taken out of the hands of the people, but, it will be noted, the legislative power cannot be "wholly entrusted in their hands with a moment's safety: the poor and the vicious would instantly rob the rich and virtuous, spend their plunder in debauchery, or confer it upon some idol, who would become the despot; or, to speak more intelligibly, if not more accurately, some of the rich, by debauching the vicious to their corrupt interest, would plunder the virtuous and become more rich, until they acquired all the property, or a balance of property and of power, in their own hands, and domineered as despots in an oligarchy." [1]   The rich as a class should therefore have

---

[1] This propensity of the propertyless to confiscation and of the rich to intrigue in self-defence and self-aggrandizement, Adams noted in a letter written to the Revolutionary hero, Samuel Adams, in 1790, in which he said: "Without these

a permanent safeguard in the upper house of the legislature, the senate.

Another institution well calculated to maintain the balance between the rich and poor — the *status quo* —is an "independent" judiciary. Under majority rule, the rights of property cannot even be adequately protected in courts dependent on majorities. "An upright, independent, judiciary tribunal, in a simple democracy, is impossible. The judges cannot hold their commissions but durante bene placito of the majority : if a law is made, that their commissions shall be made quamdiu se bene gesserint, this may be repealed whenever the majority will, and, without repealing it, the majority are only to judge when the judges behave amiss, and therefore have them always at mercy. When disputes arise between the rich and poor, the higher and the lower classes, the majority in the house must decide them ; there is no possibility, therefore, of having any fixed rule to settle disputes and compose contentions ; but in a mixed government the judges cannot be displaced but by the concurrence of two branches, who are jealous of each other, and can agree in nothing but justice ; — the house must accuse, and the senate condemn ; this cannot be without a formal trial, and a full defence. In the other [a simple government], a judge may be removed, or condemned to infamy, without any defence or hearing or trial."

This inherent incapacity of the people for restrained direct government does not mean of course that they are to be excluded entirely from all share in the government. On

[proper checks], the struggle will ever end only in a change of impostors. When the people, who have no other property, feel the power in their own hands to determine all questions by a majority, they ever attack those who have property, till the injured men of property lose all patience, and recur to finesse, trick, and stratagem, to outwit those who have too much strength, because they have too many hands to be resisted in any other way." John Adams, *Life and Works*, Vol. VI, p. 418.

the contrary, "the people's fair, full, and honest consent to every law by their representatives must be made an essential part of the constitution : but it is denied that they are the best keepers, or any keepers at all, of their own liberties when they hold collectively or by representation the executive and judicial power, or the whole and uncontrolled legislative ; on the contrary, the experience of all ages has proved that they instantly give away their liberties into the hands of grandees, or kings, idols of their own creation. The management of the executive and judicial powers together always corrupts them, and throws the whole power into the hands of the most profligate and abandoned among themselves. The honest men are generally nearly equally divided in sentiment, and therefore the vicious and unprincipled always follow the most profligate leader, who bribes the highest, and sets all decency and shame at defiance : it becomes more profitable and reputable too, except with a very few, to be a party man than a public-spirited one."

This "balanced" system based upon the recognition of the division of society into rich and poor and of the necessity of preventing either class from conquering the other, by having an independent executive and judiciary to act as "mediators" laid Adams open to the charge of being a monarchist and an aristocrat at heart. In fact, however, he was not much concerned with titles as such ; he was more concerned with the substance than the fictions of government. Nedham's doctrine that the children of the common people should be educated into dislike and enmity for kingly government, Adams contended, was "a most iniquitous and infamous aristocratical artifice, a most formidable conspiracy against the rights of mankind, and against that equality between gentlemen and the common people which nature has established as a moral right, and law should ordain as a political right, for the preservation of liberty. By kings, and kingly power, is meant, both by our author and me, the executive power in a single person. American common people are too enlightened, it is hoped, ever to fall into such a hypocritical snare; the gentlemen, too, it is hoped are too enlightened, as well as too equitable, ever to attempt such a measure; because they must know that the consequence will be, that, after suffering all the evils of contests and dissensions, cruelty and oppression, from the aristocratics, the common people will perjure themselves, and set up an unlimited monarchy instead of a regal republic."

Nevertheless, if the proper balance of classes in the government will not obviate the evils of factious democracy, there is, in Adams' opinion, but one other recourse: "neither philosophy nor policy has yet discovered any other cure, than by prolonging the duration of the first magistrate and senators. The evil may be lessened and postponed, by elections for longer periods of years, till they become for life; and if this is not found an adequate remedy, there will remain no other but to make them hereditary. The delicacy or the dread of unpopularity that should induce any man to conceal this important truth from the full view and contemplation of the people would be a weakness, if not a vice."

That Adams contemplated the creation of an hereditary aristocracy is not to be supposed, but his notion of a senate was far removed from the idea of rotation in office and social equality which is associated with Jeffersonian democracy — often quite erroneously. Adams saw the objections to the descent of titles through the eldest son, no matter how, depraved to the exclusion of other sons, no matter how excellent; and he likewise saw the objections to maintaining decayed families in power on grounds of birth alone. But he asks : "Are not the senators, whether they be hereditary or elective, under the influence of powerful motives to be tender and concerned for the security of liberty?" The spirit and genius of the state are preserved by living tradition. "What stronger motive to virtue, and to the preservation of liberty, can the human mind perceive, next to those of rewards and punishments in a future life, than the recollection of a long line of ancestors who have sat within the walls of the senate and guided the councils, led the armies, commanded the fleets, and fought the battles of the people? . . . If the people have the periodical choice of these, we may hope they will generally select those, among the most conspicuous for fortune, family, and wealth, who are most signalized for virtue and wisdom. . . . Let the people have a full share, and a decisive negative : and, with this impregnable barrier against the ambition of the senate on one side, and the executive power with an equal negative on the other, such a council will be found the patron and guardian of liberty on many occasions, when the giddy, thoughtless multitude, and even their representatives, would neglect, forget, or even despise and insult it."

Moreover, the one constitution which most nearly approaches the ideal of the perfectly balanced government so highly praised by Adams is the English Constitution. "A science," he says, "certainly comprehends all the principles in nature which belong to the subject. The principles in nature which relate to government cannot all be known without a knowledge of the history of mankind. The English constitution is the only one which has considered and provided for all cases that are known to have generally, indeed to have always, happened in the progress of every nation; it is, therefore, the only scientific government. To say then that standing powers have been erected, as mere artificial devices of great men, to serve the ends of avarice, pride, and ambition of a few, to the vassalizing of the community, is to declaim and abuse. Standing powers have been instituted to avoid greater evils, corruption, sedition, war, and bloodshed, in elections; it is the people's business, therefore, to find out some method of avoiding them without standing powers. The Americans flatter themselves they have hit upon it; and no doubt they have for a time, perhaps a long one; but this remains to be proved by experience.''

Adams' system of political science may be summed up in the following manner:

1. Society is divided into contending classes, of which the most important and striking are the gentlemen and common people, or to speak in economic terms, the rich and the poor.

2. The passion for the acquisition of property or the augmentation of already acquired property is so great as to override considerations arising out of religious or moral sentiments.

3. Inevitably the rich will labor to increase their riches at the expense of the poor, and if unchecked, will probably, on account of their superior ingenuity and wisdom, absorb nearly all of the wealth of the country.

4. Out of the contest for economic goods arise great political contests in society, particularly between the rich and the poor. Such contests have ended for the most part in the poor committing themselves to an absolute monarch to secure protection against the predatory rich.

5. The other possible outcome of the contest is the spoliation of the rich by the poor, and this is what happens in

a simple democracy where the majority, unchecked by other than moral considerations, is permitted to rule.

6. Liberty, that is, the preservation of the right of the poor against further spoliation and the rich against attacks by communistic levellers, depends entirely upon the maintenance of order and the *status quo*.

7. Moral and religious considerations or mere theoretical notions about freedom, however widely entertained, are not sufficient to maintain liberty against the assaults of the contending factions.

8. Therefore, the constitution must embody in it a representation of the rich and poor as distinct orders; and a *tertium quid* in the form of an independent executive holding for as long a term as possible should be introduced as a check on both the contending classes. Finally, an independent judiciary should be established as a check on all the other branches and subject to removal only by the coöperation of the representatives of the two contending classes, from whose ambitions dangerous attacks on liberty and property may be expected.

There are one or two features of Adams' system of political science which deserve special consideration in relation to the fortunes of the Federalist and Jeffersonian parties. Although Adams frankly believed that the doctrine of direct popular sovereignty was dangerous to the acquired rights of the rich, he by no means believed in the right of the rich to practise their innate predatory habits on the poor. His society and his balanced government were static. He did not contemplate the possibility of new and extraordinary modes of accumulating wealth. In his system there was no inherent opposition between landed property and personalty. But it appears that his philosophy of **personalty** did not carry him so far as to approve the methods of financial accumulation associated with Hamilton's policy. In fact, Adams was often declared to be a foe of the funding system and its accessories. He believed in the protection of the rights of the rich against the poor and the creation of a system of government that would guarantee the permanence of that protection. For this he received the cordial approbation of the Federalist school. But most of the Federalist leaders were involved in the speculative methods of accumulation which flourished with the funding system, and they could hardly have been expected to look upon any of the lawful modes employed by themselves as predatory in character.

, Such being the practical views of Adams, it is not difficult to discover an important ground of difference between him and Hamilton in matters of public policy. The former feared the rich almost as much as the poor, believing that they were as prone to use the government in spoliation as the latter. Hamilton does not seem to have regarded the rich as a danger to the state. On the contrary, he viewed the rich and well born as the safest depositaries of public power, although he advocated the admission of the propertyless to a speaking voice in the government. Adams did not view the conflict as a struggle between personalty and real property owners but between the rich and poor, although in his classification most of the farmers and petty tradesmen were placed in the latter category. Hamilton was essentially the spokesman of the commercial and financial classes. Contrary to contemporary misrepresentation, it would appear that Adams' property was in land rather than stock and bonds.[1] In fact his biographer says that "in Mr. Adams's vocabulary, the word property meant

[1] *Life and Works*, Vol. I, p. 638.

land. He had no confidence in the permanence of anything else." Such a man was not temperamentally fitted to become the leader of a party founded principally upon capitalistic as opposed to landed interests. Hamilton believed that his fiscal and commercial policy was advantageous to the beneficiaries and the nation at large; he wanted positive action in support of those policies, not "mediation" between contending factions. Under the circumstances it is not surprising that Adams had about as much sympathy for Jefferson as for Hamilton.

Another feature of Adams' system was his grouping of the poor, urban and agrarian, in one mass and his attribution to them of an inclination, fortified by passion and interest, to despoil the rich. This was not very flattering to the ethical standards of the masses, and may have helped to turn against the Federalist party the laboring classes that were steadily increasing in the cities and that had been, apparently, in support of the adoption of the Constitution during the contest over ratification. In an age when most of the political writings exalted popular sovereignty and flattered the people, Adams had the courage of his convictions and wrote out with great labor and pains his disbelief in simple direct popular rule. What many other statesmen before and since have said privately, Adams published in a laboriously systematic form. Only one other man of the period expressed similar political doctrines with equal clarity, and that was the man whom Jefferson selected to succeed him in the presidency — James Madison, author of Number Ten of *The Federalist*, — but Madison announced his views anonymously.

Although the system of political economy laid down in the *Defence of American Constitutions* had no direct reference to the course of party politics in the United States, there is no doubt that Adams thought it entirely applicable to the situation in America. He had no delusions about special dispensations for the new nation; and in a tract prepared in 1808 he showed the bearing of his doctrines upon the problems of his fellow countrymen, saying: "We do possess one material which actually constitutes an aristocracy that governs the nation. That material is wealth. Talents, birth, virtues, services, sacrifices are of little consideration with us. The greatest talents, the highest virtues, the most important services are thrown aside as useless unless they are supported by riches or parties, and the object of both parties is chiefly wealth. . . . In the Roman history we see a constant struggle between the rich and the poor from Romulus to Cæsar. The great division was not so much between patricians and plebeians, as between debtor and creditor. Speculation and usury kept the state in perpetual broils. The patricians usurped the lands and the plebeians demanded agrarian laws. The patricians lent money at exorbitant interest and the plebeians were sometimes unable and always unwilling to pay it. These were the causes of dividing the people into two parties, as distinct and jealous, and almost as hostile to each other, as two nations. Let Mr. Hillhouse [to whom the tract is directed] say whether we have not two parties in this country springing from the same sources? Whether a spirit for speculation in land has not always existed in this country, from the days of William Penn, and even long before? Whether this spirit has not become a rage from Georgia to New Hampshire, within the last thirty years? Whether foundations have not been laid for immense fortunes in a few families, for their posterity? Whether the variations of a fluctuating medium and an unsteady public faith have not raised vast fortunes in personal property, in banks, in commerce, in roads, bridges, &c.? Whether there are not distinctions arising from corporations and societies of all kinds, even those of religion, science, and literature, and whether the professions of law, physic, and divinity are not distinctions? Whether all these are not materials for forming an aristocracy? Whether they do not in fact constitute an aristocracy that governs the country? On the other side the common people, by which appellation I designate the farmers, tradesmen, and laborers, many of the smaller merchants and shopkeepers, and even the unfortunate and necessitous, who are obliged to fly into the wilderness for a subsistence, and all the debtors, cannot see these inequalities without grief and jealousy and resentment. . . . They throw themselves naturally into the arms of the party whose professed object is to oppose the other party. Two such parties, therefore, always will exist, as they always have existed, in all nations, especially in such as have property, and most of all, in commercial countries. Each of these parties must be represented in the legislature, and the two must be checks on each other. But, without a mediator between them, they will oppose each other in all things and go to war till one subjugates the other. The executive authority is the only one that can maintain peace between them." [1]

[1] *Life and Works*, Vol. VI, p. 530.

CHAPTER XII

JOHN ADAMS' theory that an aristocracy of wealth must exist in every society and that every constitution of government must be based upon this inexorable fact was assailed by John Taylor, of Caroline county, Virginia, who may be called the philosopher and statesman of agrarianism. Like Adams, Taylor was a man of affairs as well as a close student of history. He served his party acceptably in the House of Representatives and the Senate of the United States; he was the most trenchant and pertinent of all the Republican pamphleteers; and he was, perhaps, the most systematic thinker that his party produced within the two decades which followed the adoption of the Constitution. During his legislative career, he wrote powerful Anti-Federalist tracts which must have seriously disconcerted the opposition, and during his later years he carefully worked into a somewhat coherent philosophy the preconceptions upon which he had based his program of practical action.

This system of politics, embraced in a weighty volume of 636 pages, was published at Fredericksburg in 1814. It bears the title of *An Inquiry into the Principles and Policy of the Government of the United States*. Without doubt it may be justly accepted as the text-book of agrarian political science, conceived in opposition to capitalism and dedicated to a republic of small farmers. Certainly the great leader of the Republican party, Jefferson, received it as such.[1] Whatever its shortcomings in prolixity of style, it deserves to rank among the two or three really historic contributions to political science which have been produced in the United States. Even if we admit that the author was looking backward, still must his book be reckoned among the first pieces of American political literature, in that it sought some genuine economic foundations for the equalitarian political democracy to which the country was theoretically committed.

At the outset of his plea for a republic based upon substantial equality, Taylor is compelled to face Adams' fundamental proposition that such a system of government is impossible because the sources of inequality "are founded in the constitution of nature," and cannot be eradicated, no matter what institutional devices are invented.[2] The Virginia author does not shrink from the task of meeting this formidable dogma which looks like an axiom in mathematics. He simply denies its validity. He will not admit that the great differences in wealth, the abysmal division into rich and poor, are historically the product of the industry of the few and the sloth of the many. On the contrary, he holds that the older aristocracies, clergy and feudal lords, were begotten of fear of the gods and military conquest [p. 27], in a word, by exploitation, not by thrift and savings.

Feudal institutions built upon this class foundation are therefore not schemes of government devised to protect the accumulations springing from the exercise of primitive virtues, but mere juristic justifications of a *status quo*, originally established by craft and material forces. Such legal institutions, however, in time, come to be merely the

---

[1] *Works* (Washington ed.), Vol. VII, p. 191.
[2] For Adams' reply to Taylor, see John Adams, *Life and Works*, Vol. VI, pp. 445 ff.

safeguard of that of which they were originally the expression, and thus the overthrow of the clerical and feudal classes can be brought about by dissolving their economic foundations. For instance, follow the example of Henry VIII in seizing the property of the church, or of the French Revolutionists in abolishing feudal rights, and the priestly and feudal classes as ruling castes will disappear. Prohibit primogeniture and introduce the division and subdivision of great landed estates and the landed aristocracy will go to pieces. This is what has happened in Europe, and accordingly, it is futile [concludes Taylor] to speak of the aristocracies of the old world as inevitable products of human nature and the experience of Europe as a guide to the makers of American institutions.

The older and more obvious aristocracies simply cannot arise in America. Diversity of religion and diffusion of learning will prevent the appearance of a priestly caste, and alienation of estates will exclude a landed class from our shores. An aristocracy of "talents and virtues" cannot endure because education is so widespread. An aristocracy cannot spring up through commercial transactions because in the course of trade there is "a natural distribution of riches"; in other words free competition will keep down the mighty. Consequently, in shaping their political institutions, the people of the United States need have no fear of such aristocracies. "Why has Mr. Adams written volumes to instruct us how to manage an order of nobles, the sons of the Gods, of exclusive virtue, talents and wealth, and attended by the pomp and fraud of superstition; or one of feudal barons, holding great districts of unalienable country, warlike and high spirited, turbulent and dangerous; now that these orders are no more [p. 15]."

While wasting time in drawing illustrations from Europe,

Adams overlooks the real sources of danger to American republicanism, namely, a capitalistic aristocracy of "paper and patronage, more numerous, more burdensome, unexposed to public jealousy by the badge of title, and not too honorable or high spirited to use and serve executive power, for the sake of pillaging the people [p. 15]." This new aristocracy, built upon modern fiscal and banking institutions, has abandoned "a reliance on the monopoly of virtue, renown and abilities, and resorted wholly to a monopoly of wealth, by the system of paper and patronage. Modern taxes and frauds to collect money, and not ancient authors, will therefore afford the best evidence of its present character [p. 29]." This new form of exclusive wealth, built upon "monopoly and incorporation," — legal privileges, — is the most formidable source of aristocracy with which mankind has to deal, and it can only be prevented by heroic remedies [p. 10]. It is "without rank or title; regardless of honor; of insatiable avarice." It is not conspicuous for virtue and knowledge, and it is "not capable of being collected into a legislative chamber." Nevertheless "differing in all its qualities from Mr. Adams' natural aristocracy and defying its remedy, it is condensed and combined by an interest, exclusive and inimical to public good [p. 15]." Strong as it is in the United States where it has no natural aristocracies to oppose it solidly, it is equally strong in feudal Europe, and is able to dominate other classes.

How much greater is the power of a capitalist aristocracy than that of priestcraft or feudalism may be imagined by supposing the result if the people of England should attempt to abolish the monarchy. "Both the aristocracy of the present age, and the nobility would arrange themselves in its defence. Which would be most formidable? The remnant or hieroglyphick of the feudal system, would indeed display a ridiculous pomp, and imbecile importance; it would appear armed with title, ribbon and symbol, and evince its weakness by tottering under shadows. But the real aristocracy of the present age; neither begotten by the Gods, the curse of conquest, nor the offspring of nature; the aristocracy of patronage and paper would draw out its fleets, armies, public debt, corporate bodies and civil offices. Which species of aristocracy, I ask again, would be the strongest auxiliary for despotism, and the most dangerous enemy to the nation? And yet Mr. Adams has written three volumes, to excite our jealousy against the aristocracy of motto and blazen, without disclosing the danger from the aristocracy of paper and patronage; that political hydra of modern invention, whose arms embrace a whole nation, whose ears hear every sound, whose eyes see all objects, and whose hands can reach every purse and every throat [p. 22]."

Having thus warned his readers in general terms against the new aristocracy, Taylor proceeds to describe its methods in detail and compare it with the aristocracies that have gone before. It divides society into contending classes and brings class hatred; it cannot be checked and watched like a legally recognized class; it is just as burdensome to the producers as were the feudal and priestly classes; it is more implacable in its demands and is never softened by human considerations as were the priests and landlords through their personal relations with the exploited; its methods are so subtle that they almost escape notice; and it defends itself by a serried array of "catch" phrases as did the aristocracies of old. These charges we may take up *seriatim* in Taylor's own language.

Paper and patronage are an infallible source of oppression and hatred in society. "Human conception is unable to invent a scheme, more capable of afflicting mankind with these evils, than that of paper and patronage. It divides a nation into two groups, creditors and debtors; the first supplying its want of physical strength, by alliances with fleets and armies, and practising the most unblushing corruption. A consciousness of inflicting or suffering injuries, fills each with malignity toward the other. . . . A legislature, in a nation where the system of paper and patronage prevails, will be governed by that interest, and legislate in its favour. It is impossible to do this without legislating to the injury of the other interest, that is, the great mass of the nation. Such a legislature will create unnecessary offices, that themselves or their relations may be endowed with them. They will lavish the revenue to enrich themselves. They will borrow for the nation, that they may lend. They will offer lenders great profits that they may share in them [39]."

It is impossible to place any effective check upon this aristocracy of paper. If the wealth of a class "consists of land, it may be measured and balanced. Suppose a nation should establish a landed nobility, and should conclude that the possession of one-third of the lands would confer a share of wealth on this order so unequal as to make it unmanageable, and of course despotick; this nation might restrict their landed order to one-fourth of all the lands in the state, concluding that the three-fourths divided among all other orders, might suffice to check the power arising from condensing one-fourth in one interest. This is what Lord Shaftesbury meant by a 'balance of property.' But if an order of paper and patronage is erected, (remember that nothing makes an order but one interest,) in what manner is its power to be checked by a balance of property? The wealth of paper and patronage is daily growing, wherefore it cannot be measured or limited; it is therefore impossible to balance it; and yet without this balance of property, the power which clings to wealth, will destroy liberty, even in the opinion of the English theorists [p. 51]."

The aristocracy of paper is a burden upon the producers. Like the Physiocrats, Taylor traces the source of wealth to the products or profits of the land, and by an ingenious method he endeavors to show that a paper aristocracy subsisting upon the profits of the land is a no less burdensome aristocracy than one of rank and title. "By taxation, the profit arising from land may be apportioned between the possession and the system of paper and patronage; or it may be wholly transferred to the system. If then an order, such as the late nobility and clergy of France, by an income consisting of the profit of one-third of the lands of France, attracted a degree of power oppressive to the nation; does it not evidently follow, whenever the system of paper and patronage, has acquired one-third of the profit produced by all the lands of a nation, that it will also acquire the oppressive degree of power, interwoven with that degree of wealth [p. 52]." [1]

Taylor then applies this theory to the United States to show that the American agrarian has as much reason for hating the oppressive burden of the capitalistic system as the French peasant had for hating the feudal burden imposed upon him by privileged orders. "All the exports from the United States, may probably amount to the whole profit yielded by land, allowing subsistence to the possessors, which forms no part of rent or profit. This amount has never extended to sixty-millions of dollars annually, yet for the purpose of including the whole, we will

---

[1] For a Republican estimate of the comparative wealth of the "paper aristocracy," see above, p. 220.

estimate the annual profit of the land at that sum. If the interest of paper and patronage received twelve millions annually from direct taxation, and eight millions annually from indirect, by bounties and the circulation of bank paper, then this system would possess that degree of wealth, which rendered the former civil and religious nobility of France, dangerous and oppressive; and it would be obvious, that a system, which had so rapidly absorbed one-third of the profit of the land of the United States, possessed a capacity of extending that third to a moiety, or even beyond a moiety, as in England [p. 52]."

A paper aristocracy is more inhuman and more implacable in the pursuit of its interest than an aristocracy of conquest. "A nation exposed to a paroxysm of conquering rage, has infinitely the advantage of one subjected to this aristocratical system. One is local and temporary; the other is spread by law and is perpetual. One is an open robber, who warns you to defend yourself; the other a sly thief, who empties your pockets under a pretense of paying your debts. One is a pestilence, which will end of itself; the other a climate deadly to liberty. After an invasion, suspended rights may be resumed, ruined cities rebuilt, and past cruelties forgotten; but in the oppressions of an aristocracy of paper and patronage, there can be no respite; so long as there is anything to get, it cannot be glutted with wealth; so long as there is anything to fear, it cannot be glutted with power; other tyrants die; this is immortal. A conqueror may have clemency; he may be generous; at least he is vain, and may be softened by flattery. But a system founded in evil moral qualities, is insensible to human virtues and passions, incapable of remorse, guided constantly by the principles which created it, and acts by the iron instruments, law, armies and tax gatherers. With what prospect of success, reader, could you address the clemency, generosity, or vanity of the system of paper and patronage [p. 41]?"

Of course the paper system makes fine pretensions to national usefulness. "It promises to diminish, and accumulates; it promises to protect, and invades. All political oppressors deceive, in order to succeed. When did an aristocracy avow its purpose? Sincerity demanded of that of the third age [the paper aristocracy] the following confession: 'Our purpose is to settle wealth and power upon a minority. It will be accomplished by national debt, paper corporations, and offices, civil and military. These will condense king, lords and commons, a monied faction and an armed faction, in one interest. This interest must subsist upon another, or perish. The other interest is national, to govern and pilfer which, is our object; and its accomplishment consists in getting the utmost a nation can pay. Such a state of success can only be maintained by armies, to be paid by the nation and commanded by this minority; by corrupting talents and courage; by terrifying timidity; by inflicting penalties on the weak and friendless, and by distracting the majority by deceitful professions. That with which our project commences is invariably a promise to get a nation out of debt; but the invariable effect of it, is to plunge it irretrievably into debt' [p. 40]."

The methods of the paper or capitalist aristocracy are so subtle and so closely wrapped up in public policy that it is almost impossible to lay them bare. Moreover, it has its system of moral and philosophical defence which frightens off the investigator. "The difficulty of producing a correct opinion of the cause and consequences of the new born aristocracy of paper and patronage, surpasses the same difficulty in relation to the aristocracies of the first and second ages, as far as its superior importance. The two last being substantially dead, their bodies may be cut up, the articulation of their bones exposed, and the convolution of their fibres unravelled; but whenever the intricate structure of the system of paper and patronage is attempted to be dissected, we moderns surrender our intellects to yells uttered by the living monster, similar to those with which its predecessors astonished, deluded, and oppressed the world for three thousand years. The aristocracy of superstition defended itself by exclaiming, the Gods! the temples! the sacred oracles! divine Vengeance! the Elysian fields! — and that of paper and patronage exclaims, national faith! sacred charters! disorganization! and security of property [p. 31]!'"

So great is the spell cast over the intellect by the moral devices of the paper aristocracy that the credulous American public is thoroughly deceived by fine words. The devices of the old privileged orders — titles, ribbons, splendors, pomp, honors, eternal and temporal penalties — have been penetrated and exploded; they can be no longer used in the United States to keep the masses satisfied. But the sham defences of the new order of paper are treated seriously: "We moderns; we enlightened Americans; we who have abolished hierarchy and title; and we who are submitting to be taxed and enslaved by patronage and paper, without being deluded or terrified by the promise of heaven, the denunciation of hell, the penalties of the law, the brilliancy and generosity of nobility, or the pageantry and charity of superstition. A spell is put upon our understandings by the words 'public faith and national credit,' which fascinates us into an opinion that fraud, corruption and oppression constitute national credit; and debt and slavery, public faith [p. 61]."

This is all very curious indeed, for on the eve of the

Revolution, the Americans were quick enough to see that they were being exploited by Great Britain through taxes and other devices. At that time they scornfully rejected Dr. Johnson's celebrated argument that taxation was no slavery. They were able to see that they were being robbed when they were taxed by another nation, but now they are not keen enough to discover exploitation by a class at home. Yet, "it is strange, that it is so difficult to distinguish between honest and fraudulent taxes, imposed by a minor interest on the public interest, and so easy to discern the real design of taxes imposed by one nation upon another. In the latter case, monopoly is clearly understood to be an indirect mode of taxation. The United States know that the monopoly of their commerce by the English, was a tribute; but they refused to know, that the monopoly of a circulating medium by banking is also a tribute. Useless offices, established here by the English government, were clearly perceived to be a tribute; but useless offices established by our own government are denied to be so. Pretexts for taxation invented by England were detected by dullness herself; but pretexts invented at home seem to deceive the keenest penetration. . . . Dr. Johnson's maxim could never convince us, that taxation by banking, funding systems, protecting duties or patronage was no slavery, if the profits arising from such institutions were received by English capitalists: does the substitution of a different receiver [*i.e.,* American capitalists] alter the case [pp. 48–50]?"

Powerful as the system of paper and patronage is and insidious and dangerous as are its methods, the Constitution strangely enough makes no safeguards against it. "The Americans devoted their effectual precautions to the obsolete modes of title and hierarchy, erected several barriers against the army mode, and utterly disregarded the mode of paper and patronage. The army mode was thought so formidable, that military men are excluded from legislatures and limited to charters or commissions at will; and the paper mode so harmless, that it is allowed to break the principle of keeping legislative, executive, and judicative powers separate and distinct, to infuse itself into all these departments, to unite them in one conspiracy, and to obtain charters or commissions for unrestricted terms, entrenched behind publick faith and out of the reach, it is said, of national will; which it may assail, wound, and destroy with impunity. This jealousy of armies and confidence in paper system can only be justified, if the following argument of defence is correct : . . . 'Soldiers, admitted to the legislature, would legislate in favour of soldiers; but stock jobbers will not legislate in favour of stockjobbers [p. 42].' ''

Having thus disposed of Adams' contention that an aristocracy of wealth inevitably springs up out of inequalities in human nature and set up the hypothesis that the paper or capitalistic aristocracy of the United States is founded on exploitation fostered by the policy of the government, Taylor then turns to an examination of the fiscal system which is the source of this new danger to republican institutions. In two long and elaborate chapters he analyzes funding and banking as economic processes and as significant factors in politics, and expounds with considerable precision, though not without diffuseness, his own doctrines of political economy.

Broadly speaking, these doctrines may be summarized in a preliminary fashion as follows : (1) Funded debts, banks authorized to issue paper, and protective tariffs are capitalistic devices for wringing money out of the producers of real wealth — commodities; in fact Taylor sometimes speaks of "the paper stock capitalists." (2) Commerce, if let alone, would perform a useful social function of exchange and would not be guilty of exploitation if not involved with paper stock capitalism. (3) The paper stock group thrives as a parasite upon the landed class particularly; it concentrates in cities; it draws to it the best brains of the country; and it enjoys a power altogether out of proportion to its numerical strength. (4) The landed class being numerous, greatly divided through the minute division of landed property, and without many of the advantages of education enjoyed by the capitalist class in the towns, is likely to be overwhelmed by the latter in contests for power. (5) This class division is the source of party divisions. (6) The landed interest is the only true basis of democracy — a defence against communism on the one hand and capitalistic exploitation on the other. (7) The solution of the contradictions is the destruction of the "paper aristocracy" by the destruction of its government privileges. These several principles we may now examine as they are stated in Taylor's own words.

(1) To the first proposition, namely, that funded debts, paper issuing banks, and protective tariffs are engines for exploiting the producers of wealth, Taylor devotes the most attention. With regard to the funded debt, he comes to the conclusion that it is a fraud upon the present and future generations when considered from an economic point of view alone. Anticipation in the form of debt, he says, "does not conjure into real existence, the commercial, agricultural or manufactured products of futurity. It does not add to the corn or coin of the realm. . . . It cannot bring up from futurity a gun, a soldier, a ration or a cartridge. The present generation suffers every hardship and cost of war, although anticipation pretends that it is

suffered by future generations. And this delusion is used to involve nations in wars, which they would never commence, if they knew that all the expense would fall upon themselves. It is twice suffered; by the living, who supply all the expenses of war; and by the unborn, who supply an equivalent sum, to take up certificates of the expenses paid by the living. No item of the expense of war is more transferable from the living to the unborn, than the blood it sheds. . . . A maniac, whose income in kind is just sufficient to support him, takes it into his head to give his bonds to sundry people annually for its value, whilst he is consuming it. At the end of fourteen years his whole income is gone, though he has only expended its annual amount. Such is anticipation to nations. But those who use it to deceive, plunder and enslave them, artfully liken it to the case of a man who buys an estate on credit, or who gives bonds to himself [p. 249]."

A funded debt is not only economically a fraud at the outset, but it continues to be an ingenious method whereby one class may take from another. "It only conjures the wealth of existing people out of some hands into others; and the credit with which to buy property of the living given by the certificate, constitutes all the solid wealth gained by anticipation [p. 249]." It is a shrewdly contrived engine for confiscation. "All paper systems are, in fact, indirect laws of confiscation, used for the purposes which induced the French revolutionists to transfer more directly, a great mass of landed property from their antagonists to themselves. These purposes simply were to enrich themselves and establish their power. It was to enrich, and establish the power of the Whigs, at the expense of the Tories that Walpole used a paper system. In America, a paper confiscation system, conferred wealth and power on a monarchical party at the expense of the Whigs. In both countries, those who furnished the riches, lost much of their power and property; those who received them, gained it. The French confiscations went boldly to their object, like a direct tax. The English and American confiscations, secretly and circuitously effected their design, by the complication of a paper system; like an indirect tax. One seized and transferred the land itself. The others, mortgaged it; artfully leaving to the owner the appearance of property, whilst he is only a receiver of the profits for the benefit of the mortgage [p. 255]."

In his long and diffuse chapter on banking, Taylor identifies bank stock and bank currency with debt stock so far as their exploitative character is concerned. In fact, in his opinion, coin permits exploitation, for he says "even the precious metals have furnished to the contrivers of pillage and oppression a medium for extracting indirectly from nations, a far greater proportion of their labor than they ever could be made to pay directly by the feudal or any other regimen [p. 292]." The only reason why the precious metals do not afford unlimited means for "pillage" is because their supply cannot be indefinitely extended by operations of the human will.

Bank stock and currency, however, are not subject to the limits imposed by nature on money made of the precious metals. "An artificial currency is subject to no such check, and possesses an unlimited power of enslaving nations, if slavery consists in binding a great number to labor for a few. Employed, not for the useful purpose of exchanging, but for the fraudulent one of transferring property, currency is converted into a thief and a traitor, and begets, like an abuse of many other good things, misery instead of happiness. Mankind soon discovered that money was easily converted into

a medium for oppression as well as for commerce, and hence
arose nearly as strong a dislike to heavy taxes in money as
in kind; it being clearly seen that labor and property were
transferred by money. This plain truth, awakened the
exertion of avarice and ambition, to deceive the vigilance
of labor and industry; the objects of pillage. The first
intricacy with which they endeavored to hide their design
was woven of indirect taxes travelling in mazes; the second,
of loaning obscured by the mist of futurity; and third, of an
artificial currency or banking, complicated by the crooked-
ness of its operation, flattering to industry, and restrained
by no natural check, as a medium of fraud and tyranny
[p. 292]."

In other words, the banking system is simply a "paper
feudal system." It represents no real wealth; it creates no
real wealth. It is nothing more nor less than another
scheme for beguiling the nation and taxing labor and land.
"The certainty and simplicity with which a bank inflicts
and collects its profit, becomes still more visible. The
operation is carried on between a nation and a banking
corporation. The nation, through the channel of its
members, exchanges a thing called credit, reduced to the
form of bonds or notes for the payment of money, with the
corporation, giving a boot, profit or difference, of about
eight per centum per annum, which the bank bond, note or
credit, is arbitrarily made by law to be worth, beyond the
national bond, note or credit. This effect is produced by
subjecting the members of the nation to the payment of a
compound interest to the corporation on their bonds, notes
or credit, and absolving the corporation from the payment
of any interest to the members of the nation, on its bonds,
notes or credit; and exhibits both the inevitability of the
tax, and a mode of its collection [p. 297]." In short, the

nation permits a private corporation, in return for a small payment, to coin its credit into notes and then borrows those notes at a high rate of interest, thus taxing itself for the benefit of a bank stock aristocracy.

But it may be objected that the bank levy is simply a tax on the voluntary borrower. "Should bread and water be placed in abundance, before a hungry and thirsty multitude, could their eating and drinking be fairly said to be merely voluntary? Currency is the medium for exchanging necessaries. If gold and silver, the universal medium, are legislated out of sight, all human wants unite to compel men to receive the tax collecting substitute. This is banking. By the help of law it creates a necessity for its own currency; and this extreme hunger is misnamed volition. The coin currency being expelled or drawn out of circulation, to an extent sufficient to create a necessity for some substitute, the power possessing the right of supplying and regulating that substitute, can inevitably so manage it, as to enrich itself by means of that necessity. It can supply the needed currency upon the terms and in the quantities it pleases. And if fluctuations in currency, produced and managed by chartered monopolies, can affect price or value, it follows that, through his income, his money, and his property, an individual is reached by the tax of this currency, though he never borrowed or used it. Such sufferers do not exercise the least formality of volition [p. 298]."

The bank stock scheme as "a machine for transferring property" is "more effectual than that made of hereditary or exclusive wisdom. Both machines have been invented for this purpose. The hereditary magnifies the defects incident to human government in its best form, to hide its own greater vices. The credit machine, in strict imitation of this example, seizes upon the errors of paper money, as reproaches against national credit; and hides under them its own greater aptitude to shrink from danger, and also its capacities for corrupting governments and plundering nations. Of the bad features in the face of paper money, corporation credit makes two masks, one to hide its hideousness, the other to hide the benefits of national credit. If all the banks in the United States circulate fifty millions of paper dollars, five millions of real property will thereby be collected. . . . Are these great sums of wealth no property? If they are property, to whom do they belong? If they belong to anybody, can they be transferred by laws and charters, under a policy, which considers property as sacred [p. 308]?"

Although Taylor directs his heaviest attack against the funded debt and banking systems of exploitation created by law, he by no means overlooks the protective tariff as another capitalistic device for conjuring money out of the pockets of the producers of real wealth. Of course, in his day the latter engine had not developed to such formidable proportions, but he had no doubt as to its capitalistic and exploitative character. In fact, he flatly declares: "The policy of protecting duties to force manufacturing, is of the same nature, and will produce the same consequences as that of enriching a noble interest, a church interest, or a paper interest; because bounties to capital are taxes upon industry and a distribution of property by law. And it is the worst mode of encouraging aristocracy, because, to the evil of distributing wealth at home by law, is to be added the national loss arising from foreign retaliation upon our own exports. An exclusion by us of foreign articles of commerce, will beget an exclusion by foreigners of our articles of commerce, or at least corresponding duties; and the wealth of the majority will be as certainly diminished to enrich capital, as if it should be obliged to export a million of guineas to bring back a million of dollars, or to bestow a portion of its guineas upon this separate interest [p. 569]."

(2) Having outlawed funding, banking, and protective tariffs as schemes designed to exploit the landed classes, Taylor is compelled to pass judgment upon commerce as well. Inasmuch as commerce is generally in the hands of a group closely allied to the capitalistic circles, we might expect to find Taylor condemning that economic interest as roundly as the others; but he refuses to put the men of trade among the exploiters. He admits that "commerce, monarchy, paper stock, legislative corruption, privileged orders, charters of exclusive commerce, and hierarchy exist together in England," but he holds that this is an unnatural alliance, because there is no real affinity between paper stock and commerce. The latter has a useful and productive function to perform, *i.e.*, buying in the cheapest market and selling in the dearest, and monopolies and paper charters are its avowed enemies. The very fact that England, with all her paper stock capital, is compelled to go to war for commercial advantages, Taylor thinks, is conclusive proof that paper stock is no friend to free commerce — perhaps the most unsuccessful piece of reasoning in which he indulges.

In spite of this enmity between commerce and artificial restraints of various kinds, Taylor is forced to admit that stocks, both national and commercial, are a goad to commercial activities, but he believes that a far better stimulant is to be found in "free and moderate government," allowing trade to flow into natural channels where it can "buy cheap and sell dear." The fact that commerce flourished so vigorously under the Articles of Confederation without the aid of paper capital is sufficient proof to him that no such aid is needed now. Commerce must, therefore, break with these unnatural alliances and return to "free" methods. In other words, Taylor seems to have anticipated, in this respect, the Manchester school. Or perhaps it would be better to say that he had learned his lessons from Adam Smith so far as this branch of his political economy is concerned.

(3) That the paper stock group is a parasite upon the landed class, Taylor has no doubts. He sketches the history of the rise of the capitalistic Whigs in England as an element deliberately imposed upon the landed gentry and adds: "A paper system followed the revolution produced by the present form of our general government, and operated upon the landed Whigs here exactly as it had done upon the landed Tories in England. It taxes them, enriches a credit or paper faction; changes property; forms a party; and transforms its principles as in England [p. 254]." Sometimes Taylor introduces labor also, but he has in mind principally labor upon the land. On one occasion he remarks that the funding system is "an engine having no resemblance in interest to land, labor or talents; therefore it cannot be a friend to either [p. 254]." And on another occasion he speaks of the income of the paper stock aristocracy as drawn from "land and labor [p. 271]."

Being a form of exploitation not unlike feudal dues, it must perforce fall principally upon land in the United States, for land constitutes the major interest, and, so far as the eye of prophecy can see, is destined to remain the major interest far into the future, if not forever. "Those who furnish the subsistence, pay all the taxes. As subsistence flows from the earth, that may be called the mother of men, liable to make all the disbursements they need. Hence all, or nearly all, taxes must be ultimately paid by agriculture, and ought of course to be inflicted by her, if the doctrine is true, that the payer is the only just imposer of taxes. Agriculture cannot be partial, because she cannot shift the tax from her own shoulders. . . . In the United States, speculation, as it was called, bought of the family of the earth an hundred millions at one shilling in the pound, and then compelled it to repurchase it at twenty. This family of the law soon disclosed its affection for its relations, monarchy and aristocracy. Here too bank stock is already annually extracting from the family of the earth, of labor and of property, five times as much as the civil government of the United States costs [p. 333]."

While thus thriving upon the landed proprietors, this capitalistic aristocracy will steadily increase in power, because "the weight of talents will follow leisure and wealth." Moreover, political power concentrates as wealth accumulates: "If wealth is accumulated in the hands of the few, either by a feudal or a stock monopoly, it carries the power also; and a government becomes as certainly aristocratical, by a monopoly of wealth, as by a monopoly of arms [p. 275]." Accumulated wealth gives leisure and talents and political power — the logic is inexorable. "As paper property is accumulated, the leisure and income of the holders will be increased. The weight of talents will follow leisure and wealth; and these will gradually acquire a locality, corresponding to the abodes of the receivers of stock taxation. This superiority of talents and wealth will invest individuals, and the cities in which they will chiefly reside, with an influence, well calculated to acquire an ascendancy over the landed interest, gradually impoverished by division [p. 262]."

Particularly insidious is the power of the banking corporation endowed with special privileges by the government and always ready to bring sinister influences to bear in the legislature. On this point Taylor writes with great feeling. He had observed at first hand the course of politics during the first administration and had unearthed by some skilful investigation the actual participation of interested stockholders and speculators in the proceedings of Congress.[1] He is not speaking of an academic matter, therefore, when he says: "As all separate interests prefer themselves, and bend governments into subserviency to their designs; so one neither responsible, nor weakened by division, nor made up of distinct independent interests, by means of different departments and unconnected offices, will act with a degree of concert and force, for its own aggrandizement, which would be impracticable to the several governments in America. The banking power is therefore a stronger, as well as a richer, power than the civil. The holders of both will use the latter as an ally of the former; the two powers will unite in one, and all the checks invented to control the civil power will be silently lost in the illimitable influence of the stock power. A power of regulating property is engendered of a capacity to enslave nations surpassing a power to regulate the press, as far as an influence over a whole nation, or great factions, exceeds one over a poor author [p. 312]."

(4) That the landed class is ill equipped to cope with this powerful, insidious, and closely knit aristocracy of capitalism, Taylor is thoroughly convinced. The very democracy of our landed system — the division of land into innumerable small farms tilled by owners of limited knowledge — makes it more difficult for the landed group to unite in a solid opposition to the oppressors. A landed aristocracy

---

[1] For his pamphlet on the security and bank stockholders in the early Congresses, see above, p. 203.

built upon great estates would be more effective for this purpose, but such is impossible and undesirable in the United States. Consequently there is grave danger that capitalism will triumph in time. Taylor thinks it is only a question of years : "Though this landed interest may not suddenly sink into an ignorant, scattered, disunited peasantry, taxed by paper operations, to enrich, instruct and elevate a new species of feudal capitalists, yet the tendency of the system is exactly to that point, and the arrival of an unobstructed tendency is inevitable. If the division of landed property has a tendency to increase the ignorance of the numerous and valuable portion of society which cultivate it, a defect of the American policy in not providing some remedy to meet this evil is disclosed. From preventing an accumulation of landed wealth, and providing for a monied or stock monopoly of knowledge, a reason arises for placing the best education within the reach of that great mass of people, called the landed interest; instead of which its inability to purchase knowledge is studiously increased, by a division of inheritances, and by the annual draughts upon it for the interest and dividends of debt and bank stock. The ignorance of land holders will thus in time be brought to a standard exactly sufficient to render them tame, and subservient to the interest of a stock aristocracy; an event which may even be accelerated, by taxing them for the purpose of diffusing a knowledge of the vulgar tongue and vulgar arithmetic. These laws for dividing landed property, and levelling landed knowledge, form a striking contrast with those for accumulating stock wealth, and of course stock knowledge. . . . Is an accumulation of wealth and knowledge by law in a few hands to be found in any receipt for making a free republick [p. 263] ?"

(5) To this conflict between the agrarian and capitalistic

interests Taylor traces the origin of party divisions. He erroneously represents Marshall as attributing the rise of parties to the "intrigues of Mr. Jefferson, to French influence, and to other transitory and fluctuating causes,"[1] and adds that if this opinion had been correct, parties would have disappeared with the supposed causes. As a matter of fact the parties sprang from the economic antagonism: "Being in truth produced by the mass of property transferred by funding, banking and patronage, creating (to borrow Mr. Hume's phrase) an aristocracy of interest, they [political parties] yet exist, because these laws divided the nation into a minority enriched, and a majority furnishing the riches; and two parties, seekers and defenders of wealth, are an unavoidable consequence. All parties, however loyal to principles at first, degenerate into aristocracies of interest at last; and unless a nation is capable of discerning the point where integrity ends and fraud begins, popular parties are among the surest modes of introducing an aristocracy [p. 569]."

During the battle of the Republicans against Hamilton's system, Taylor looked to his party to relieve the nation of the paper incubus, but he has now (1811) apparently lost faith in the willingness of that party to destroy the parasitical class against which it has waged war.[2] "Individuals and entire parties, to a vast extent, have loudly reprobated and calmly defended this power; and the folly or knavery of those who first represented it as an usurpation dangerous to free government, and afterwards seized upon it, ought to be a memorial to nations against reposing an excessive degree of confidence in parties or individuals; in judges or legislatures; in governments or patriots. The history of

---

[1] For Marshall's correct view, see above, p. 237.

[2] For Jefferson's use of the "fiscal squadron" for party purposes, see below, p. 447.

man proves that all will often avail themselves of the precedents established by their predecessors and reprobated by themselves. Every precedent, however clearly demonstrated to be unconstitutional and tending 'towards monarchy and an iron government' by a party out of power, will be held sacred by the same party in it ; and those who clearly discerned the injustice and impolicy of enriching and strengthening the federalists by bank or debt stock, at the publick expense, will seldom refuse to receive a similar sinecure. In short, a power in the individuals who compose legislatures, to fish up wealth from the people, by nets of their own weaving, whatever be the names of such nets, will corrupt legislative, executive and judicial publick servants, by whatever systems constituted [p. 304]."

The fact is, the Republican party has been captured by the law-created special interests — paper stock, banking, and protected capital engaged in manufacturing. "The United States exhibit four parties, the republican, monarchical, stock, and patronage. The two parties of principle, unsophisticated by the parties of separate interest, would discuss with moderation, and decide with integrity ; but the last two, accepted on both sides as recruits, by an ardor for victory, though known to be allies who serve for plunder, empoison them all by the contamination of an interest, distinct from the publick ; and by all the animosities, aristocracies of interest inspire. Aristocracy or separate interest in our case, at present, takes refuge under the one and then under the other of our parties, because it is not yet able to stand alone ; but whilst it is fondling first one and then the other of its nurses, it is sucking both into a consumption and itself towards maturity [p. 568]."

While thus appearing to assume that two parties of pure theoretical principles, monarchical and republican, would exist were there no special interest, Taylor, at another point, clearly identifies agrarianism with republicanism and the paper interest with monarchical predilections. "The landed interest of the United States, being indissolubly betrothed to commerce, has been considered as so completely covering the interests of the society, that it is used in several states as a substratum of civil government [landed qualifications on the suffrage] recognised as republican, by the guarantee in the federal constitution. And where the range of suffrage is wider, but attended either by a greater portion of bank stock or executive patronage, the tendency towards monarchy or aristocracy is more visible, than where suffrage has been in some degree limited to land, but attended with less stock or patronage [p. 555]."

(6) In spite of all the difficulties and discouragements confronting the American people, land is the real basis of democracy, the only genuine and enduring basis. It alone has no special, law-made privileges, and seeks no favors from the government. It stands on an independent foundation. "Land is not created by law; therefore it is under no apprehension of its death stroke from law. It does not subsist upon other interests; therefore it is not beset by an host of enemies, whose vengeance it is conscious of deserving. By the operation of laws adverse to its monopoly, it quickly adjusts itself to the interest of a majority of the nation; thenceforward it is incapable of the avarice and injustice of a factitious legal interest, because no temptation to seduce it into either exists. To this point of improvement, a landed interest will invariably be brought, by laws for dividing lands; nor can it be corrupted, except by laws which confine lands to a minority [p. 260]."

Like most defenders of a class interest against the assaults of another class which they deem predatory, Taylor does not inquire too narrowly into the origins and rights of private property in land. He repeatedly speaks of labor as the true and natural distributor of wealth where unimpeded by governmental intervention, but he can hardly regard property in land as a "reward" justly distributed by nature to labor. Neither does he bring under review the simple exploitation of slave labor by the planters for whom he was himself the special spokesman. "Governments were instituted," he says, "to enable men to keep their property, but in these evils days (and in fact quite commonly in history), they use public powers to transfer property from the owners to factitious, legally created special interest [p. 561]."

Under no circumstances should the government interfere with the distribution of wealth. "No form of civil government can be more fraudulent, expensive, and complicated than one which distributes wealth and consequently power by the act of the government itself [p. 244]. . . . Our policy is founded upon the idea, that it is both wise and just, to leave the distribution of property to industry and talents ; that what they acquire is all their own, except what they owe to society ; that they owe nothing to society except a contribution equivalent to the necessities of government ; that they owe nothing to monopoly or exclusive privilege in any form ; and that whether they are despoiled by the rage of a mob, or the laws of a separate interest, the genuine sanction of private property is equally violated [p. 282]."

The landed interest, in addition to being the enduring basis of democracy, is a true preservative of the rights of private property against invasion by exploiting paper stock interests and the levelling poor. "There are two modes," said Taylor, "of invading private property ; the first, by which the poor plunder the rich, is sudden and violent ; the second, by which the rich plunder the poor, slow and legal.

. . . Whether the law shall gradually transfer the property of the many to the few, or insurrection shall rapidly divide the property of the few among the many, it is equally an invasion of private property, and equally contrary to our constitutions. If equalizing and accumulating laws are the same in principle, it is inconceivable how the same mind should be able to detest the one, and approve the other. Integrity is compelled to reject both and spurning at doctrines, calculated to incite the few to plunder the many, or the many to plunder the few, leaves every man under the strongest excitement to labor for his own and national prosperity [p. 280]."

Taylor repudiates therefore the communistic principles of Godwin with the same zeal that he attacks the special interests. The very philosophy of communism, he traces to the exploitation of the producers of real wealth by fictitious interests. "To the indignation inspired by the fraudulent legal modes for acquiring wealth, mankind are indebted for the pernicious and impracticable idea of equalizing property by law. This speculation has been considered by philosophers, in contrast with its opposite. It seemed to them more reasonable and just, that property should be made equal, than unequal, by law. Destroy the alternative by assailing both its branches with the benefits arising from leaving property to be distributed by industry, and the argument would assume a new aspect. It would be discovered, that arts and sciences, peace and plenty, have never been found disunited from metes and bounds [p. 563]."

Just how "labor" had "distributed" property in land Taylor does not attempt to explain.

However, in a contest between wealth and the propertyless bent upon levelling all property rights, Taylor holds, fraudulent and honest property will unite in common defence. "Legal, factitious or fraudulent property, comprising every species resulting from direct and indirect modes of accumulation by law, at the expense of others, has been able in all civilized countries to unite itself with substantial, real or honest property, comprising accumulations arising from fair and useful industry and talents. The equalizing speculation, by proposing to destroy both, united these two opposite moral beings in a defensive war; just as a good and bad man would unite against an assassin, indifferently determined to murder them both. Had philosophers wisely avoided this snare and confined the discussion to a discrimination between the useful and pernicious kinds of property, they would never have given to the latter the benefit of an alliance by which it is sustained; and might have long since settled some definition of private property, sufficiently perspicuous, to defend mankind against the pecuniary oppressions that they are forever suffering for the want of it. Instead of associating honest and fraudulent property in one interest, by the chimerical and impracticable equalizing project, they would have established a rational and practicable distinction, between that species of private property founded only in law, such as is gained by privilege, hierarchy, paper, charter, and sinecure; and that founded also in nature, arising from industry, arts, and sciences [p. 564]."

(7) The agrarian interest being the only true basis of democracy and the defender of the rights of private property against exploiters and communists, it is in duty bound to destroy that great enemy of the republic — the capitalistic paper interest, root and branch, without compensation. Of this remedy Taylor has no doubts. A landed aristocracy can be destroyed by alienation and a capitalistic aristocracy can be destroyed by the abolition of all special privileges.

It is therefore incumbent upon the agrarian democracy of America to fall upon its great enemy without mercy, remembering that "all societies have exercised the right of abolishing privileged, stipendiary, or factitious property, whenever they become detrimental to them; nor have kings, churches, or aristocracies ever hesitated to do the same thing, for the same reason. The king of England joined the people and judges, in abolishing the tenures and perpetuities of the nobles; the king and nobles united in abolishing the property of the popish clergy; the consistory of Rome suppressed the order of Jesuits and disposed of its property; and several of these states have abolished entails, tithes, and hierarchical establishments. What stronger ground can be occupied by any species of law-begotten wealth than by these [p. 562]?"

Taylor's system may be summed up in the following manner:

1. The masses have always been exploited by ruling classes, royal, ecclesiastical, or feudal, which have been genuine economic castes sustaining their power by psychological devices such as "loyalty to the throne and altar."

2. Within recent times a new class, capitalistic in character, has sprung up, based on exploitation through inflated public paper, bank stock, and a protective tariff, likewise with its psychological devices, "public faith, national integrity, and sacred credit."

3. In the United States, this class was built up by Hamilton's fiscal system, the bank, and protective tariff, all of which are schemes designed to filch wealth from productive labor, particularly labor upon the land.

4. Thus was created a fundamental conflict between the capitalistic and agrarian interests which was the origin of parties in the United States.

5. Having no political principles, capitalism could fraternize with any party that promised protection, and in fact after the victory of the Republicans successfully intrenched itself in power under the new cover.

6. The only remedy is to follow the confiscatory examples of other classes and destroy special privilege without compensation.

CHAPTER XIII

THE GREAT BATTLE OF 1800

PRESIDENT ADAMS' systematic treatise on politics plagued him throughout his administration.[1] The Republicans never wearied in referring to it as a work conceived in the spirit of aristocracy and flatly contradictory to all American doctrines and practices. It is true that he publicly announced himself as a believer in simplicity by saying in his first inaugural address that robes and diamonds could add nothing beyond ornament and decoration to the majesty of a self-governing nation, and received a faint applause from the Republicans for his democratic sentiments. But the land was full of political trouble, and Adams was no man to ride a popular storm successfully. He had a high sense of honor and was conscious of it. He was austere and unbending and there was little in his career or bearing to attract the enthusiasm of the populace. And it added nothing to his good humor to reflect upon the bitter fact that he was President "by three votes." From the day that he took the oath of office until the cold dawn of March 4, 1801, when he hurried away from Washington to escape the hateful spectacle of his rival's inauguration, Adams did not perform an official act or make a public pronouncement that did anything to conciliate permanently the opposition party, and it may be justly said that he added to the unpopularity with his own party from which he suffered in the beginning. Moreover, the march of events at home and abroad did

[1] See The Aurora, September 12, 1800.

not contribute to Adams' ease of mind or to the happy administration of affairs. When Washington was gone, the last restraint on party criticism was broken, and Federalist measures could be attacked without incurring the odium of slurring the impeccable "Father of his Country." And opportunity for criticism was not wanting. Adams inherited an unfortunate legacy in the Jay treaty. Although that agreement contained a declaration to the effect that it should in no way conflict with the obligations of the United States to France, the Federalists interpreted it in such a fashion as to give umbrage to that country. In retaliation, France began to prey upon American commerce. In the closing weeks of Washington's administration, the Republican Monroe who had shown undue enthusiasm for the revolutionary cause in France had been recalled from his post as American representative to that country; and the French government, which was closely in touch with the political situation in the United States through its keen-sighted agents,[1] refused to receive Monroe's successor, that Federalist of the old school, Charles Coatesworth Pinckney.

Then followed two years of anxious negotiation with France, during which period the army and navy were greatly increased, to the terror of all faithful Republicans, and preparations were made for open war, with Washington and Hamilton in command. Although the conduct of the French government was in many ways disgusting even to the Republicans, they insisted that the breach with a sister Republic engaged in a death grapple with the recent foe of American liberty, Great Britain, was, in the main, due to Federalist machinations, to Federalist sympathy with monarchical institutions and fear of the revolutionary tendencies of French republicanism. Whatever may have been the truth

[1] See above, p. 217.

of the matter, and undoubtedly there was much to be said in justification of the Republican position, it is certain that the whole affair with France augmented partisan feeling in the country and gave support to the deep and inveterate Republican suspicion that Federalism was allied with British commercial and financial interests — which was true, though not in the sinister sense in which pamphleteers took it.

Meanwhile the expenditures of the Federal government mounted upwards, giving new cause for complaint on the part of the "tax-burdened people." They were in round numbers $5,800,000 in 1796, $6,000,000 in 1797, $7,600,000 in 1798, $9,300,000 in 1799, and $10,800,000 in 1800. The national debt, instead of decreasing, was augmented by the extraordinary military expenses; and the war on the stock-jobbers became more vociferous than ever. It was not diminished when, by a law approved July 14, 1798, a direct tax was laid upon houses, lands, and slaves, to meet the increasing demands upon the federal revenue. Although this law was made somewhat more palatable to the Republican members of Congress by placing a heavy progressive tax on houses in cities, it was not received with satisfaction by the Southern states, for in addition to the land tax, Congress laid a tax of fifty cents on every slave between the ages of twelve and fifty.[1]

[1] See a letter of Gouverneur Morris to Rufus King, Morrisania, June 4, 1800. After expressing the opinion that fear of their opponents would cause the Republicans to use moderation in office, he said: "Truth is that a direct Tax, unpopular everywhere, is really unwise in America, because property here is not productive. Of course their Democrats and their demagogues have had just cause to complain of the manner in which money is raised; and our expenditure is so far from economical, that no applause is to be expected on that score. But the thing which in my opinion has done most mischief to the federal party is the ground given by some of them to believe that they wish to establish a monarchy." *Life and Correspondence of Rufus King*, Vol. III, p. 252. On January 26, 1797, Fisher Ames wrote to Hamilton: "The anti-gents make their calculations no doubt that a direct tax will sharpen popular feelings, augment clamors against the debt, bank, &c., enfeeble

The Federalists then poured oil on the fire by passing in the same year the famous Alien and Sedition Acts. The first of these measures, directed against Frenchmen in the United States, authorized the President to expel from the country aliens whom he deemed dangerous to public peace and safety. The second measure, approved on July 14, the same day as the direct tax law, was designed to facilitate the suppression of Republicans who attacked the administration in public print. It made liable to fine and imprisonment any one who counselled or attempted rioting or insurrection against the authority of the United States or who was guilty of issuing false, scandalous, or seditious writings against the government of the United States, the President, the Senate, or the House of Representatives. The federal courts began at once to enforce the Sedition Act with evident enthusiasm.

These rash measures no doubt alienated many Federalists, for even the reliable Marshall opposed both of them on grounds of law and expediency. The Virginia and Kentucky legislatures protested against them in their famous "Resolutions." The protest of the latter state was drafted by Jefferson and amounted in fact to a nullification of federal law within the borders of that commonwealth. The philosophical leader of the Republicans, John Taylor, even went so far as to propose the dissolution of the union and the formation of a southern confederacy, but the cautious

and discredit the other species of revenue, especially internal. . . . Our proceedings smell of anarchy. We rest our hopes on foolish and fanatical grounds — on the superior morals and self-supporting theories of our age and country — on human nature being different from what it is and better here than anywhere else. . . . Internal revenues demand systems and vigor. The collection must be watched and enforced. We want officers, courts, habits of acquiescence in our country and the principles in Congress would hardly begin to form any of these. The western country scarcely calls itself dependent on the Union. France is ready to hold Louisiana. The thread of connection is slender and that event I fear would break it. Yet we disband regiments." *Hamilton Mss.*, January 26, 1797.

Jefferson shrank from such a violent measure. Nevertheless it is easy to overestimate the disturbing influence of these laws upon the country.[1] Certainly their immediate effect was not to diminish seriously the power of the Federalist party as the elections of 1799 and the replies of the states to the Kentucky and Virginia doctrines conclusively demonstrate. It may, perhaps, be said, with some show of reason, that they only served to strengthen the conviction of the Republicans that an aristocracy of wealth was prepared to go any length in fastening its rule upon the country.

It is true that if one takes the mass of materials in the newspapers and pamphlets as reflecting the relative importance of the issues of the campaign of 1800, one may assign to freedom of the press, Jefferson's irreligion, and the attacks on the aristocrats the very first rank among the questions of the day. But these matters, which were especially inviting to verbosity, did not obscure the old economic problems which had been at the centre of the political conflicts since the days of the Philadelphia Convention. The Federalist holder of public securities, investor in bank or industrial stocks, manufacturer, or shipowner may have had some misgivings about the expediency of a law which imposed a fine on a Republican who wished that the wad of a cannon fired to salute John Adams, President of the United States, had hit that eminent gentleman in the broadest part of his breeches,[2] but there could be no doubt about the danger of placing in power at Washington a man who was a known enemy to the funding system, the bank, commerce, and industry.

---

[1] See Professor F. M. Anderson's articles on the subject in the American Historical Review, Vol. V, especially p. 244.

[2] A Jerseyman by the name of Baldwin was fined for using this highly seditious expression in public.

Jefferson's views on fundamental economic questions were not matters of speculation. In his *Notes on Virginia* he had denounced the arts of the merchant and the financier, and declared the landowning farmer to be the only true hope of a republic. He had made it plain that the methods of capitalism were not only highly objectionable to him personally, but that, in his opinion, an extensive development of them was incompatible with the perpetuity of American institutions.[1] In his letter to Mazzei, made public before the campaign of 1800 in a somewhat garbled form, Jefferson had, in effect, declared the battle to be between agrarianism and capitalism, by placing on his side the whole landed interest, and on the Federalist side "British merchants and Americans trading on British capital, speculators and holders in banks and public funds, a contrivance invented for the purpose of corruption." The clew to the campaign thus furnished by the leader was taken up by his partisans, who exhausted every implement their ingenuity could devise in making the fiscal policies of the Federal administration odious and even treasonable in the minds of the people from New Hampshire to Georgia.

The contest over economic issues, the alignment of agrarian mass against the capitalistic class, which Jefferson and his followers deliberately made, was likewise accepted by the leading Federalists as fundamental. Even in the smaller and also the more completely agrarian states the economic note was sounded in the campaign. The Vermont Republicans smote the speculators hip and thigh;[2] the New Jersey Republicans fell upon the fiscal party which had long fattened upon the public treasury, and

---

[1] Below, pp. 422 ff.
[2] Vermont Gazette, quoted in The Aurora, August 27, 1800.

sought security in nominating farmers for the House of Representatives;[1] Delaware Republicans placed direct taxes, heaving imposts, an army and navy in time of peace, and "a variety of stock-jobbing acts which have given birth to a system of speculation, fraud, and bankruptcy" among the issues of the hour;[2] and in Virginia, where there were no large centres of capitalism, the dwindling Federalists sought to close their ranks by making Jefferson's letter to Mazzei the crucial document of the campaign and by giving the voters a choice between Washington's system and a sail on "the boisterous sea of liberty."[3]

In the larger states which had important financial and commercial towns, Massachusetts, Connecticut, New York, Pennsylvania, and South Carolina, the economic character of the antagonism between agrarianism and capitalism was naturally more pronounced, more definite, and more precisely avowed. Blows called forth blows; as the campaign proceeded the smoke of the battle lifted and revealed more clearly than in other states the ranks of the two great contending classes with their numerous camp followers. In Massachusetts, the spirit of the fray was accurately reflected in two papers by "Decius" published in the Columbia Centinel. It would be easy to gather a cloud of witnesses, but the words of Decius are so terse, so eloquent, and so direct that they call for nothing in addition by way of illustration. After an examination of Jefferson's doctrines, he says: "If he [Jefferson] *had been* personally a friend to the funding system, without which public credit cannot be supported, still it would be impossible for him or any other man to withstand the torrent of prejudice, which his party

---

[1] The Aurora, October 4, 1800, and December 17, 1800. See also the address of the "Federal" Republicans in the Connecticut Courant, November 24, 1800.

[2] Wilmington Mirror, quoted in The Aurora, September 22, 1800.

[3] Connecticut Courant, June 16, 1800.

feel on this subject. — The sagacious Jacobins have so long and so perpetually labored to excite false and unfounded objections and opposition to the funding system, that the *more ignorant* of their party have finally believed them sincere and accordingly entertained a cordial hatred for the whole system of public credit. — In *Virginia* more particularly from whence Mr. Jefferson's support will be principally derived, there are certain other causes which will and have contributed to render this system more odious, — they possess little or no part of the public debt — they feel jealous and envious of their brethren in the Eastern states, who with more œconomy and foresight have possessed themselves of their full share of it. . . . To satisfy the clamours of the multitude who have been taught to consider the reign of Jefferson as a Jubilee which was to free them from all tithes and taxes, Mr. Jefferson, if he valued public credit, would be compelled to favor its extinction. But Mr. Jefferson is himself the most deadly foe to the system itself and of course his interest and his feelings will happily coincide. . . . Tremble then in case of Jefferson's election, all ye holders of public funds, for your ruin is at hand. Old men who have retired to spend the evening of life upon the fruits of the industry of their youth. Widows and orphans with their scanty pittances. Public banks, insurance companies, literary and charitable institutions, who confiding in the admirable principles laid down by Hamilton and adopted by Congress, and in the solemn pledges of the national honor and property, have invested their moneys in the public debt, will be involved in one common, certain, and not very distant ruin. . . . I believe that he [Jefferson] was sincere in his hatred of the funding system and that he will do everything in his power to overthrow it. — I believe it because he has expressed it confidentially to his friend Mazzei[1] — because Virginians possess but little or nothing of the public debt — because Jefferson possesses *none* of it." [2]

In a later paper, "Decius" adds to his objections to Jefferson: "His contempt for commerce and commercial men — and his despicable opinion of the morals and principles of mechanics,[3] and his attachment to foreign manufactures — and to foreign *carrying* trade. . . . His rooted antipathy to the Federal Constitution and his fixed determination to overthrow it. . . . The ruinous effects upon our external relations, by uniting us in a close connection with France and involving us in a war with *Great Britain*." [4]

In the state of Connecticut, where was a large number of embryo capitalists and commerce and manufacturing were making vigorous beginnings, Jefferson's champion, Abraham Bishop, challenged the new order and demanded a return to agriculture as the main stay of a Republican government.[5] He attacked the funding system as the basis of the "Aristocracy," and he made a special point of assailing commerce as a burden upon the farmers, compelling them to support a defensive navy for the benefit of ship owners and builders when foreign carriers would be glad to compete for the carrying trade and assume the heavy burden of protecting it by battle ships. Bishop's doctrines were set forth in an oration delivered at New Haven and were spread abroad in pamphlet form.[6]

The challenge of the agrarian was at once taken up by

---

[1] See below, p. 430.

[2] "Decius" in the Columbian Centinel, August 27, 1800.

[3] See below, p. 425.

[4] Columbian Centinel (Boston), September 20, 1800.

[5] See his *Connecticut Republicanism* (1800).

[6] Jefferson rewarded Bishop with a public office, and the Federalists in New Havun set up "a hideous Bawling" on account of it. *Jefferson Mss.*, 2d Series, Vol. XXXII, No. 24.

Connecticut Federalists,[1] and a keen pamphleteer replied to Bishop in a tract bearing the title, *A Rod for a Fool's Back*. The author of this work was highly wrought up over Bishop's attack on commerce: "One of the most daring as well as most pernicious opinions which our Democrats have ventured to broach and defend . . . is that *commerce is a great public evil* — that it costs more to defend it than it is worth, that if we will sell or burn our ships, turn all our seamen, ship-builders, rope makers and riggers out of their employment, and let trade take care of itself, then foreigners will come and purchase our produce at our doors, and give us more than we can get in foreign markets; in which case we avoid the expense of a navy. . . . To inculcate this doctrine, to make trade odious to the people, to discourage our seamen, and to ruin the persons who are in trade or are in any way connected with it is a principal object of Mr. Bishop in his Oration.

"To preach such a doctrine in a town which depends mostly on commerce for its support; and which, at this moment, is growing rich and flourishing by commerce, requires more than common affrontery. . . . If the multitudes of industrious seamen and mechanics who derive their subsistence from trade were not better citizens and less disposed to sedition and riots than the preacher of such heresies, he could not escape a coat of tar and feathers. . . . The Chinese policy is recommended by the Democrats as a model for us! A most unfortunate model! The Chinese are subject to the most severe despotism now on the globe! . . . Commerce has not only civilized but *en-*

---

[1] For democracy as a scheme for pillaging the "earnings of the honest and industrious for the purpose of enriching the prodigal, the pickpocket, and the demagogue," see the Connecticut Courant, October 20, 1800. See "Burleigh's" series in the Courant (beginning June 20, 1800), in which the Jeffersonians are denounced as enemies of the Constitution, the funding system, the bank, and direct taxes.

franchised the most of Europe — it is the parent of civilization and humanity as well as wealth. . . . *Commerce first shook off the shackles of slavery* [in Europe]. . . . This is an indubitable truth — That commerce is the friend of freedom and to that we are greatly indebted for the freedom of our country."

In reply to Bishop's charges that the funding system had enriched a few, the author of *A Rod for a Fool's Back,* declared that the public debt was widely distributed in Connecticut: "A few men and a very few indeed made fortunes by speculation. — It happens that I know the facts on this point. I was Notary Public in Hartford at the time of the funding of the debts and the great speculations and most of the transfers of stock were made through my hands. I *know* that much the greatest part of the certificates of this state were funded in the hands of the *original holders,* most of whom were the farmers of the country, who thus received the real value of their honest debts. Some of them sold their funded stock at *twenty-four shillings* on the pound — others sold at par — and many yet hold their stock — and the funding of the debt has thus been a principal means of enriching our farmers." [1]

Without venturing into the troublesome question of a possible economic interpretation of theological biases, it is interesting to note also that the clergy of New England, in the main, saw eye to eye with the wealthy occupants of the pews, in the matter of Jefferson's candidature, and fortunately for them his liberal views on Christianity offered them abundant opportunities to attack him on religious grounds. In many places, the clergymen were closely related to the dominant commercial and trading families. They were frequently sons of wealthy men or connected

---

[1] *The Connecticut Courant,* September 22, 1800. See above, p. 183.

with wealthy families through ties of marriage. An interesting illustration of this interrelation of the clergy with politics is afforded by the following "Family Compact of Connecticut," compiled by some loyal follower of Jefferson and given to the public through the party press:

THE FAMILY COMPACT OF CONNECTICUT

1. Dr. Timothy Dwight, President of Yale, generally known as the Pope.

2. James Hillhouse, United States Senator. He and Dwight married sisters.

3. Theodore Dwight, Candidate for Congress. A brother to the Pope.

4. Mr. Morris, the extraordinary chairman of Sedgwick in Congress. Married Pope Dwight's sister.

5. Mr. Hosmer, Member of Congress. Related to Hillhouse by marriage.

6. Chauncy Goodrich, member of Congress. Married Oliver Wolcott's sister.

7. Oliver Walcott, Secretary of Treasury.

8. Elizur Goodrich, brother of Chauncy.

9. Long John Allen, brother-in-law of Elizur Goodrich.

10. Mr. Austin, Collector of Customs at New Haven, is the step-father of Long John Allen.

11. Son of Gov. Trumbull married the daughter of

12. Jeremiah Wadsworth.

13. Roger Griswold, Candidate for Congress, a cousin of Hillhouse.

Dr. Dwight dictates the policy and prayers of the Illuminati; Mr. Hillhouse holds the purse, as Treasurer.[1]

While the rude language of The Aurora jarred on the nerves of persons with refined tastes, the contention of that paper that Connecticut was ruled by a small, compact group was sustained by a no less competent observer of New England politics, than President Adams. In a review

[1] The Aurora, September 12, 1800.

of some propositions advanced by Hillhouse for amending the Constitution, Adams declared : "The state of Connecticut has always been governed by an aristocracy, more decisively than the empire of Great Britain is. Half a dozen, or, at most a dozen families, have controlled that country when a colony, as well as since it has been a state. . . . Mr. Hillhouse says, 'the United States do not possess the materials for forming an aristocracy.' But we do possess one material which actually constitutes an aristocracy that governs the nation. That material is wealth." [1] Hartford and New Haven were centres of considerable capital in Connecticut ; the families which The Aurora enumerates were, most of them at least, noteworthy holders of public funds ; [2] and the clerical members of those families were convinced that Jefferson's theology and economics were equally unsound.

At Yale, the Reverend Timothy Dwight, president of the college, was thundering away at the atheists and blasphemers who were undermining the foundations of Christian morals and "good" government by insidious philosophical speculations ; [3] and in his Fourth of July orations he was skilfully attacking the Jeffersonian party by depicting the horrors that befell those who went the way of the illuminati, the philosophers, the atheists, and the deists. "For what end," he exclaimed, "shall we be connected with men of whom this is the character and the conduct ? Is it that we may assume the same character and pursue the same conduct ? Is it that our churches may become temples of reason, our Sabbath a decade, and our

---

[1] C. F. Adams, *Works of John Adams*, Vol. VI, p. 530.
[2] Loan Office Records (Connecticut), Treasury Department, Washington, D.C.
[3] See *The Nature and Danger of Infidel Philosophy Exhibited in Two Discourses Addressed to the Candidates for the Baccalaureate in Yale College*, September 9, 1797. New York Public Library.

psalms of praise Marseillais hymns? Is it that we may change our holy worship into a dance of Jacobin phrenzy and that we may behold a strumphet personating a Goddess on the altars of JEHOVAH? Is it that we may see the Bible cast into a bonfire, the vessels of the sacramental supper borne by an ass in public procession, and our children, either wheedled or terrified, uniting in chanting mockeries against God, and hailing in the sounds of ça ira, the ruin of their religion and the loss of their souls? Is it that we may see our wives and daughters the victims of legal prostitution; soberly dishonoured; speciously polluted; the outcasts of delicacy and virtue, the loathing of God and man? . . . Shall we, my brethren, become partakers of these sins? Shall we introduce them into our government, our schools, our families? Shall our sons become the disciples of Voltaire, and the dragoons of Marat; or our daughters the concubines of the Illuminati?" [1]

In New York, the months preceding the election of Jefferson were filled with hot contests between the Federalists and Republicans. And pertinently enough Hamilton, the champion of the Constitution when its adoption was pending, led the Federalists against George Clinton, the astute manager of those who had sought to defeat the ratification of the new instrument of government. This time victory was with Clinton. Adams had alienated many Federalists and Hamilton had alienated many more, but in the main it was the old battle between the financial and commercial interests against agrarianism and the propertyless. Such at least is the view which many private letters and newspaper reports give us, and it is supported by some important detailed election figures.[2]

---

[1] *Duty of Americans, at the Present Crisis, Illustrated in a Discourse, Preached on the Fourth of July, 1798 . . . at the Request of the Citizens of New Haven.* New York Public Library. [2] Below, pp. 383 ff.

In a letter to Rufus King, Robert Troup said of the election of 1799 in New York City: "The election was the most animated I have ever experienced. All men of property stood forth and appeared to act as if they were persuaded that everything valuable in society depended upon the success of their efforts. The merchants in particular were zealous and active. . . . We have broken the democratic fetters with which we have been bound." [1] That the merchants and men of property were fully as active in the city during the contest of the next year is clearly evident from the maps of the elections published below (p. 385).

In the rural districts, the Republicans seem to have been equally busy enrolling the farmers under the banner of agrarianism. An up-state writer frankly avowed that Jefferson was the friend of the farmers and the enemy of the financiers. This partisan publicist, after quoting from Jefferson's works to show that he was no atheist and calling attention to various passages in the *Notes on Virginia*, declared of the party leader: "He has on all occasions shown himself the friend and patron of agriculture. You then whose lives are devoted to agricultural pursuits cannot surely approve of those who unjustly asperse his well-earned reputation. Hear him on the subject which must be nearest to your hearts, since it is most intimately connected with your interests." Here the writer quotes at length from the *Notes on Virginia* the passages to the effect that those who labor in the earth are God's chosen people and the mercantile and laboring element of the towns the measure of a nation's decay.[2]   To this the writer adds: "Such is the language of Mr. Jefferson, but such is not the language of his political enemies, — of that

[1] *Life and Correspondence of Rufus King*, Vol. III, p. 14.
[2] See below, p. 425.

mushroom race of speculators who have acquired wealth without the exercise of industry and have risen into political preëminence without possessing a single spark of that public virtue which alone should entitle men to preëminence in a free government. These men immersed in luxury and debauchery, think only of gratifying their avarice and ambition at the expense of the honest and industrious farmer: — paltry and imperious upstarts; the mere muck worm of corruption, they look upon you as totally incapable of comprehending what is right or wrong in the administration of your government." [1] In commending their candidate for Congress, the Republicans of the ninth district declared: "He is a respectable farmer; the inhabitants of the 9th district are composed of cultivators of the soil; did not but practical farmers represent the agricultural interest throughout the union, we should not be burdened with an intolerable load of taxes." [2]

In view of such clear-cut declarations on the part of the Republicans in New York, it is small wonder that Jefferson's alignment of the agrarian masses against the large capitalistic interests was more than once made the text of a Federalist argument. "Marcellus" in the New York Spectator of April 26, 1800, dealt specifically with Jefferson's letter to Mazzei and declared that with the election of Jefferson and the ousting of the Federalists, "the whole system of finance will tumble into ruin at a stroke. The funding system has ever been the subject of the loudest clamours among the Jacobins. When they have the power, will they not subvert it? They commonly use all the powers they possess for the purpose of mischief. . . . When the funding system is annihilated, what becomes of our national debt? The interest will be unpaid and the

[1] The Albany Register, April 8, 1800.   [2] *Ibid.*, April 18, 1800.

value of the stock destroyed. The consequence of this will be the foulest breach of national faith, and wide-spread misery and beggary to the proprietors." Furthermore, urged Marcellus, commerce will be ruined with the decline of the navy, and high wages in the towns will come down with the destruction of commerce.

It is certain that the New York Federalists were desperately frightened at the prospects of an agrarian President. So deep seated was their conviction that the Republican victory meant disaster to the capitalistic interests that Hamilton proposed, as a last resort, an ingenious plan for regaining the lost battlefield, which even his ardent ▸eulogist, Mr. Lodge, thought unworthy of the great statesman.[1] As is pointed out below, under the law then prevailing, presidential electors were chosen in New York by the state legislature and such was the requirement when the elections for members of the legislature were held in May, 1800. Five days after the election of the new legislature, that is, on May 7, 1800, Hamilton wrote to Governor John Jay informing him of the probable victory of the Republicans and proposing the calling of the old legislature for the purpose of providing for the choice of presidential electors in districts by popular vote. Hamilton's

---

[1] How far Hamilton should be held personally responsible for this proposal is a matter for conjecture, because it was evidently agreed to in a party caucus. The scheme was soon made public through the Republican press. For example, The Aurora of May 7, 1800, reported: "Their despondency approaches to the melancholy of despair; at a party meeting last night, it was suggested that Mr. Jay should immediately call the old legislature of this state together, and that they should invest him with the power of chusing the electors of President and Vice-President, in order to prevent the effects of the recent change in the people's minds from taking effect. Whether this will be attempted by Mr. Jay or not is uncertain. But when it was urged that it might lead to a civil war, if the obvious temper of the public were opposed, a person present observed that a civil war would be preferable to having Jefferson for President. This expression hurt one or two but there were many more who warmly supported him and seemed to think a contest at arms would be desirable." The Philadelphia Aurora, May 7, 1800.

letter containing this plan is such a remarkable and informing document that it deserves reproduction at length. He said : "You have been informed of the loss of our election in this city. It is also known that we have been unfortunate throughout Long Island and in Westchester. According to the returns hitherto, it is too probable that we lose our senators for this district. The moral certainty therefore is, that there will be an anti-federal majority in the ensuing Legislature ; and the very high probability is that this will bring *Jefferson* into the chief magistracy, unless it be prevented by the measure which I shall now submit to your consideration, namely, the immediate calling together of the existing legislature. I am aware that there are weighty objections to the measure, but the reasons for it appear to me to outweigh the objections ; and in times like these in which we live, it will not do to be over-scrupulous. *It is easy to sacrifice the substantial interests of society by a strict adherence to ordinary rules.* In observing this, I shall not be supposed to mean that anything ought to be done which integrity would forbid, but merely that the scruples of delicacy and propriety, as relative to a common course of things, ought to yield to the extraordinary nature of the crisis. They ought not to hinder the taking of a *legal* and *constitutional* step to prevent an atheist in religion, and a fanatic in politics from getting possession of the helm of state. You, sir, know, in a great degree, the anti-federal party ; but I fear you do not know them as well as I do. It is a composition, indeed, of very incongruous materials ; but all tending to mischief — some of them to the OVERTHROW of the GOVERNMENT, by stripping it of its due energies ; others of them, to a REVOLUTION, after the manner of BONAPARTE. I speak from indubitable facts, not from conjectures and inferences. In proportion as the true character of the party is understood, is the force of the considerations which urge to every effort to disappoint it; and it seems to me, that there is a very solemn obligation to employ the means in our power. The calling of the Legislature will have for its object the *choosing of electors by the people in districts;* this (as Pennsylvania will do nothing) will ensure a majority of votes in the United States for a Federal candidate. The measure will not fail to be approved by all the federal party; while it will, no doubt, be condemned by the opposite. As to its intrinsic nature, it is justified by unequivocal reasons of PUBLIC SAFETY. The reasonable part of the world will, I believe, approve it. They will see it as a proceeding out of the common course, but warranted by the particular nature of the crisis and the great cause of social order. If done, the motive ought to be frankly avowed. In your communication to the Legislature they ought to be told that temporary circumstances had rendered it probable that, without their interposition, the executive authority of the general government would be transferred to hands hostile to the system heretofore pursued with so much success, and dangerous to the peace, happiness, and order of the country; that under this impression, from facts convincing to your own mind, you had thought it your duty to give the existing Legislature an opportunity for deliberating whether it would not be proper to interpose, and endeavor to prevent so great an evil by referring the choice of electors to the people distributed into districts. In weighing this suggestion you will doubtless bear in mind that popular governments must certainly be overturned, and, while they endure, prove engines of mischief, if one party will call to its aid all the resources which vice can give, and if the other (however pressing the emergency) confines itself within all the ordinary forms of delicacy and decorum. The Legislature can be brought together in three weeks, so that there will be full time for the object; but none ought to be lost. Think well, my dear sir, of this proposition — appreciate the extreme danger of the crisis; and I am unusually mistaken in my view of the matter, if you do not see it right and expedient to adopt the measure." This remarkable letter met with Jay's disapproval, for he merely indorsed it with the words: "Proposing a measure for party purposes which it would not become me to adopt." [1] This decisive stand on the part of the Federalist governor put an end to Federalist hopes in New York.

In Pennsylvania, the chief objects of Republican attack were the stock-jobbers, the aristocrats, the fiscal squadron, and the artful financiers. Whoever wades through the files of The Aurora will find such phrases repeated with tiresome iteration. Adams was attacked for putting merchants among his "simplemen," [2] and the "sagacious" doctrines of Jefferson's letter to Mazzei were indorsed. [3] In the country districts the farmers were rallied to battle against "the fiscal crew." The Republicans of Bucks, Chester, and Montgomery counties put in their bill of indictment against the Federalists the heavy loans, the funding system, "a mock insurrection," the excise laws, the house and stamp taxes, the increase in the public debt, and the official robbery of the public coffers, and cited Jefferson's letter to Mazzei with approval. [4] The Chester, Delaware, Bucks, and Montgomery Republicans in presenting their candidates for the state legislature and for Congress

[1] Hamilton, *Works* (Lodge ed.), Vol. VIII, pp. 549 ff.
[2] The Aurora, August 15, 1800.
[3] *Ibid.*, August 23, 1800.
[4] *Ibid.*, September 26, 1800.

declared that "most of them are farmers, the occupation of all others that leads most to virtue." [1] The Lancaster Intelligencer portrayed the Federalists as old Tories, British "agents, factors, riders, and partners of manufacturing and commercial houses," military adventurers, and other patriots who looked upon the public treasury as private booty.

Far to the South we catch the echoes of the same economic conflict. That converted champion of Jeffersonian Democracy, Charles Pinckney, who in the constitutional Convention had wanted to establish a $50,000 property qualification for President of the United States and suitable amounts for other officers and who thought the people did not have enough intelligence to elect even the House of Representatives,[2] appeared as the leader of the agrarian and planting interests against the commercial and financial interests. In a series of papers signed "A Republican" which appeared in the Charleston City Gazette and Daily Advertiser from August 28, 1800, to October 14, 1800, he discussed every issue of the campaign : the alien and sedition laws, the judiciary, the system of taxation, and the personal claims of Jefferson to the office of President.[3]

In the sixteenth number of the Republican, Pinckney analyzes the economic issues at stake in the contest and brings out the conflict between the "monied" interest and agriculture. In this number, also, he quiets any alarms which the slave owners might have entertained on account of Jefferson's academic views on slavery, by assuring them, on Jefferson's authority, that they need fear no adverse action in case Jefferson is elected.

In opening his sharp attack Pinckney declares that

---

[1] *Ibid.*, August 1 and 2, 1800.
[2] See above, p. 56.
[3] On October 12, 1800, Pinckney wrote to Jefferson that he had circulated these papers as widely as possible. American Historical Review, Vol. IV, p. 114.

the public debt had been increased $10,000,000 notwithstanding all of the taxes which the Federal Government had devised. The direct tax he brands as a scheme to shift a large part of the burden to agriculture. "How then does it happen," he continues, "that in laying a direct tax, the whole of it is laid on *lands and slaves only*, and on no other species of property? Why is the whole of it laid on the agricultural interest and the land-holder? Are the planters and land-holders obnoxious classes of citizens to the government, that they are to bear these exclusive burdens? Or, what have they done to draw down upon them this *penalty* or punishment? For certainly, wherever one class of citizens is taxed and obliged to raise contributions, and all others excused, it operates both in the nature of a punishment and a stigma; it shows clearly that the government are least inclined to favor them, or even to protect their equal rights; and proves that in this country, whenever *extraordinary burdens* are to be imposed, the *land-holders and planters* are to bear them alone. . . . Our government by this *invidious distinction*, has placed the land-holder and the planter in an oppressive and degrading predicament. And what is this done for? Why, clearly, to exempt all the *monied interest*, which is by far the largest in the northern states and the greatest favorite of the federal party, from bearing any share of the public burdens, and throwing all direct taxes entirely upon the landed and planting interests; that if any man in a northern state is worth half a million of stock or money at interest, he shall not pay a shilling to a direct tax, while a poor Virginia or Carolina planter, who owns a little land and a few negroes, and perhaps owes for a part of them, is obliged to contribute his share.

"For instance, that Mr. Adams, owning as he probably

does, a large estate in stock, shall not pay for his stock a shilling, while Mr. Jefferson, *whose whole estate is in land and negroes,* will have to pay a heavy tax. And yet there are men who will tell you Mr. Jefferson is an unsafe president for you; he, whose whole estate is exactly like that of your own planters, who owns two hundred negroes himself, and who, in order to remove all doubts upon the subject, has explicitly authorized his friends to declare as his assertion: 'That the Constitution has not empowered the federal legislature to touch in the remotest degree the question respecting the condition or property of slaves in any of the states, and that any attempt of that sort would be unconstitutional and a usurpation of rights Congress do not possess.'

"I shall not trouble you with any further remarks on the direct tax; it is so clear an oppression of our land holder and planter, that I wish them to read the act with attention; and, if, after this, they agree to support one of the federal party, I shall suppose them to be content to be more oppressed and degraded, and to bear heavier and more unequal burdens, than I, at present, believe they are." [1]

With the results of the campaign in which he took such a conspicuous and vigorous part, Charles Pinckney had every reason to be highly elated. In a series of letters to Jefferson he recounted the experiences of the contest and informed him of the satisfactory outcome, incidentally revealing the economic causes of the party divisions. On October 12, 1800, he wrote a long letter to Jefferson.[2]

---

[1] "A Republican," Charleston City Gazette and Daily Advertiser, October 3, 1800. The following foot-note occurs with this address: "It is confidently asserted, that in North Carolina, so reprobate is this *unequal direct tax*," that the tax was not collected before the election.

[2] These letters are in the American Historical Review, Vol. IV, pp. 111 ff.

Concerning Republican prospects in the election that would be held in South Carolina in a few days for choice of members of the next legislature (presidential electors were chosen by the legislature in that state), he said : "The influence of the officers of the Government and of the Banks and of the British and Mercantile interest will be very powerful in Charleston. I think we shall in the City as usual lose 2/3rds of the representation, but the City has generally not much influence at Columbia. our Country Republican interest has always been very strong, I have no doubt will be so now. I have done everything to strengthen it and mean to go to Columbia to be present at the election of electors. the 24 numbers of The Republican which I have written have been sent to you, and I trust you have received and approved them. they are written in much moderation and have been circulated as much as possible. so has the little Republican Farmer I shewed you in Philadelphia and which has been reprinted in all our *Southern States*. With these and my speeches on Juries, Judges, Ross' Bill, the Intercourse Bill and the Liberty of the Press, we have literally sprinkled Georgia and No. Carolina *from the mountains to the ocean*."

Before mailing his letter of October 12, Pinckney on October 16th and 17th added more, saying : "Since the within was written we have had the election for Charleston, which by dint of the Bank and federal interest, is reported by the Managers to be against us 11 to 4 — that is the federalists are reported to have 11 out of 15 the number for the City representation. . . . to shew you what has been the Contest and the abuse I have been obliged to bear, I enclose you some of the last days Publications. I suppose this unexpected opposition to my Kinsman who has never been opposed here before as member for the City, will sever and

divide me from him and his Brother forever, for the federalists all charge me with being the sole cause of any opposition
in this State, where all our intelligence from the country
convinces me that we shall have a decided majority in our
Legislature. besides we mean to dispute the Election of
Charleston on the ground that many have Voted who had
no right and are not Citizens — I am told 200 — and that
a scrutiny is to be demanded. . . . I left off yesterday
and now resume my pen. since this our accounts from the
Country are still more favorable, I expect to-morrow to
hear further and more favorably. I never before this
knew the full extent of the federal Interest connected with
the British and the aid of the Banks and the federal Treasury, and all their officers. they have endeavored *to shake
Republicanism in South Carolina to its foundations,* but we
have resisted it firmly and I trust successfully. our Country interest out of reach of Banks and Custom Houses and
federal officers is I think as pure as ever. I rejoice our
Legislature meets 130 or 40 miles from the Sea. as much
as I am accustomed to Politics and to study mankind this
Election in Charleston has opened to me a new view of
things. never certainly was such an Election in America.
we mean to contest it for 8 or 9 of the 15. it is said that
several Hundred more voted than paid taxes. *the Lame,
Crippled, diseased and blind were either led, lifted or brought
in carriages to the Poll.* the sacred right of ballot was
struck at, for at a late hour, when too late to counteract
it, in order to know how men, who were supposed to be
under the influence of Banks and federal officers and English Merchants, Voted, and that they might be watched
to know whether they Voted as they were directed, the
Novel and Unwarrantable measure was used of Voting with
tickets printed on Green and blue and red and yellow

paper and Men stationed to watch the votes." On October 26th, Pinckney added to this letter: "Our accounts respecting our State Legislature are every day more favorable. from those We have heard of We are sure now to have a decided majority and We still have to hear from other counties which have been always republican and which in fact we consider our strong ground."

When the returns of the great election were all in it was discovered that the Federalist candidates, Adams and Pinckney, had sixty-five and sixty-four electoral votes respectively, and that Jefferson and Burr had seventy-three each and were tied, thus throwing the election in the House of Representatives where the vote had to be taken by states and the Federalists, under this arrangement, had a majority. In several of the states, all the electors were chosen by the legislature on a general ticket and the party divisions within the state did not appear in the electoral vote. This was the case in New Hampshire, Vermont, Connecticut, New York, New Jersey, Delaware, Pennsylvania, and other states.[1] Therefore, maps based upon the electoral vote of the several states are practically worthless for an economic study of the politics of the period. This is well illustrated in the case of New York which appears on the political map as a solid Republican State, whereas, as shown below, the heart of New York City, the old Federalist stronghold, was as loyal as ever to Federalism and the Constitution.[2]

Even the gross popular vote where the presidential electors were chosen by ballot does not yield to an economic analysis until broken into the smallest possible units. For ex-

---

[1] In only one of these states, Pennsylvania, was the electoral vote divided, and that was due to the fact that the Federalists had a majority in the upper house of the state legislature.

[2] Below, p. 383.

ample, we find the most recalcitrant opponent of the Constitution, Rhode Island, returning four Federalist electors with apparent unanimity; but an examination of the vote more closely makes some startling revelations. Of the thirty towns in that state, the Republicans carried eighteen in the election of November 19, 1800, at which presidential electors were chosen. If it had been a question of the ratification of the Constitution by a state convention composed of delegates from the towns on the rotten borough system of apportionment which prevailed at that time, Rhode Island would have rejected the Constitution in 1800 by an overwhelming vote—that is, counting the Jeffersonian vote against the Constitution. Rhode Island went Federalist in 1800 because in one of the minority of twelve towns that the party carried, — the commercial town of Providence, which had even threatened to secede from the state and join the Union some years before when ratification was long delayed, — the Federalist majority was 456, a majority sufficiently large to wipe out the majority of 164 with which the Republicans rolled up to the gates of the city. The Federalist majority in Providence more than counterbalanced the Republican majorities in fifteen of the eighteen towns which they carried, that is, Little Compton, Tiverton, Newport, Jamestown, Portsmouth, Warren, Smithfield, Gloucester, Foster, Johnston, Cranston, Exeter, North Kingston, Richmond, and Charlestown. The Federalist majority in the whole state was only 292. The Federalist majorities in the three towns of Bristol, Coventry, and Providence totalled 665 which more than offset the total majority of 629 with which the Republicans carried the eighteen towns that fell to their portion. In other words, the former paper money regions were, for the most part, loyal to their traditions and voted for the agrarian candidate, but the commercial and financial centre of Providence, true to her traditions also, saved the day for John Adams.[1]

The gross vote in Massachusetts in 1800 is particularly misleading. According to the returns for the election of governor in that year the Federalists were victorious, but it was no overwhelming victory, for the vote stood 21,620 to 17,019. Curiously enough, the proportions were almost those of the votes for and against the Constitution in the state ratifying convention of 1788 — 187 to 168. But we are informed that political sentiment taken by districts seems to have been reversed and that Boston went Republican.[2] This is true, but as has been pointed out, only if we take the gross vote by large districts. Boston went Republican in 1800 by a majority of twenty-four votes polled by Gerry, the Anti-Federalist of 1788, who by a series of most dextrous political somersaults had been elected to Congress on a moderate platform in 1789, had voted for Hamilton's fiscal system from which he derived large personal benefits, had voted for Adams for President in 1796, accepted an appointment under him, and then ended as an "ardent" Republican. But as has been shown, the total vote in Boston in 1800 was about four times the vote on the Constitution some twelve years before, and the population had by no means doubled in the period. Until a narrower analysis is made of the Boston vote of 1800 we may still believe with Henry Adams that the "wealth and talents" of the state were Federalist.

If we divide Massachusetts into three parts, the Maine region, the east part, and the west part, we undoubtedly find what appears to be reversal of the vote on the Consti-

[1] The election statistics here given are taken from The Aurora, Philadelphia, December 4, 1800. The totals given there are corrected.
[2] See above, p. 31.

tution. The Maine and western regions went Federalist in the election of governor in 1800. An examination of the figures shows, however, that the vote in the Maine district was 3883 for the Federalist candidate and 3111 for the Republican candidate; in other words, that the old Anti-Federalist district of 1788 went Federalist in 1800 by a small margin. We do not know the popular vote of the earlier period, but reasoning from similar conditions elsewhere we may reasonably assume an enormous increase. Though we must reverse the Republican and Federalist colors on a political map, it may be that each party was loyal to its traditions but that the augmentation of the forces of one party or the other was responsible for the political change. If we take the western region, which was Anti-Federalist by a considerable majority in 1788, we find what appears to be a radical change in sentiment, but how far this was a real change in personal opinions and how far it was due to the rise of new forces we cannot tell. The election figures are puzzling. The Republicans polled in the gubernatorial election of 1800 in the west, 3226 votes, but this was a loss of only twenty-five votes as against the number polled in 1796, namely, 3251. While the Republican vote fluctuated greatly between 1796 and 1800, once falling as low as 304 in this district, the Federalist vote steadily increased without a single relapse from 4850 in 1796 to 9550 in 1800. It may very well be, therefore, that the Republicans of 1787 remained loyal to their party, in the main, but that the Federalist victory was due to the rise of new forces. In the eastern district, the Republican candidate for governor, Gerry, polled 10,682 votes as against 8197 cast for Strong, the Federalist candidate. This was an increase of about 6000 votes over the number polled in 1796 and how great an increase over the number cast in the town elections of 1787 no one can ever tell. From 1796 to 1800 the Federalist vote rose steadily, except in 1799, when owing to the extraordinary popularity of the Federalist candidate for governor it made a leap to 11,000. The vote in the eastern district in 1800 was larger by 6000 votes than in 1796, and, if the figures of Boston are typical, three or four times larger than the popular vote when delegates to the state ratifying convention were chosen.[1] It would be a bold person, therefore, who would say in the face of the gross returns that Federalists of 1787 had become Republicans and that Anti-Federalists of 1787 had become Federalists. Before coming to statistical conclusions, we must await a long and careful search into the minutiæ of the election returns for Massachusetts.

The gross vote in New York State would also seem to show a reversal of the party division of 1788, but a close examination of one small group of the election returns, those for New York City, proves the utter unreliability of general estimates ; and, as far as it goes, proves the Federalist party to have derived its strength in 1800 from the commercial and capitalistic interests. Fortunately, the statistics of election in that city, by wards, have come down to us and it is possible to discover from the tax rolls where the people of wealth resided. It is true, that, at the time, presidential electors were chosen by the state legislature, and no direct vote was taken upon the merits of Adams and Jefferson. Nevertheless, the election, on May 2, 1800, of the members of the state legislature, who were to select the presidential electors, was fought definitely on the momentous question whether Adams or Jefferson should be President and the issue at stake was fully understood by the leaders and the voters.

[1] Figures here from Morse, *The Federalist Party in Massachusetts*, p. 179, note.

Under the prevailing suffrage qualifications only free-holders of property worth at least one hundred pounds could vote for members of the state senate. In the election to the senate on May 2, 1800, Haight, the Federalist candidate standing highest on the list, received 1126 votes in New York City and Denning, the Republican candidate standing highest, received 877 votes, making a total of 2003 votes cast in the election. The Federalist was thus victorious in the City proper, but he was unable to overcome the heavy majority cast against him in the outlying rural regions of the senatorial district. The votes of these two highest candidates were distributed among the various wards of the City as follows: [1]

WARD	HAIGHT	DENNING
1	130	47
2	213	74
3	185	75
4	179	124
5	147	139
6	108	187
7	164	231
	1126	877

In the election of assemblymen on the same day, at which a wider suffrage prevailed,[2] 5757 votes were cast for Furma, the Federalist, and Clinton, the Republican — the candidates standing highest on their respective tickets. This vote was distributed among the wards of the City as follows:

[1] Figures from The New York Spectator, Saturday, May 10, 1800.
[2] In addition to freeholders and a few freemen, any person who rented a house or tenement worth forty shillings a year could vote for assemblymen. Figures from The New York Spectator, May 7, 1800.

WARD	FURMA	CLINTON
1	245	172
2	434	200
3	438	250
4	330	412
5	370	458
6	363	814
7	485	786
	2665	3092

These tables reveal many interesting aspects of contemporary politics. They show, for example, how widespread was the disfranchisement worked by the freehold qualifications placed on voters for the state senate, for at least 3700 more men participated in the election of assemblymen than in the election of senators. They show also that the number of voters who took part in the election of 1800 in the City alone was twice the number that voted in the entire county of New York in the election of delegates to the state convention which ratified the Federal constitution in 1788. In other words, taking the increase of population into account, a relatively larger percentage of the adult males took part in the election of 1800 than in the election on the Constitution when no property qualification at all was placed on the suffrage.[1]

From the point of view of an economic interpretation, the figures, taken into connection with the distribution of wealth in the City, are striking, indeed. The City of New York had almost doubled in population between 1790 and 1800, but this growth did not add much to the congestion of the lower end of the City because the additional popu-

[1] *Economic Interpretation*, p. 244.

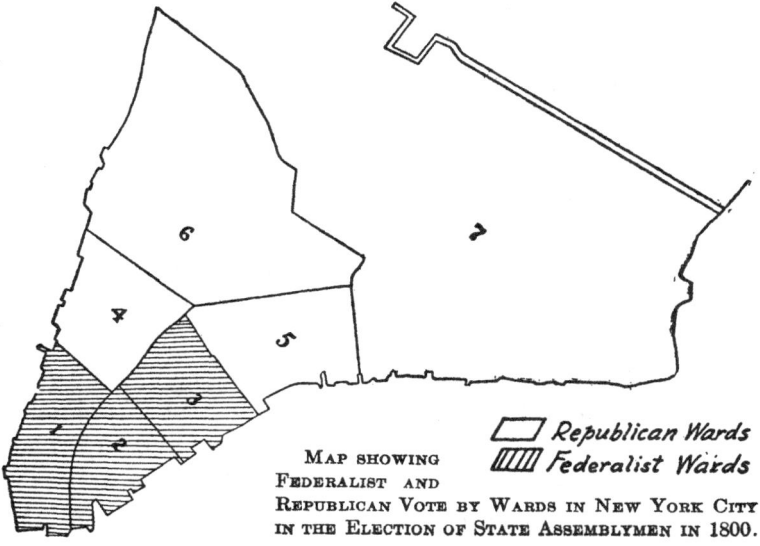

MAP SHOWING
FEDERALIST AND
REPUBLICAN VOTE BY WARDS IN NEW YORK CITY
IN THE ELECTION OF STATE ASSEMBLYMEN IN 1800.

☐ *Republican Wards*
▨ *Federalist Wards*

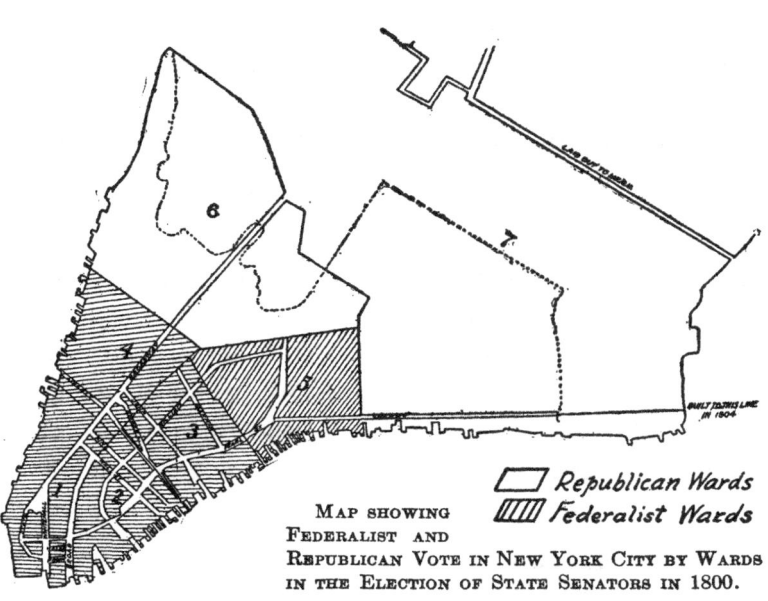

MAP SHOWING
FEDERALIST AND
REPUBLICAN VOTE IN NEW YORK CITY BY WARDS
IN THE ELECTION OF STATE SENATORS IN 1800.

☐ *Republican Wards*
▨ *Federalist Wards*

lation spread out into what are represented as the fifth, sixth, and seventh wards on the maps (p. 385). The first, second, third, and fourth wards were the districts in which the most of the wealthy men of the city lived. This is not a matter of conjecture for the assessment rolls, show that practically all of the houses valued at £2000 and over were on Pearl, Broad, Whitehall, State, Wall, William, Front, Water, Pine, Liberty, Beekman, John, and Cherry streets and on Broadway, Sloat Lane, and Maiden Lane.[1] An examination of the map, illustrating the senatorial election, shows that these streets were almost all confined to the limits of the first four wards — the Federalist strongholds. In those days, "there were no 'down town' and 'up town' as we have since learned to understand these terms. The attorney, the merchant, the shop keeper carried on their business in the house that was their dwelling. . . . The parts now devoted to business only, where homes, except the humblest, are unknown, were then also the haunts of business, but at the same time presented the more cheery aspect of ordinary habitation and betrayed the dainty and tidy touch of the house-wife. While there were not many shops on Broadway, in William, in Broad, in Wall Street and others, offices, and stores and counting houses were mingled in busy array."[2]

An examination of the map shows that in the election of state senators, when the higher property qualifications were applied, the Federalists carried the first, second, third, fourth, and fifth wards, that is, practically every street in which the houses of the rich men of the City were located. In the Wall Street region, appropriately enough, there were only seventy-four Jeffersonians, while the Federalists polled

---

[1] Wilson, *Memorial History of the City of New York*, Vol. III, p. 150.
[2] *Ibid.*, Vol. III, p. 148.

213 votes. As we move outward into the districts inhabited by laborers, carters, truck gardeners, and small folk generally, the Jeffersonian vote increases and the Federalist vote diminishes.

The economic element appears in a still more startling fashion when we examine the vote for assemblymen. In that election, the freehold qualifications were not applied and practically any man who had a settled habitation, whether an owner or renter, could cast his ballot. In this election, the Jeffersonian element captured two more of the upper wards from the Federalists, the fourth and fifth, and greatly increased the proportion of their vote in the first, second, and third wards. For example, the Jeffersonians polled about one-third as many votes as the Federalists in the Wall Street ward when the high property qualifications were imposed and nearly one-half as many when the low property qualifications were applied.

Of course, a perfect mathematical analysis would require us to have the names and property holdings of all the voters and to know their political views as well, but surely the evidence here presented is conclusive as to the fact that the "wealth and talents" of New York City, that is, the capitalists, merchants, financiers, brokers, shippers, and traders, were against Jefferson and his party, and the poorer orders were on his side. When an equally fine analysis is made of the entire country, we may be able to answer decisively the question as to the relation of the constitutional struggle to the political conflict which followed. Meanwhile, it may be safely guessed that the great bulk of those who supported the Constitution in 1788 in New York City voted the Federalist ticket in 1800.

If we take the vote for members of the lower house of the Pennsylvania legislature on October 14, 1800, we find quite a contrast to the returns in Massachusetts. The Federalists elected five out of the six members from the old centre of Federalism, Philadelphia; and they carried the old Federalist counties of Delaware, Chester, Lancaster, and Huntington. The Republicans, on the other hand, carried the old Anti-Federalist regions embracing Alleghany, Washington, Greene, Fayette, Westmoreland, Cumberland, Dauphin, and Berks. Large areas of the Pennsylvania political map, showing the elections of 1800, correspond exactly with the respective Federalist and Anti-Federalist areas of 1787. However, the Republicans made many gains. In 1800 they carried the regions which had been embraced in the Federalist counties (1787) of Northumberland, Luzerne, Northampton, Bucks, Montgomery, Mifflin, and a part of York. The only Federalist gain appears to have been in the former Anti-Federalist county of Bedford which had been divided. In the election, the Republicans carried fifty-five seats in the lower house and the Federalists twenty-two seats, but the latter by virtue of their possession of the upper house were able to secure seven of the fifteen presidential electors. When we remember that only about 13,000 out of 70,000 voters took part in the elections of 1787 and that the Republican *majority* in the congressional battle in 1800 was 18,230 [1] we recognize the difficulty of making comparisons between the two elections; but still it is evident that the Anti-Federalists more than held their old ground and gained at the expense of the Federalists. The overwhelming victory of the Republicans in 1800 makes us wonder whether radically different results would not have occurred in 1787 if the Federalists had given their opponents ample time to rouse the sleeping giants in the country districts against the Constitution.[2] One thing seems reasonably certain and

[1] The Aurora, November 17, 1800.   [2] *Economic Interpretation*, pp. 231 ff.

that is that very few Anti-Federalists of 1787 went over to the Federalist party by 1800.

To the southward the gross election returns as measured by the electoral vote were on the whole highly favorable to the Republicans. Maryland alone was equally divided in the popular election of presidential electors. The Republicans carried the northwest district over against the Republican counties of Pennsylvania, and four of the northeastern districts, including. Baltimore and Annapolis. The Federalists carried their old areas around the city of Washington and on both of the lower shores.[1] Unlike New York, Philadelphia, and Charleston, the city of Baltimore went Republican by an overwhelming majority, the vote for the Republican elector being 1497 and for the Federalist elector 438 or less than half the Federalist vote cast for the ratification of the Constitution in 1788.[2] The Federalists carried only the third ward of Baltimore, between the east side of Light Street and the west side of Calvert Street, a strip right in the heart of the city.[3]   The heaviest Jeffersonian vote was in the seventh and eighth wards at Fell's Point, a newer district of the city.

In Virginia, Jefferson secured every presidential elector. In that state the Constitution had been ratified with great difficulty by a close vote — the popular vote very probably being in the gross against it.   The assumption of state debts and the transference of nearly all the Virginia debt to speculative purchasers, the excise tax, the Jay treaty, and finally the tax on lands and slaves must have turned many Federalists to the Republican party, even if state pride and a growing dislike for the commercially minded Yankees had

[1] The Aurora, December 4, 1800.
[2] *Ibid.*, November 14, 1800.   This is, of course, a Republican source.
[3] Scharf, *Chronicles of Baltimore*, p. 281; for a contemporary map see *Records of the City of Baltimore, 1797–1813*, appendix.

not been sufficient to roll up Jefferson's majorities. But when the tide was at its flood some vestiges of the old Federalist landmarks appeared above the surface. "Practically complete returns," says Ambler, "gave Jefferson a majority of 13,363 votes in a total of 20,797. Loudon and Augusta were the only counties which gave majorities to Adams, though several counties of the lower Tidewater and the Shenandoah Valley gave him large minorities. The vote in the eastern towns and cities was also almost evenly divided." [1]

The one surprise of the South was North Carolina which gave four of her twelve electoral votes to Adams. The northern tier of counties went Republican readily, but it seems that the districts in the southern part of the state which had been Tory strongholds during the war of the Revolution went, some of them quite heavily, for Adams.[2] The backwoods western regions were Republican by a vote of four to one, but on the southeastern coast the Federalists made a very respectable showing.

In South Carolina, the former lines marking the capitalistic and agrarian interests remained, but the Republicans made severe inroads upon the old Federalist areas.[3] Notwithstanding the Jay treaty, the tax on slaves, and the protective measures in behalf of Northern trade and manufactures, the old friends of the Constitution in Charleston stuck by their guns and returned Federalist members to the state legislature that was to choose presidential electors. However, the Republican gains in the country were too heavy for them and the legislature selected a solid delegation of Republican presidential electors.

---

[1] Ambler, *Sectionalism in Virginia*, p. 79.

[2] Data from the United States Gazette, Philadelphia, November 20 and November 28, 1800, and from The Aurora, December 1, 1800.

[3] American Historical Review, Vol. IV, pp. 111 ff.

Although the detailed researches have not yet been made which warrant many broad generalizations as to the total results of the elections of 1800, certain features of the vote deserve consideration in relation to the conflict over the Constitution in 1787–1788 and to the contending economic interests of the period. Taking the gross electoral vote, it will be discovered that, with the exception of divided North Carolina (eight for Jefferson and four for Adams), the entire South below Maryland was Republican. On the other hand, New England, Delaware, and New Jersey were solidly Federalist; Pennsylvania and Maryland were divided, and New York was the only solid Republican state north of the Potomac. This is, in the main, the division which Madison noted when, on July 14, 1787, he remarked in the constitutional convention: "It seems now to be pretty well understood that the real difference of interests lay, not between the large and small, but between the Northern and Southern states. The institution of slavery and its consequences formed the line of discrimination." [1]

Although Madison is correct in locating the commercial interests in the North and the agricultural interest in the South, this does not mean that there were no commercial interests in the South or no vocal agrarian interests in the North. Nevertheless, the dominant class in New England, dominant by virtue of its wealth, its consciously developed solidarity of interest, and its cultural cohesion, was undoubtedly the mercantile and financial group. The predominance of this class was further strengthened by the thrifty farmers near the seashore who frequently had money invested in the public funds or were concerned in minor shipping ventures and by small manufacturers who began their tiny enterprises in little villages scattered throughout

[1] Farrand, *Records*, Vol. II, p. 10.

the rural districts. As Hildreth remarked long ago : "In the division of parties which took place on the question of the funding system and the general policy of the new federal government, the lawyers, the clergy, the merchants and capitalists, the great land holders in the Middle States, almost all the educated and intelligent men of the North, united quite generally in favor of Hamilton's measures." [1]

The funded debt and the control of the United States bank had largely centralized in the Northern states by 1795. Take, for example, the bank directors elected on October 21, 1791. Thomas Willing, Robert Morris' partner in Philadelphia, was made President, and James Watson, Philip Livingston, Rufus King, Nicholas Low, Joseph Anthony, Herman Le Roy, Jonathan Mason, Jr., Jeremiah Wadsworth, John Lawrence, Joseph Barrill, John Watts, Joseph Ball, William Bingham, James Cole Fisher, Robert Smith, Archibald M'Call, Charles Carroll, Charles Pettit, John M. Nesbit, George Cabot, Fisher Ames, James McClurg, Samuel Johnston, and William Smith were named directors. All of the prominent men whose views are known to us were Federalists. Practically all are from the North. McClurg, from Virginia, Samuel Johnston, from North Carolina, and William Smith, from South Carolina, constituted the Southern contingent.[2] In the second election of bank directors, January 3, 1792, only two men from south of the Potomac were chosen, two Federalist politicians, William Smith, of South Carolina, and Samuel Johnston, of North Carolina.[3]

In the distribution of the holdings of public debt there was likewise a remarkable concentration in the Northern states, particularly, the cities. The speculators from the North,

[1] *History of the United States*, Vol. IV, p. 348.
[2] Dunlap's Daily Advertiser, October 23, 1791.
[3] Gazette of the United States, January 7, 1792.

where the seat of the government was located during the funding process, almost stripped the South of its paper at a low figure, because they had "inside" information. The four New England states, New Hampshire, Massachusetts, Connecticut, and Rhode Island, received $440,800 in the interest and capital disbursements on the public debt in 1795 out of a total national disbursement of $1,180,909.19 in that year. Massachusetts alone received in interest on the funds one-third more than did all of the Southern states : Maryland, Virginia, North Carolina, South Carolina, and Georgia.[1] The thrifty Yankees of Connecticut held more of the public debt than all the creditors in Virginia, North Carolina, and Georgia. The only large holdings were in South Carolina and they were concentrated in the city of Charleston where Federalism held out vigorously long after the other Southern states had gone hopelessly over to Republicanism. The only Northern state with holdings comparable to those of Massachusetts was New York, which appears Republican on the national political map of 1800, but an examination of the Treasury Records for that state reveals a heavy concentration in New York City and Albany, where Federalism was most strongly intrenched.[2]

The student who fixes his eye on the solid color which represents New England as Federal must remember that in spite of the great strength and organization of the commercial and fiscal interests, New England, in 1800, even as in 1787, was sharply divided against itself. In Connecticut alone, where the public security holdings and small industries were perhaps most widely distributed, were the Federalists without formidable opposition. New Hampshire had to be driven into ratifying the Constitution by skilful ma-

---

[1] *Economic Interpretation*, p. 36.
[2] See the Loan Office Books in the Treasury Department at Washington, D.C.

nœuvring, and in 1800 the Vermont region of that state sent to Congress a Republican Representative, Israel Smith, formerly of the old Anti-Federalist town of Suffield, Connecticut. The vote on the ratification of the Constitution had been close in Massachusetts in 1788, and the vote in the campaign of 1800 was divided almost in the same proportions. From the rebellious western region of Stockbridge, the Republicans sent as Representative, John Bacon, a Princeton graduate who had been driven out of the old South Church in Boston for "diversity of opinion." From Bristol County the Republicans sent Captain Phanuel Bishop, a former Shays adherent, who had worked and voted against the ratification of the Constitution in the Massachusetts convention of 1788. Bishop had as a colleague in the House of Representatives, Richard Cutts, who had stood shoulder to shoulder with him in the fight in the convention against the Constitution. Three other Republicans found their way into the House of Representatives that greeted Jefferson, Eustis, Josiah Smith, and Joseph Varnum, the last two having been Federalist members of the state convention who renounced their former allegiance. Thus Massachusetts was divided in 1800.

Connecticut, as has been remarked, doubtless on account of the wide distribution of capitalistic interests noted, was solidly Federalist in its delegation to the House. Rhode Island sent one Republican Representative. All of the New York electors were Republican in 1800 and the entire delegation in the House was of the same party. In view of the attitude of that state in the ratification contest of 1788, this is significant, for the popular vote in that year had been overwhelmingly against the Constitution, the Federalists carrying only the regions about New York City. In 1800, the Federalists retained their strength in New York and Albany, but the growth of Republicanism, added to Anti-Federalism, was too great for them to overcome.

The New Jersey electors were Federalist, but the delegation in the House was composed of farmers, according to The Aurora for December 17, 1800, and was appropriately enough solidly Republican. New Jersey had ratified the Constitution unanimously. Delaware, where the ratification had likewise been unanimous, sent Bayard, a faithful Federalist, to the House.

In Pennsylvania, the Federalists secured seven presidential electors by manipulation,[1] but the state was undoubtedly Republican, for only three Federalist Representatives were elected as against ten Republicans. Three of the Republican Representatives, Hanna, Heister, and Smilie, had been members of the state ratifying convention and had worked and voted against the Constitution. This was altogether fitting. Pennsylvania had been driven into ratifying the Constitution by the shrewd management of the Federalists, four-fifths of the voters failing to take part in the elections. The Federalists probably held their own, but were submerged by the rising tide of new voters.[2]

The South was almost, but not quite solid. Maryland which had ratified the Constitution by a large majority was equally divided as to presidential electors and sent three Federalist Representatives to Congress. Virginia sent a solid Republican delegation to the House and gave all her electoral votes to Jefferson. Virginia had ratified the Constitution with great reluctance in 1788, and holding little of the public debt and having practically no commercial and manufacturing interests, she found no consolation in the policies of the government established under the Constitution. North Carolina which had rejected the Con-

[1] See above, p. 388.   [2] Ibid.

stitution and finally accepted it under compulsion was divided in the electoral vote and sent four Federalists out of a delegation of eleven Representatives to Congress. With the exception of Huger, Lowndes, and Rutledge, the South Carolina Representatives were Republican. The advocates of ratification in South Carolina had a comfortable majority in 1788, and it is clear that the fiscal policies of the administration had driven a number of former Federalists into the Republican camp by 1800. All of the Georgia delegation were Republicans. Georgia had ratified the Constitution unanimously, but under the stress of an Indian invasion which threatened the state with destruction if national aid was not to be secured.

From the point of view of earlier affiliations in the constitutional conflict of 1787–1788, the roll of the House of Representatives of the Seventh Congress is interesting. There were three Federalist members who had voted for the ratification of the Constitution as members of their respective state conventions: Davenport, of Connecticut, and Grove and Hill, of North Carolina. There were seven Republican Representatives who had likewise voted for the Constitution in state ratifying conventions, and then had allied themselves with the opposition: Smith and Varnum, of Massachusetts, Smith and Van Cortlandt, of New York, Jackson, of Virginia, and Johnston and Wynns, of North Carolina. But there were twelve Republican members of the House who had been Anti-Federalists in 1787–1788, and had voted in their respective state conventions against the Constitution: Bishop and Cutts, of Massachusetts, Stanton, of Rhode Island, Hanna, Heister, and Smilie, of Pennsylvania, Cabell, the two Triggs, of Virginia, Fowler, of Kentucky which had been a part of Virginia in 1788, and Butler and Sumter, of South Carolina. Not an Anti-Federalist convention member of the constitutional conflict found his way into the House on a Federalist ticket. Seven Federalists of that conflict had gone over to the Republicans. But twelve Anti-Federalists had been loyal through thick and thin to the cause of opposition.

From an economic point of view the almost solid South is what we should naturally expect. Georgia and North Carolina held practically none of the public debt. The large holdings in South Carolina were concentrated in Charleston which was the very citadel of Federalism. Charleston, with a population of about fifteen thousand, was the only Southern city of any importance. Richmond, Virginia, had 3761 inhabitants in 1790, and was the metropolis of the state. North Carolina did not have a town with over two thousand at that date. There was practically no manufacturing south of the Potomac.[1] Nearly all of the requests for protection which Hamilton received in 1790 and the following years, were from the North. The registered shipping of Boston alone, in 1799, was larger than that of Virginia and North Carolina combined.[2] Nevertheless, the net duties on imported goods paid by Virginia alone, in 1792, were almost equal to those of Massachusetts and Connecticut combined.[3] The South exported the raw products of agriculture while the exports of manufactures, such as they were, went from the North.[4] The following description of Virginia, sent by Heth to Hamilton, in 1792, applies to the entire South, except Federalist Charleston : "The trade of this state [Virginia] is carried on chiefly with foreign capital. Those engaged in it hardly deserve the name of merchants, being factors, agents, and shopkeepers of the merchants and manufacturers of Gt. Britain, and their

---

[1] Jedediah Morse, *American Geography* (2d ed.), 1792.
[2] *State Papers: Commerce and Navigation*, Vol. I, p. 455.
[3] *Ibid.*, p. 165.   [4] *Ibid.*, p. 157.

business to dispose of the goods of that, for the produce of this country, and remit it to the order of their principals with whom the profits of the trade, of course, centre. And *this commerce* is so divided that it will be extremely difficult to find unanimity enough to fix upon the place for establishing the bank. Richmond, Petersburg, Norfolk, and, perhaps, Alexandria may contend for this honor. . . . If the principal object is discount, I question much whether it will defray its expenses. For the reasons already given, *there is no considerable mercantile, circulating capital and there are but few monied men in the country*: consequently the deposits in specie will be inconsiderable, and the merchants or those who carry the trade, having no attachment to the country, no fixed or permanent residence in it, or any visible property except their goods and debts, discounts will be uncertain. . . . [The bank] should receive the *countenance and protection* of the state before a branch is fixed here. Otherwise it might give rise to such an opposition as would defeat the end. And in my humble opinion the last essential would be difficult to obtain unless some leading and influential members of our legislature should become stock-holders in the bank. . . . Besides the operation of the government hath by no means been pleasing to the people of this country. On the contrary the friends to it are daily decreasing. Some of the highest in rank and ability among us who supported it in our convention are now extremely dissatisfied and loud in abusing its measures." [1]

However natural was the antagonism between the small farmers of the South and the rich planters, yet in a contest with the power of capitalism they were united. The southern planters formed the "natural aristocracy" of the South,

[1] *Hamilton Mss.*, June 28, 1792.

readily consolidated because they possessed the leisure and the intelligence requisite for travel, communication, and correspondence which fused them into a social group conscious of identical interests. It is a curious freak of fortune that gives to a slave-owning aristocracy the leadership in a democracy of small farmers, but the cause is not far to seek. In a conflict with capitalism, the agrarians rallied around that agrarian class which had the cultural equipment for dominant direction. This fundamental economic interpretation of American politics was made more than half a century ago, by that penetrating historian Hildreth : "South of the Potomac the planters were all powerful, while the other sections of the natural aristocracy [lawyers and clergy and capitalists] counted in those states for little or nothing in comparison ; and as the planters were generally opposed to the funding system, they had little difficulty in carrying those states into an opposition to the federal administration, an opposition into which the outcry so loudly raised in those states against the Constitution itself was by this time pretty generally merged. Looking only to fundamentals, no two classes in the community might seem more naturally antagonistic than the small, self-working agricultural proprietors of the Northern states, and the possessors of large plantations cultivated by slaves. There were, however, some accidental circumstances which brought these two classes into close sympathy, giving rise to relations which produced a remarkable effect on the politics of the United States, through the traditionary influence of party names and associations, prolonged, in some degree, even to the present time [1856]. The expenses and efforts of the Revolutionary war had left not only the states and the confederacy, but individuals also, greatly burdened with debt. Almost all the small land-holders had been obliged to struggle at once against tax-gatherers, state and national, and their own creditors. . . . But this pecuniary embarrassment was not confined to the small landholders. It extended in almost equal degree to the greater part of the southern planters, who, besides their more recent debts, found hanging over their heads, in consequence of the powers given to the general government to enforce the treaty with Great Britain, that large mass of ante-Revolutionary claims on the part of English merchants already more than once referred to.[1] . . . It was on this common ground of pecuniary distress that so many, both of the aristocratic planters and of the democratic farmers, had united against the Federal Constitution, which they justly regarded as the work of the creditor party, intended and likely to lead to a strict enforcement of contracts, both public and private. A common reluctance to pay, a common dread of taxation, a common envy of the more fortunate moneyed class, whose position had been so palpably improved by the funding of the public debt — though little more so, in reality, than the position of everybody else — made both farmers and planters join in those clamors against the funding system, into which Jefferson and his co-operators, not content with a mere re-echo of them, sought to infuse a new bitterness by dark charges of corruption and alarming insinuations of anti-Republican designs." [2]

In this general war of the planters and small farmers on capitalism, it appears that a considerable portion of the poorer orders in the cities joined. At all events, the Republican vote in the cities was very large in 1800, and judging from the demonstrated facts of the New York City election, we may assume that it was the smaller folk, not "wealth

---

[1] See above, p. 270.

[2] Hildreth, *History of the United States* (1856 ed.), Vol. IV, pp. 348-350.

and talents," that supported Jefferson.[1] This is not surprising. The working class was then small, partly recruited
from foreign elements, German and Irish, that had fled from
the oppressions of Europe. The Jeffersonian appeal was
to the "masses" against the "aristocracy of riches," and it
doubtless captured hundreds of the mechanics in Boston,
New York, Philadelphia, and Baltimore. It is true, that
the Jeffersonian leaders had no intention of widening the
suffrage, if their performances during the first decade
of their dominance are to be regarded as an evidence of
their intentions, but the masses, then as now, seem to have
been more stirred by denunciation of the rich and mighty
than by constructive proposals on their own behalf. So
we have "the mobs of the great cities" whom Jefferson
personally despised,[2] united under his banner with the small
farmers and the slave-owners against the capitalists. That
the Republicans were victorious in 1800 is not surprising.
The wonder is that the small, compact group of capitalists
were able to hold the reins of power for so long a period in a
country predominantly agrarian.

When, in the late autumn of 1800, the news of the presidential elections at length crept into the urban centres,
Boston, Hartford, New York, Philadelphia, and Charleston,
the Federalists were in utter dismay. All those capitalist
interests which were collectively known in agrarian lexicon
as "the stock jobbing crowd," the holders of the funded
debt of the United States, the stockholders in the federal
Bank, and the protected commercial and manufacturing
classes saw, or thought they saw, in Jefferson's victory a
vision of complete financial ruin. Had not one of their
spokesmen in the Columbian Centinel, of August 27, 1800,

[1] Above, p. 386.   [2] Below, p. 425.

warned the voters against the agrarian leader from Virginia in terrifying strains : "Tremble then in case of Mr. Jefferson's election, all ye holders of public funds, for your ruin is at hand. Old men who have retired to spend the evening of life upon the fruits of the industry of their youth. Widows and orphans with their scanty pittances. Public banks, insurance companies, literary and charitable institutions, who confiding in the admirable principles laid down by Hamilton and adopted by Congress and in the solemn pledges of national honor and property have invested their moneys in the public debt will be involved in one common, certain and not very distant ruin." [1] Had not the Democrats in their campaign against the Federalists waged a bitter word war against the "aristocrats," the "fiscal corps," the "stock gamblers," the "plunderers of the people," the "thieves on the farmers' backs," and the "corrupt squadron" in general? The noble farmer had been called upon by the Republicans to follow the example of '76 and expel from the United States the "monocrats" who fattened on the people, and every person who had a dollar to invest had been solemnly and repeatedly warned by the Federalists to vote against "the enemies of public credit and of commerce." The issue had been clearly set and the agrarians were triumphant over the capitalists. But at length a ray of hope penetrated the gloomy circles of Federalism. The defeat was not unconditional. Jefferson and Burr were tied for the presidency and the election devolved upon the House of Representatives, where the Federalists were strong enough to decide the day. And parties that can cast the die can make terms.

The astute leaders of Federalism were quick to see the strategic position which they occupied, and they began at

[1] Above, p. 360.

once to consider the problem : "Who is more dangerous to the fiscal interests, Jefferson or Burr?" The Federalist leaders in Congress, Gouverneur Morris, of New York, Bayard, of Delaware, Sedgwick, of Massachusetts, and Rutledge, of South Carolina, brought the keen edge of their analysis to the situation at once, and came to the conclusion that finance and commerce had less to fear from Burr. On January 10, 1801, Sedgwick wrote a letter to Hamilton,[1] saying that after considering the dangerous and democratic notions entertained by Jefferson, he was inclined to support Burr. Sedgwick then went on to give his estimate of Burr's character : "He holds to no pernicious theories, but is a mere matter-of-fact man. His very selfishness prevents his entertaining any mischievous predilections for foreign nations. The situation in which he lives [New York City] has enabled him to discern and justly appreciate the benefits resulting from our commercial and national systems ; and the same selfishness will afford some security that he will not only patronize their support but their invigoration. . . . If Burr should be elected by the Federalists against the hearty opposition of the Jacobins, the wound mutually given and mutually received will probably be incurable — each will have committed the unpardonable sin. Burr must depend on good men [*i.e.*, the Federalists] for his support and that support he cannot receive but by conformity to their views." It is thus clear that Sedgwick, who was little acquainted with Jefferson, thought the sage of Monticello was a wild doctrinnaire who would seek to apply his theories immediately and remorselessly, upsetting the financial and commercial interests of the country in his vain strivings after "democracy."

On the same day that Sedgwick wrote this letter, John Rutledge, a Federalist from South Carolina, also in Wash-

[1] *Hamilton Mss.* (Library of Congress), January 10, 1801.

ington at the time and a member of Congress, sent to Hamilton his impressions of the impending battle: "The federalists think their preferring Burr will be the least mischief they can do. His promotion will be prodigiously afflicting to the Virginia faction and must disjoint the party. If Mr. B.'s presidency be productive of evils, it will be very easy for us to excite jealousy respecting his motives and to get rid of him. Opposed by the Virginia party, it will be his interest to conciliate the federalists and we are assured by a gentleman who lately had some conversation with Mr. B. on this subject that he is disposed to maintain and expand our systems. Should he attempt an usurpation, he will endeavour to accomplish his ends in a bold manner and by the union of daring spirits — his project in such a shape cannot be very formidable and those employed in the execution of it can very easily be made way with. Should Mr. Jefferson be disposed to make (as he would term it) an improvement (and as we should deem it a subversion) of our Constitution, the attempt would be fatal to us, for he would begin by democratizing the people and throwing everything into their hands." [1]

It is abundantly evident from the letters in the Hamilton Manuscripts preserved in the Library of Congress that the Federalist leaders in Congress approached Burr and negotiated with him.[2] It would appear also that they received aid and comfort from him, although he was wily enough to avoid committing himself too positively to the Federalist programme. At all events the news was spread in Federalist circles to the effect that Burr would not attack but would "invigorate" the Federalist "systems."

---

[1] *Hamilton Mss.*, January 10, 1801.

[2] On January 9, 1801, James Gunn wrote Hamilton that "Genl. Smith had an interview with Burr at Philadelphia last Saturday." *Hamilton Mss.*, January 9, 1801.

Then the masterly Hamilton came to the rescue. He knew Jefferson better than any Federalist leader in Congress. He had served as Secretary of the Treasury while Jefferson was in the State Department under Washington. He had analyzed Jefferson's character and sounded the depths of his principles. He believed that Jefferson, although the accredited thinker of his party, was also a practical man, for had he not negotiated at Jefferson's house and with his coöperation the arrangement whereby one of the pillars of the Federalist system, the assumption of state debts, had been secured in exchange for the location of the capital on the mud banks of the Potomac?[1] In his terse and vigorous language he warned the Federalists against Burr and all his promises and doings and at the same time he delineated the character of Jefferson in no unmistakable manner. In his letter to Oliver Wolcott, then Secretary of the Treasury, dated New York, December 16, 1800, Hamilton cautioned his Federalist friend against preferring Burr: "There is no doubt but that, upon every virtuous and prudent calculation, Jefferson is to be preferred. He is by far not so dangerous a man; and he has pretensions to character. As to *Burr* there is nothing in his favor. . . . He is truly the Catiline of America; and, if I may credit Major Wilcocks, he has held very vindictive language respecting his opponents. . . . Yet it may be well enough to throw out a lure for him, in order to tempt him to start for the plate, and then lay the foundation of dissension between the two chiefs. You may communicate this letter to *Marshall* and *Sedgwick*."[2]

In a letter written the following day to Wolcott, Hamilton told him that Burr had the boldness and daring to give success to the Jacobin system, whereas Jefferson "for want of that

---

[1] Above, p. 171.   [2] *Works* (Lodge ed.), Vol. VIII, p. 565.

quality, will be less fitted to promote it." [1]   In a long letter
to James A. Bayard, the Representative from Delaware,
Hamilton gave fuller expression to his view that Jefferson,
in spite of his radical doctrines, was, from his character and
principles, less likely than Burr to attempt any application
of them to practical politics: "Perhaps myself the first,
at some expense of popularity, to unfold the true character
of Jefferson, it is too late for me to become his apologist;
nor can I have any disposition to do it.   I admit that his
politics are tinctured with fanaticism; that he is too much in
earnest with his democracy; that he has been a mischievous
enemy to the principal measures of our past administrations;
that he is crafty and persevering in his objects; that he is
not scrupulous about the means of success, nor very mindful
of truth, and that he is a contemptible hypocrite.   But it is
not true, as is alleged, that he is an enemy to the power of
the Executive, or that he is for confounding all the powers in
the House of Representatives.   It is a fact which I have
frequently mentioned, that, while we were in the administration together, he was generally for a large construction of
the Executive authority and not backward to act upon it
in cases which coincided with his views.   Let it be added that
in his theoretic ideas he has considered as improper the par-
ticipations of the Senate in the Executive authority.   I have
more than once made the reflection that, viewing himself
as the reversioner, he was solicitous to come into the possession of a good estate.

"*Nor is it true that Jefferson is zealot enough to do anything
in pursuance of his principles which will contravene his popularity or his interest.   He is as likely as any man I know to
temporize — to calculate what will be likely to promote his own
reputation and advantage; and the probable result of such a*

[1] *Works* (Lodge ed.), Vol. VIII, p. 566.

temper is the preservation of systems, though originally opposed, which, being once established, could not be overturned without danger to the person who did it.   To my mind a true estimate of Mr. Jefferson's character warrants the expectation of a temporizing rather than a violent system.   That Jefferson has manifested a culpable predilection for France is certainly true; but I think it is a question whether it did not proceed quite as much from her *popularity* among us as from sentiment and, in proportion as that popularity is diminished, his zeal will cool.   Add to this that there is no fair reason to suppose him capable of being corrupted, which is a security that he will not go beyond certain limits." [1]

While trying to convince the Federalists at Washington that Jefferson was not a man who would allow his theoretical principles to interfere with the practical economic interests which were the special care of the Federalist party—fiscal, commercial, and manufacturing — Hamilton advised them that they would do well to be doubly secure by obtaining from Jefferson, if possible, definite promises as to his policy on these matters, if elected.   To Wolcott he wrote, after warning him against Burr: "Far better will it be to endeavor to obtain from Jefferson assurances on some cardinal points :

"1st. The preservation of the actual fiscal system.

"2d. Adherence to the neutral plan.

"3d. The preservation and gradual increase of the navy [the bulwark of commerce].

"4th. The continuance of our friends in the offices they fill, except in the great departments, in which he ought to be left free." [2]

---

[1] *Ibid.*, p. 581.   Italics mine.
[2] *Ibid.*, p. 569.
To James A. Ross, a Senator from Pennsylvania, a foremost leader among the Federalists, Hamilton also wrote: "Let the Federalists vote for Jefferson. But,

There is absolutely no doubt that the Federalist managers in Washington were convinced that Burr, through his financial and banking connections in New York and his more intimate knowledge of commercial affairs, was less dangerous to the capitalistic interests than was Jefferson.[1] But they wanted to receive from the former definite assurances on the capital points at issue before they elected him to the office of President. It is highly probable that had Burr "committed himself" positively on the propositions laid before him by the Federalists, he would have received their support, in spite of Hamilton's advice. The chief negotiator for the Federalists, James A. Bayard, who held the election in the hollow of his hand, wrote to Hamilton after the election was over that he would have taken Burr if he could have detached him completely from the Republicans, and he added: "I was enabled soon to discover that he [Burr] was determined not to shackle himself with Federalist principles and it became evident that if he got in without being absolutely committed in relation to his own party he would be disposed and obliged to play the [double] game."[2]

as they have much in their power, let them improve the situation to obtain assurances from him:

"1. The preservation of the actual system of finance and public credit.

"2. The support and the gradual increase of the navy.

"3. A bona fide neutrality towards belligerent powers.

"4. The preservation in office of our friends, except in the great departments, in respect to which and to future appointments he ought to be at liberty to promote his friends." In the same strain, Hamilton wrote to Gouverneur Morris, then Senator from New York, authorizing him to make discreet use of the letter. *Works* (Lodge ed.), Vol. VIII, p. 577. *Ibid.*, pp. 572, 573.

[1] George Baer, a Federalist member of the House from Maryland wrote: "They [the Federalists] were less certain of the hostility of Mr. Burr to Federal policy than of Mr. Jefferson which was known and decided. Mr. Jefferson had identified himself with, and was at the head of the party in Congress who had opposed every measure deemed necessary by the Federalists for putting the country in a posture of defence. . . . His speculative opinions were known to be hostile to the independence of the judiciary, to the financial system of the country, and to internal improvements." Davis, *Memoirs of Aaron Burr*, Vol. II, p. 116.

[2] *Hamilton Mss.*, March 8, 1801.

At a later date, April, 1806, while the matter was still fresh in his mind, Bayard declared upon his oath, that he had conducted negotiations with Jefferson, through an intimate friend, General Smith, and had received assurances that Jefferson would maintain the three Federalist policies in question; namely, the support of the public credit, the maintenance of the navy, and the retention of the subordinate officers of the government. Bayard swore that he had first attempted the negotiation with Jefferson through John Nicholas, a member from Virginia and a particular friend of Jefferson, but without avail, for Nicholas would do no more than assure Bayard of Jefferson's soundness on the propositions at issue. Bayard then turned to General Smith and the latter replied on his own authority that Jefferson could be trusted as to the three points raised. Bayard then added : "I told him [General Smith] *I should not be satisfied or agree to yield till I had the assurance of Mr. Jefferson himself; but, that if he would consult Mr. Jefferson, and bring the assurance from him, the election should be ended.* The general made no difficulty in consulting Mr. Jefferson and proposed giving me his answer the next morning. The next day, upon our meeting, General Smith informed me that he had seen Mr. Jefferson, and stated to him the points mentioned, and was authorized by him to say that they corresponded with his views and intentions, and that we might confide in him accordingly. The opposition of Vermont, Maryland and Delaware was immediately withdrawn, and Mr. Jefferson was made President by the votes of ten states." [1]

But it may be said that this is all second-hand evidence and is not proof that any propositions ever reached Jefferson himself. Fortunately, Jefferson has not left us in the dark

[1] Davis, *Memoirs of Aaron Burr*, Vol. II, p. 132. Italics mine.

in this matter, for in a letter written to Monroe on February 15, 1801, he said: "Many attempts have been made to obtain terms and promises from me. I have declared to them unequivocally, that I could not receive the government in capitulation, that I would not go into it with my hands tied."[1] Indeed it would be surprising if he had not been approached, for he was at the time dining at the same boarding house with Nicholas, Langdon, General Smith, Albert Gallatin, and other friends and hot partisans.[2] To suppose that these men, knowing full well the terms proposed by the Federalists, never mentioned them to their chief, whose fortunes depended upon a little turn of the wheel, would be to think them capable of enduring a greater strain than human nature can bear.

The next question that arises is whether Jefferson authorized any one to speak for him and convey to the Federalists his promise to sustain the public credit, uphold the navy, and keep the Federalists (or at least some of them) in the subordinate offices. On this point we have a flat denial from Jefferson, who wrote on April 15, 1806: "Bayard pretends to have addressed me, during the pending of the presidential election in February, 1801, through General Smith, certain conditions on which my election might be obtained, and that General Smith, after conversing with me, gave answer for me. This is absolutely false. No proposition was ever made to me on that occasion by General Smith, or any answer authorized by me; and the fact General Smith affirms at this moment."[3] If this denial is true—if General Smith did not approach Jefferson— who did approach him, for he admits that propositions reached him from the Federalists?

---

[1] *Works* (Washington ed.), Vol. IV, p. 355.
[2] Adams, *Life of Gallatin*, p. 253; letter of January 15, 1801, to his wife.
[3] *Works* (Ford ed.), Vol. I, p. 312.

As to the truth of Jefferson's denial, however, we have a sworn statement by General Smith, made in 1806, which speaks for itself. General Smith swore that shortly before the termination of the election dispute, a Federalist, Colonel Josiah Parker, held a private conversation with him and asked him what would be Jefferson's conduct, if elected, in regard to the public debt, commerce, and the navy. General Smith, saying that he had heard Jefferson converse on those points, informed Parker about what he understood were the opinions of that gentleman. Smith then continued : "I lived in the house with Mr. Jefferson, and, that I might be certain that what I said was correct, I sought and had a conversation that evening with him on those points, and, I presume, though I do not precisely recollect, that I communicated to him the conversation which I had with Colonel Parker." [1]

The next day, the Federalist politician, General Dayton, approached General Smith and privately inquired as to Jefferson's opinions respecting the navy, commerce, and the public debt. Smith's account of his answer is most informing : "I said that I had last night had conversation with Mr. Jefferson on all those subjects ; that he had told me that any opinion he should give at this time might be attributed to improper motives ; that to me he had no hesitation in saying that, as to the public debt, he had been averse to the manner of funding it, but that he did not believe that there was any man who respected his own character who would or could think of injuring its credit at this time ; that on commerce, he thought that a correct idea of his opinions on that subject might be derived from his writings, and particularly from his conduct while he was minister at Paris, when he thought he had evinced his attention to the

---

[1] Davis, *Memoirs of Aaron Burr*, Vol. II, p. 134.

commercial interest of his country; that he had not changed his opinion, and still did consider the prosperity of our commerce as essential to the true interest of the nation; that on the navy he had fully expressed his opinions in his Notes on Virginia; that he adhered still to the ideas then given; that he believed our growing commerce would call for protection; that he had been averse to a too rapid increase of our navy; that he believed a navy must naturally grow out of our commerce, but thought prudence would advise its increase to progress with the increase of the nation, and that in this way he was friendly to the establishment." [1] To this Smith adds that Dayton appeared pleased with the conversation.

In a little while, General Smith was approached by another Federalist, the chief negotiator, Bayard, who stated that he had it in his power to end the election contest and wanted information on certain points alluded to by Parker and Dayton. Smith thereupon rehearsed his conversation with Jefferson on these points, and Bayard then added a fourth; namely, the retention of certain Federalist office-holders, notably George Latimer, of Philadelphia, and Mr. M'Lane, collectors of the port at Philadelphia and Wilmington respectively. Smith said that he had not heard Jefferson speak on that subject. Bayard asked him to inquire of Jefferson and inform him next day. Smith's sworn statement then continues: "*I did so. And the next day (Saturday) told him that Mr. Jefferson had said that he did not think that such officers ought to be dismissed on political grounds only, except in cases where they had made improper use of their offices to force the officers under them to vote contrary to their judgment. That, as to Mr. M'Lane, he had already been spoken to in his behalf by Major Eccleston, and, from the character given him by that gentleman, he considered him a meritorious officer; of course, that he would not be displaced, or ought not to be displaced. I further added that Mr. Bayard might rest assured (or words to that effect) that Mr. Jefferson would conduct, as to those points, [evidently about the debt, commerce, and navy] agreeably to the opinions I had stated as his. Mr. Bayard then said, We will give the vote on Monday."* [1]

Twenty-four years after making this sworn declaration, General Smith wrote to Bayard's sons to the effect that he had never stated that he had received any proposition from Mr. Jefferson to be made to Mr. Bayard or any other person — and that he had never communicated any proposition of any kind from Jefferson to Bayard. In speaking of the way in which he obtained information from Jefferson on the points which the Federalists had at heart, Smith said : "I lodged with Mr. Jefferson, and that night [after my conference with Bayard] had a conversation with him, *without his having the remotest idea of my object.* . . . Satisfied with his opinion on the third point, I communicated to your father the next day — that from the conversation that I had had with Mr. Jefferson, I was satisfied in *my own mind,* that his conduct on that point would be so and so. But I certainly never did tell your father that I had any authority from Mr. Jefferson to communicate anything to him or to any other person." [2]

From the evidence thus presented, students will draw various conclusions as to its meaning and significance, but it cannot be denied that Jefferson was approached in behalf of the main interests of the capitalistic group, and that General

---

[1] *Ibid.*, p. 136.

[2] *Ibid.*, p. 108. Gallatin writing nearly fifty years after the election said that some of his friends had intermeddled in the election and confounded their opinions and wishes with those of Jefferson and thus given rise to very unfounded surmises. Adams, *Life of Gallatin,* p. 250. Gallatin liked to think of himself as the chief actor in that scene. *Ibid.,* p. 251.

Smith, known to be living in the house with Jefferson and very close to him as a warm friend and partisan, assured the Federalists that they could count upon Jefferson not disturbing the established order. That there was a "bargain" it is not necessary to suppose, when we remember the skill which the gentlemen concerned had previously shown in diplomacy and practical politics.[1] That Jefferson might have been elected had there been no intermediary to convey Federalist opinions to him and his views to the Federalists is entirely probable. But that his election immediately followed what the Federalists regarded as "a proper understanding" is clearly established.

[1] Mr. Charles Francis Adams has said that "even if the terms of the agreement had been acknowledged, they do not seem to imply any conditions for which the parties had reason to make excuse." *Memoirs of John Quincy Adams*, Vol. I, p. 428, note.

CHAPTER XIV

JEFFERSON'S ECONOMICS AND POLITICS

JEFFERSON never wrote anything approaching a treatise on government or political science, and his philosophy of politics must, therefore, be sought among his letters and public papers.[1] In many ways this must be an unsatisfactory method of procedure, for these scattered documents were written for varying purposes and directed to particular circumstances, so that there are among them many contradictions, both real and apparent. It would be easy, by selecting passages and tearing them from their historical connections, to build up a Jeffersonian political theory quite at variance with the fundamental doctrines which he entertained. Like all men of a speculative turn of mind, he doubtless hoped for a system too ideal for the world of fact, and accordingly it is a question whether one should construct his philosophy out of occasional theoretical utterances or out of statements directed to immediate practical ends which were in large part determined by outward con-

[1] Although Jefferson wrote no treatise on government expounding his system of politics, it is interesting to note that he thoroughly indorsed Taylor's *Inquiry into the Principles and Policy of the Government of the United States* (see above, Chap. XI) and declared that Col. Taylor and he had never differed on any political principle of importance. *Works* (Washington ed.), Vol. VII, p. 191. How much stress to lay upon this indorsement it is difficult to say, for Jefferson also spoke highly of John Adams' system of political science. On February 23, 1787, Jefferson wrote to Adams from Paris commending his *Defence of the American Constitutions*, which was the text-book of those who frankly believed in the necessity and desirability of class rule. "I have read your book with infinite satisfaction and improvement. It will do great good in America. Its learning and its good sense will, I hope, make it an institute for our politicians, old as well as young." *Works* (Washington ed.), Vol. II, p. 128.

ditions over which the idealist had no control. In other words, the problem is whether we should accept as the Jeffersonian system the theories of government which he entertained for a reasonably perfected humanity, or those theories which he sought to apply when called upon to make decisions in the world of practical politics.

The matter of the Virginia constitution of 1776 affords an interesting illustration of this difficulty. It seems reasonably certain that about that time Jefferson had come to believe in what he vaguely called "a general suffrage," and yet in making a draft of a state constitution for the use of his friends in Virginia he proposed to limit the suffrage to freeholders and taxpayers. Furthermore, twenty-four years afterward, in a private letter, he wrote that had he been in the Virginia convention he would "probably have proposed a general suffrage; because my opinion has always been in favor of it. Still I find some very honest men who, thinking the possession of some property necessary to give due independence of mind, are for restraining the elective franchise to property." [1] Just why he thought it advisable to suggest a suffrage restricted by property qualifications when drafting a plan of a constitution, and yet declared that could he have been present in the convention he would have proposed a "general suffrage" is not at all clear. Neither is it clear whether we should take as his doctrine on the suffrage, a theoretical statement made after the fact, or the statement directed to immediate ends. Students will probably choose according to their predilections and sympathies.

A further interesting illustration of the difficulty of getting at the true Jeffersonian system is afforded by the case of the judiciary. It has been the fashion of opponents of judicial control over legislation to call to their support the

[1] *Writings* (Ford ed.), Vol. VII, p. 454 (1800).

vigorous criticisms of the judiciary made by Jefferson, and perhaps no one ever made more effective use of them than did Lincoln after the Dred Scott decision.[1] An examination of the citations, however, shows that they are all taken from papers written after Jefferson became President and during that long period of conflict between his party and the bold warrior of Federalism, Chief Justice Marshall. It is undeniable that at the time of the formation of the Constitution, Jefferson privately entertained the belief that the judiciary should have been given the express power to negative acts of Congress.[2] It is also certain that at the same time Jefferson feared legislative despotism, that tyranny of majorities, which judicial control was designed to obviate.[3]

With the reconciliation of these apparent contradictions we are not concerned here. The problem at hand is to ascertain whether underlying all his general doctrines there was not in Jefferson's political science a reasonably clear recognition of economic forces as the basis of party divisions. Here, too, we come face to face with apparent contradictions. In a long and important letter written to Judge Johnson, on June 12, 1823, Jefferson expounds his view of the causes of the cleavage between the Federalists and Republicans, and in this document he ascribes the origin of the two parties to psychological differences, holding that the Republicans "cherished" the people and the Federalists "feared and distrusted" them.[4] "The fact is," he says, "that at the formation of our government, many had formed their political opinions on European writings and practices, believing the experience of old countries, and especially of England, abusive as it was, to be a safer

[1] Haines, *The American Doctrine of Judicial Control*, p. 225.
[2] Beard, *The Supreme Court and the Constitution*, p. 127.
[3] *Writings* (Ford ed.), Vol. V, p. 83.
[4] *Works* (Washington ed.), Vol. VII, p. 290.

guide than mere theory.   The doctrines of Europe were, that men in numerous associations cannot be restrained within the limits of order and justice, but by forces physical and moral, wielded over them by authorities independent of their will.   Hence their organization of kings, hereditary nobles, and priests.   Still further to constrain the brute force of the people, they deem it necessary to keep them down by hard labor, poverty, and ignorance, and to take from them, as from bees, so much of their earnings, as that unremitting labor shall be necessary to obtain a sufficient surplus barely to sustain a scanty and miserable life.   And these earnings they apply to maintain their privileged orders in splendor and idleness, to fascinate the eyes of the people, and excite in them an humble adoration and submission, as to a superior order of beings."

Here we have in concise form Jefferson's statement of the Old World theory of politics : The rule of classes originates in the nature of man ; the masses are so brutish that they can be restrained only by physical and moral forces.   The exploitation of the masses is necessary to keep them down, and the application of the revenues of exploitation to luxury and dazzling splendor is a further requisite of social order. Thus Jefferson appears to believe that European governments rested upon a *theory* about the moral depravity of the masses, according to which class rule was to be viewed as an instrument for the maintenance of public order, and exploitation was a mere incident to the process.   In other words, he reverses the facts in his theory, for most scholars hold to-day that exploitation was itself the origin of the state and class rule, and that government and good order were incidental products.[1]

---

[1] Jenks, *History of Politics*.   Ponder also the significant words of the profoundest student of law that England has produced : "If we use the term in this wide sense (the barbarian conquests being given us as an unalterable fact) feudalism means

But with the correctness of Jefferson's interpretation we are not concerned. For our purposes, the point is that he apparently rests his concept of government upon a theory of human nature. He does not, however, accuse all of the Federalists of entertaining the doctrine of class rule in its pristine purity. "Although few among us," he continues, "had gone all these lengths of opinion, yet many had advanced, some more, some less, on the way. And in the Convention which formed our government, they endeavored to draw the cords of power as tight as they could obtain them, to lessen the dependence of the general functionaries on their constituents, to subject to them those of the states, and to weaken their means of maintaining the steady equilibrium which the *majority of the convention* had deemed salutary for both branches, general and local. To recover, therefore, in practice the powers which the nation had refused, and to warp to their own wishes those actually given, was the steady object of the Federal party."

It will be here noted that Jefferson does not admit for a moment that the majority of the Convention which drafted the Constitution entertained Old World notions of class rule [1] or sought to draw too tightly the cords of power in the new instrument of government, or to lessen the dependence of the general functionaries on their constituents, or to subject state to national authorities. He cannot admit that the Constitution was a class instrument or that the

civilization, the separation of employments, the division of labor, the possibility of national defence, the possibility of art, science, literature, and learned leisure. . . . When we therefore speak . . . of forces which make for the subjection of the peasantry to seigniorial justice and which substitute the manor with its villeins for the free village, we shall . . . be speaking not of abnormal forces, not of disease, but in the main of normal and healthy growth. Far from us indeed is the cheerful optimism which refuses to see that the process of civilization is often a cruel process." Maitland, *Domesday Book and Beyond*, p. 22.

[1] See *Economic Interpretation*, Chap. VI.

party of state's rights was not in a majority in the Convention which drafted it.   On the contrary the Federalist party has "usurped" authority which the Convention did not intend to convey to the national government.   The Constitution is a Republican document; Federalist class rule is sheer usurpation.[1]   To have assailed the Ark of the Covenant would have been impolitic in the Republicans. Consequently they chose the better course of seizing it for themselves.

Having disposed of the Federalists as a small group of usurpers who had violated the spirit of the Constitution and based their theory of government on the doctrine of human depravity, Jefferson sets forth the high principles which actuated his party, and first among them he puts devotion to the Constitution.   "Our [object], on the contrary," he continues, "was to maintain the will of the *majority* of the convention and of the people themselves. We believed, with them, that man was a rational animal, endowed by nature with rights and with an innate sense of justice;   and that he could be restrained from wrong and protected in right, by moderate powers, confided to persons of his own choice and held to their duties by dependence on his own will. . . .   We believed that men, enjoying in ease and security the full fruits of their own industry, enlisted by all their interests on the side of law and order, habituated to think for themselves, and to follow their reason as their guide, would be more easily and safely governed, than with minds nourished in error, and vitiated and debased, as in Europe, by ignorance, indigence and oppression.   The cherishment of the people was our principle, the fear and distrust of them, that of the other party."[2]

[1] See above, Chaps. I and II.

[2] In two letters written about the same time, Jefferson attributes the origin of political parties to differences in temperament.   In a letter to Lafayette, Novem-

Although Jefferson thus based his explanation of the source of the party antagonism on a theory of human nature, it must not be supposed that he was unaware of the economic character of the masses aligned on his side. Curiously enough in the very passages in which he attributes the party cleavage to the distribution of the capacity for cherishing or distrusting the people, he positively states that his party was composed of "the landed and laboring interests of the country," and that the cities were "the strongholds of Federalism." Thus he recognizes that the divergence in views concerning human nature which caused the split into parties was not fortuitous, but ran along distinctly economic lines. The landed and laboring interests cherished the people; the movable property, or capitalistic, interests distrusted them.

The landed interests being in an overwhelming majority naturally could cherish themselves, but it is not so evident that they or their leader, Jefferson, so cordially cherished the laboring interests of the cities. On the contrary, Jefferson, repeatedly and with great deliberation, declared, before his campaign for the presidency, both in public and private, his profound distrust of the working-classes of the great cities. And after he was elected President he consciously directed his policy in such a manner as to make it appeal first of all to the agricultural sections of the country.[1] His very democracy was founded upon an

ber 4, 1823, he says: "In truth, the parties of Whig and Tory, are those of nature. They exist in all countries, whether called by these names or by those of Aristocrats and Democrats, *Coté Droite* and *Coté Gauche*, Ultras and Radicals, Serviles, and Liberals. The sickly, weakly, timid man fears the people and is a Tory by nature. The healthy, strong and bold, cherishes them and is formed a Whig by nature. . . . The Tories [in the United States] are for strengthening the executive and general government; the Whigs cherish the representative branch, and the rights reserved by the states, as the bulwark against consolidation, which must immediately generate monarchy." *Works* (Washington ed.), Vol. VII, p. 325. See also to the same effect a letter to H. Lee, *ibid.*, p. 376.   [1] See below, p. 436.

economic system of small land-owning farmers — upon that wide distribution of property which was possible only where land was cheap and plentiful. It did not embrace a working-class as that term is conceived in modern life. The incompatibility of an immense proletariat and an equalitarian political democracy, he clearly recognized, but he never attempted to solve the problem which it presented. In fact, he apparently believed that the problem was insoluble and that the only hope of American democracy was to escape from it by preventing its appearance on the soil of the United States.

All this is set forth in a wonderful chapter in his *Notes on Virginia* written in the winter of 1781 and 1782, in response to certain queries put to him by M. de Marbois, then secretary of the French legation in the United States, and printed for private circulation in Paris, in 1784. In the chapter, entitled "Query XIX : The present state of Manufactures, Commerce, Interior and Exterior trade," Jefferson made it clear in a few cogent sentences that he fully understood the drift of economic tendency toward manufacturing, the effect of this new economic force on politics, and the relation of a proletariat to democracy.[1] Here he is writing without any immediate practical purpose in view. The momentous future, with its immense constitutional and political changes, is veiled to him. He is letting his mind play freely upon the relation of economics to politics.

He is well aware of the fact that European political economists advocate the policy of encouraging manufactures for the purpose of making their respective nations self-sufficient, but he urges that the people of the United States are in a totally different economic position. "The

[1] *Works* (Washington ed.), Vol. VIII, pp. 405 ff.

political economists of Europe," he says, "have established it as a principle, that every state should endeavor to manufacture for itself; and this principle, like many others, we transfer to America, without calculating the difference of circumstance which should produce often a difference of result. In Europe the lands are either cultivated or locked up against the cultivator. Manufacture must, therefore, be resorted to of necessity, not of choice, to support the surplus of their people. But we have an immensity of land courting the industry of the husbandman. Is it best then that all our citizens should be employed in its improvement, or that one half should be called off from that to exercise manufactures and handicraft arts for the other?"

In Jefferson's mind, the answer to this question depends upon an appreciation of the intimate relation of fundamental economic processes to human character and thus inevitably to that independence and equality which are the very essence of democracy. It is no agrarian's scorn for the shopkeeper which he displays. He knows that the merchant or manufacturer has hands, organs, dimensions, senses, affections, and passions like those of the farmer; but he believes that different modes of acquiring a livelihood give such different directions to the senses, affections, and passions as to produce fundamental differences in character. The farmers, owning their own soil, tilling it with their own hands, looking not to their fellow-men but to the sun, the earth, and their labor for their sustenance, must perforce have an independence of character which corresponds to their economic independence. Subservience, corrupting luxury, and venality cannot flourish where labor is necessary to a livelihood and yet is certain of its reward. "Those who labor in the earth," exclaims Jefferson, "are the chosen people of God, if ever He had a chosen people, whose breasts He has made his peculiar deposit for substantial and genuine virtue. It is the focus in which He keeps alive that sacred fire, which otherwise might escape from the face of the earth. Corruption of morals in the mass of cultivators is a phenomenon of which no age nor nation has furnished an example. It is the mark set on those, who, not looking up to heaven, but to their own soil and industry, as does the husbandman, for their subsistence, depend for it on casualties and caprice of customers."

That confidence in the reasonableness and virtue of man which Jefferson made the basis of his party's faith, wide as it was, did not extend to all men regardless of their economic interests and occupations, but was restricted to the free, stalwart farmer secure in his economic basis. "Dependence," says Jefferson, "begets subservience and venality, suffocates the germ of virtue, and prepares fit tools for the designs of ambition. This, the natural progress and consequence of the arts, has sometimes perhaps been retarded by accidental circumstances; but generally speaking, the proportion which the aggregate of the other classes of citizens bears in any state to that of its husbandmen, is the proportion of its unsound to its healthy parts, and is a good enough barometer whereby to measure its degree of corruption."

For this disease which destroys society and makes impossible the democracy of equality and independence, there is no remedy. The only hope is to bar it from our shores forever: "While we have land to labor, then, let us never wish to see our citizens occupied at a work-bench or twirling a distaff. Carpenters, masons, smiths are wanting in husbandry; but, for the general operations of manufacture, let our workshops remain in Europe. It is better to carry provisions and materials to workmen there, than bring them to the provisions and materials, and with them their manners and principles. The loss by the transportation of commodities across the Atlantic will be made up in happiness and permanence of government. The mobs of great cities add just so much to the support of pure government, as sores do to the strength of the human body. It is the manners and spirit of a people which preserve a republic in vigor. A degeneracy in these is a canker which soon eats to the heart of its laws and constitution." [1]

This thoroughgoing distrust of the artisan class was not an outburst of momentary feeling, but the expression of a reasoned conviction based upon an analysis of the economic foundations of democracy. It is formulated in his *Notes on Virginia* with more precision than in any other of Jefferson's writings, but traces of it are to be found more or less completely in other places. For example, when John Jay wrote him in the summer of 1785, asking him whether "it would be useful to us, to carry all our own productions or none," he replied: "Were we perfectly free to decide this question, I should reason as follows. We have now lands enough to employ an infinite number of people in their cultivation. Cultivators of the earth are the most valuable citizens. They are the most vigorous, the most independent, the most virtuous, and they are tied to their country, and wedded to its liberty and interests, by the

[1] Washington, to a certain extent, shared Jefferson's view. He wrote to the latter in 1788: "I perfectly agree with you that an extensive speculation — a spirit of gambling — or the introduction of anything which will divert our attention from agriculture must be extremely prejudicial if not ruinous to us. But I conceive under an energetic general government such regulations might be made and such measures taken as would render this country the asylum of pacific and industrious characters from all parts of Europe — would encourage the cultivation of the earth by the high price which its products would command — and would draw the wealth and wealthy men of other nations into our own bosom, by giving security to property and liberty to its holders." *Documentary History of the Constitution*, Vol. IV, p. 429.

most lasting bonds. As long, therefore, as they can find employment in this line, I would not convert them into mariners, artisans, or anything else. But our citizens will find employment in this line, till their numbers, and of course their productions, become too great for the demand, both internal and foreign. This is not the case as yet, and probably will not be for a considerable time. As soon as it is, the surplus of hands must be turned to something else. I should then, perhaps, wish to turn them to the sea in preference to manufactures; because, comparing the characters of the two classes, I find the former the most valuable citizens. I consider the class of artificers [artisans] as the panders of vice, and the instruments by which the liberties of a country are generally overturned." [1]

Even when urging most strongly the principle of majority rule and reliance upon the mass of the people as the surest safeguard of republican government, Jefferson qualified his doctrines by making them inapplicable to an industrial population. Writing to James Madison, on December 20, 1787, he said that the democratic principle of a mild government dependent upon the intelligence of the masses would be very well "as long as we remain virtuous; and I think we shall be so, as long as agriculture is our principal object, which will be the case, while there remain vacant lands in any part of America. When we get piled upon one another in large cities, as in Europe, we shall become corrupt as in Europe, and go to eating one another as they do there." [2]

[1] *Works* (Washington ed.), Vol. I, p. 403.

[2] *Ibid.*, Vol. II, p. 332. In a pamphlet entitled *An Inquiry into the Present State of the Foreign Relations of the Union*, published at Philadelphia in 1806 (Library of Congress Miscellaneous Pamphlets, Vol. 1011) a writer makes the following interesting commentary on Jefferson's opposition to industrial and commercial pursuits: "Wrapt up in the fulness of self-consequence and strong enough, in reality, to defend ourselves against every invader, we might enjoy

In view of his avowed hostility to a working-class and to the arts and artifices of commerce, finance, and manufactures and his whole-hearted devotion to agriculture, it is impossible to believe that Jefferson did not consciously and purposely direct his public policies and his political appeal to the agricultural sections of the population. Of course, it may be said that after his election to the presidency he softened his social antipathies and tempered his administration to commerce and manufacture. In a sense this is true. As we shall see later, Jefferson was, what

an eternal rusticity and live, forever, thus apathised and vulgar under the shelter of a selfish, satisfied indifference. I know that a reduction of things to this uncharitable state is the wish of certain high characters among us who deem themselves wise. The author of the *Notes on Virginia* began the clamour against a foreign commerce of the United States, and stated as one of his many pretty theoretical impossibilities that it would be better for us to 'abandon the ocean.' Mr. Gallatin almost denounced commerce in his speeches upon the establishment of the navy and the cry has been steadily kept up by all the gentlemen of that party. But I will not insult the understanding and taste of Americans by asking them if they are willing to live under such monkish discipline. . . . Indulgent thus far, it becomes us to protest, in the name of reason and the peace of our country, against the remotest attempts to apply this dark, unsocial scheme to any practical purpose. Harmless as it may be in theory, it is full of ruin when brought into real operation. To strike a blow at our foreign commerce from any quarter of the country is to sever the union of the states. The question is not whether it would be better for us to direct the resources and population of America entirely to agriculture and internal navigation, leaving the rest for strangers to fetch and carry. The decision is already made. It is indifferent whether or not in the halls of academies or in the studies of the learned, but a strong decision, from which there is no appeal, is made in the practices, the habits, and the pursuits of our citizens; and the impulse of commercial enterprise which they have gotten will operate in all its vigor, to the rolling up of the records of time. It is too late to think of drawing off the overflowings of the spirit of adventure that urges our countrymen to have the honors of the ocean and to divert it to the wilds of Georgia and Maine. . . . We are not only, to all intents and purposes a commercial people, but after Great Britain, there is no nation whose commerce bears any proportion to that of America. . . . We legislate for commerce, we fight for it, we negociate for it, we derive our national resources from it. . . . All Europe strain every nerve for commercial advantages and fight for commercial interests; and what are the reasons which have so much cogency for the obtaining of these great points? It is because commerce creates, both by its direct and indirect operation, a wealth which contributes in a prodigious degree, to the enlargement and strength of what has been emphatically called the sinews of a state, its revenues. . . . In a word, commerce has become the mainspring of nations."

Hamilton declared him to be, a theorist who never allowed his dogmas to interfere with the pressing exigencies of practical affairs. But when all is done and said, it yet remains true that, within the limits of stern realities, Jefferson was agrarian in his principles and practices. Had he left no other records than those just cited, we should be impelled to look to agrarianism as the source of the political party that gathered about him as a leader. He was not dealing in the fustian of a demagogue when he expressed his deep and firm faith in the virtue of the farmer and in the fitness of the farming class to maintain a stable republican government. His faith was a class faith and his appeal was a class appeal.

There is, however, plenty of evidence to show that Jefferson's antagonism to the Federalist administration grew out of his belief that it was being used to advance the interests of financiers and manufacturers. As early as February 4, 1791, he sensed the opposition of the Southern states to the fiscal policy of the new government, and proposed as a remedy for the "corruption" in the form of government "the augmentation of the numbers in the lower house, so as to get a more agricultural representation, which may put that interest above that of the stock jobbers." [1]

When Washington remarked to Jefferson early in 1792 that serious dissatisfaction had arisen with the new government, the latter replied that the fiscal system of the Treasury Department was responsible for the trouble, saying: "I told him, that in my opinion, there was only a single source of these discontents. Though they had indeed appeared to spread themselves over the War department also, yet I considered that as an overflowing only from their real channel, which would never have taken

[1] *Writings* (Ford ed.), Vol. V, p. 275.

place, if they had not first been generated in another department, to wit, that of the Treasury."[1]

The superficial observer, on encountering again and again in Jefferson's writings, the linking of Federalism with "stock-jobbing" and "paper operations," might suppose that this was merely a trick of a politician seeking to put his opponents in a bad light, but implied no fundamental economic antagonism. Nothing could be further from the truth. The fact is that the capitalist mode of accumulation was foreign to Jefferson's personal economic experience and of the planting class to which he belonged — a class based, as Calhoun long afterward pointed out, upon the simple exploitation of slave labor and not upon the arts of finance and commerce.[2] Undoubtedly the heavy indebtedness of the planting interests to British creditors and the accumulation of the national debt in urban centers embittered his antipathy to capitalist methods. But it is not necessary to introduce this element to account for the psychology and economics of the slave-owning planter.

There is no doubt at all that Jefferson believed the landed interest to be the economic foundation of the Republican party.[3] This would be inferred, of course, from

---

[1] *Works* (Washington ed.), Vol. IX, p. 104. See above, pp. 110 ff.

[2] *The Works of John C. Calhoun* (1870), Vol. II, pp. 629 ff.

[3] In a letter of May 13, 1793, Jefferson made the following economic analysis of the political alignment: "The line is now drawn so clearly as to show on one side, 1. The fashionable circles of Philadelphia, New York, Boston, and Charleston, (natural aristocrats). 2. Merchants trading on British capital. 3. Paper men, (All the old tories are found in some one of the three descriptions). On the other side are, 1. Merchants trading on their own capital. 2. Irish merchants. 3. Tradesmen, mechanics, farmers, and every other possible description of our citizens." *Works* (Washington ed.), Vol. III, p. 557. Jefferson said in a private letter in 1786: "I own it to be my opinion that good will arise from the destruction of our credit. I see nothing else which can restrain our disposition to luxury, and to the change of those manners which alone can preserve republican government." *Ibid.*, Vol. I, p. 518. When on August 6, 1793, Washington called on Jefferson to converse with him about his withdrawal from the office of the Secretary of State, the latter remarked upon the particular uneasiness of his situation in the place,

his general notion that agriculture was the only enduring basis of republican government, but on more than one occasion he referred to that interest as the object of his solicitude in politics and the chief support of the Republican party. In his famous letter to Mazzei, an Italian friend, written on April 24, 1796, he aligns the landed interest on one side and the capitalistic interests on the other side. In fact, this letter is such a succinct statement of Jefferson's economic interpretation of contemporary politics that it deserves quotation here at length : "The aspect of our politics has wonderfully changed since you left us. In place of that noble love of liberty and republican government which carried us triumphantly through the War, an Anglican monarchical aristocratical party has sprung up, whose avowed object is to draw over us the substance, as they have already done the forms, of the British government. The main body of our citizens, however, remain true to their republican principles ; *the whole landed interest is republican*, and so is a great mass of talents. Against us are the executive, the judiciary, two out of three branches of the legislature, all the officers of the government, all who want to be officers, all timid men who prefer the calm of despotism to the boisterous sea of liberty, *British merchants and Americans trading on British capitals, speculators and holders in the banks and public funds*, a contrivance invented for the purposes of corruption, and for assimilating us in all things to the rotten as well as the sound parts of the British model. It would give you a fever were I to name to you the apostates who have gone over to these

---

" where," he added, "the laws of society oblige me always to move exactly in the circle which I know to bear me peculiar hatred ; that is to say, the wealthy aristocrats, the merchants connected closely with England, the new created paper fortunes ; that thus surrounded, my words were caught, multiplied, misconstrued, and even fabricated and spread abroad to my injury." *Works* (Washington ed.), Vol. IX, p. 166.

heresies, men who were Samsons in the field and Solomons in the council, but who have had their heads shorn by the harlot England. In short, we are likely to preserve the liberty we have obtained only by unremitting labors and perils. But we shall preserve it; and our mass of weight and wealth on the good side is so great as to leave no danger that force will ever be attempted against us. We have only to awake and snap the Lilliputian cords with which they have been entangling us during the first sleep which succeeded our labours." [1] From this private letter in which Jefferson wrote with unrestrained frankness, it is clear that he regarded the antagonism as existing mainly between the landed and capitalistic interests. The latter had captured the former during the lull which followed the Revolution, but the agrarians were destined in good time to recover their liberty.

A year later in a letter to Colonel Arthur Campbell, dated at Monticello, September 1, 1797, Jefferson gave a similar interpretation of the political cleavage : capitalism *versus* agrarianism. "It is true," he says, "that a party has risen up among us, or rather has come among us, which is endeavoring to separate us from all friendly connection with France, to unite our destinies with those of great Britain, and to assimilate our government to theirs. Our lenity in permitting the return of the old tories, gave the first body to this party ; they have been increased by large importations of British merchants and factors, by American merchants dealing on British capital, and by stock dealers and banking companies, who, by the aid of a paper system, are enriching themselves to the ruin of our country, and swaying the government by their possession of the printing presses, which their wealth commands, and by other means, not

[1] *Writings* (Washington ed.), Vol. IV, p. 139. The italics are mine.

always honorable to the character of our countrymen. Hitherto their influence and their system have been irresistible, and they have raised up an executive power which is too strong for the Legislature. But I flatter myself they have passed their zenith. The people, while these things were doing, were lulled into rest and security from a cause which no longer exists. No prepossessions will now shut their ears to truth. They begin to see to what port their leaders were steering during their slumbers, and there is yet time to haul in, if we can avoid a war with France. All can be done peaceably, by the people confining their choice of Representatives and Senators to persons attached to republican government and the principles of 1776, not office hunters, *but farmers whose interests are entirely agricultural. Such men are the true representatives of the great American interest, and are alone to be relied on for expressing the proper American sentiments.*" [1]

Even Jefferson's foreign policy had its economic aspects. His deep antipathy toward capitalistic interests in general was partly responsible for his opposition to Hamilton's conciliatory policy in dealing with Great Britain. Naturally he entertained some bitter feelings toward Britain as a result of the revolutionary struggle and sympathized with the French on account of his theoretical objections to monarchy as such, but there is reason to believe that much of his hostility toward the mother-country may be traced to the fact that the English sympathizers who remained in America and the English who came over to trade after the Revolution were closely associated with the economic interests which supported Federalism.[2] Jefferson was therefore

---

[1] *Works* (Washington ed.), Vol. IV, p. 197. Italics mine.

[2] Naturally the leading Federalists, being residents of the cities, came into closer contact with the British merchants and sympathizers and entertained less bitterness toward things British than did the countrymen. As members of the mercan-

using no figure of speech when he declared that the Federalist party was British in sympathy and affiliation. This he made clear on several occasions, but nowhere more specifically than in a letter written to Elbridge Gerry in 1797. In this letter, Jefferson remarked that he wished the United States to take a neutral and independent stand in the matter of foreign policy and that he had on many occasions, in a private and also an official capacity, informed

tile class, the Federalists also had close relations with the former enemies of the new Republic. This was irritating, of course, to the Republicans. A very interesting example of the way in which relations were renewed after the heat of the war had died down is afforded by the following letter by Sir John Temple, British Consul General in the United States to the British foreign office, concerning Doctor William Samuel Johnson, who had been a member of the Convention which framed the Constitution and was elected one of the first United States Senators from Connecticut:

                                                    " New York, 2d of Octo : 1788
" Dear Sir,

"This morning after I had closed my Letter to My Lord Carmarthen, Doctor Johnson now President of Columbia College in this City a most Respectable Character who hath been constantly attached to his Majesty & to his Government called on me to supplicate a favor from Lord Carmarthen. There are it seems several Vacancies in the Council of Bermuda, and very few fit and suitable people there, as I am informed to fill those Vacancies. Doctor Johnson has a son, Practicing the Law in that Island, a Worthy Man of Abilities & good Education, Whom he wishes to have appointed to one of those Vacancies. There is not a Shilling Emolument to the Appointment but merely a feather and Rank to those who have them. I do not presume to Ask a favor of Lord Carmarthen but I trust his Lordship will not be displeased at my requesting of you to inform him that the Obliging such a Person as Dr. Johnson in the appointment I have mentioned may very probably be of essential service to His Majesty's Interest in this part of the World. . . . I have since my Residence here found him undeviating in his Attachment to the Interests of our Nation and I have had some useful information from him. Though much Courted and Solicited by the people, he would have nothing to do with public affairs during the late contest, nor until his Majesty had granted Independence to these States, after that he took a seat in Congress, had a great share in framing the new Constitution and would now probably be sent Minister to London if the States were not fearful for his being too much attached to the Interests and Government of Gt. Britain. His Son (whose name is William Johnson) I know to be a Respectable Character able in the Law & to Whom the Collector of the Customs at Bermuda hath recourse (from the insufficiency of the Attornies there) for Law Council upon all Necessary Occasions in his office.
"I am Dr Sir
                           "Your Most Obedt. Servant
                                                              .".J. Temple."..
Columbia University Alumni News, October 23, 1914.

the British that they could expect equal treatment if they would only be content with it.   In spite of his reassurances, however, they had demanded nothing less than a monopoly of commerce and influence in America and had in the course of economic development secured it.   The weakness of the nascent capitalistic interests in the United States gave British financiers and merchants an extraordinary power in directing the trend of American banking and trade, and of this Jefferson was fully aware, for he was at great pains to explain to Gerry in detail the varieties of American economic servitudes to Great Britain.   "When we take notice," he said, "that theirs is the workshop to which we go for all we want; that with them center, either immediately or ultimately, all the labors of our hands and lands; that to them belongs either openly or secretly the great mass of our navigation; that even the factorage of their affairs here, is kept to themselves by factitious citizenships; and these foreign and false citizens now constitute the great body of what are called our merchants, fill our sea-ports, are planted in every little town and district of the interior country, sway everything in the former places by their own votes, and those of their dependants, in the latter, by their insinuations and the influence of their ledgers; that they are advancing fast to a monopoly of our banks and public funds, and thereby placing our public finances under their control; that they have in their alliance the most influential characters in and out of office; when they have shown that by these bearings on the different branches of the government, they can force it to proceed in whatever direction they dictate, and bend the interest of this country entirely to the will of another; when all this, I say, is attended to, it is impossible for us to say we stand on independent ground, impossible for a free mind not to see and to groan under the bondage in which it is bound. If anything after this could excite surprise, it would be that they have been able so far to throw dust in the eyes of our own citizens, as to fix on those who wish merely to recover self-government the charge of subserving one foreign influence, because they resist submission to another." [1]

Surely no further citation of authority is necessary to show conclusively that Jefferson believed the agricultural interest to be the very basis of the Republican party, although he looked upon the petty merchants, tradesmen, and mechanics [2] as valuable recruits for that organization. It is equally well established that Jefferson regarded the larger capitalistic interests — the security holding, banking, commercial, and manufacturing groups — as the economic foundation of the Federalist party and the real enemy against which the forces of the Republican party were to be hurled. While it may not be profitable to join in an interminable argument as to whether this constitutes an economic "interpretation" of Jefferson's politics, men of a practical turn of mind will be satisfied with its significance in the world of fact.

It is now fully apparent from Jefferson's letters and other writings that his sympathies and affiliations were with the agrarian class and that he recognized the agricultural interest as the main body of his party. To complete the circle of his system it is necessary to show that he and his party consciously directed their public policies toward the satisfaction of the demands of that interest, of course, within the limits of practical politics. In directing our inquiries

---

[1] *Works* (Washington ed.), Vol. IV, p. 173.

[2] The term " mechanic" was then applied to the carpenter, blacksmith, and other village workmen and was somewhat sharply distinguished from the term " artisan" which was reserved for the mass of workmen in cities.

to this branch of the subject we must remember, however, that we are now dealing with Jefferson in a responsible official position, not merely with the partisan leader concerned primarily in stirring the agrarian masses to action. We should naturally expect less precision and clarity in his public utterances; but we are not surprised to find him expressing privately to his friends his solicitude for the concerns of the class that installed him in power.

For example, when Dupont de Nemours suggested to Jefferson that his message of December, 1801, to Congress might call forth objections worthy of consideration, the President replied that he did not have the city dwellers particularly in mind when he wrote the document in question, but was directing his appeal to the agricultural population with whose sentiments he was well acquainted. "Placed as you are in a great commercial town," Jefferson said, "with little opportunity of discovering the dispositions of the country portions of our citizens, I do not wonder at your doubts whether they will generally and sincerely concur in the sentiments and measures developed in my message of Jany 7 [*sic*]. But from 40 years of intimate conversation with the agricultural inhabitants of my country, I can pronounce them as different from those of the cities, as those of any two nations known. The sentiments of the former can in no degree be inferred from those of the latter. . . . The majority of the present legislature are in unison with the agricultural part of our citizens, and you will see that there is nothing in the message to which they do not accord. Some things may perhaps be left undone from motives of compromise for a time, and not to alarm by too sudden a reformation, but with a view to be resumed at another time. . . . When this government was first established, it was possible to have kept it going on true principles, but the contracted, English, half-lettered ideas of Hamilton, destroyed that hope in the bud. We can pay off his debts in 15 years : but we can never get rid of his financial system. It mortifies me to be strengthening principles which I deem radically vicious, but this vice is entailed on us by the first error. In other parts of our government I hope we shall be able by degrees to introduce sound principles and make them habitual. What is practicable must often control what is pure theory." [1]

In this private letter we have the real key to Jefferson's public policies. His sympathies were with the agrarians, but the capitalistic interests built up around Hamilton's system could not be suddenly overthrown. Compromise was therefore necessary, unpalatable as it was. Nevertheless the main lines of Republican policy were directed toward the fulfilment of the promises made to the farmers — particularly the pledge to reduce the burden of taxation and the public debt. Gallatin, an old opponent of the Constitution and one of the most truculent enemies of the funding system devised by Hamilton, was called to the post of Secretary of the Treasury, and set himself to the task of cutting away those features of the fiscal system which had been most obviously irritating to the Republicans. The student of the legislation of the period from 1801 onward will readily recall the chief measures of the Jeffersonian party.

The expenses of the federal government for military purposes were immediately pared down by a reduction of the army to the footing of 1796. The construction of war vessels, designed particularly by the Federalists to protect American shipping on the high seas and in all the markets of the world, was discontinued. The new circuit courts

---

[1] *Works* (Ford ed.), Vol. VIII, p. 125.

created by the Federalists and filled with good party members were abolished and the "princely" salaries of the judges covered back into the Treasury. Savings were made in a few branches of the civil service, much to the pain of the Federalist office-holders at whose expense the tax-burdened farmer was relieved. All in all, these reductions were very considerable. The net expenditures for ordinary purposes, exclusive of interest on the public debt, were brought down from $7,500,000 for the fiscal year 1800 to less than $5,000,000 for the next year, and for the three succeeding years a reduction to about $4,000,000 annually was effected.[1]

These economies made possible the abolition of the excise duties which had been so thoroughly hated by the farmers,[2] whose little distilleries were regularly visited by the tax-gatherer. This was a bold and clever stroke on the part of the Republicans. No more convincing evidence of the solicitude of the party for agrarian interests could have been devised. Of course, it was mildly suggested by the Federalists that a reduction might better be made in the taxes on the necessaries of life, like tea, coffee, sugar, and salt, than in those on a luxury like whiskey, but the Republicans who made whiskey did not think it a luxury. At all events, the tax on that commodity, falling as it did on thousands of little distillers, was keenly felt, while the tax through the customs-house was in no sense disturbing to the Republican conscience. So the tax which fell principally on the small producing farmer was repealed and the more impalpable tax on the necessaries of life remained untouched.

While cutting down expenditures, the Republicans were

---

[1] Dewey, *Financial History of the United States*, p. 120.
[2] Above, pp. 248 ff.

able to make effective inroads upon the public debt which stood at $83,000,000 in round numbers in 1801. Year after year it was steadily reduced until it stood at $57,000,000 in 1809 and at $45,200,000 in 1812. The only apparent extravagance of the government under Jefferson's administration was the purchase of Louisiana, but the acquisition of this enormous domain of unsettled land at what was then considered a great sum of money was wholly in line with the interests of the Jeffersonian party. It meant that many generations would elapse before the vacant lands would be all taken up and the people of the United States turned from agriculture to the demoralizing and destructive pursuits of finance, manufacturing, and commerce. It was more than acceptable to the slave-owning planters already beginning to awaken to the inexorable demand for new lands to exploit, which the rapid cropping system produced. With all the economic interests of the agrarian party in support of the purchase, it is not surprising that Jefferson was able to overcome his scruples as to its constitutionality.

Finally we may enumerate among the chief measures which followed the Republican triumph, the abolition of the United States Bank at the end of its charter period in 1811. Since the inauguration of that financial institution, a large number of state banks had sprung up and they were exceedingly jealous of the special privileges which it enjoyed. Indeed many of the local banks were political as well as financial rivals of the central concern and its branches. The opposition to a rechartering of Hamilton's bank was too powerful to be overcome. Gallatin had discovered the financial and political advantages of the institution and favored its continuance, but he was overborne in the contest. It is true, the Republicans a few years later established a second United States Bank, but that was only after a bitter experience with state banking and after a trying time with war finances.[1]

Although the leading measures of Jefferson's administration were directly designed in the interest of the agrarian party, it must not be thought that he was rash in advancing his policies. When he came to the presidency, the Federalists were too strong to be brushed lightly aside. They had too large an economic power in the country to be ignored, and Jefferson, as Hamilton remarked, was a practical man unwilling to sacrifice immediate political advantages for a remote ideal. Instead of declaring a frontal assault on the Federalists, he conciliated them, and as time wore on he took a leaf from the book of their experience in the use of the United States Bank for political purposes.

At the very outset he felt his way carefully. Take, for instance, the first inaugural. Of course, the touch of the theorist is there, for would not his followers scan every line for words of comfort and good cheer? "A wise and frugal government, which shall restrain men from injuring one another, which shall leave them otherwise free to regulate their own pursuits of industry and improvement, and shall not take from the mouth of labor the bread it has earned. This is the sum of good government, and this is necessary to close the circle of our felicities." Government banks, funded debts with circulating money based indirectly thereon and supported by government credit, protective tariffs, and discriminating commercial regulations, the objects of such bitter attacks during the campaign, of course, were no part of a scheme of government which merely restrained men from injuring one another and otherwise

---

[1] A fuller review of the political economy of the Republicans after the inaugural of Jefferson will be given in a forthcoming volume on agrarianism and slavocracy.

left them free to follow their pursuits. Jefferson's broad principle of *laissez faire* might be interpreted by any eager disciple to mean war on the various Federalist fiscal devices; but it is immediately counterbalanced by a guarantee of "the honest payment of our debts and sacred preservation of the public faith; encouragement of agriculture, and of commerce as its handmaid." The financial system of Hamilton is to be strictly upheld and commerce is to receive protection. Well might Jefferson exclaim, "We are all Republicans — we are all Federalists." Why should Federalists not be Republicans if they ask for bread and receive it?

When the Inaugural was published, many leading Federalists made fun of the grammar, but rejoiced in the doctrines. Almost immediately, the doughty old warrior, Henry Knox, wrote to Jefferson congratulating him on his splendid appreciation of "the motives of the two parties"; and while avowing his political enmity, he assured the new President of his high esteem. "The great extent of our country and the different manners of the respective parts," concluded Knox, "claim forcibly the superintendence and direction of an enlarged mind to consolidate the interests and affections. And if you should happily affect this much to be desired object, an imperishable fame will be attached to your character." [1]

[1] "I cannot refrain from expressing to you the heartfelt satisfaction I have experienced in perusing your address of the 4th of the present month. The just manner in which you appreciate the motives of the two parties which have divided the opinions, and which sometimes have seemed to threaten to divide the territory and government of the country; and the strong incitement you display for cementing more closely our union, the essential principle of our prosperity, evince conspicuously at one view your intelligence, patriotism and magnanimity. . . . The respect and attachment however, that I have ever entertained for you, enhanced by your acquaintance and confidence have never been in the least impaired. The great extent of our country, and the different manners of the respective parts claim forcibly the superintendence and direction of an enlarged mind to consolidate their interests and affections. And if you should happily affect this much to be desired

Some months after this auspicious and conciliatory beginning, Jefferson set about the preparation of his first message to Congress. Although the draft of that important paper may have been sketched in the quiet study at Monticello, it is certain that the philosopher-statesman was unwilling to risk his personal views until they were tried out on the practical men around him.

One of Jefferson's most trusted advisers was his Attorney-General, Levi Lincoln, of Massachusetts, and to him the new President sent a draft of his proposed message. Although the paper which Jefferson placed in Lincoln's hands does not seem to have been preserved, the latter's interesting notes on the draft are to be found in Jefferson's manuscripts in the Library of Congress, and among other proposed changes is the suggestion that more attention should be given to conciliating the manufacturing and commercial interests. Lincoln's emendation of Jefferson's draft ran as follows : "Considering the importance that agriculture and manufacture are to our country and the ideas too prevalent in the northern states, that the administration and the southern states are hostile to our navigation and commerce, *quere* if it would not have a good effect to add to the address some such general expressions as the following, viz. — 'It is

object an imperishable fame will be attached to your character." H. Knox, to Jefferson (March 16, 1801). Jefferson Papers, 2d Series, Vol. XLVIII, No. 8. On March 27, 1801, Jefferson replied to Knox: "I have received with great pleasure your favor of the 16, and it is with the greatest satisfaction I learn from all quarters that my inaugural address is considered as holding out a ground for conciliation and union. I am the more pleased with this, because the difference of opinion therein stated as to the real ground of the difference among us (to-wit, the measures rendered most expedient by French enormities) is that which I have long entertained. I was always satisfied that the great body of those called Federalists were real republicans as well as Federalists. . . . Union is already effected from N. York southwardly almost completely. In the N. England states it will be slower than elsewhere from peculiar circumstances better known to yourself than to me. But we will go on attending with the utmost solicitude to their interests and doing them impartial justice, and I have no doubt they will in time do justice to us." *Works* (Ford ed.), Vol. VIII, p. 35.

with Congress to consider whether the agriculture and manufacturing of our country require immediate attention, beyond the private patronage of individuals, and whether any legislative efforts are necessary or practicable for securing, encouraging, or preventing the abridgment of the carrying trade, particularly important to the prosperity of the northern states.'" [1]

It would seem that Jefferson heard the voice of the commercial and manufacturing interests speaking through Lincoln, and perhaps he heard it gladly, for he had written to Knox that in spite of the opposition to him in New England "we will go on attending with the utmost solicitude to their interests, doing them impartial justice, and I have no doubt they will in time do justice to us." [2]   What he had written on the subject of commerce and manufactures in his first draft, if he had written anything, we cannot say; but it would appear that he had not mentioned the subject, for the other notes by Lincoln cite the specific paragraphs to which they belong and this note on the protection of commerce and manufactures does not refer to any paragraph. In fact, Lincoln distinctly speaks of "adding" his statement. Under the circumstances the following passage in Jefferson's first message may be tentatively attributed to Levi Lincoln's plea for the conciliation of the special economic interests of New England : "Agriculture, manufactures, commerce, and navigation, the four pillars of our prosperity, are the most thriving when left most free to individual enterprise.   Protection from casual embarrassments, however, may sometimes be seasonably interposed.   If in the course of your observations or inquiries they should appear to need any aid within the limits of our constitutional powers, your sense

<hr />

[1] *Jefferson Mss.*, 2d Series, Vol. LII, No. 15 (Library of Congress).

[2] Above, p. 441, note.

of their importance is a sufficient assurance they will occupy your attention. We cannot, indeed, but all feel an anxious solicitude for the difficulties under which our carrying trade will soon be placed. How far it can be relieved, otherwise than by time, is a subject of important consideration."

A study of the two passages shows that Jefferson's tender to the commercial and manufacturing interests was more skilful than that of Lincoln and less liable to offend the agrarian regions of the South. He starts out with the broad principle of no government intervention, but modifies it by saying that "protection for casual embarrassments, however, may be sometimes seasonably interposed." Lincoln bluntly suggests that it is for Congress to consider whether agriculture and manufacturing require immediate attention. Jefferson arrives at the same point by a circumlocution which rids himself of all responsibility in the matter: "If in the course of your observations or inquiries they should appear to need any aid within the limits of our constitutional powers, your sense of their importance is a sufficient assurance they will occupy your attention." Lincoln frankly suggests that Congress should consider whether the carrying trade needs government aid, but Jefferson modifies it by saying, "How far it can be relieved, otherwise than by time, is a subject of important consideration."

Though the evidence is not forthcoming, there is good reason for believing that Jefferson's paragraph is built up out of Lincoln's suggestions. Lincoln speaks of "the private patronage of individuals" and Jefferson of "individual enterprise." Lincoln suggests that it is for Congress to consider whether the protection of agriculture and manufacturing requires "immediate attention"; and Jefferson says that if these interests appear to need aid, their importance is sufficient guarantee that they will "occupy" the "attention" of Congress. Lincoln suggests that Congress should consider "whether any legislative efforts" were necessary to encourage or prevent the abridgment of the carrying trade; and Jefferson says that "how far it can be relieved" is a subject of important consideration for Congress. Interestingly enough, in the next to the final draft (signed on the day it was sent to Congress) Jefferson had written "whether" the carrying trade can be relieved is for Congress to consider, and then he made a subtle change by substituting "how far," as if there was no doubt in his mind that it might be relieved to a certain extent.

It was not merely the manufacturing and commercial interests that Jefferson sought to conciliate after his election. It is true that he had spoken of the banks and public funds as "a contrivance invented for the purposes of corruption";[1] but he was too shrewd an observer of the course of events not to desire the support of the interests which he and his partisans had so roundly denounced. He had assured the public creditors in his first inaugural, that they had nothing to fear, and through the Secretary of the Treasury, Gallatin, he soon began to conduct private negotiations with the representatives of the fiscal interests, as he put it himself, "to engage the individuals who belong to them in support of the reformed order of things or at least an acquiescence under it."[2]

The fact is that the local financial interests which had sprung up widely throughout the country began to take advantage of what Jefferson called "the reformed order of things" to secure charters from the Republican legislatures in several states; and knowing full well how deeply dyed with Federalism the United States Banks and its branches

[1] Above, p. 430.   [2] *Works* (Ford ed.), Vol. VIII, p. 172.

were, Jefferson and his advisers deliberately adopted a policy of manipulating the government funds in such a way as to build up local Republican moneyed machines in order to resist the force of the Federalist interests and provide competitors that would give the Republicans the power in the economic world which they so earnestly desired. In other words, they decided that the country could not be ruled without the active support, or at least the acquiescence, of the capitalistic interests.

That this was a conscious policy of Jefferson's administration there can be no doubt. At first Jefferson was inclined not to intermeddle with the banking interests. When Gallatin wrote him on June 18, 1802, about a plan for relieving the Bank of Pennsylvania without alienating the United States Bank, Jefferson replied: "The monopoly of a single bank is certainly an evil. The multiplication of them was intended to cure it; but it multiplied an influence of the same character with the first, and completed the supplanting the precious metals by a paper circulation. Between such parties, the less we meddle the better." [1] In this case, however, it should be remarked that the Bank of Pennsylvania, which was applying for aid at the hands of the administration in the form of deposits, was in a notoriously bad financial condition, and non-intervention was obviously the wisest thing.[2]

A few months later when the Baltimore Bank applied to the administration for aid, Jefferson had either changed his mind about the matter of policy, or the circumstances were such as to lead him to favor the use of the government funds for political purposes. On October 7, 1802, he wrote to Gallatin: "The application of the Bank of Baltimore

---

[1] *Works* (Washington ed.), Vol. IV, p. 440.
[2] H. Adams, *The Writings of Gallatin*, Vol. I, p. 80.

is of great importance. The consideration is very weighty that it is held by citizens, while the stock of the United States Bank is held in so great a proportion by foreigners. Were the Bank of the United States to swallow up the others and monopolize the whole banking business of the United States, which the demands we furnish them with tend shortly to favor, we might, on a misunderstanding with a foreign power, be immensely embarrassed by any disaffection in that bank. It is certainly for the public good to keep all the banks competitors for our favors by a judicious distribution of them and thus to engage the individuals who belong to them in support of the reformed order of things or at least in an acquiescence under it." [1]

The following year, Jefferson had fairly launched out on the policy of employing the government's power to detach the banking interests from the Federalists and to fasten them to the Republican party. Although he had treated Hamilton's actions based on the identical principle as highly corrupt and corrupting, Jefferson was conscious of the rectitude of his own intentions. The difference lay in the fact that he was using the financial interests to support what he called "the reformed order of things," and Hamilton had used them for the benefit of the interests themselves and the Federalist party. On July 12, 1803, Jefferson wrote to Gallatin that he favored turning all the banks into Republican banks and capturing the mercantile interest. In reply to a communication about the Bank at Providence, Rhode Island, which was a notorious Federalist stronghold,[2] Jefferson said : "As to the patronage of the Republican Bank at Providence, I am decidedly in favor of making all the banks Republican, by sharing deposits among them in proportion to the dispositions they show ; if the law now forbids it,

---

[1] *Works* (Ford ed.), Vol. VIII, p. 172.   [2] See above, p. 379.

we should not permit another session of Congress to pass without amending it. It is material to the safety of Republicanism to detach the mercantile interest from its enemies and incorporate them into the body of its friends. A merchant is naturally a Republican, and can be otherwise only from a vitiated state of things." [1]

Although Jefferson's use of the economic interests which he had so vigorously denounced was probably not known to Hamilton, the latter was highly gratified to find the new President unwilling to make any dangerous innovations in the established fiscal system. In an address to the voters of New York, in 1801, Hamilton rejoiced in the fact that the change in the presidential office promised no changes of great moment in economic affairs, and he found great difficulty in discovering in Jefferson's policy anything worthy of his heaviest batteries. [2] "Happily for our country," declared Hamilton, "there has just beamed a ray of hope that these violent and absurd notions [about the fiscal system] will not form the rule of conduct of the person whom the party have recently elevated to the head of our national affairs. In the speech of the new President upon assuming the exercise of his office, we find among the articles of his creed, — 'the honest *payment of our* DEBT, *and sacred preservation of the* PUBLIC FAITH.' The funding system, the national debt, the British treaty, are not therefore in his conception abuses, which, if no longer to be tolerated,

---

[1] *Works* (Ford ed.), Vol. VIII, p. 252. This idea of fighting Federalist fiscal interests by setting up Republican interests of a kindred nature appears as early as July 3, 1792, in a letter from Jefferson to Madison in which he says: "It seems nearly settled with the Treasury bankites that a branch shall be established at Richmond; could not a counter bank be set up to befriend the agricultural man by letting him have money on a deposit of tobo. notes or even wheat for a short time and would not such a bank enlist the legislature in its favor and against the Treasury bank?" Jefferson, *Works* (Ford ed.), Vol. VI, p. 97.

[2] See Hamilton's long criticism of Jefferson's message. *Works* (Lodge ed.), Vol. VII, pp. 200 ff.

would be of course to be abolished. But we think ourselves warranted to derive from the same source, a condemnation still more extensive of the opinions of our adversaries. The speech characterizes our present government 'as republican in the *full tide* of successful *experiment.*' Success in the *experiment* of a government is success in the *practice* of it, and this is but another phrase for an administration, in the main, wise and good. That administration has hitherto been in the hands of the Federalists. Here then, fellow citizens, is an open and solemn protest against the principles and opinions of our opponents, from a quarter which as yet they dare not arraign. In referring to this speech we think it proper to make a public declaration of our approbation of its contents. We view it as virtually a candid retraction of past misapprehensions, and a pledge to the community that the new President will not lend himself to dangerous innovations, but in essential points will tread in the steps of his predecessors. In doing this, he prudently anticipates the loss of a great portion of that favor which has elevated him to his present station. Doubtless, it is a just foresight. Adhering to the professions he has made, it will not be long before the body of the Anti-Federalists will raise their croaking and ill-omened voices against him. But in the talents, the patriotism, and the firmness of the Federalists, he will find more than an equivalent for all that he shall lose." [1] Certainly, if the Federalists had actually had a preëlection arrangement with Jefferson, they could not have won from him a clearer recognition of the interests which they represented. Whether Jefferson ever seriously contemplated a war on the great capitalistic interests which he had so strenuously denounced, or later came to realize the futility of such a campaign, or discovered

[1] *Works* (Lodge ed.), Vol. VII, p. 194.

how much easier it was to make use of them than to destroy them is a matter for interesting speculation. The immediate outcome, however, was the same, whatever the political motive behind his policies.

Although it seems well established that Jefferson regarded the party conflict which originated in Washington's administration as a conflict of divergent economic interests and conducted his campaign on that understanding, it appears worth while to inquire into the validity of his oft-repeated assertion that temperamental differences divided the parties, the Federalists "fearing" and the Republicans "cherishing" the people. That the former did truly regard with misgivings any constitutional arrangements which would vest in the whole body of adult males the power to rule directly and simply on the mere majority principle, through representative machinery, cannot be denied. The limited suffrage, the check and balance system, the indirect method of electing certain branches of the government, and special property qualifications on the suffrage and office-holders were the institutional devices which expressed their fear of direct majority rule. But in this did the Federalists differ from the Republicans? The fleeting emotions which the leaders of both parties entertained as they contemplated the course of democracy are not recorded, but many of their schemes of government, projected and realized, have come down to us for study and analysis.

It has been more than once said that Jefferson's confidence in the people is evidenced in his faith in majority rule. The term was constantly on his lips; it appears with striking frequency in his public and private papers — particularly after his party became the majority in the nation. Until his election to the presidency the will of the people had been perverted by corrupt representatives, or at best the people had been lulled into a false and deceptive security. After "the great revolution" of 1800, Jefferson spoke freely of "the will of the people." In his first inaugural address, he placed "absolute acquiescence in the decision of the majority" as "the vital principle of republics, from which there is no appeal but to force, the vital principle and immediate parent of despotism." In a letter written shortly afterward, he declared the will of the people to be "the only legitimate foundation of any government," and added that "to protect its free expression should be our first object." [1]

But these are vague assertions with which the most ardent Federalists could hardly have quarrelled. Everybody at the time talked vaguely about the rule of the people, but no one sought to explore all of its implications. When the monarchy was destroyed, there was no other basis of sovereignty than "the will of the people." Social and economic conditions did not permit of any claims to rule on the part of a legally recognized aristocracy. The sovereignty of the king and parliament was gone, and a transfer to a popular basis was inevitable. Every one agreed on that, but the agreement on such an obvious generality left unanswered the far more significant question: "What people and how organized?" In fact no statesman at the time seems to have considered that matter in the abstract. In forcing the adoption of the national Constitution in the place of a system which permitted the populations of the petty states like Delaware and Rhode Island to have equal weight with the populations of the great states like Virginia and Pennsylvania, the Federalists talked long and eloquently about majority rule, protesting that, on the principles of American liberty and right reason, such glaring examples of minority

[1] *Works* (Washington ed.), Vol. IV, p. 379.

rule as those afforded under the Articles of Confederation could not be tolerated. Yet when the same Federalists were considering the evils inflicted upon property by popular majorities in state legislatures they were equally vehement in their defence of the rights of minorities. The Federalists' attitude toward majority rule depended wholly upon the angle from which they viewed it.

In this regard it is difficult to see just wherein Jefferson and his party differed from the Federalists. In fact, when speaking of the will of the people in his first inaugural, Jefferson was careful to add "according to the rules of the Constitution" — rules which prevented simple majority government by giving states (not people) equal representation in the Senate, the South representation in the House for its slaves, the President, indirectly elected, a veto over acts of the legislature, and the judiciary control over legislation. With the Federalist system of "refining popular will," to use the phrase of Madison (on whose shoulders Jefferson placed his mantle) or, to speak accurately, preventing simple majority rule, Jefferson had no quarrel. His letters written at the time of the formation and adoption of the Constitution show that he approved the general structure of the government based on the check and balance principle, favored giving the judiciary an express veto power, and shared Federalist distrust of the legislature.[1]

[1] Jefferson's chief objection to the federal Constitution as drafted at Philadelphia was the absence of a bill of rights securing personal and property rights from federal interference save in accordance with time-honored Anglo-Saxon usages. The check and balance idea upon which the Constitution was based, he cordially approved. Writing to Madison from Paris, on December 20, 1787, he said: "I like the organization of the government into Legislative, Judiciary, and Executive. . . . And I like the negative given to the Executive with a third of either house, though I should have liked it better had the judiciary been associated for that purpose, or invested with a similar and separate power." *Writings* (Ford ed.), Vol. IV, pp. 475–476. It is thus apparent that Jefferson went further than Hamilton in his doctrine of judicial control, for under his scheme the judges could veto laws on grounds of policy as well as law. This principle he wished to see

In fact, the constitutional amendments on behalf of private rights, which he did so much to secure, like all other constitutional limitations, were an expression of distrust and fear of the legislative branch of the government.

Nevertheless, he went so far as to say that *the fundamental difference* between the Federalists and the Republicans was over the respective powers to be enjoyed by the executive and the legislative departments of the government.[1] The former, he said, were inclined to support the executive branch at the expense of the legislative department, while the Republicans were by principle committed to the view that the legislature was the more appropriate depository of public confidence. This view was commonly circulated throughout the country and on the basis of this distinction the Federalists were branded with having "monarchical" tendencies as contrasted with the "democratic" tendencies of the Republicans.

Yet, if we search for any extraordinary deference on the part of Jefferson to legislative will we shall hardly find it. It is true that as President he did not exercise the veto power, but on no fundamental matter did he differ from the legislature controlled by his party and under his leadership. What he might have done had he found himself confronted by a Federalist legislature bent on capitalistic and commercial policies which he did not approve, we can only conjecture. Nevertheless we may draw some conclusions from the fact

written into the federal Constitution. That the judiciary would exercise a control over the legislature under the Constitution as drafted he clearly understood, for he favored a bill of rights because of "the legal check which it puts into the hands of the judiciary." *Ibid.*, Vol. V, p. 81.

[1] "I consider the pure federalist as a republican who would prefer a somewhat stronger executive; and the republican as one more willing to trust the legislature as a broader representation of the people and a safer deposit of power for many reasons. But both sects are republican, entitled to the confidence of their fellow citizens. Not so their quondam leaders, covering under the mask of federalism hearts devoted to monarchy." *Works* (Ford ed.), Vol. VIII, p. 76.

that Jefferson believed in the power of the courts to declare acts of Congress null and void and that he even went so far as to hold that the President had the constitutional right to pronounce invalid acts of Congress duly signed by his predecessor.

This fact is not commonly known, or is not known at all, but it can be proved by reference to the draft of Jefferson's first message to Congress, signed by him on December 8, 1801. This draft lies among his papers preserved in the Library of Congress and in it appears the following astounding passage which, for some reason, was struck out of the document at the last moment, just before it was sent to Congress: "Our country has thought proper to distribute the powers of its government among three equal and independent authorities constituting each a check upon one or both of the others in all attempts to impair its constitution. To make each an effectual check it must have a right in cases which arise within the line of its proper function, where equally with the others, it acts in the last resort and without appeal, to decide on the validity of an act according to its own judgment and uncontrolled by the opinions of any other departments. . . . On my accession to the administration, reclamations against the sedition act were laid before me by individual citizens claiming the protection of the Constitution against the sedition act. Called on by the position in which the nation had placed me to exercise in their behalf my free and independent judgment, I took that act into consideration, compared it with the Constitution, viewed it under every respect of which I thought it susceptible, and gave it all the attention which the magnitude of the case demanded. On mature deliberation, in the presence of the nation and under the solemn oath which binds me to them, and to my duty, I do declare that I hold that act to be in palpable and unqualified contradiction to the Constitution. Considering it then as a nullity, I have relieved from oppression under it those of my fellow citizens who were within the reach of the functions confided to me. In recalling our footsteps within the limits of the Constitution, I have been actuated by a zealous devotion to that instrument." [1]

Why Jefferson cut this passage out of the draft on the eve of sending it to Congress is a subject for interesting conjecture. But it does not matter what the motive, it is clear that he was prepared to set himself up as a sort of high tribunal and declare null and void, as unconstitutional, an act of Congress, duly passed and approved. That he treated the law in fact as null and void by refusing to execute it against his friends is well known, but [that he was prepared to do what John Marshall did two years later in Marbury v. Madison has apparently escaped the historians who write their books from printed documents. It would have been interesting to have read the comments of those newspapers which had been exalting the legislative branch of the government if Jefferson had let that passage stand in his message.

This proposal solemnly to annul the sedition law, passed by an undoubted majority "according to the rules of the Constitution," is an evidence that he was as little ready as any one "to acquiesce in the will of the majority" when that will conflicted with his views of sound public policy. In fact, as if dimly aware of his inconsistency on this point, Jefferson was quick to add, in his first inaugural, a limitation on the principle of obedience to the majority. "All too will bear in mind this sacred principle that though the will of

---

[1] *Jefferson Papers*, 1st Series, Vol. VIII, No. 252. This draft signed by Jefferson, December 8, 1801.

the majority is in all cases to prevail, that will, to be rightful, must be reasonable; that the minority possess their equal rights, which equal laws must protect, and to violate which would be oppression."

The only part of the Federal government which Jefferson and his party vigorously attacked was the judicial branch. They destroyed the new circuit courts created by Congress, but those positions were filled by the most relentless foes of Republicanism that John Adams could discover throughout the whole American empire. With Jefferson's sanction his party waged war publicly and privately upon the Supreme Court of the United States, but that eminent tribunal was under the dominion of perhaps the most cordially hated Federalist in the country, John Marshall. If Jefferson had not indorsed judicial control before he found himself thwarted by it, we might more readily accept the pleasing theory that in warring upon Marshall he was fighting the battle of "the people" against "judicial oligarchy." By a sort of poetic justice, the party which Jefferson led against the Supreme Court with such vigor, long afterward looked upon the Dred Scott decision, pronounced it good, and solemnly declared in its platform that it would abide by the decisions of the Supreme Court in "all questions of constitutional law"!

It would appear that in the field of federal law and politics, the conflict between the Republicans and the Federalists was over economic issues and not over any nice readjustments of the Constitutional system with a view of making it more amenable to simple majority rule. It may be said, however, that the national system was by the nature of circumstances necessarily a compromise and therefore built upon no consistent theory of constitutional democracy. Accepting this for the sake of argument, we may turn to

JEFFERSON'S ECONOMICS AND POLITICS   457

an examination of Jefferson's doctrines for the government of commonwealths where no questions of large and small states entered to complicate the simple problem of forming the constitutional structure.

Fortunately we have ample materials from Jefferson's pen on this point of state constitutions, and the development of constitutional democracy in the Republican states can be traced with precision. Jefferson was not a member of the Virginia convention of 1776 which drafted the constitution of the commonwealth. He was at that time serving in the national Congress at Philadelphia, but he drew up a plan for the guidance of his fellow-citizens, which, although it did not reach them in time to be made the basis of their new scheme of government, reveals his leading ideas as to the exact manner in which " the people " were to rule.[1]

In providing the basis of the government Jefferson thought it wise or expedient to stipulate that only those males "having a freehold estate in one quarter of an acre of land in any town or twenty-five acres in the country," or those who had paid scot and lot to the government for the two preceding years should enjoy the right to vote, for members of the lower house of the state legislature. This was a broader suffrage than the convention decided upon, and Jefferson would have made it practically manhood suffrage by requiring the government of the state to grant to non-landholders small estates out of the public domain. Thus he would have made land the basis of the government, but he would have widened it as far as possible by making all males landholders. This was in harmony with his theory that small farmers were the safeguard of republican institutions.

With reference to the structure of the government, Jeffer-

---

[1] Jefferson's plan is in *Works* (Ford ed.), Vol. II, p. 7.   C. R. Lingley, *Transition in Virginia from Colony to Commonwealth*, Chap. VII (Columbia University Studies).

son provided for direct election of only the lower house of the legislature — to be chosen annually. He proposed that the senators should be chosen by the lower house, and he at first advanced the proposition that they should enjoy a life tenure, but this he later modified in favor of a nine-year term. To refine popular whims he provided that only one-third of the senators should go out every three years, thus preventing a complete renewal of the government at one election.

The executive branch of the government Jefferson made subordinate to the lower house by providing that the "administrator" should be chosen annually by that body and checked by a privy council likewise selected by that chamber. The judiciary he removed as far as possible from direct election. The county judges were to be appointed by the administrator and the privy council and to be removable only by the court of appeals. The judges of the general court and high court of chancery were to be appointed in the same manner, to hold office during good behavior, and to be removable by the court of appeals for cause. The judges of the court of appeals were to be selected by the lower house of the legislature, to serve during good behavior, and to be recalled only by act of the legislature.

In commenting upon this plan of government, Mr. W. C. Ford remarks : "It would naturally be expected that Jefferson would favor a democratic constitution — one, that is, which embodied the idea that all powers rested with the people ; yet his plan was less democratic than the instrument adopted by the convention, for he would allow the people to participate directly only in the election of the lower house of the Assembly. All else was based upon this narrow foundation." [1]

[1] The Nation, Vol. LI, p. 108. Jefferson considered it the normal function of the judiciary to declare void any law contrary to a formally drawn constitution. *Works* (Washington ed.), Vol. IX, p. 290.

Deeply as Jefferson cherished the people, he was as fearful as any Federalist of "the despotism of elected persons." His chief objection to the Virginia constitution was its vesting of extensive powers in the legislature. "The concentrating these in the same hands," he says, "is precisely the definition of despotic government. It will be no alleviation that these powers will be exercised by a plurality of hands, and not by a single one. One hundred and seventy-three [legislative] despots would surely be as oppressive as one. Let those who doubt it turn their eyes on the republic of Venice. As little will it avail us that they are chosen by ourselves. An *elective despotism* was not the government we fought for." [1] This is just the danger that Madison, Jefferson's chosen successor, feared, when he wrote, in 1788, to the latter : "Wherever the real power in a government lies, there is the danger of oppression. In our Governments, the real power lies in the majority of the community, and the invasion of private rights is chiefly to be apprehended, not from acts of Government contrary to the sense of its constituents, but from acts in which the government is the mere instrument of the major number of the constituents." [2]

The fact is that, notwithstanding his generous use of the phrase "popular rule," Jefferson was as anxious as any Federalist to guard against "the tyranny of majorities," [3] and like that stanch Federalist, Charles Coatesworth Pinckney, he thought a good senate representing wealth was a desirable feature of constitutional government. Commenting on the Virginia legislature, he says : "The senate is, by its constitution, too homogeneous with the house of delegates. Being chosen by the same electors, at the same time, and

---

[1] *Works* (Washington ed.), Vol. VIII, p. 361.
[2] *Documentary History of the Constitution*, Vol. V, p. 88.
[3] *Works* (Ford ed.), Vol. V, p. 83.

out of the same subjects, the choice falls of course on men of the same description. The purpose of establishing different houses of legislation is to introduce the influence of different interests or different principles. . . . In some of the American states, the delegates and senators are so chosen, as that the first represent the persons, and the second the property of the state. But with us [in Virginia] wealth and wisdom have an equal chance for admission into both houses. We do not, therefore, derive from the separation of our legislature into two houses those benefits which a proper complication of principles are capable of producing, and those which can alone compensate the evils which may be produced by their dissensions." [1]

When, however, Jefferson was called upon a few years later to draft another plan of a constitution for the state of Virginia, he did not introduce this idea of differentiating between the senate and the lower house on the basis of wealth. Instead he proposed to refine the popular will by having the senators chosen indirectly by electors chosen by the voters. The selection of the judges of the high and supreme courts of the state he would have vested in the legislature and their term of office he would have made "during good behavior." As a check upon the legislative branch of the government, he suggested a council of revision composed of the governor, two councillors of state (the governor and council to be elected by the legislature), and three judges of high courts, and invested with the power of rejecting measures of the legislature, subject to the provision that any measure so rejected might be enacted into law by a two-thirds vote.[2]

[1] *Works* (Washington ed.), Vol. VIII, p. 361.

[2] This plan was drawn up in the summer of 1783 when it was thought that a convention would soon be called to draft a new constitution for Virginia. The text is in Jefferson's *Works* (Washington ed.), Vol. VIII, pp. 441 ff.

In his plan of 1783,[1] however, Jefferson did propose a wider suffrage than in 1776, for he suggested that the ballot should be given to all free males who possessed a certain amount of real property or who had served in the militia.[2] In 1800 he declared that had he been in the Virginia constitutional convention he would "probably have proposed a general suffrage" and from time to time thereafter he expressed himself in favor of general manhood suffrage. In taking this advanced step he was not followed at all by the Republican party in Virginia, and more than half a century after the Declaration of Independence we find the non-freeholders of Virginia petitioning for the right to vote, but in vain. The doctrine of universal manhood suffrage was academic with Jefferson[3] and was not generally accepted by his party during his lifetime. In fact, the South was most tenacious in holding to property qualifications.

There was one point, however, on which Jefferson differed from most of his contemporaries; he believed that state constitutions should not go into effect until ratified by popular vote. He accordingly proposed in 1776 that the constitution based on his draft "shall be referred by them [the convention] to the people to be assembled in their respective counties; and that the suffrages of two-thirds

---

[1] *Works* (Washington ed.), Vol. VIII, p. 444.

[2] Jefferson's plan for a constitution usually placed under the date of 1794 was a fantastic affair and its purpose is unknown. It may be neglected so far as its practical bearings are concerned.   The Nation, Vol. II, p. 107.

[3] Jefferson's view as to the possibility of woman suffrage is curious and interesting. He said: "Were our state a pure democracy, in which all its inhabitants should meet together to transact all their business, there would yet be excluded from their deliberations, 1. infants until arrived at years of discretion. 2. Women, who, to prevent depravation of morals and ambiguity of issue, could not mix promiscuously in the public meetings of men. 3. Slaves." *Works* (Washington ed.), Vol. VII, p. 36. Contrary to popular impression, Hamilton believed in universal manhood suffrage for the lower house of the national legislature and like Jefferson relied on adequate checks in the other branches of the government.

of the counties shall be requisite to establish it." Jefferson looked upon a constitution as a fundamental law, as a solemn compact controlling the legislature and not subject to alteration by mere majorities; for his plan of government provided that amendments to the constitution must be approved by the voters of two-thirds of the counties. The Virginia convention of 1776 did not accept Jefferson's plan for requiring popular ratification, and seven years later the supreme court of the state held that acquiescence in the constitution by the people was itself ratification.[1]

We may now sum up the conclusions as to Jefferson's political philosophy on the basis of the evidence here presented:

He clearly recognized the antagonism between the capitalistic and agrarian interests and frankly declared that the former was the basis of the Federalist party and the latter the basis of the Republican party.

As the leader of the latter party he made a distinct appeal to the agricultural interests granting only those concessions to the capitalistic interests which he, as a practical man, deemed necessary.

The Constitution with its elaborate system of checks and balances, indirect election and judicial control, designed to soften the rigors of popular rule, Jefferson claimed as a Republican not a Federalist instrument of government.

In designing state constitutions, Jefferson nowhere committed himself to simple majority rule through representative institutions.

He was in favor of judicial control over legislation as a principle, but was led to modify his views by his practical experience at the hands of his bitter political enemy, Chief Justice Marshall.

[1] Lobingier, *The People's Law*, p. 145.

He accepted the Federalist principle and practice of distrusting the intelligence and character of the section of the people that was opposed to him. The Federalists distrusted the fiat-money agrarian party, and Jefferson distrusted capitalists and the "mobs of the great cities." Early in his career he proposed property qualifications on the suffrage but he later came to believe in the theory of a wide suffrage, extended to all men who paid taxes or served in the militia. But this was an academic matter with him, for neither he nor his party regarded universal manhood suffrage as an essential element of Republican faith. Among the very last states to surrender the dominion of the landed class, based on freehold property qualifications on the suffrage, were Jefferson's own state, Virginia, and the neighboring commonwealth of North Carolina. In fact, a study of the history of the suffrage in the Republican and the Federalist states shows that the former were no more enamored of an equalitarian political democracy than the latter. Long after Jefferson's death, the slave-owning planters of the South ruled by virtue of their superior wealth and talents and buttressed their natural power by property qualifications either on the suffrage or office-holding or both.[1]

[1] This restriction of popular rule by one form of property qualification or another was the subject of frequent commentary by the more radical sections of the Republican party, but these sections had no very great influence in the councils of the party in the first two decades of its organization. For example, a Maryland pamphleteer in 1806 makes the following remarks on the "strange inconsistency" of Virginia as well as his own state: "Maryland has of late years progressed considerably in her advances towards a pure and simple form of Republican Government: she has proclaimed universal suffrage to all her citizens who have attained the years of majority. She has one step further to go, and that is to declare all electors capable of being elected to any office in the state. Property, under every form of government, will retain fully more than its just weight; the rich man, when in competition with a poor man of equal merit, will most generally be successful. Why then grant wealth additional influence in society. . . . By the Constitution of this state it is required that to render a citizen capable of being elected to certain offices, he must be worth so many hundred pounds current money. A member to

GENERAL CONCLUSIONS

No one can spend the leisure of several years in the study of the period which saw the formation of the Constitution and the rise of Jeffersonian democracy without arriving at certain general reflections, which may or may not be worthy of the name conclusions, concerning the drift of events. Such conclusions as have been reached in the course of preparation of the essay on the Constitution and this volume are here set down for whatever value they may have. No pretence is made to infallibility, but there appears to be satisfactory historical evidence to support them.

It is established upon a statistical basis that the Constitution of the United States was the product of a conflict between capitalistic and agrarian interests. The support for the adoption of the Constitution came principally from the cities and regions where the commercial, financial, manufacturing, and speculative interests were concentrated

the House of Delegates, for instance, must be worth five hundred pounds. . . . He who is free from debt, he who though counted poor by society in general, is as independent of the world as the world is of him; and Maryland can boast of her thousands who may be ranked in this list; industrious farmers and mechanics who render her more real service and do her more real honor than all of the overgrown rich men in the state. And here let me ask a question : is the majority of the citizens of Maryland worth five hundred pounds current money each? If they are the state is much richer than I supposed ; but if the reverse is the case, then a majority of the people are actually excluded from a participation in the government, excluded even from the lowest grade of public offices. . . . I cannot here pass over in silence the strange inconsistency exhibited in Virginia [where only freeholders may vote], a republican state in the gross, yet leaning to aristocracy in detail. Is there no industrious patriot in that state, who will bring forward an elective system more in unison with the principles of republicanism? Now is the time. . . .

"In regard to the election of governor, I can see no substantial reason why he should not be elected by the voice of the people as 'every remove from the voice of the people is a departure from the principles of Republicanism,' besides in ten of the states, viz. in Massachusetts, Connecticut, New Hampshire, Rhode Island, Vermont, New York, Pennsylvania, Delaware, Kentucky and Tennessee, governors are chosen by the people at the same time that elections are held for other purposes." *An Address to the People of Maryland* (1804) [by R. Smith?] (Duane Collection, Library of Congress, Vol. 116, No. 7).

and the bulk of the opposition came from the small farming and debtor classes, particularly those back from the sea board.

The capitalistic interests whose rights were especially safeguarded by the Constitution had been harried almost to death, during the few years preceding the adoption of the Constitution, by state legislation and by the weaknesses and futility of the government under the Articles of Confederation. They were, therefore, driven into a compact mass, cemented by a conscious solidarity of interest. In the contest for the Constitution, they formed the aggressive party, and though a minority of the nation, they were able to wring from the reluctant voters a ratification of the new instrument of government, because the backwoods agrarians were uninformed and indifferent and from two-thirds to three-fourths of the electorate failed to vote one way or the other on the Constitution. In other words, though numerically in a minority, the party of the Constitution was able by virtue of its wealth, talents, solidarity, and political skill to carry through ratification in the face of a powerful opposition representing very probably the majority of the country.

The men who framed the Constitution and were instrumental in securing its ratification constituted the dominant group in the new government formed under it, and their material measures were all directed to the benefit of the capitalistic interests — i.e., were consciously designed to augment the fluid capital in the hands of security holders and bank stock owners and thus to increase manufacturing, commerce, building, and land values, the last incidentally, except for speculative purposes in the West. The bulk of the party which supported these measures was drawn from the former advocates of the Constitution.

The spokesmen of the Federalist and Republican parties,

Hamilton and Jefferson, were respectively the spokesmen of capitalistic and agrarian interests. Their writings afford complete and abundant proof of this fact.

The party of opposition to the administration charged the Federalists with building up an aristocracy of wealth by the measures of the government and appealed to the mass of the people, that is, the farmers, to resist the exactions of "a moneyed aristocracy." The Republicans by thus declaring war on the rich and privileged drew to themselves the support not only of the farmers, but also of a considerable portion of the smaller tradesmen and mechanics of the towns, who had no very great liking for the "rich and well born." By the ten years' campaign against the ruling class, they were able to arouse the vast mass of the hitherto indifferent voters and in the end swamp the compact minority which had dominated the country.

Jefferson was peculiarly fitted to become the leader of the opposition party. He was a planter and thus regarded as the spokesman of the agrarian interest. As a slave-owner and member of the ruling aristocracy in Virginia he conciliated that portion of the South which might have been disturbed by some of the violent democratic theories associated with his name. He had taken no part in the making and ratification of the Constitution, and it was known that he gave aid and comfort to the opponents of ratification while avowing his approval of certain parts of that instrument of government. He was known to oppose slavery in theory, but his agents skilfully spread abroad his statement that the federal government could not interfere with that peculiar institution under the powers conferred upon it by the Constitution. In private correspondence, Jefferson had vigorously denounced the bank and funded debt as schemes for robbing the agrarian interests, and his views were widely circulated by his friends and enemies.   But he did not commit himself to any radical schemes for repudiation or irregular reduction and upon his election he skilfully used and conciliated the very classes that he had denounced.   His academic views assiduously circulated by his partisans pleased the temper of the agrarian masses, and his practical politics propitiated, rather than alienated, the capitalistic interests.

Jeffersonian Democracy did not imply any abandonment of the property, and particularly the landed, qualifications on the suffrage or office-holding; it did not involve any fundamental alterations in the national Constitution which the Federalists had designed as a foil to the levelling propensities of the masses; it did not propose any new devices for a more immediate and direct control of the voters over the instrumentalities of government.   Jeffersonian Democracy simply meant the possession of the federal government by the agrarian masses led by an aristocracy of slave-owning planters, and the theoretical repudiation of the right to use the Government for the benefit of any capitalistic groups, fiscal, banking, or manufacturing.

INDEX